주한미군지위협정(SOFA)

서명 및 발효 8

주한미군지위협정(SOFA)

서명 및 발효 8

| 머리말

미국은 오래전부터 우리나라 외교에 있어서 가장 긴밀하고 실질적인 우호 · 협력관계를 맺어 온 나라다. 6 · 25전쟁 정전 협정이 체결된 후 북한의 재침을 막기 위한 대책으로서 1953년 11월 한미 상호방위조약이 체결되었다. 이는 미군이 한국에 주둔하는 법적 근거였고, 그렇게 주둔하게 된 미군의 시설, 구역, 사업, 용역, 출입국, 통관과 관세, 재판권 등 포괄적인 법적 지위를 규정하는 것이 바로 주한미군지위협정(SOFA)이다. 그러나 이와 관련한 협상은 계속된 난항을 겪으며 한미 상호방위조약이 체결로부터 10년이 훌쩍 넘은 1967년이 돼서야 정식 발효에 이를 수 있었다. 그럼에도 당시 미군 범죄에 대한 한국의 재판권은 심한 제약을 받았으며, 1980년대 후반 민주화 운동과 함께 미군 범죄 문제가 사회적 이슈로 떠오르자 협정을 개정해야 한다는 목소리가 커지게 되었다. 이에 1991년 2월 주한미군지위협정 1차 개정이 진행되었고, 이후에도 여러 사건이 발생하며 2001년 4월 2차 개정이 진행되어 현재에 이르고 있다.

본 총서는 외교부에서 작성하여 최근 공개한 주한미군지위협정(SOFA) 관련 자료를 담고 있다. 1953년 한미 상호방위조약 체결 이후부터 1967년 발효가 이뤄지기까지의 자료와 더불어, 이후 한미 합동위원회을 비롯해 민 · 형사재판권, 시설, 노무, 교통 등 각 분과위원회의 회의록과 운영 자료, 한국인 고용인 문제와 관련한 자료, 기타 관련 분쟁 자료 등을 포함해 총 42권으로 구성되었다. 전체 분량은 약 2만 2천여 쪽에 이른다.

2024년 3월

한국학술정보(주)

| 일러두기

· 본 총서에 실린 자료는 2022년 4월과 2023년 4월에 각각 공개한 외교문서 4,827권, 76만여 쪽 가운데 일부를 발췌한 것이다.

· 각 권의 제목과 순서는 공개된 원본을 최대한 반영하였으나, 주제에 따라 일부는 적절히 변경하였다.

· 원본 자료는 A4 판형에 맞게 축소하거나 원본 비율을 유지한 채 A4 페이지 안에 삽입하였다. 또한 현재 시점에선 공개되지 않아 '공란'이란 표기만 있는 페이지 역시 그대로 실었다.

· 외교부가 공개한 문서 각 권의 첫 페이지에는 '정리 보존 문서 목록'이란 이름으로 기록물 종류, 일자, 명칭, 간단한 내용 등의 정보가 수록되어 있으며, 이를 기준으로 0001번부터 번호가 매겨져 있다. 이는 삭제하지 않고 총서에 그대로 수록하였다.

· 보고서 내용에 관한 더 자세한 정보가 필요하다면, 외교부가 온라인상에 제공하는 『대한민국 외교사료요약집』 1991년과 1992년 자료를 참조할 수 있다.

| 차례

정/리/보/존/문/서/목/록

기록물종류	문서-일반공문서철	등록번호	920 9593	등록일자	2006-07-27
분류번호	741.12	국가코드	US	주제	
문서철명	한.미국 간의 상호방위조약 제4조에 의한 시설과 구역 및 한국에서의 미국군대의 지위에 관한 협정 (SOFA) 전59권. 1966.7.9 서울에서 서명 : 1967.2.9 발효 (조약 232호) *원본				
생산과	미주과/조약과	생산년도	1952 - 1967	보존기간	영구
담당과(그룹)	조약	조약	서가번호	--	
참조분류					
권차명	V.22 실무교섭회의, 제45-50차, 1964.3-4월				
내용목차	1. 제45차 회의, 3.6 (p.2~56) 2. 제46차 회의, 3.13 (p.57~94) 3. 제47차 회의, 3.20 (p.95~143) 4. 제48차 회의, 4.3 (p.144~212) 5. 제49차 회의, 4.10 (p.213~239) 6. 제50차 회의, 4.23 (p.240~275) * 일지 : 1953.8.7 이승만 대통령-Dulles 미국 국무장관 공동성명 - 상호방위조약 발효 후 군대지위협정 교섭 약속 1954.12.2 정부, 주한 UN군의 관세업무협정 체결 제의 1955.1월, 5월 미국, 제의 거절 1955.4.28 정부, 군대지위협정 제의 (한국측 초안 제시) 1957.9.10 Hurter 미국 국무차관 방한 시 각서 수교 (한국측 제의 수락 요구) 1957.11.13, 26 정부, 개별 협정의 단계적 체결 제의 1958.9.18 Dawling 주한미국대사, 형사재판관할권 협정 제외 조건으로 행정협정 체결 의사 전달 1960.3.10 정부, 토지, 시설협정의 우선적 체결 강력 요구 1961.4.10 장면 국무총리-McConaughy 주한미국대사 공동성명으로 교섭 개시 합의 1961.4.15, 4.25 제1, 2차 한.미국 교섭회의 (서울) 1962.3.12 정부, 교섭 재개 촉구 공한 송부 1962.5.14 Burger 주한미국대사, 최규하 장관 면담 시 형사재판관할권 문제 제기 않는 조건으로 교섭 재개 통고 1962.9.6 한.미국 간 공동성명 발표 (9월 중 교섭 재개 합의) 1962.9.20~1965.6.7 제1-81차 실무 교섭회의 (서울) 1966.7.8 제82차 실무 교섭회의 (서울) 1966.7.9 서명 1967.2.9 발효 (조약 232호)				

마/이/크/로/필/름/사/항

촬영연도	*롤 번호	화일 번호	후레임 번호	보관함 번호
2006-11-22	I-06-0068	07	1-275	

0001

1. 제45차 회의, 3.6

0002

기 안 용 지

자체통제		기안처	미주과 이근팔	전화번호	근거서류접수일자

	과장	국장	차관	장관		
	(서명)	(서명)	(서명)	(서명)		

관계관 서명	

기안 년월일	1964. 3. 4.	시행 년월일		보존 년한		정서	기장
분류 기호	외구미 722.2	전체 통제		종결			

경유 수신 참조	건의	발신	장관

제목	제 45 차 주둔군지위협정 체결교섭회의에 임할 우리측 입장

3 월 6 일 개최될 제 45 차 주둔군지위협정 체결을 위한 한.미간 교섭회의에서는 형사재판관할권, 공위물 및 용역, 및 노무에 관한 조항을 토의하도록 예정하고 있는바 이에 대하여 우리측 교섭실무자는 3 월 3 일 회합을 갖고 제 45 차 회의에서 취할 태도를 별첨과 같이 결정하였아오니 재가하여 주시기 바랍니다.

유 첨: 제 45 차 주둔군지위협정 체결교섭회의에 임할 우리측 태도. 끝.

1966,12,31 에 예고문에 의거 일반문서로 재분류됨

~~보통문서로 재분류(1966.12.31)~~

승인서식 1-1-3 (11 00900-03) (195mm×265mm16절지)

0003

1. 공익물 및 용역

(1) 미측은 제 44 차 회의에서 우리측 합의의사록 1항에 대하여 제시한 대안에서 미군에 적용되는 공익물 및 용역의 사용우선권, 조건, 사용료 및 tariffs 의 변경이 있을 경우에는 발효기일전에 합동위원회에서 협의해야 한다고 구정하고 있는바 우리측은 다음과 같은 양해사항을 유보하고 미측대안을 수락한다.

(ㄱ) 한국정부에서 결정한 변경사항을 발효일 전에 합동위원회에서 협의하는 것은 변경결정사항을 미측에 통고하고 미측의 의사를 청취할 기회를 제공하는데 끝이며 이미 결정된 사항을 변경시키는 것은 아니다.

(ㄴ) 변경사항이 결정된 후 발효일까지 협의할 시간적여유가 없을 경우(예: 12 월 31 일 결정되어 익년 1 월 1 일 ~~~~에 발효되는 때)에는 예외로 한다.

(2) 미측은 3항의 대안에서 한국은 비상시 미군의 수요에 필요한 공익물 및 용역의 제공을 위하여 적절한 수단을 취하는데 동의할 것을 요구하고 있는 바 우리측은 (ㄱ) 한국이 취하여야 할 "appropriate measures "라함은 양국정부가 협의하여 결정하는 "적절한 수단"임을 뜻한다는 양해사항을 유보하고 이를 수락한다.

2. 노무문제

(1) 미군의 노무자 채용은 한국인에 한정할 것을 규정한 우리초안 1항에서 한국인 채용을 원칙으로 하되 특수한 경우에 한하여 제 3 국인을 채용하는 것은 한국정부당국과 상의하여 해결을 모색할 용의가 있다.

(2) 노무자 조달은 한국정부의 조력을 통하여 하는 것을 주로 하되 미측이 필요하다고 인정하는 ~~때에는~~ 직접고용을 ~~하는 것을 인정할 수 있다.~~ 대상을 구체적으로 명기한 것을 요구하고 답변에 따라 재고하도록 한다.

(3) 우리초안은 미군의 군기 유지 및 안전에 의한 해고만을 규정하고 있으나 미군이 감군, 예산의 삭감 기타 정당한 이유로 공정한 표준에 따라 해고시킬 수 있는 것은 한국법에서도 보장하고 있음을 명백히 한다.

0004

(4) 미측이 K.S.C. 가 한국정부의 피고용자라는 근거를 제시할 것을 요구하고 만일 제시 못 할 경우에는 우리측은 K.S.C. 의 인원 조달 및 한국군인을 배속시키 운영면에서 협조함에 불과하며 임금, 해고 기타 모든 노무관리등 실질적인 문제를 미측이 장악하고 있음으로 미측의 노무자라고 주장한다.

(5) 한국의 노동관계법은 노동조건의 최저수준을 규정하고 있는 것이기 때문에 미측이 한국법에 위반되지 않는 범위내에서 노동조건을 결정하는 것은 무방하나 미측이 노동조건의 결정 기준으로 한국의 노동관계법 외에 customs and practices를 삽입한 의도를 질문하여 불리한 것이라면 삭제할 것을 요구한다.

(6) 가사사용인에 대하여서는 우리 나라 노동법에서 적용을 배제하고 있음으로 본문에서 삭제할 것을 주장한다.

3. 형사재판관할권

(1) 우리측 초안과 미국측 초안의 차이점을 지적하여 우리측 초안에 대한 제안설명을 하고 우리 초안에 입각하여 축조적으로 심의할 것을 제안한다. 끝.

SOFA NEGOTIATION

Agenda for the 45th Session

14:00 March 6, 1964

1. Continuation of Discussions on:

    a. Utilities and Services Article

    b. Labor Article

    c. Criminal Jurisdiction Article

2. Other Business

3. Agenda and Date of the Next Meeting

4. Press Release

0006

Submitted by U.S. side on March 6 '64

AGREED MINUTE

2. The undertaking of the United States Government to conform to Korean labor laws, customs, and practices, does not imply any waiver by the United States Government of its immunities under international law. Moreover, the United States Government may terminate employment whenever the continuation of such employment would materially impair the accomplishment of the mission of the United States armed forces.

0007

Submitted by
U.S. Side
on March 6, '64

AGREED MINUTE

3. It is understood that the Government of the Republic of Korea shall be reimbursed for direct costs incurred in providing assistance requested pursuant to paragraph 2.

0008

Mar. 6 '64

United States Statement on Labor Article
at 6 March 1964 Meeting

I would like first to make a general comment on the Labor Article. In 1945 both Japan and Germany were conquered enemy countries. US forces occupied those countries in a military occupation. As a defeated enemy country the Japanese Government, in so far as it was allowed to govern, did so only as an agent of the Supreme Commander of the Allied Powers. As for labor, the Japanese government was simply called upon to provide it wherever the Supreme Commander required it. It was provided free, without any cost to the United States. In both Japan and Germany the wages of this labor were paid by the Japanese or German governments, without any reimbursement by the United States. They were part of the Occupation Costs paid by a defeated enemy country. This was the origin of the system of indirect hire we have today in Japan. As both Japan and Germany went through successive stages and were converted from enemies to allies, the nature of the US military presence changed from military occupiers to visiting forces and the occupation costs came to be shared between us with the United States taking over the payment of some of them, including labor costs. But the system of indirect hire, which still exists in Japan, in which the Japanese government obtains our labor force for us, is a carryover from our military occupation of a defeated enemy country. We do not have such an arrangement with any of the other free countries in the Pacific area. In China, in the Philippines, in Australia, in Okinawa, in Vietnam, in Thailand, and here in Korea, we hire labor directly in the free labor market. We do not have it impressed for us by the host government. It would not be proper for us to do so. Such an arrangement would be typical of a military occupation. We of course are not here as military occupiers but are here at your invitation and in response to the call of the United Nations. Our relationship with you is that of guest and host. We are free and equal allies in a common cause. Our employment of labor here has been that typical of a free employer on the one hand and a free labor force on the other. We have tried to be a good employer in conformity with your labor laws and practice. We will continue to be such. But it would be grossly improper and a very backward step after 19 years of free labor practice for us here to adopt the Japanese labor article based on an impressed labor system imposed (also 19 years ago) upon a defeated enemy nation.

All of this is the reason that our draft labor article is worded as it is and is not based on the Japanese article. At the last session in which this article was discussed you raised certain objections to our draft and in consequence of your suggestions we have obtained authority to make certain changes in our draft which we believe you desire. These changes are not taken from the Japanese article with

0009

its entirely different origin but instead are designed to make our free labor draft more fully representative of your stated preferences.

First, in paragraph 1 (b), we offer to delete the phrase "who is an employee of the Government of Korea." This was suggested by your side.

Second, in paragraph 2, we offer to add the words, "and upon request by the employer, with the assistance of the authorities of the Republic of Korea." This is based upon a suggestion from your side. It is not, we realize, exactly what you suggested, but it is absolutely as far as we can go in this direction. We simply can not be bound to obtain no employees at all except through your governmental agencies. In an agreement designed to create a status for our forces somewhat better than that of mere tourists and businessmen we cannot accept a limitation on employing a labor force which is more restrictive than those placed upon such businessmen, whether Korean or third-national who do business here. This would seem so obvious on the face of it that we ask you to give serious consideration to our proposed language. This language which we are proposing today is very similar to that in the labor article of our new SOFA with Australia. Australia is certainly an important ally of the United States and is a first-class power in the Pacific area and in your consideration of this proposal we ask you to give weight to that fact.

Third, in paragraph 3, we offer to delete the words "provided, however that an employer may terminate employment whenever the continuation of such employment would materially impair the accomplishment of the mission of the United States armed forces" and to place them instead in the agreed minutes as the second sentence of agreed minute 2 where they would read: "Moreover the United States government may terminate employment whenever the continuation of such employment would materially impair the accomplishment of the mission of the United States armed forces." This proposal of our side is designed to meet an objection from your side.

Fourth, we offer to add a new agreed minute as follows: "It is understood that the Government of the Republic of Korea shall be reimbursed for direct costs incurred in providing assistance requested pursuant to paragraph 2." This offer is made to comply with a suggestion made by your side at our last discussion of this article.

Fifth, we are authorized to convey to you that the principle of US forces withholding employee contributions to social security and income tax is acceptable to the United States. We consider that such an obligation is included in our commitment of general conformity with the labor laws, customs, and practices of the Republic of Korea. Should you desire a specific reference in the agreement to this obligation to withhold taxes, suitable language may be worked out. I would like to add one additional comment about the language in our paragraph 3 calling for general conformity with Korean labor laws, customs, and practices. The United States fully recognizes the sovereignty of the Republic of Korea within Korean territory. At the same time it should be remembered that the United States is also a sovereign nation and under accepted principles of international law it is not proper for one sovereign to hail another sovereign into its courts as a defendant or before its administrative tribunals as a respondent. It is precisely for this reason that we cannot now nor at any time in the future agree to comply with any law which requires the United States to appear when summoned before a court or board. I may say that this is not done, either, in Japan or Germany but that in those states the judicial or administrative actions brought by employees or their representatives are defended or responded to by the governments of Japan and Germany, not by the government of the United States. We are most willing to be helped and advised by the competent ministries of your government in the settlement of any labor dispute but we cannot agree that the United States give up a right inherent in every sovereign state not to be brought against its will before the tribunals of another sovereign. Out position on this point cannot change, here or anywhere else in the world. It is a universal principle of international law.

Now we ask you to consider our five proposals, all made in a desire on our part to be responsive to your legitimate requirements. They do not fully meet your position as expressed in our previous discussion but they are as far as we can go toward meeting you. Please give them full consideration and convey your views to us at the next meeting.

ARTICLE XXV

Revised US Draft of Labor Procurement Article
(As tabled on 6 March 64)

1. In this Article the expression:

(a) "employer" refers to the United States armed forces (including nonappropriated fund activities) and the persons referred to in the first paragraph of Article__________.

(b) "employee" refers to any civilian (other than a member of the civilian component) employed by an employer, except (1) a member of the Korean Service Corps and (2) a domestic employed by an individual member of the United States armed forces, civilian component or dependent thereof.

2. Employers may accomplish the recruitment, employment and management of employees directly, and on the request of the employer with the assistance of the authorities of the Republic of Korea.

3. The condition of employment, the compensation, and the labor-management practices shall be established by the United States armed forces for their employees in general conformity with the labor laws, customs and practices of the Republic of Korea.

4. (a) An employee shall have the same right to strike as an employee in a comparable position in the employment of the armed forces of the Republic of Korea. Such an employee may voluntarily organize and join a union or other employee group whose objectives are not inimical to the interests of the United States. Membership or nonmembership in such groups shall not be a cause for discharge or non-employment.

(b) Employers will maintain procedures designed to assure the just and timely resolution of employee grievances.

0012

5. (a) Should the Republic of Korea adopt measures allocating labor, the United States armed forces shall be accorded employment privileges no less favorable than those enjoyed by the armed forces of the Republic of Korea.

(b) In the event of a national emergency, employees who have acquired skills essential to the mission of the United States armed forces shall be exempt from Republic of Korea military service or other compulsory service. The United States armed forces shall furnish to the Republic of Korea lists of those employees deemed essential.

6. Members of the civilian component shall not be subject to Korean laws or regulations with respect to their terms and conditions of employment.

AGREED MINUTES

1. The Republic of Korea will make available, at designated induction points, qualified personnel for Korean Service Corps units in numbers sufficient to meet the requirements of United States armed forces. The employment of a domestic by an individual member of the United States armed forces, civilian component or dependent thereof shall be governed by applicable Korean law and in addition by wage scales and control measures promulgated by the United States armed forces.

2. The undertaking of the United States government to conform to Korean or laws, customs, and practices, does not imply any waiver by the United States Government of its immunities under international law. Moreover, the United States Government may terminate employment whenever the continuation of such employment would materially impair the accomplishment of the mission of the United States armed forces.

3. It is understood that the Government of the Republic of Korea shall be reimbursed for direct costs incurred in providing assistance requested pursuant to paragraph 2.

0013

기 안 용 지

자 체 통 제	외무사무관 손익종	기안처	미주과 이근팔	전화번호	근거서류접수일자
	과장	국장	차관	장관	
관계관 서명					
기안 년월일	1964. 3. 11.	시행 년월일			정서기장
분류 기호	외구미 722.2	전체 통제			
경유 수신 참조	대통령 (참조: 비서실장) 국무총리			발신	
제목	제 45 차 주둔군지위협정 체결 교섭 실무자회의 보고				

1964. 3. 6. 하오 2 시부터 동 4 시 10 분 까지 외무부장관 회의실에서 개최된 제 45 차 주둔군지위협정 체결 교섭 실무자회의에서 토의된 내용을 별첨과 같이 보고합니다.

유 첨: 제 45 차 교섭회의 보고서 1 부. 끝.

1966, 12, 31, 에 예고문에 의거 일반문서로 재분류됨

승인서식 1—1—3 (11 00900 03) (195mm×265mm16절지)

0014

제 45 차

한미간 주둔군지위협정 체결교섭 실무자회의

보 고 서

1. 일 시: 1964 년 3 월 6 일 하오 2 시부터 동 4 시 10 분 까지.

2. 장 소: 외무부장관 회의실

3. 토의사항:

가. 공의물 및 용역

(1) 양측은 미군에 적용되는 공익물 및 용역의 요금 기타 조건에 변경이 있을 경우에는 발효기일전에 합동위원회에서 협의하는데 대하여 우리측의 다음과 같은 양해사항을 유보하고 합의하였다.

(ㄱ) 미측의 견해를 청취하기 위하여 협의하되 그 협의가 한국정부의 변경에 대한 결정사항을 다시 변경할 수는 없다.

(ㄴ) 변경사항 결정 후 발효일까지 협의할 시간적 여유가 없을 때에는 사전협의를 하지 않는다.

(2) 양측은 한국이 비상시 미군의 수요에 필요한 공익물 및 용역의 제공을 위하여 적절한 조치를 취함에 있어 (ㄱ) 한국정부가 취할 적절한 조치라 함은 양국정부당국이 협의하여 결정하는 조치라는 양해사항을 유보하고 수락하였다.

나. 노무조달

미측은 자유우방제국에 주둔하고 있는 미군의 노무조달이 직접 자유조달원칙하에 이루어 지고 있으며 미측초안은 그 원칙에 입각하여 한국의 노동관계법규에 대체로 합치시켜서 노무조달을 기하려고 한다는 설명을 하고 다음과 같은 수정사항을 제의하였다.

(1) K.S.C. 가 한국정부의 피고용인이라고 주장하지는 않겠다.

(2) 미군의 노무조달은 직접고용을 원칙으로 하되 미군이 한국관계당국에 요청하면 한국정부가 협조한다.

(3) 미측은 노무관리를 규정한 사항중 "고용자는 미국군대의 사명수행에 중대한 지장을 초래할 시에는 피고용자를 해고할 수 있다"라는 용어를 삭제하여 합의의사록에 추가 삽입한다.

0015

66-3-31

64-3-10 (4)

외정 109-3(4)

0016

(4) 미측은 또한 미측이 한국정부 관계당국에 노무조달을 요청하는 경우에 한국당국의 노무조달을 위한 협조에서 필요한 직접적인 비용은 미당국이 상환할 것을 제의하였다.

(5) 미군은 미군노무자의 임금으로 부터 소득세 및 사회보장기금을 공제토록 강구하는데 동의한다. 그러나 미국은 주권국가로서의 특권을 포기하여서 까지 노무분쟁에 관련하여 한국법정 또는 노동위원회의 결정에 복할 수는 없으며 이러한 미국의 입장은 한국이나 기타 어떤 국가에서도 변경될 수 없는 원칙이다.

다. 형사재판관할권

(1) 미측은 형사재판관할권에 관한 미측의 입장을 다음과 같이 밝혔다.

(ㄱ) 미군지휘관이 군기를 유지하기 위하여서는 형사재판관할권을 행사할 수 있는 권리를 장악하는 것이 긴요하다.

(ㄴ) 전투태세를 위하여 배치되어 있는 미군을 주둔군지위협정으로 규정하려는 것은 한국에서의 특수사정이며 미군은 전투지역의 설정을 필요로 하고 있다. 그러나 그 구역한계는 교섭에서 결정될 문제이다.

(ㄷ) 관할권이 경합될 경우 한국측에 대한 관할권 포기 요청은 독일, 일본, 희랍등 국가에서도 인정된 원칙이다.

0017

64-3-32

(다음 면으로 계속)

64-3-10
기.모 109-3
0018

(ㄹ) 행정적, 징계적 제재에 관한 전속관할권 포기 요청은 합리적이며 또 인도적면을 고려한 것이다.

(ㅁ) 한국군인이 범하면 군법회의에 회부될 범죄에 관련된 미군을 미군군법회의에 회부하려는 것은 당연한 주장이다.

(ㅂ) 한국의 구금시설은 미측에 만족할 만한 것이 못됨으로 재판전의 피의자를 미측이 구금하기를 원하며 그 것은 한국측에 경제적일 것이다. 독일에서도 그렇게 하고 있다.

(ㅅ) 재판후 기결수의 보호도 미측에서 하려는 것이며 1961년에 외무부측에서 제의한바 있다.

(ㅇ) 미군의 공무집행중 범죄에 관련하여 군지휘관이 증명을 발행하는 것은 각국에서 인정된 일반적 원칙이다.

(ㅈ) 가족도 미측 관할권에 복하여야 하며 미대심원의 판례에서도 명시되어 있으며 1960 년도 이후의 주둔군지위협정은 가족을 포함시키고 있다.

(ㅊ) 전쟁 발발시 조치 및 협정 발효전 범죄에 관하여서도 규정함이 필요하다.

(ㅋ) 미측은 미군인으로 하여금 한국의 계엄령 선포하에서 군법재판에 복하게 할 수는 없다.

(2) 한국측은 한국측 입장을 다음과 같이 밝혔다.

(ㄱ) 미측안은 한국의 민사당국의 관할권에만 복하기로 되어 있고 군사재판에는 복하지 않게 되어 있는바 한국법에 의하면 특정한 경우 민간인도 군법에 복하며 대법원이 최고심이 되어 인권의 보장을 기하고 있다.

(ㄴ) 한국이 미군사당국이라고 규정한데 대하여 미측은 미국당국이 관할권을 행사하는 것으로 되어 있는데 이것은 미군당국이 않인 기타 당국도 포함하는 것이 않인가 염려된다.

(ㄷ) 한국은 전투지역을 이유로 한 관할권의 지역적 제한을 인정할 수 없다.

(ㄹ) 공무집행에 관한 한국측 입장은 해석상의 분쟁을 미연에 방지하려는 것이다.

0019

6(0-1-3)

64-3-70
미일 109-3
0020

(ㅁ) 가족은 군인, 군속과는 그 성격이 판이함으로 한국의 관활권에 복하여야 한다.

(ㅂ) 미국법에 의하여 처벌될 수 없으나 한국법에 의해서 처벌될 수 있는 범죄는 한국의 전속관활권에 복한다는 것은 당연의 것이며 포기될 수 없다.

(ㅅ) 관활권의 경합 시 제 1 차 관활권을 포기할 것을 요구하는 것은 서로가 제 1 차 관활권을 인정한 원칙에 위배된다.

4. 기타 사항: 차기 회의 일자: 1964 년 3 월 13 일 하오 2 시 부터. 끝.

0021 64-3-34

64-5-10 (4)

기획, 문 105-3 (4)

0022

March 6, 1964

Utilities and Services

1. Mr. Chang opened the meeting by recalling that at the previous meeting, agreement had been reached on the text of the utilities and services provisions and Agreed Minute #2. He said the Korean negotiators were prepared to agree to the revised Agreed Minute #1 tabled at the previous meeting by the U.S. negotiators. The Korean negotiators did so with two understandings to be recorded in the negotiating record. The first understanding was that consultation in the Joint Committee, which will provide an opportunity for the U.S. authorities to make known their views concerning proposed changes, will in no way prejudice the right of the ROK authorities to make the final decision regarding such changes. The second understanding was that there might be rare occasions on which the ROK authorities would not be able to provide advance consultation. One such occasion might occur, for instance, if the National Assembly should pass a law on December 31 providing for rate changes to go into effect on January 1. Mr. Chang stated that this would be an extreme case and the Korean negotiators did not anticipate its occurrence.

2. Mr. Chang stated that the Korean negotiators were also prepared to agree to the revised Agreed Minute #3 tabled at the previous meeting by the U.S. negotiators, with the understanding that the measures to be taken by the ROK authorities would be such measures as were determined to be appropriate by the ROK and U.S. authorities through consultation.

3. Mr. Habib replied that the U. S. negotiators agreed to the first understanding stated by the Korean negotiators with regard to Agreed Minute #1. The second understanding did not appear to pose any great problems. The U.S. negotiators ASSUMED that if there were pending in the National Assembly a bill dealing with rate changes, the provisions of the bill would be known and discussed in the Joint Committee prior to the bill's passage. The U.S. negotiators accepted both understandings, since the Joint Committee would be capable of handling the situations to which they pertained. The U.S. negotiators also agreed to the understanding by the Korean negotiators with regard

0023

to Agreed Minute #3.

4. Full agreement was thereupon reached on the text of the provisions dealing with utilities and services.

Accounting Procedures

5. The negotiators confirmed the agreement reached at the previous meeting to make paragraph 4 of the U.S. draft of the utilities and services provisions into a separate article in the Status of Forces Agreement.

Labor Procurement

6. Turning to discussion of the Labor Procurement Article, Brig. Gen. Fuller stated that the U.S. negotiators wished to make a general comment. In 1945, he pointed out, both Japan and Germany were conquered enemy countries. U.S. forces occupied those countries in a military occupation. As a defeated enemy, the Japanese Government, in so far as it was allowed to govern, did so only as an agent of the Supreme Commander of the Allied Powers. As for labor, the Japanese Government was simply called upon to provide it wherever the Supreme Commander required it. It was provided free, without any cost to the United States. In both Japan and Germany the wages of this labor were paid by the Japanese or German governments, without any reimbursement by the United States. These wages were part of the occupation costs paid by a defeated enemy. This was the origin of the system of indirect hire which the U.S. armed forces use today in Japan. As both Japan and Germany went through successive stages and were converted from enemies to allies, the nature of the U.S. military presence changed from that of military occupiers to that of visiting forces and the occupation costs came to be shared, with the United States Government taking over the payment of some of them, including labor costs. But the system of indirect hire, which still exists in Japan, in which the Japanese Government obtains

0024

the labor force for the U.S. armed forces, is a carryover from the military occupation of a defeated enemy country. The U.S. armed forces do not have any such arrangement with any of the other free countries in the Pacific area. In China, the Philippines, Australia, Okinawa, Vietnam, Thailand, and Korea, the U.S. armed forces hire labor directly in the free labor market. It is not impressed by the local government for the U.S. armed forces in any of these countries. Such an arrangement would not be proper, for it would be typical of a military occupation. The U.S. armed forces are in Korea not as military occupiers but at the invitation of the ROK Government and in response to the call of the United Nations. The relationship between the ROK Government and the U.S. armed forces is that of Host and guest. They are free and equal allies in a common cause. The employment of labor by the U.S. armed forces in Korea has been that typical of a free employer on the one hand and a free labor force on the other. The U.S. armed forces have tried to be a good employer in conformity with Korean labor laws and practice. They will continue to be such. But it would be grossly improper and a very backward step after 19 years of free labor practice for the [illegible] SOFA negotiators now to adopt the Japanese labor article based on an impressed labor system imposed upon a defeated enemy.

7. Gen. Fuller explained that it was for the foregoing reasons that the U.S. draft of the Labor Procurement Article is worded as it is and is not based on the Japanese article. During the previous discussion of this article, the Korean negotiators had raised certain objections to the U.S. draft. In consequence, the U.S. negotiators wished to propose certain changes in the U.S. draft which they believed would meet the desires of the Korean negotiators. These changes are taken not from the Japanese article but instead are designed to make the U.S. draft more fully representative of the stated preferences of the Korean negotiators.

8. In paragraph 1(b), Gen. Fuller continued, the U.S. negotiators offered to delete the phrase "who is an employee of the Government of Korea", as had been

0025

suggested by the Korean Negotiators.

9. In paragraph 2, the U.S. negotiators proposed the addition of the words "and upon request by the employer, with the assistance of the authorities of the Republic of Korea". This also was based upon a suggestion by the Korean negotiators. Gen. Fuller pointed out that while this language was not exactly that suggested by the Korean negotiators, it was absolutely as far as the U.S. negotiators could go in that direction. The U.S. armed forces simply can not be bound to obtain no employees at all except through ROK governmental agencies. In an agreement designed to create a status for the U.S. armed forces somewhat better than that of tourists and businessmen, the U.S. armed forces cannot accept a limitation on employing a labor force which is more restrictive than those placed upon businessmen operating in the Republic of Korea, whether Korean or third-country nationals. Gen. Fuller pointed out that the revised language proposed by the U.S. negotiators was very similar to that in the labor article of the recently negotiated SOFA with Australia. Australia is an important ally of the United States and is a first-class power in the Pacific area. The U.S. negotiators asked the Korean negotiators to give weight to these facts in their consideration of this proposal.

10. From paragraph 3 of the U.S. draft, Gen. Fuller continued, the U.S. negotiators offered to delete the words "provided, however, that an employer may terminate employment whenever the continuation of such employment would materially impair the accomplishment of the mission of the United States armed forces" and to place them instead in the Agreed Minutes as the second sentence of Agreed Minute #2, where they would then read: "Moreover, the United States Government may terminate employment whenever the continuation of such employment would materially impair the accomplishment of the mission of the United States armed forces". Gen. Fuller remarked that this proposal was designed to meet an objection previously made by the Korean negotiators.

0026

11. As their fourth proposal, Gen. Fuller continued, the U.S. negotiators

offered to add a new Agreed Minute to read as follows:

"3. It is understood that the Government of the Republic of Korea shall be reimbursed for direct costs incurred in providing assistance requested pursuant to paragraph 2."

This proposal was being made in response to a suggestion made by the Korean negotiators during previous discussion of this article.

12. Finally, Gen. Fuller stated, the U.S. negotiators had been authorized to state that the principle of withholding by the U.S. armed forces of employee contributions to social security and of income tax payments is acceptable to the United States Government. The U.S. authorities believed that an obligation to withhold such contributions and payments is included in the commitment in the U.S. draft to establish labor practices "in general conformity" with Korean labor laws, customs, and practices. However, should the Korean negotiators desire to include in the article a specific reference to this obligation to withhold taxes, the U.S. negotiators believed that suitable language could be worked out.

13. Gen. Fuller stated that the U.S. negotiators would like to make one additional comment concerning the language in paragraph 3 of the U.S. draft, which calls for general conformity with Korean labor laws, customs, and practices. The United States fully recognizes the sovereignty of the Republic of Korea. At the same time, it should be remembered that the United States is also a sovereign nation and that under accepted principles of international law, it is not proper for one sovereign government to hail another sovereign government into its courts as a defendant or before its administrative tribunals as a respondent. It is precisely for this reason that the U.S. armed forces cannot now nor at any time in the future agree to comply with any law which requires the Government of the United States to appear when summoned before a court or board. This is not done in Japan or Germany. In those states, the judicial or administrative actions brought by employees or their representatives are defended or responded to by the Governments of Japan and Germany, not by the United States

0027

Government. The U.S. armed forces are most willing to be helped and advised by the competent ministries of the ROK Government in the settlement of any labor dispute but the U.S. negotiators cannot agree that the United States Government give up a right inherent in every sovereign state not to be brought against its will before the tribunals of another sovereign state. The position of the United States Government on this point cannot change, either in Korea or anywhere else in the world. It is a universal principle of international law.

14. Gen. Fuller reiterated that the five proposals just made by the U.S. negotiators had been made out of a desire to be responsive to the legitimate requirements of the Korean negotiators. The proposals do not fully meet the Korean position, as expressed in the previous discussion of this article, but they are as far as the U.S. negotiators can go toward meeting the Korean position. He asked the Korean negotiators to give full consideration to these proposals and state their views at the next meeting.

15. Mr. Chang thanked Gen. Fuller for his explanation of the U.S. proposals and stated that the Korean negotiators would comment on them at the next meeting.

Criminal Jurisdiction

16. Turning to the Criminal Jurisdiction Article, Mr. Habib stated that the U.S. negotiators had carefully examined the statement made by Mr. Chang at the previous meeting, in presenting the comments of the Korean negotiators on the U.S. draft of this article. The U.S. negotiators would respond to the six points made by Mr. Chang and would discuss a number of points which he had not mentioned. Before doing so, however, Mr. Habib said the U.S. negotiators would like to make a general statement.

17. Mr. Habib said Mr. Chang had stated that, in general, it appeared to be the U.S. intention to retain jurisdiction over members of the U.S. armed forces in Korea, to the maximum possible. This is indeed the U.S. intention,

0028

for the reason spelled out in full in the Agreed Minutes of the U.S. draft. The reason is that it is the primary responsibility of any military commander to maintain good order and discipline among his troops and associated personnel. To do so, he must have jurisdiction over them. In all of its Status of Forces agreements, the U.S. Government attempts to preserve maximum control by a commander over his troops and associated personnel. This is done in two ways: first, by providing in the agreement a legal basis for the exercise of jurisdiction by the military commander and second, by providing in Agreed Minutes or in other less formal arrangements for the waiver to the United States by the host country of a maximum number of cases in which the host country has jurisdiction. This is the world-wide practice of the U.S. Government. It is reflected in the U.S. draft.

18. Referring to the six points which Mr. Chang had discussed in his statement, Mr. Habib recalled that Mr. Chang had questioned the U.S. proposal to designate a combat zone in which the military commander would have exclusive jurisdiction. This proposal is designed to take into account the military purpose of the presence of the U.S. armed forces in Korea and to take into account the unique conditions which exist here. Korea is the only area in the world in which it is proposed to bring under a status of forces agreement U.S. combat troops deployed in battle position against an active enemy. It is essential in such a combat area that the combat troops be instantly responsive to the will of their military commander. Their situation is not at all the same as that of administrative troops living in rear areas in England, France, Italy, and Japan. In those countries, U.S. troops live in and among the civilian population and carry on their duties much as any civilian would do. By contrast, the troops in the forward areas in Korea live in their battle positions with their weapons ready to fight off an aggressor. It is not appropriate that they should be hailed away from these positions upon

complaint made in some distant court. They are totally amenable to a rigid code of military justice and any criminal act of theirs does not go unpunished. The U.S. commanders must retain their power to punish these troops and under U.S. law they are well able to do so.

19. Mr. Habib stated that if the Korean negotiators had some question about the geographical extent of such a combat zone, as had been indicated by Mr. Chang at the previous meeting, the U.S. negotiators were quite willing to discuss what its proper boundaries should be. While the Korean negotiators had referred to certain major offenses which had occurred in this zone, there have also occurred numerous incursions from North Korea. These have been met by the armed action of both U.S. and ROK forces. At this point, the U.S. negotiators displayed a map of the area, on which were delineated the Demilitarized Zone, the Civilian Control Line, and the proposed boundary of the combat zone. Pinpointed on the map were the sites of North Korean incursions which had occurred since October, 1962. Mr. Habib pointed out that the map did not take into account the almost nightly disturbances in the DMZ.

20. Mr. Habib then referred to the second point regarding which Mr. Chang had expressed concern: the U.S. proposal for waiver of cases where there are concurrent rights of jurisdiction. Mr. Habib pointed out that this is a standard provision in most of the U.S. status of forces agreements. He cited particularly the Netherlands and Greek bilateral agreements with the United States in the NATO area; the West Indies agreement in the western hemisphere; the new German agreement, which applies to the situation which is the closest approach to the combat conditions existing in Korea; and the 12 years of practice under the Japanese agreement in the Pacific area. He then provided to the Korean negotiators a copy of Department of Defense Statistics on the Exercise of Criminal Jurisdiction by Foreign Tribunals over United States Personnel, 1 December 1961 - 30 November 1962, an annual shows the percentages of waiver in

0030

all countries where U.S. forces are stationed. This book shows that during the latest year for which published reports are available, of all cases in which the host government had the primary right to exercise jurisdiction about 60% were waived to the United States. In Japan over 90% of such cases were waived to the United States. Mr. Habib remarked that these figures have been fairly constant over the entire 12-year experience of the U.S. armed forces with status of forces agreements. There appears to be nothing objectionable to the host governments in waiving jurisdiction granted to them under these agreements.

21. The third point to which Mr. Chang had objected, continued Mr. Habib, was the Agreed Minute proposed by the U.S. negotiators which asked the ROK Government to give sympathetic consideration to the waiver of cases in which the Agreement would give the Korean authorities exclusive jurisdiction. In many cases of offenses committed by members of the civilian component and dependents, an administrative or disciplinary sanction may be appropriate instead of a criminal penalty. In such a case, both the ROK Government and the U.S. Government may be willing to forego a criminal penalty. The U.S. proposal states merely that the ROK Government will give sympathetic consideration to such a proposal. It does not seem reasonable to the U.S. negotiators that the Korean negotiators would object to such a humanitarian statement, which does not commit the ROK Government to any action in a particular case but merely states that it will give sympathetic consideration. The ultimate decision in any such case is left totally to the discretion of the ROK Government.

22. Mr. Habib then referred to the objection of the Korean negotiators to the U.S. proposal that if an offense committed by a member of the ROK armed forces would have been tried by court-martial, then such an offense committed by a member of the U.S. armed forces would also be subject to trial by court-martial, convened under the authority of a U.S. military commander. If a ROK soldier is to be tried for an offense by a court-martial under ROK law, then a U.S. soldier committing the same offense should be tried by a court-martial under U.S. law. This seems fair and

0031

reasonable to the U.S. negotiators. Asking why it did not seem fair and reasonable to the Korean negotiators, Mr. Habib pointed out that if the Korean negotiators insisted that a U.S. soldier committing such an offense should be tried by a Korean civil court, they would be making a special provision outside of present Korean law to handle such a case and they would be disregarding the military status of the offender, a status which ROK law does recognize for ROK soldiers.

23. Mr. Habib noted that the Korean negotiators had also raised the question of pre-trial custody. The U.S. negotiators had proposed that such custody be retained by the U.S. armed forces. They had made this proposal partly because an examination of the ROK pre-trial detention facilities had indicated that they are not satisfactory places for an American soldier, civilian employee, or dependent to be confined while awaiting trial and partly because of the many cases reported in Korean newspapers in which persons awaiting trial in Korean courts have been subjected to torture and compulsion to incriminate themselves. The U.S. armed forces do not intend to subject their personnel to such pre-trial treatment. The U.S. armed forces will undertake to guarantee that accused persons will be held in Korea if they are to be tried in Korean courts and will not be allowed to escape ROK jurisdiction. With such an undertaking on the part of the U.S. armed forces, there should be no need for the Korean negotiators to insist upon pre-trial custody in ROK facilities. Mr. Habib pointed out that the U.S. proposal would provide economic benefits to the ROK Government since it would avoid making it necessary for the ROK authorities to make any special provisions for detention of U.S. personnel awaiting trial. He also noted that the U.S. armed forces in Germany retain full pre-trial custody in all cases.

24. Mr. Habib recalled that Mr. Chang had also questioned the U.S. proposal that the ROK Government give sympathetic consideration to a request from the U.S. authorities that an offender serve his post-trial sentence in a U.S. prison rather than in a Korean prison. He pointed out that this proposal had been made first not

0032

by the U.S. negotiators but by Foreign Ministry officials during a conference with Embassy officers in 1961. This proposal also would be economically beneficial to the ROK Government.

25. Having thus discussed the six points raised by the Korean negotiators in Mr. Chang's statement of February 28, Mr. Habib said he would like to discuss several points not mentioned in that statement. A major point of difference between the two drafts is the manner in which they deal with the "performance of duty certificate". While the U.S. draft makes it clear that the issuance of this certificate by U.S. military authorities is conclusive, the Korean draft provides that the final determination of the validity of such a certificate would be made not by the U.S. authorities, nor even by a Korean court, but instead would be made administratively by a local prosecutor. The U.S. position expresses world-wide practice in status of forces agreements since their beginning in 1952. There is no precedent anywhere for the Korean proposal. In the case of NATO, the negotiating record makes it clear that it was the understanding of the negotiators that the question of the performance of duty could be determined only by the authorities of the visiting forces. This has been the universal practice in NATO ever since. In only one case did a NATO government question a duty certificate. In the Martin case in France, the Court of Cassation, the highest court in France, decided for all time that such a certificate was final and could not be questioned by the French Government. In many agreements, the finality of the duty certificate is spelled out; in those cases where it is not spelled out, it has been accepted in practice. This is entirely reasonable, as no one other than a military commander is competent to determine whether one of his soldiers is or is not performing an assigned duty.

26. A further difference between the two drafts, Mr. Habib continued, is that in many critical paragraphs the Korean text omits the word "dependent" and limits the coverage of this article to members of the armed forces and the civilian component.

0033

The United States Government is certainly as much concerned about the treatment of dependents as about the treatment of members of the armed forces and civilian employees. The U.S. negotiators must insist, therefore, that dependents be covered in the SOFA with the ROK Government in the same way that they are covered in the agreements with Japan and all the NATO governments. If the Korean negotiators were concerned about the effect of the U.S. Supreme Court decisions in 1960 regarding military jurisdiction over civilians, Mr. Habib stated, the U.S. negotiators would like to point out that: (a) the U.S. armed forces have as much jurisdiction over dependents as they do over the civilian component, which has been included in the Korean draft; and (b) all of the status of forces agreements concluded since the 1960 decisions have included the word "dependent", just as the earlier ones did.

27. Mr. Habib then noted that the Korean draft omits any reference to the outbreak of hostilities, which is covered by paragraph 11 of the U.S. draft. In the event of a reopening of hostilities and any penetration of the ROK by Communist forces, the full strength of the U.S. armed forces will be needed to fight them off. U.S. personnel cannot be left to be overrun in ROK prisons or be absent from their duties while defending themselves in civilian courts. The U.S. military justice system will deal adequately with any wrongdoing.

28. Mr. Habib also noted that the Korean draft makes no provision for the disposition of cases which may have arisen prior to the coming into effect of the SOFA. This is covered by paragraph 12 of the U.S. draft, which is based exactly on the corresponding paragraph of the SOFA with Japan. The U.S. negotiators do not believe the Korean negotiators can have any serious objection to it.

29. Mr. Habib stated that during disorders of the sort which would justify the imposition of martial law, the U.S. armed forces could not allow their personnel to be tried by the summary procedures of ROK military courts. The U.S. draft provides against such an eventuality; the Korean draft does not.

0034

30. The U.S. draft, Mr. Habib pointed out, lists trial safeguards which

have been shown to be necessary as a result of a study of Korean criminal procedure, laws, and practices. These safeguards relate to public trial, confidential access to counsel, a right to examine the evidence and to be present when it is received, and many other points.

31. Mr. Habib then referred to the U.S. Agreed Minute regarding the provision of assistance in providing witnesses in each other's courts. He stated that this is a fair and equal Minute, with reciprocal provisions. The corresponding Agreed Minute in the Korean draft is entirely one-sided, has no equivalent in any other status of forces agreement, and is not acceptable to the U.S. negotiators. Among its other objectionable features, it is so broad as to permit U.S. officials to be called into Korean courts to testify on their conduct of their duties and on the official business of the United States Government. This is contrary to international practice and is not called for in any other SOFA. It is not acceptable to the U.S. negotiators.

32. Mr. Habib stated that the Korean draft is unduly restrictive on the military police powers of the U.S. armed forces and would prevent U.S. military police from being able to control such allied forces as the Thai and Turk contingents. This limitation is not desirable neither for the U.S. armed forces nor for the ROK Government.

33. Mr. Habib stated that a number of other differences exist between the two drafts but that some of them are related to the major differences already discussed; when the major differences have been resolved, the minor ones may be more easily reconciled. Mr. Habib indicated that the U.S. negotiators had now responded to the statement made at the previous meeting by the Korean negotiators. In addition, he had made some preliminary comments on points which had not been mentioned by the Korean negotiators. The U.S. negotiators, in giving their views on the key elements of this article, had suggested that some of the differences between the two drafts were

0035

not as great as the Korean negotiators might have thought. They had referred to precedents in other status of forces agreements and in actual practice under those agreements, so that the present negotiations might benefit from those precedents. The U.S. negotiators had also pointed out the uniqueness of the conditions under which the U.S. armed forces operated in Korea and the effect of this uniqueness on the provisions of this article. In discussing this article, the U.S. negotiators had identified those facts in the situation which create problems for them and for the U.S. armed forces. If they had been critical, they hoped that the Korean negotiators would take the criticism in the spirit in which it had been given. The U.S. negotiators believed that a basis had now been laid for negotiation of this article. They were prepared to listen to any comments which the Korean negotiators might wish to make.

34. Mr. Chang replied that at the previous meeting, the Korean negotiators had not attempted to mention all of the differences between the two drafts because they had wished to concentrate on the most important points. They now wished to make some further remarks, including some indirect comments on the remarks just made by Mr. Habib.

35. Mr. Chang stated that the Korean negotiators had noticed that the U.S. draft used the term "civil authorities of the Republic of Korea" rather than "authorities of the Republic of Korea". This appeared to imply that members of the U.S. armed forces would be subject to Korean civilian courts but not to Korean military courts. However, under Korean law, even civilians are subject to court-martial in circumstances, for specific offenses under special. Nevertheless, the Korean Supreme Court has final appellate jurisdiction over courts-martial, thereby guaranteeing to every defendant his basic human rights to the maximum extent.

36. Mr. Chang noted that the Korean draft uses the term "military authorities of the United States" whereas the U.S. draft uses the term "authorities of the United States". The Korean negotiators that this did not imply that the U.S.

0036

Korean nationals ought to equality ... and Constitution. Consequently, the Korean negotiators were not in the position to differentiate the benefits of law, protection and means of redress on the basis of difference in locality. In this respect also, the concept of combat zone

negotiators were thinking in terms of some U.S. authority other than U.S. military authorities having jurisdiction in the Republic of Korea. If that is the case, the Korean negotiators found no difficulty for the U.S. side to accept the Korean draft.

37. Referring to the concept of the combat zone, Mr. Chang recalled that at the last meeting the Korean negotiators had objected to this apparent intention on the part of the U.S. negotiators to restrict the jurisdiction of the ROK authorities over a portion of ROK territory. ~~He said the Korean negotiators were not in a position to agree to restrictions on the jurisdiction of ROK authorities on the basis of geography.~~ Such a restriction would hardly be compatible with the spirit of the ROK Constitution.

38. With regard to the question of duty certificates, Mr. Chang said the Korean negotiators had defined specific procedures in the Korean draft in order to prevent this matter from becoming a controversial issue in the future in actual application. They had tried to avoid ambiguity by defining the exact meaning of "duty offenses".

39. Mr. Chang stated that the position of the Korean negotiators with regard to dependents had been made clear during discussion of other articles. They believed that, in application of judicial rights also, a clear distinction should be made between dependents and members of the armed forces and the civilian component who are performing military missions. They believed that dependents should be excluded from the application of this article.

40. Regarding exclusive jurisdiction, Mr. Chang stated that both drafts give to the ROK Government the right to exercise exclusive jurisdiction with respect to offenses punishable by Korean law but not by U.S. law. In such cases, the Korean negotiators believe the right of the ROK Government to exercise jurisdiction is inalienable and not subject to waiver.

41. Mr. Chang noted also that the U.S. draft provides for a general waiver of the primary right to exercise jurisdiction. He said such a provision is not consonant with the principle of mutual recognition by each government of the primary right of jurisdiction of the other which was specifically set forth in both texts. With regard to precedents in other status of forces agreements regarding waiver, Mr. Chang indicated that ~~the Korean negotiators did not intend~~

0037

the Korean authorities prepared waive in many cases as in the precedents referred to by the U.S. negotiator, ~~to rule out waiver completely~~ but believed that this Agreement should contain the same language and expressions as other status of forces agreements.

42. Mr. Chang stated that the Korean negotiators would respond more specifically at the next meeting to the statement made at today's meeting by the U.S. negotiators. Mr. Habib suggested that the next meeting be devoted to answering questions regarding the two drafts. It was agreed to hold the next meeting on March 13 at 2:00 p.m. The meeting was then adjourned.

0038

JOINT SUMMARY RECORD OF THE 45TH SESSION

1. Time and Place: 2:00-4:10 P.M. March 6, 1964 at the Foreign Ministry's Conference Room (No. 1)

2. Attendants:

ROK Side:

Mr. Chang, Sang Moon	Director European and American Affairs Bureau
Mr. Yoon, Doo Sik	Director Prosecutor's Bureau Ministry of Justice
Mr. Shin, Kang Sup	Director Employment Security Bureau Office of Labor Affairs
Mr. Koo, Choong Whay	Chief, American Section Ministry of Foreign Affairs
Mr. Chung, Tai Kyun	Chief Prosecutor's Section Prosecutor's Bureau Ministry of Justice
Col. Kim, Won Kil	Chief, Military Affairs Section Ministry of National Defense
Mr. Oh, Jae Hee	Chief, Treaty Section Ministry of Foreign Affairs
Mr. Chung, Woo Young (Rapporteur and Interpreter)	3rd Secretary Ministry of Foreign Affairs
Mr. Lee, Chung Bin	3rd Secretary Ministry of Foreign Affairs
Mr. Lee, Keun Pal	3rd Secretary Ministry of Foreign Affairs
Mr. Kim, Nai Sung	Staff Officer Europe Section Ministry of Foreign Affairs

U.S. Side:

Mr. Philip C. Habib	Counselor American Embassy
Brig. Gen. G.G. O'Connor	Deputy Chief of Staff 8th U.S. Army

0039

Brig. Gen. L.J. Fuller	Staff Judge Advocate United Nations Command
Col. Howard Smigelow	Deputy Chief of Staff 8th U.S. Army
Col. Kenneth C. Crawford	Staff Judge Advocates Office 8th U.S. Army
Mr. Benjamin A. Fleck (Rapporteur and Press Officer)	First Secretary Americnn Embassy
Mr. James Sartorius	2nd Secretary American Embassy
Mr. Robert A. Kinney	J-5 8th U.S. Army
Mr. Robert D. Peckham	Staff Officer, JAG 8th U.S. Army
Mr. Kenneth Campen	Interpreter
Mr. D.C. Reed	Director Office of Civil Personnel 8th U.S. Army

Utilities and Services

1. Mr. Chang opened the meeting by recalling that at the previous meeting, agreement had been reached on the text of the utilities and services provisions and Agreed Minute #2. He said the Korean negotiators were prepared to agree to the revised Agreed Minute #1 tabled at the previous meeting by the U.S. negotiators. The Korean negotiators did so with two understandings to be recorded in the negotiating record. The first understanding was that consultation in the Joint Committee, which will provide an opportunity for the U.S. authorities to make known their views concerning proposed changes, will in no way prejudice the right of the ROK authorities to make the final decision regarding such changes. The second understanding was that there might be rare occasions on which the ROK authorities would not be able to provide advance consultation. One such occasion might occur, for instance, if the National Assembly should pass a law on December 31 providing for rate

0040

changes to go into effect on January 1. Mr. Chang stated that this would be an extreme case and the Korean negotiators did not anticipate its occurrence.

2. Mr. Chang stated that the Korean negotiators were also prepared to agree to the revised Agreed Minute #3 tabled at the previous meeting by the U.S. negotiators, with the understanding that the measures to be taken by the ROK authorities would be such measures as were determined to be appropriate by the ROK and U.S. authorities through consultation.

3. Mr. Habib replied that the U.S. negotiators agreed to the first understanding stated by the Korean negotiators with regard to Agreed Minute #1. The second understanding did not appear to pose any great problems. The U.S. negotiators assumed that if there were pending in the National Assembly a bill dealing with rate changes, the provisions of the bill would be known and discussed in the Joint Committee prior to the bill's passage. The U.S. negotiators accepted both understandings, since the Joint Committee would be capable of handling the situations to which they pertained. The U.S. negotiators also agreed to the understanding stated by the Korean negotiators with regard Agreed Minute #3.

4. Full agreement was thereupon reached on the text of the provisions dealing with utilities and services.

Accounting Procedures

5. The negotiators confirmed the agreement reached at the previous meeting to make paragraph 4 of the U.S. draft of the utilities and services provisions into a separate article in the Status of Forces Agreement.

0041

Labor Procurement

6. Turning to discussion of the Labor Procurement Article, Brig. Gen. Fuller stated that the U.S. negotiators wished to make a general comment. In 1945, he pointed out, both Japan and Germany were conquered enemy countries. U.S. forces occupied those countries in a military occupation. As a defeated enemy, the Japanese Government, in so far as it was allowed to govern, did so only as an agent of the Supreme Commander of the Allied Powers. As for labor, the Japanese Government was simply called upon to provide it wherever the Supreme Commander required it. It was provided free, without any cost to the United States. In both Japan and Germany the wages of this labor were paid by the Japanese or German governments, without any reimbursement by the United States. These wages were part of the occupation costs paid by a defeated enemy. This was the origin of the system of indirect hire which the U.S. armed forces use today in Japan. As both Japan and Germany went through successive stages and were converted from enemies to allies, the nature of the U.S. military presence changed from that of military occupiers to that of visiting forces and the occupation costs came to be shared, with the United States Government taking over the payment of some of them, including labor costs. But the system of indirect hire, which still exists in Japan, in which the Japanese Government obtains the labor force for the U.S. armed forces, is a carryover from the military occupation of a defeated enemy country. The U.S. armed forces do not have any such arrangement with any of the other free countries

0042

in the Pacific area. In China, the Philippines, Australia, Okinawa, Vietnam, Thailand, and Korea, the U.S. armed forces hire labor directly in the free labor market. It is not impressed by the local government for the U.S. armed forces in any of these countries. Such an arrangement would not be proper, for it would be typical of a military occupation. The U.S. armed forces are in Korea not as military occupiers but at the invitation of the ROK Government and in response to the call of the United Nations. The relationship between the ROK Government and the U.S. armed forces is that of host and guest. They are free and equal allies in a common cause. The employment of labor by the U.S. armed forces in Korea has been that typical of a free employer on the one hand and a free labor force on the other. The U.S. armed forces have tried to be a good employer in conformity with Korean labor laws and practice. They will continue to be such. But it would be grossly improper and a very backward step after 19 years of free labor practice for the SOFA negotiators now to adopt the Japanese labor article based on an impressed labor system imposed upon a defeated enemy.

7. Gen. Fuller explained that it was for the foregoing reasons that the U.S. draft of the Labor Procurement Article is worded as it is and is not based on the Japanese article. During the previous discussion of this article, the Korean negotiators had raised certain objections to the U.S. draft. In consequence, the U.S. negotiators wished to propose certain changes in the U.S. draft which they believed would meet the

0043

desires of the Korean negotiators. These changes are taken not from the Japanese article but instead are designed to make the U.S. draft more fully representative of the stated preferences of the Korean negotiators.

8. In paragraph 1(b), Gen. Fuller continued, the U.S. negotiators offered to delete the phrase "who is an employee of the Government of Korea", as had been suggested by the Korean Negotiators.

9. In paragraph 2, the U.S. negotiators proposed the addition of the words "and upon request by the employer, with the assistance of the authorities of the Republic of Korea". This also was based upon a suggestion by the Korean negotiators. Gen. Fuller pointed out that while this language was not exactly that suggested by the Korean negotiators, it was absolutely as far as the U.S. negotiators could go in that direction. The U.S. armed forces simply can not be bound to obtain no employees at all except through ROK governmental agencies. In an agreement designed to create a status for the U.S. armed forces somewhat better than that of tourists and businessmen, the U.S. armed forces cannot accept a limitation on employing a labor force which is more restrictive than those placed upon businessmen operating in the Republic of Korea, whether Korean or third-country nationals. Gen. Fuller pointed out that the revised language proposed by the U.S. negotiators was very similar to that in the labor article of the recently negotiated SOFA with Australia. Australia is an important ally of the United States and is a first-class power in the Pacific area. The U.S. negotiators asked the Korean negotiators to give weight to these facts in their consideration of this proposal.

0044

10. From paragraph 3 of the U.S. draft, Gen. Fuller continued, the U.S. negotiators offered to delete the words "provided however, that an employer may terminate employment whenever the continuation of such employment would materially impair the accomplishment of the mission of the United States armed forces" and to place them instead in the Agreed Minutes as the second sentence of Agreed Minute #2, where they would then read: "Moreover, the United States Government may terminate employment whenever the continuation of such employment would materially impair the accomplishment of the mission of the United States armed forces". Gen. Fuller remarked that this proposal was designed to meet an objection previously made by the Korean negotiators.

11. As their fourth proposal, Gen. Fuller continued, the U.S. negotiators offered to add a new Agreed Minute to read as follows:

> "3. It is understood that the Government of the Republic of Korea shall be reimbursed for direct costs incurred in providing assistance requested pursuant to paragraph 2."

This proposal was being made in response to a suggestion made by the Korean negotiators during previous discussion of this article.

12. Finally, Gen. Fuller stated, the U.S. negotiators had been authorized to state that the principle of withholding by the U.S. armed forces of employee contributions to social security and of income tax payments is acceptable to the United States Government. The U.S. authorities believed that an obligation to withhold such contributions and payments is included in the commitment in the U.S. draft to establish labor practices "in general conformity" with Korean labor laws, customs, and practices. However, should the Korean negotiators desire to include in the article

0047

a specific reference to this obligation to withhold taxes, the U.S. negotiators believed that suitable language could be worked out.

13. Gen. Fuller stated that the U.S. negotiators would like to make one additional comment concerning the language in paragraph 3 of the U.S. draft, which calls for general conformity with Korean labor laws, customs, and practices. The United States fully recognizes the sovereignty of the Republic of Korea. At the same time, it should be remembered that the United States is also a sovereign nation and that under accepted principles of international law, it is not proper for one sovereign government to hail another sovereign government into its courts as a defendant or before its administrative tribunals as a respondent. It is precisely for this reason that the U.S. armed forces cannot now or at any time in the future agree to comply with any law which requires the Government of the United States to appear when summoned before a court or board. This is not done in Japan or Germany. In those states, the judicial or administrative actions brought by employees or their representatives are defended or responded to by the governments of Japan and Germany, not by the United States Government. The U.S. armed forces are most willing to be helped and advised by the competent ministries of the ROK Government in the settlement of any labor dispute but the U.S. negotiators cannot agree that the United States Government give up a right inherent in every sovereign state not to be brought against its will before the tribunals of another sovereign state.

0046

The position of the United States Government on this point cannot change, either in Korea or anywhere else in the world. It is a universal principle of international law.

14. Gen. Fuller reiterated that the five proposals just made by the U.S. negotiators had been made out of a desire to be responsive to the legitimate requirements of the Korean negotiators. The proposals do not fully meet the Korean position, as expressed in the previous discussion of this article, but they are as far as the U.S. negotiators can go toward meeting the Korean position. He asked the Korean negotiators to give full consideration to these proposals and state their views at the next meeting.

15. Mr. Chang thanked Gen. Fuller for his explanation of the U.S. proposals and stated that the Korean negotiators would comment on them at the next meeting.

Criminal Jurisdiction

16. Turning to the Criminal Jurisdiction Article, Mr. Habib stated that the U.S. negotiators had carefully examined the statement made by Mr. Chang at the previous meeting, in presenting the comments of the Korean negotiators on the U.S. draft of this article. The U.S. negotiators would respond to the six points made by Mr. Chang and would discuss a number of points which he had not mentioned. Before doing so, however, Mr. Habib said the U.S. negotiators would like to make a general statement.

17. Mr. Habib said Mr. Chang had stated that, in general, it appeared to be the U.S. intention to retain jurisdiction over members of the U.S. armed forces in

0047

Korea, to the maximum extent possible. This is indeed the U.S. intention, for the reason spelled out in full in the Agreed Minutes of the U.S. draft. The reason is that it is the primary responsibility of any military commander to maintain good order and discipline among his troops and associated personnel. To do so, he must have jurisdiction over them. In all of its status of forces agreements, the U.S. Government attempts to preserve maximum control by a commander over his troops and associated personnel. This is done in two ways: first, by providing in the agreement a legal basis for the exercise of jurisdiction by the military commander and second, by providing in Agreed Minutes or in other less formal arrangements for the waiver to the United States by the host country of a maximum number of cases in which the host country has jurisdiction. This is the world-wide practice of the U.S. Government. It is reflected in the U.S. draft.

18. Referring to the six points which Mr. Chang had discussed in his statement, Mr. Habib recalled that Mr. Chang had questioned the U.S. proposal to designate a combat zone in which the military commander could have exclusive jurisdiction. This proposal is designed to take into account the military purpose of the presence of the U.S. armed forces in Korea and to take into account the unique conditions which exist here. Korea is the only area in the world in which it is proposed to bring under a status of forces agreement U.S. combat troops deployed in battle position against an active enemy. It is essential in such a combat area that the combat troops be instantly

0048

responsive to the will of their military commander. Their situation is not at all the same as that of administrative troops living in rear areas in England, France, Italy, and Japan. In those countries, U.S. troops live in and among the civilian population and carry on their duties much as any civilian would do. By contrast, the troops in the forward areas in Korea live in their battle positions with their weapons ready to fight off an aggressor. It is not appropriate that they should be hailed away from these positions upon complaint made in some distant court. They are totally amenable to a rigid code of military justice and any criminal act of theirs does not go unpunished. The U.S. commanders must retain their power to punish these troops and under U.S. law they are well able to do so.

19. Mr. Habib stated that if the Korean negotiators had some question about the geographical extent of such a combat zone, as had been indicated by Mr. Chang at the previous meeting, the U.S. negotiators were quite willing to discuss what its proper boundaries should be. While the Korean negotiators had referred to certain major offenses which had occurred in this zone, there have also occurred numerous incursions from North Korea. These have been met by the armed action of both U.S. and ROK forces. At this point, the U.S. negotiators displayed a map of the area, on which were delineated the Demilitarized Zone, the Civilian Control Line, and the proposed boundary of the combat zone. Pinpointed on the map were the sites of North Korean incursions which had occurred since October, 1962. Mr. Habib pointed out that the map did not take into account the almost nightly disturbances in the DMZ.

0049

20. Mr. Habib then referred to the second point regarding which Mr. Chang had expressed concern: the U.S. proposal for waiver of cases where there are concurrent rights of jurisdiction. Mr. Habib pointed out that this is a standard provision in most of the U.S. status of forces agreements. He cited particularly the Netherlands and Greek bilateral agreements with the United States in the NATO area; the West Indies agreement in the western hemisphere; the new German agreement, which applies to the situation which is the closest approach to the combat conditions existing in Korea; and the 12 years of practice under the Japanese agreement in the Pacific area. He then provided to the Korean negotiators a copy of Department of Defense Statistics on the Exercise of Criminal Jurisdiction by Foreign Tribunals over United States Personnel, 1 December 1961 - 30 November 1962, an annual publication which shows the percentages of waiver in all countries where U.S. forces are stationed. This book shows that during the latest year for which published reports are available, of all cases in which the host government had the primary right to exercise jurisdiction about 60% were waived to the United States. In Japan over 90% of such cases were waived to the United States. Mr. Habib remarked that these figures have been fairly constant over the entire 12-year experience of the U.S. armed forces with status of forces agreements. There appears to be nothing objectionable to the host governments in waiving jurisdiction granted to them under these agreements.

0050

21. The third point to which Mr. Chang had objected, continued Mr. Habib, was the Agreed Minute proposed by the U.S. negotiators which asked the ROK Government to give sympathetic consideration to the waiver of cases in which the Agreement would give the Korean authorities exclusive jurisdiction. In many cases of offenses committed by members of the civilian component and dependents, an administrative or disciplinary sanction may be appropriate instead of a criminal penalty. In such a case, both the ROK Government and the U.S. Government may be willing to forego a criminal penalty. The U.S. proposal states merely that the ROK Government will give sympathetic consideration to such a proposal. It does not seem reasonable to the U.S. negotiators that the Korean negotiators would object to such a humanitarian statement, which does not commit the ROK Government to any action in a particular case but merely states that it will give sympathetic consideration. The ultimate decision in any such case is left totally to the discretion of the ROK Government.

22. Mr. Habib then referred to the objection of the Korean negotiators to the U.S. proposal that if an offense committed by a member of the ROK armed forces would have been tried by court-martial, then such an offense committed by a member of the U.S. armed forces would also be subject to trial by court-martial, convened under the authority of a U.S. military commander. If a ROK soldier is to be tried for an offense by a court-martial under ROK law, then a U.S. soldier committing the same offense should be tried by a court-martial

0051

under U.S. law. This seems fair and reasonable to the U.S. negotiators. Asking why it did not seem fair and reasonable to the Korean negotiators, Mr. Habib pointed out that if the Korean negotiators insisted that a U.S. soldier committing such an offense should be tried by a Korean civil court, they would be making a special provision outside of present Korean law to handle such a case and they would be disregarding the military status of the offender, a status which ROK law does recognize for ROK soldiers.

23. Mr. Habib noted that the Korean negotiators had also raised the question of pre-trial custody. The U.S. negotiators had proposed that such custody be retained by the U.S. armed forces. They had made this proposal partly because an examination of the ROK pre-trial detention facilities had indicated that they are not satisfactory places for an American soldier, civilian employee, or dependent to be confined while awaiting trial and partly because of the many cases reported in Korean newspapers in which persons awaiting trial in Korean courts have been subjected to torture and compulsion to incriminate themselves. The U.S. armed forces do not intend to subject their personnel to such pre-trial treatment. The U.S. armed forces will undertake to guarantee that accused persons will be held in Korea if they are to be tried in Korean courts and will not be allowed to escape ROK jurisdiction. With such an undertaking on the part of the U.S. armed forces, there should be no need for the Korean negotiators to insist upon pre-trial custody in ROK facilities.

0052

Mr. Habib pointed out that the U.S. proposal would provide economic benefits to the ROK Government since it would avoid making it necessary for the ROK authorities to make any special provisions for detention of U.S. personnel awaiting trial. He also noted that the U.S. armed forces in Germany retain full pre-trial custody in all cases.

24. Mr. Habib recalled that Mr. Chang had also questioned the U.S. proposal that the ROK Government give sympathetic consideration to a request from the U.S. authorities that an offender serve his post-trial sentence in a U.S. prison rather than in a Korean prison. He pointed out that this proposal had been made first not by the U.S. negotiators but by Foreign Ministry officials during a conference with Embassy officers in 1961. This proposal also would be economically beneficial to the ROK Government.

25. Having thus discussed the six points raised by the Korean negotiators in Mr. Chang's statement of February 28, Mr. Habib said he would like to discuss several points not mentioned in that statement. A major point of difference between the two drafts is the manner in which they deal with the "performance of duty certificate". While the U.S. draft makes it clear that the issuance of this certificate by U.S. military authorities is conclusive, the Korean draft provides that the final determination of the validity of such a certificate would be made not by the U.S. authorities, nor even by a Korean court, but instead would be made administratively by a local prosecutor. The U.S. position expresses world-wide practice in status of forces agreements since their beginning in 1952. There is no precedent anywhere for the Korean proposal. In the

0053

case of NATO, the negotiating record makes it clear that it was the understanding of the negotiators that the question of the performance of duty could be determined only by the authorities of the visiting forces. This has been the universal practice in NATO ever since. In only one case did a NATO government qudstion a duty certificate. In the Martin case in France, the Court of Cassation, the highest court in France, decided for all time that such a certificate was final and could not be questioned by the French Government. In many agreements, the finality of the duty certificate is spelled out; in those cases where it is not spelled out, it has been accepted in practice. This is entirely reasonable, as no one other than a military commander is competent to determine whether one of his soldiers is or is not performing an assigned duty.

26. A further difference between the two drafts, Mr. Habib continued, is that in many critical paragraphs the Korean text omits the word "dependent" and limits the coverage of this article to members of the armed forces and the civilian component. The United States Government is certainly as much concerned about the treatment of dependents as about the treatment of members of the armed forces and civilian employees. The U.S. negotiators must insist, therefore, that dependents be covered in the SOFA with the ROK Government in the same way that they are covered in the agreements with Japan and all the NATO governments. If the Korean negotiators were concenred about the effect of the U.S. Supreme Court decisions in 1960 regarding military jurisdiction over civilians, Mr. Habib stated, the U.S. negotiators would like to point

0054

out that: (a) the U.S. armed forces have as much jurisdiction over dependents as they do over the civilian component, which has been included in the Korean draft; and (b) all of the status of forces agreements concluded since the 1960 decisions have included the word "dependent", just as the earlier ones did.

27. Mr. Habib then noted that the Korean draft omits any reference to the outbreak of hostilities, which is covered by paragraph 11 of the U.S. draft. In the event of a reopening of hostilities and any penetration of the ROK by Communist forces, the full strength of the U.S. armed forces will be needed to fight them off. U.S. personnel cannot be left to be overrun in ROK prisons or be absent from their duties while defending themselves in civilian courts. The U.S. military justice system will deal adequately with any wrongdoing.

28. Mr. Habib also noted that the Korean draft makes no provision for the disposition of cases which may have arisen prior to the coming into effect of the SOFA. This is covered by paragraph 12 of the U.S. draft, which is based exactly on the corresponding paragraph of the SOFA with Japan. The U.S. negotiators do not believe the Korean negotiators can have any serious objection to it.

29. Mr. Habib stated that during disorders of the sort which would justify the imposition of martial law, the U.S. armed forces could not allow their personnel to be tried by the summary procedures of ROK military courts. The U.S. draft provides against such an eventuality; the Korean draft does not.

30. The U.S. draft, Mr. Habib pointed out, lists trial safeguards which have been shown to be necessary as a result of a study of Korean criminal procedure, laws, and practices. These safeguards relate to public trial, confidential access to counsel, a right to examine the evidence and to be present when it is received, and many other points.

31. Mr. Habib then referred to the U.S. Agreed Minute regarding the provision of assistance in providing witnesses in each other's courts. He stated that this is a fair and equal Minute, with reciprocal provisions. The corresponding Agreed Minute in the Korean draft is entirely one-sided, has no equivalent in any other status of forces agreement, and is not acceptable to the U.S. negotiators. Among its other objectionable features, it is so broad as to permit U.S. officials to be called into Korean courts to testify on their conduct of their duties and on the official business of the United States Government. This is contrary to international practice and is not called for in any other SOFA. It is not acceptable to the U.S. negotiators.

32. Mr. Habib stated that the Korean draft is unduly restrictive on the military police powers of the U.S. armed forces and would prevent U.S. military police from being able to control such allied forces as the Thai and Turk contingents. This limitation is not desirable either for the U.S. armed forces or for the ROK Government.

33. Mr. Habib stated that a number of other differences exist between the two drafts but that some

0056

of them are related to the major differences already discussed; when the major differences have been resolved, the minor ones may be more easily reconciled. Mr. Habib indicated that the U.S. negotiators had now responded to the statement made at the previous meeting by the Korean negotiators. In addition, he had made some preliminary comments on points which had not been mentioned by the Korean negotiators. The U.S. negotiators, in giving their views on the key elements of this article, had suggested that some of the differences between the two drafts were not as great as the Korean negotiators might have thought. They had referred to precedents in other status of forces agreements and in actual practice under those agreements, so that the present negotiations might benefit from those precedents. The U.S. negotiators had also pointed out the uniqueness of the conditions under which the U.S. armed forces operated in Korea and the effect of this uniqueness on the provisions of this article. In discussing this article, the U.S. negotiators had identified those facts in the situation which create problems for them and for the U.S. armed forces. If they had been critical, they hoped that the Korean negotiators would take the criticism in the spirit in which it had been given. The U.S. negotiators believed that a basis had now been laid for negotiation of this article. They were prepared to listen to any comments which the Korean negotiators might wish to make.

34. Mr. Chang replied that at the previous meeting, the Korean negotiators had not attempted to mention all of the differences between the two drafts because

0057

they had wished to concentrate on the most important points. They now wished to make some further remarks, including some indirect comments on the remarks just made by Mr. Habib.

35. Mr. Chang stated that the Korean negotiators had noticed that the U.S. draft used the term "civil authorities of the Republic of Korea" rather than "authorities of the Republic of Korea." This appeared to imply that members of the U.S. armed forces would be subject to Korean civilian courts but nor to Korean military courts. However, under Korean law, even civilians are subject to court-martial for specific offenses under special circumstances. Nevertheless, the Korean Supreme Court has final appellate jurisdiction over courts-martial, thereby guaranteeing to every defendant his basic human rights to the maximum extent.

36. Mr. Chang noted that the Korean draft uses the term "military authorities of the United States" whereas the U.S. draft uses the term "authorities of the United States". The Korean negotiators hoped that this did not imply that the U.S. negotiators were thinking in terms of some U.S. authority other than U.S. military authorities having jurisdiction in the Republic of Korea. If that is the case, the Korean negotiators found no difficulty for the U.S. side to accept the Korean draft.

37. Referring to the concept of the combat zone, Mr. Chang recalled that at the last meeting the Korean negotiators had objected to this apparent intention on the part of the U.S. negotiators to restrict the jurisdiction of the ROK authorities over a portion of

0058

ROK territory. Korean nationals ought to be equally treated before the law and constitutions. Consequently, the Korean negotiators were not in a position to differentiate the benefits of law, protection and means of redress on the basis of difference in locality. In this respect also, the concept of combat zone would hardly be compatible with the spirit of the ROK Constitution.

38. With regard to the question of duty certificates, Mr. Chang said the Korean negotiators had defined specific procedures in the Korean draft in order to prevent this matter from becoming a controversial issue in the future in actual application. They had tried to avoid ambiguity by defining the exact meaning of "duty offenses".

39. Mr. Chang stated that the position of the Korean negotiators with regard to dependents had been made clear during discussion of other articles. They believed that, in application of judicial rights also, a clear distinction should be made between dependents and members of the armed forces and the civilian component who are performing military missions. They believed that dependents should be excluded from the application of this article.

40. Regarding exclusive jurisdiction, Mr. Chang stated that both drafts give to the ROK Government the right to exercise exclusive jurisdiction with respect to offenses punishable by Korean law but not by U.S. law. In such cases, the Korean negotiators believe the right of the ROK Government to exercise jurisdiction is inalienable and not subject to waiver.

0059

41. Mr. Chang noted also that the U.S. draft provides for a general waiver of the primary right to exercise jurisdiction. He said such a provision is not consonant with the principle of mutual recognition by each government of the primary right of jurisdiction of the other which was specifically set forth in both texts. With regard to precedents in other status of forces agreements regarding waiver, Mr. Chang indicated that the Korean authorities were prepared to waive in as many cases as in the precedents refered to by the U.S. negotiator, but believed that this Agreement should contain the same language and expressions as other status of forces agreements.

42. Mr. Chang stated that the Korean negotiators would respond more specifically at the next meeting to the statement made at today's meeting by the U.S. negotiators. Mr. Habib suggested that the next meeting be devoted to answering questions regarding the two drafts. It was agreed to hold the next meeting on March 13 at 2:00 p.m. The meeting was then adjourned.

0060

2. 제46차 회의, 3.13

0061

기 안 용 지

자체 통제		기안처	미주과 이근팔	전화번호	근거서류접수일자

	과장	국장	차관	장관		
	(서명)	(서명)	(서명)	(서명)		

관계관 서명	

기안 년월일	1964.3.12.	시행 년월일		보존 년한		정서	기장
분류 기호	외구미722.2	전체 통제		종결			

경유 수신 참조	건의	발신	

제목	제 46 차 주둔군지위협정 체결교섭회의에 임할 우리측 입장

3 월 13 일 개최될 제 46 차 주둔군지위협정 체결을 위한 한.미간 교섭회의에서는 금전청산절차, 현지조달, 노무조달, 형사재판 관할권, 및 보호조치에 관한 조항을 토의하도록 예정하고 있는바 이에 대하여 우리측 교섭실무자는 3 월 10 일 회합을 갖고 제 46 차 회의에서 취할 태도를 별첨과 같이 결정하였아오니 재가하여 주시기 바랍니다.

유 첨: 제 46 차 주둔군지위협정 체결교섭회의에 임할 우리측 태도. 끝.

(1966.12.31.)

승인서식 1-1-3 (11-00900-03) (195mm×265mm16절지)

1966.12.31에 예고문에 의거 일반문서로 재분류됨

0062

가. 금전청산절차

(1) 미측은 공의물 및 용역조항 4항에서 금전청산절차에 관하여 규정하고 있는데 우리측은 다음과 같은 양해사항을 유보하고 동 규정을 별개조항으로 신설하는 것은 승락한다.

(ㄱ) 한.미 양국당국간에 체결된 기존 협정은 별도로 합의되지 않는 한 계속 효력을 갖인다.

나. 현지조달

(1) 미국군대의 현지조달 물품에 대한 면세에 관한 미측초안 제 3항 및 동 합의의사록 3 항의 규정은 미측안대로 수락하되 다음과 같은 합의의사록 4항 및 양해사항의 유보를 제안한다.

(ㄱ) 미군당국의 현지조달 물품의 사용 목적에 관한 "for official purposes " 및"for ultimate use "용어의 뜻을 명백히 규정하여 별첨과 같은 합의의사록 4 항초안을 제시한다. 단, 동 초안내용중 최종적으로 미국군대에 의하여 사용되는 물품조달의 면세 대상은 계약자의 구매거래의 최종단계에만 적용된다.(양해사항)

(ㄴ) 면제되는 조세의 종목중 traffic tax 는 bulk transportation 에만 적용된다는 양해사항을 제시한다.

(2) 합의의사록 1 항은 미측초안대로 수락한다.

(3) 미측합의의사록 2 항은 " other appropriate persons를 other appropriate representative로 대치할 것을 우리측에서 주장한바 있음으로 미측의 견해를 듣고 수락한다.

(4) 합의의사록 3항은 "an authorized agent"를 " an authorized representative "로 대치하기로 하고 수락한다.

다. 노무조달

(1) 미측이 45 차 회의에서 제시한 입장에 대하여 우리측은 우리측 입장을 다음과 같이 주장한다.

(ㄱ) K.S.C.는 한국정부의 피고용자가 않이며 우리측은K.S.C. 의 인원조달 및 한국군인을 배속시켜 운영면에서 협조하고 있음에 불과하며 미측이 임금, 해고, 기타 모든 노무관리를 장악하고

0063

있음으로 미측의 일반노무자와 하등 다를 것이 없다고 주장한다.

(ㄴ) 노무자의 조달은 미측의 제안을 참작하여 우리초안을 수정하여 가능한한 최대한도로 한국정부의 조력에 의하여 충족시킴과 동시에 필요한 정보 제공을 위하여 우리안 2항 전단에 " to the maximum extent practicable "용어를 삽입하고 동 전단 끝에 "In case the United States military authorities exercise direct recruitment and employment of labors, they shall provide the Republic of Korea with the relevant information required for labor administration "용어를 추가 삽입한다.

(ㄷ) 우리초안은 미군의 군기유지 및 안전에 의한 해고만을 규정하고 있으나 미군이 감군 예산의 삭감 기타 적당한 이유로 공정한 표준에 따라 해고시킬 수 있는 것은 한국법에서도 보장하고 있다.

(ㄹ) 한국정부당국의 노무조달을 위한 조력으로 인한 미측의 직접비용 상환에 관한 제안은 우리측 합의의사록 1항에 반영하여 " direct"용어를 삽입한다.

(ㅁ) 미측이 노무자의 임금에서 소득세 및 사회보장기금을 공제하는데 동의한바 있는데 우리초안에 반영되고 있으며 용어의 조정에 대하여서는 미측의 제안을 고려할 용의가 있다.

(ㅂ) 미측이 주권국가로서 우리 나라 재판에 복할 수 없다는 주장에 관하여서는 "나토", "아이스랜드"제국과의 주둔군지위협정의 규정 및 사실상운영실태를 질문한다.

라. <u>형사재판관할권</u>

(1) 미측이 제 45 차 회의에서 주장한 점에 대하여 우리측은 우리측 입장을 다음과 같이 밝힌다.

(ㄱ) 미측이 규정한 <u>전투지역에 대하여</u> (가) 범죄와 작전은 상이한 개념이며 (나) 한국인에게 지역적으로 불평등한 보호를 하게되는 결과가 되며 우리 나라 헌법정신에 위배된다. (다) 미국은 미측의 전속적 및 제 1 차적관할권으로 목적을 달성할 수 있을 것이다.

(ㄴ) <u>관할권이 경합될 경우</u>의 포기요청은 3 항의 입법취지에 위배된다.

(ㄷ) <u>전속관할권은</u> 본질적으로 포기 또는 양보할 수 있는 권리가 아니며 해당 범죄는 경중에 따라 처벌하는 것이지 과중한 처벌을 하려는 것은 아니다.

0064

(ㄹ) 미군은 법적지위로 보아 한국군과 같이 취급될 수 없으며 한국군인이 범하면 군법회의에 회부될 그러한 범죄를 범한 미군인은 미군법회의에 회부되어야 한다는 것은 부당한 주장이다.

(ㅁ) 재판전 구금시 우리 나라 법률상 고문은 금지되어 있으며 행형상의 경제적문제까지 걱정해 줄 필요는 없다.

(ㅂ) 한국당국에 의하여 재판받는 자는 그 형도 한국이 집행한다는 것을 전제로 하는 것이다.

(ㅅ) 대륙법계에서는 검사가 수사의 주체이며 따라서 검사가 공무집행중 범죄여부를 수사단계에서 결정하여야 하며 최종적으로는 판사가 하게 된다. 공무자체와 공무집행중 범죄가 공무와 관계가 있는가의 문제는 개념상 구별되어야 한다. 공무자체의 증명은 사령관이 할 수 있을지 몰라도 공무집행중 범죄 여부는 객관적으로 검사가 해야할 성질의 것이다.

(ㅈ) 가족은 군대의 사명을 수행하는 군인 군속과 그 지위 및 성격에 있어서 판이하기 때문에 한국이 한국법에 따라 재판권을 행사해야 한다.

(ㅊ) 한국행형법 15조 및 동 62조에 의하여 기결수 및 미결수의 수용은 천재, 지변 시 피난의 방법이 없다고 인정되는 때에는 수형자를 타처에 호송 수용하고 타처에의 호송이 불가능할 때에는 일시 석방하게 되어 있다.

(ㅋ) 협정 발효 이전의 범죄는 본 협정의 적용을 받지 않는 것은 당연한 것이며 조안을 제시하여도 좋다.

(ㅌ) 계엄하의 군법회의도 삼심제를 채택하고 있어 최종심은 대법원으로 되어 있어 민간인에 대한 인권옹호를 기하고 있다.

(ㅍ) 재판절차상의 보호는 아국헌법, 기타 형사관계법에 규정되어 있음으로 구태여 협정에 삽입할 필요가 없다.

(ㅎ) 증인소환에 있어 군비상사태를 고려하겠다. 군경찰권 행사에 있어서 한국헌법상 현행범을 제외하고는 영장없이 체포할 수 없다.

0065

다. 보호조치

(1) 우리측 주장에 대한 미측의 견해를 청취하고

(2) 안전보호의 대상으로 군대, 군인, 군속, 상기인들의 가족 외에 미측의 주장대로 군계약자 및 그들의 가족을 포함하기 위하여 우리안전단에 " the persons who are present in the Republic of Korea pursuant to Article _____ "용어를 삽입한다.

(3) 미국정부 재산의 보호를 위한 입법조치는 우리안 대로 주장한다.

(4) 형사재판관할권과 관련하여 범법자를 처벌하는 것은 미측 주장을 수락하여 우리안 후단에 " consistent with Article —— "용어를 삽입한다. 끝.

0066

SOFA NEGOTIATION

Agenda for the 46th Session

14:00 March 13, 1964

1. Continuation of Discussions on:

   a. Accounting Procedures Article

   b. Local Procurement Article

   c. Labor Article

   d. Criminal Jurisdiction Article

   e. Security Measures Article

2. Other Business

3. Agenda and Date of the Next Meeting

4. Press Release

0067

Mar 13 '64

"4. Regarding para 3, it is understood that "materials, supplies, equipment and services procured for official purposes" refers to direct procurement by the United States armed forces or its authorized procurement agencies from Korean suppliers. "Materials, supplies, equipment and services procured for ultimate use" refers to procurement by contractors of the United States armed forces from Korean suppliers of items to be incorporated into or necessary for the production of the end product of their contracts with the United States Armed Forces".

0068

기 안 용 지

자체 통제	구주라 기밀성식	기안처	미주과 이근팔	전화번호	근거서류접수일자
	과장	국장	차관	장관	
관계관 서명					
기안 년월일	1964. 3. 19.	시행 년월일		보존 년한	정서기장
분류 기호	외구미722.2	전체 통제	종결		
경유 수신 참조	대통령 (참조: 비서실장) 국무총리			발신	장관
제목	제 46 차 주둔군지위협정 체결 교섭 실무자회의 보고				

1964. 3. 13. 하오 2 시 부터 동 4 시 15 분 까지 외무부 제 1 회의실에서 개최된 제 46 차 주둔군지위협정 체결 교섭 실무자회의에서 토의된 내용을 별첨과 같이 보고합니다.

유 첨: 제 46 차 교섭회의 보고서 1 부. 끝.

1966, 12, 31 의거 일반문서로 재분류됨

승인서식 1—1—3 (11 00900—03) (195mm×265mm16절지)

0069

제 46 차

한.미간 주둔군지위협정 체결 교섭 실무자회의

보 고 서

1. 일 시: 1964 년 3 월 13 일 하오 2 시 부터 동 4 시 15 분 까지.

2. 장 소: 외무부 제1 회의실

3. 토의사항:

가. 회계절차

(1) 한.미 양측은 본 협정 체결에 관련하여 발생하는 금전거래를 위하여 회계절차를 마련함에 있어 다음과 같은 양해사항을 유보하고 완전 합의를 보았다.

(ㄱ) 한.미 양국 관계당국 간에 체결된 기존 절차는 별도로 합의되지 않는 한 계속 효력을 갖는다.

나. 현지조달

(1) 우리측은 미군당국의 현지조달 물품에 대하여 면세함에 있어

(ㄱ) 미군당국의 현지조달 물품의 "공적 사용 목적" 및 "최종적 사용 목적"의 용어의 정의를 한정하여 합의의사록 4항으로 신설 규정할 것과

(ㄴ) 최종적으로 미군당국에 의하여 사용되는 물품조달의 면세 대상은 구매거래의 최종단계에만 적용되어야 한다는 양해사항을 유보할 것을 제안하였다.

(2) 미측 합의의사록 1항은 원안대로 수락하고 동 2, 3항은 약간의 자구수정을 조건으로 수락할 것임을 표명하였다.

다. 노무조달

(1) 미측대표가 45 차 회의 석상에서 주장한 사항을 검토한 결과에 따라 우리측은 다음과 같이 우리측 입장을 제시하였다.

(ㄱ) K.S.C.는 우리 정부의 노무자가 않이며 미당국의 일반 노무자와 상의한 점이 없다.

(ㄴ) 노무자의 조달은 가능한 한 한국정부의 조력을 통하여 충족시키되 만약 미군당국이 직접적으로 노무자를 조달 또는 고용하는 경우에는 노무행정상 필요한 정보를 한국당국에 제공하여야 한다.

0070

64-3-3/

미국-12-10P-21

64-3-12(3)

0071

(ㄷ) 미군당국의 노무조달을 위하여 한국정부 당국이 지출한 직접적 비용 만을 미측이 한국정부에 상환토록 한다.

(ㄹ) 미측이 노무자의 임금으로 부터 소득세 및 사회보장기금을 공제하는데 동의한 바 있는데 우리 초안에 반영되어 있으며 용어의 조정에 대한 미측의 제안을 참작할 용의가 있다.

(ㅁ) 미측의 노무자의 해고에 관한 규정은 우리측으로서는 받아 드릴 수 없다.

(2) 미측대표는 미국이 주권국가로서 노무분쟁에 관련하여 한국의 법정이나 노무위원회의 결정에 복할 수 없으며 한국초안이 군기 유지 및 안전에 관한 해고만을 인정하고 있는데 미군이 맡은 바 사명을 수행함에 있어 중대한 지장을 초래하는 경우에는 노무자를 해고할 수 있는 권한이 인정되어야 한다고 주장하였다.

다. 형사재판관할권

(1) 미측은 우리측이 45 차회의에서 밝힌 입장에 대하여 다음과 같이 미국측 주장을 제시하였다.

(ㄱ) 한국측은 미군이 계엄령 하에서 군법재판을 받지 않겠다는 미국측 주장에 대하여 반대한바 있으나 미국이 체결한 어느 협정에서도 미군이 접수국의 군법에 복하도록 되어 있는 선례가 없으며 한국측 주장은 수락할 수가 없다.

(ㄴ) 공무집행중 범죄 여부의 증명에 관한 한국측 주장은 모순점이 있으며 현실에 반하는 것이다. 많은 국제적 선례를 보아도 공무에 관한 증명은 공무를 부과하는 자에 의하여서 가장 잘 규정될 것이다. 그러므로 미측은 국제선례에 위배되는 한국측 주장을 수락할 수 없다.

(ㄷ) 미측은 재판전 피의자의 신병을 구금함에 있어서 한국측의 요구에 응하여 수사에 협조하고 도망 방지를 기하겠다.

(ㄹ) 한국측은 과거 재판 후 기결수의 신병 구금을 미측에 인도할 의도가 있음을 표시한 바 있다. 미국의 주장은 한국측에 인도를 의무를 부과하는 것이 않이라 미측의 인도 요구에 대하여 고려하여 달라는 것이다.

0072

64-3-40

(ㅁ) 한국측은 각국의 주둔군지위협정이 가족을 포함하고 있다는 사실을 고려하기 바란다.

(ㅂ) 전속관할권의 포기 요청은 한국측이 관할권 행사를 원치 않을 경우를 생각하여 규정한 것이다.

(ㅅ) 국제적 선례에 의하면 관할권이 경합할 경우 접수국의 파견국에 대한 관할권 포기의 비율이 상당히 높으며 이 점에 대한 한국측 견해를 밝히기 바란다.

(ㅇ) 미측의 관할권 행사기관은 미당국으로 되어 있으며 일단 관할권을 부여한 이상 행사기관 여하는 내부적인 문제이다.

(ㅈ) 한국측은 전투지역 내에서 한국민에 대한 보호가 충분하지 못할 것을 우려하고 있는바 형사재판관할권은 형사책임만을 고려할 뿐이며 민사상의 책임문제는 민사관계부문에서 취급될 문제이다.

(ㅊ) 한국군인이 범하면 군법재판에 회부될 성질의 범죄를 미군이 범한 경우 그 미군인은 당연히 미군법회의에 회부되어야 한다고 보는데 한국측이 반대하는 이유를 이해하기 곤난하다.

(2) 한국측은 (ㄱ) 미군인을 군법회의에 회부하는 문제와 (ㄴ) 가족을 포함시키는 문제는 한국의 헌법정신으로 보아 미국측 주장을 수락하는 것은 곤난하나 앞으로 교섭에서 검토될 여지는 있다고 말하고 미측이 제시한 제 문제에 대하여서는 다음 회의에서 언급하기로 하였다.

다. 보호조치

(1) 안전 보호의 대상으로 미국군대, 군인, 군속, 및 그들의 가족외에 미측의 주장대로 군계약자 및 그들의 가족을 포함시키고,

(2) 미국정부 재산의 보호를 위한 입법조치는 우리 안대로 할 것과

(3) 형사재판관할권과 관련하여 범법자를 처벌하는 것은 미측주장을 수락하여 우리요안 후단에 " consistent with Article ___"용어를 삽입할 것을 미측에 제안하였다.

4. 기타 사항: 차기 회의 개최 일자: 1964 년 3 월 20 일 하오 2 시 부터. 끝.

0074

64-3-41

0075

March 13

Accounting Procedures

1. Mr. Chang opened the meeting by referring to the decision reached previously to make paragraph 4 of the U.S. draft of Article "D" a separate article in the Agreement. He said the Korean negotiators were prepared to agree to the text of the paragraph as tabled by the U.S. negotiators, with the understanding that existing arrangements for the use of utilities and services [and payment therefor] by the U.S. armed forces will continue in effect unless otherwise agreed by the two governments, which was previously confirmed by General Fuller at the 35th session.

2. Mr. Habib replied that the U.S. negotiators confirmed that understanding and believed that it was implicit in the language of Agreed Minute #2 to the Utilities and Services provisions. He noted that the negotiators had now reached full agreement on the Accounting Procedures Article.

Local Procurement

3. Turning to the article on local procurement, Mr. Chang stated that Mr. Sin would present the views of the Korean negotiators. Mr. Sin stated that the Korean negotiators accepted the U.S. draft of paragraph 3 and Agreed Minute #3, with the provision that the U.S. negotiators agree to a new Agreed Minute #4 to read as follows:

> "4. Regarding paragraph 3, it is understood that 'materials, supplies, equipment and services procured for official purposes' refers to direct procurement by the United States armed forces or their authorized procurement agencies from Korean suppliers. 'Materials, supplies, equipment and services procured for ultimate use' refers to procurement by contractors of the United States armed forces from Korean suppliers of items to be incorporated into or necessary for the production of the end product of their contracts with the United States Armed Forces."

4. In response to queries concerning his statement that the Korean negotiators accepted the text of Agreed Minute #3, Mr. Sin indicated that [in subparagraph (b)] the Korean negotiators wished ~~to make certain changes in the language of that Agreed Minute. In subparagraph (b), they wished~~ to substitute the term "authorized representative of the United States armed forces" for the term "authorized agent of the United States

0076

para. 5 - Minutes (for Embassy)

He also stated that the agreement of the Korean negotiators to paragraph 3 was conditioned upon (a) U. S. acceptance of an understanding that the U. S. will be given exemption only in the last stages of procurement unless it is agreed in the Joint Committee that the tax for which exemption is sought may be identified specifically and forms a significant part of the purchase price of the item, and (b) agreement by the U. S. negotiators to the insertion of the words "in advance" following the words "appropriate certification" in the first sentence of paragraph 3 of the U. S. draft. Further, etc

0077

armed forces". He also stated that the agreement of the Korean negotiators to paragraph 3 was conditioned upon U.S. acceptance of an understanding that the U.S. will be given exemption only in the last stages of procurement unless it is agreed in the Joint Committee that the tax for which exemption is sought may be identified specifically and forms a significant part of the purchase price of the item, and (b) agreement by the U.S. negotiators to the insertion of the words "in advance" following the words "appropriate certificate" in the first sentence of paragraph 3 of the U.S. draft. Further, that the Korean agreement to the inclusion of the traffic tax in the list of exemptions was conditioned upon the explanation given by the U.S. negotiators at the 26th negotiating meeting that this exemption would apply only to bulk purchases of transportation by the U.S. armed forces and not to purchases by individual travellers. Mr. Habib replied that the U.S. negotiators would take these proposed understandings under consideration.

6. Mr. Sin stated that the Korean negotiators would accept the text of Agreed Minute #2, provided the phrase "appropriate persons" was changed to "appropriate representatives". He said if the U.S. negotiators accepted the Korean proposals, full agreement on this article would be achieved.

7. Mr. Habib replied that the U.S. negotiators would study the Korean proposals and respond to them as soon as possible.

Security Measures

8. Turning to the Security Measures Article, Mr. Chang stated that there were three points at issue, namely, (a) should invited contractors be covered by the provisions of this article?; (b) should language be included in this article to make it consistent with the Criminal Jurisdiction Article?; and (c) should individual persons and their property be covered by the provisions of this article? He said the Korean negotiators were prepared to make concessions with regard to the first two points. They would agree to the inclusion in the Korean draft respectively of the phrases "the persons who are present in the Republic of Korea pursuant to Article ____" between the words "the civilian component" and "their dependents" and the phrase "consistent with Article ____" before the words "for the punishment of offenders" if the U.S. negotiators would agree to delete the phrase "of the persons referred to in this paragraph, and their property". Mr. Habib replied that the U.S. negotiators would study this proposal and respond at a subsequent meeting.

0078

Labor Procurement

9. Turning to the Labor Procurement Article, Mr. Chang stated that he would discuss, paragraph by paragraph, the modifications proposed by the U.S. negotiators at the previous meeting. The Korean negotiators had no objection to the deletion of the phrase "who is an employee of the Government of Korea" from paragraph 1(b). However, the Korean negotiators saw no reason why the members of the Korean Service Corps should be exempted from the application of this article. They are ordinary laborers and their exclusion from the provisions of this article would be incompatible with the Korean laws and regulations of Labour and the spirit of the Constitution of the Republic of Korea. Article 29, paragraph 1 of the Constitution states that workers shall have the right of independent association, collective bargaining and collective action for the purpose of improving their working conditions.

10. The U.S. negotiators had explained that the direct hire system in Japan was left over from an earlier period of military occupation, Mr. Chang continued. Although the situation in the Republic of Korea was not one of military occupation, the Korean authorities were seeking to avoid a situation in which surplus Korean labor could be hired under adverse conditions. Therefore, the Korean negotiators proposed the following alteration in paragraph 2 of the Korean draft of this article. In the first sentence after the word "satisfied", add the words "to the maximum extent practicable". Following the first sentence, a new sentence should be inserted, to read as follows:

> "In case the United States military authorities exercise direct recruitment and employment of laborers, they shall provide the Government of the Republic of Korea with the relevant information required for labor administration."

11. Mr. Chang stated that the Korean negotiators had been pleased by the statement of the U.S. negotiators that the United States Government accepted the principle of withholding taxes and social security contributions. However, this was provided for in paragraph 2 of the Korean draft. If the U.S. negotiators found the language in the [illegible]able, the Korean negotiators

0079

were prepared to consider any alternative language which the U.S. negotiators might wish to propose.

12. Mr. Chang recalled that the U.S. negotiators had proposed transferring the final clause of paragraph 3 of the U.S. draft to be added to Agreed Minute #2. Inasmuch as this would not change the meaning of the provision in any way, the Korean negotiators did not find the proposal acceptable. Mr. Habib stated that in that case, the U.S. negotiators withdrew the proposal.

13. Mr. Chang then referred to the previous discussion by the U.S. negotiators of the meaning of "general conformity" with Korean labor laws, customs, and practices. He said the Korean negotiators wished to have labor disputes settled in accordance with the existing Korean laws and regulations. The U.S. negotiators, however, appeared to be trying to create new regulations. They had said that it was not proper for one sovereign power to hail another sovereign power into its courts. The Korean negotiators proposed that this entire question be discussed in an informal meeting away from the negotiating table.

14. Mr. Habib replied that the U.S. negotiators were not prepared to discuss important matters of principle such as this outside of the formal negotiations. They wanted the record to show clearly that the United States Government will not submit itself to Korean courts, arbitration panels, or similar bodies. This was a logical position, taken in accordance with international law.

15. Regarding "general conformity", Mr. Habib said that the United States armed forces intended to continue to act as a good employer and to conform voluntarily to Korean laws and practices to the same extent as other Korean employers. However, the U.S. armed forces could not promise to conform precisely because of the unforeseeable nature of certain personnel and management decisions which had to be made from time to time. An example would be the necessity of terminating employment for security reasons. Questions of security could vitally affect the accomplishment

0080

by the U.S. armed forces of their mission in Korea, a mission which they had to accomplish under unique conditions. The U.S. armed forces were not prepared to submit cases involving security to ROK arbitration panels or courts. If the Korean authorities had any doubts or questions as to the manner in which the U.S. armed forces were conforming with Korean laws and regulations, they could always raise those questions in the Joint Committee.

16. Brig. General Fuller commented that agreement with the Korean position would prevent the U.S. armed forces from discharging employees for security reasons. In effect, the Korean negotiators were proposing that the U.S. armed forces be prevented from taking action which would prevent the impairment of the accomplishment of their mission in Korea.

17. Mr. Chang replied that the Korean negotiators had proposed an informal discussion for the purpose of asking questions and hearing explanations by the U.S. negotiators on the matters which had just been discussed. If the U.S. negotiators did not wish to hold an informal discussion, the Korean negotiators withdrew their proposal. With regard to the question of security cases, the U.S. negotiators misunderstood the Korean position. Mr. Chang pointed out that the Korean draft of this article fully covers the question of dismissals for security reasons.

18. In response to a question by General Fuller, Mr. Chang stated that the Korean negotiators objected to the phrase "would materially impair" in paragraph 3 of the U.S. draft. He said that interpretation of this phrase might well be controversial. There was no way of gauging the extent to which the U.S. armed forces might go in using this provision. It could be used as an excuse for any type of firing, including a reduction in force. Under the terms of the Korean draft, the U.S. armed forces could terminate employment for security reasons.

19. General Fuller stated that it was necessary for the U.S. armed forces to have the authority to terminate employment which would materially affect the accomplishment of their mission, inasmuch as their mission was the only reason for their presence in the Republic of Korea.

0081

20. General Fuller asked the Korean negotiators to explain what they meant by "relevant information required for labor administration". Mr. Chang replied that the reference was to the number of employees hired, the places of employment, the job classification of their positions, and similar information.

21. General Fuller commented that one reason why the U.S. armed forces have not made fuller use in the past of the ROK labor offices is that these offices have been able to provide only common labor, whereas the bulk of the requirements of the U.S. armed forces are for skilled and semi-skilled laborers, such as typists, clerks, plumbers, engineers, etc.

22. Mr. Chang stated that the Korean negotiators were puzzled by one comment made at the previous meeting by the U.S. negotiators. General Fuller had said that in Japan and Germany, the U.S. Government was not made the respondent in labor disputes which were taken to court. The Korean negotiators had noticed that the language of the SOFA with Iceland was similar to the language of the Korean draft. Did this mean that the U.S. Government did go to court in Iceland?

23. General Fuller replied that in Iceland, as elsewhere, the U.S. Government did not act as respondent. He said the host government, as the employer, defended the cases in court. In Iceland, the Icelandic Government is the employer and the SOFA does not call for the United States Government to act as the defendant in such cases. General Fuller pointed out that this procedure is not that which is being proposed by the U.S. negotiators. He said the U.S. negotiators would draft a statement answering the questions of the Korean negotiators, which pertained to the Korean draft.

Criminal ~~Military~~ Jurisdiction

24. Turning to the Criminal Jurisdiction Article, Mr. Habib stated that the U.S. negotiators wished to respond to the statement made at the previous meeting by the Korean negotiators and to ask some questions regarding the Korean position.

0082

25. Mr. Habib recalled that the Korean negotiators had objected to that provision of the U.S. draft which would exempt U.S. personnel from the jurisdiction of ROK military courts during time of martial law. He pointed out that in no other status of forces agreement has the U.S. Government agreed to give the host government such jurisdiction. It should not surprize the Korean negotiators, therefore, that the U.S. negotiators have no intention to agree to any such provision in the SOFA with the Republic of Korea. Although the Korean draft is silent on this point, the Korean negotiators had pointed out that U.S. personnel would be subject to Korean military courts unless the Agreement contains a provision such as that which is included in the U.S. draft. Therefore, the U.S. negotiators would like to hear the Korean negotiators state again their position on this point.

26. With regard to the official duty certificate, Mr. Habib recalled that the Korean negotiators had indicated that their reason for providing the procedures contained in paragraph 3(a)(ii) of their draft and for including a definition of official duty in the Agreed Minutes of their draft was to avoid disputes over the interpretation of "official duty". Far from avoiding disputes, the Korean provisions would foster disputes. In keeping with worldwide precedents, the U.S. negotiators believe that duty is best defined by those who assign the duty. In actual fact, the definition suggested by the Korean negotiators was illogical and contrary to reality.

27. As an example, Mr. Habib asked the Korean negotiators to consider the case of artillery firing practice on a firing range. Korean nationals wander onto the range while the firing is in progress and are hit. Under the Korean definition, firing of the shells which hit the Koreans would not be considered in line of duty, since wounding civilians is not a "normal function" of artillery practice firing. This definition is palpably unacceptable to the U.S. negotiators. Mr. Habib reminded the Korean negotiators that this article deals with criminal jurisdiction, not civil liability, which is provided for elsewhere in the Agreement. If the Korean negotiators were concerned that U.S. officers might abuse their trust in executing duty certificates, the U.S.

0083

negotiators could assure the Korean negotiators that the execution of the duty certificates would be done in a responsible manner by responsible officers. This is the procedure followed elsewhere; there is no reason to establish an entirely new precedent which is inconsistent with normal worldwide practice. The U.S. negotiators, therefore, could not agree to the Korean draft.

28. Regarding pre-trial custody, Mr. Habib asked why the Korean authorities desired it when the U.S. armed forces were prepared to obligate themselves to produce defendants on request and to prevent them from escaping Korean jurisdiction. He pointed out that in actual practice, the Japanese authorities have shown no desire for pre-trial custody.

29. Regarding post-trial custody, Mr. Habib reiterated that the U.S. authorities had previously received from the ROK Government a suggestion that the U.S. authorities might take post-trial custody of defendants convicted under ROK jurisdiction. The U.S. negotiators had thought that they were responding to this suggestion. The U.S. draft would not obligate the Korean authorities in any way but would merely call on them to entertain a request for post-trial custody. Unless this provision were included in the Agreement, the U.S. authorities would not have the right to take post-trial custody, even if the Korean authorities wanted them to do so.

30. With regard to dependents, Mr. Habib stated that the Korean negotiators apparently did not agree with the coverage given by the U.S. draft. He pointed out that the number of dependents who would be covered by the SOFA would be relatively small, since most of the military dependents in Korea were MAAG dependents who would not be covered by the SOFA. The Korean negotiators should consider the fact that dependents are covered by this article in every other status of forces agreement.

31. Mr. Habib commented that the provision of the U.S. draft which permitted waiver of exclusive jurisdiction by the ROK Government had been included as an attempt to assist the Korean authorities. It was thought

0081

desirable to provide for some procedure which would permit the ROK authorities to avoid the holding of a trial in cases over which they might not wish to exercise jurisdiction. In such cases, the U.S. authorities would take appropriate administrative action against the offenders.

32. Mr. Habib said the waiver of concurrent jurisdiction was another matter. Under other status of forces agreements, the rate of waiver had proved to be very high. The U.S. negotiators would like to hear the Korean negotiators state their position on this question, as well as on the other points which Mr. Habib had just discussed.

33. Mr. Chang stated that with regard to the questions of U.S. personnel being subject to ROK military courts and the coverage of dependents, the Korean negotiators had already stated that they found it difficult to accept the U.S. position in principle because of conflict with the ROK Constitution. However, the Korean negotiators were not adamant on these questions and there was room for further negotiation.

34. In response to a question as to what provision of the Constitution was relevant by Mr. Habib, Mr. Chang stated that the U.S. proposals on these two subjects were not in keeping with the spirit of the ROK constitution. Mr. Habib replied that the SOFA was being negotiated in connection with existing Korean laws, not just with regard to spirit.

35. Mr. Chang asked whether the U.S. negotiators had any further comments to make regarding the Korean position. Mr. Habib replied that the Korean negotiators had expressed some concern over the fact that the U.S. draft used the term "authorities of the United States" rather than "military authorities of the United States". He said this was a matter of internal concern for the United States and should not worry the Koreans. The language had been made broad enough to provide for any possible exercise of jurisdiction by U.S. authorities.

36. Mr. Habib referred to the Korean comments regarding the U.S. proposal for the recognition of a combat zone. The Korean negotiators had said that the ROKG could not sacrifice the right of a citizen of the Republic of Korea to seek redress in Korean courts simply because he in a geographical area. Mr. Habib

0085

reminded the Korean negotiators that when a U.S. soldier is prosecuted in a court of the Republic of Korea, the citizen who has been injured by the soldier obtains no redress. The punishment is by the sovereign, the Republic of Korea, and is punishment for a violation of the sovereign's laws. The criminal jurisdiction article of the SOFA, therefore, grants no Korean citizen the right of redress. He must seek redress in the civil courts, not the criminal courts. The existence of a combat zone in which the U.S. authorities would exercise exclusive jurisdiction would not mean that U.S. personnel would not be amenable to civil jurisdiction within that area. The liability of a U.S. soldier to an individual ROK citizen for a wrong committed against the latter is not within the purview of the criminal jurisdiction article but falls elsewhere in the Agreement.

37. Finally, Mr. Habib referred to the Korean proposal that U.S. soldiers should be subject to trial by ROK civilian courts, even though they were accused of committing offenses for which Korean soldiers were tried by Korean courts-martial. He said the U.S. negotiators could not understand why the Korean negotiators could not agree that if a Korean soldier is tried by a Korean court-martial, a U.S. soldier should be tried by a U.S. court-martial for the same type of offense.

38. Mr. Chang stated that the Korean negotiators would respond at the next meeting to the views expressed by the U.S. negotiators at this meeting. It was agreed to hold the next meeting on March 20 at 2:00 p.m.

0086

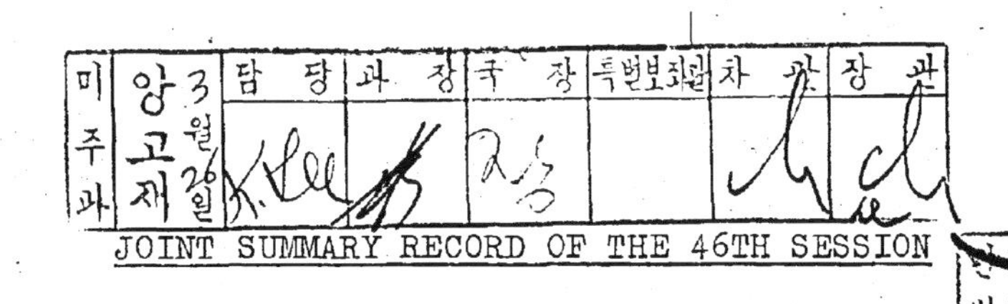

JOINT SUMMARY RECORD OF THE 46TH SESSION

1. Time and Place: 2:00-4:10 P.M. March 13, 1964 at the Foreign Ministry's Conference Room (No.1)

2. Attendants:

ROK Side:

Mr. Chang, Sang Moon	Director European and American Affairs Bureau
Mr. Yoon, Doo Sik	Director Prosecutor's Bureau Ministry of Justice
Mr. Shin, Kwan Sup	Director Customs Bureau Ministry of Finance
Mr. Koo, Choong Whay	Chief, American Section Ministry of Foreign Affairs
Mr. Chung, Tai Kyun	Chief Prosecutor's Section Prosecutor's Bureau Ministry of Justice
Col. Kim, Won Kil	Chief, Military Affairs Section Ministry of Natinnal Defense
Mr. Oh, Jae Hee	Chief, Treaty Section Ministry of Foreign Affairs
Mr. Chung, Woo Young (Rapporteur and Interpreter)	3rd Secretary Ministry of Foreign Affairs
Mr. Lee, Keun Pal	3rd Secretary Ministry of Foreign Affairs
Mr. Kim, Nai Sung	Staff Officer Europe Section Ministry of Foreign Affairs

U.S. Side:

Mr. Philip C. Habib	Counselor American Embassy
Brig. Gen. G.G. O'Connor	Deputy Chief of Staff 8th U.S. Army
Brig. Gen. L.J. Fuller	Staff Judge Advocate United Nations Command

0087

Col. Howard Smigelow	Deputy Chief of Staff 8th U.S. Army
Col. Kenneth C. Crawford	Staff Judge Advocates Office 8th U.S. Army
Mr. Benjamin A. Fleck (Rapporteur and Press Officer)	First Secretary American Embassy
Mr. James Sartorius	2nd Secretary American Embassy
Mr. Edward Hurwitz	2nd Secretary American Embassy
Mr. Robert A. Kinney	J-5 8th U.S. Army

Accounting Procedures

1. Mr. Chang opened the meeting by referring to the decision reached previously to make paragraph 4 of the U.S. draft of Article "D" a separate article in the Agreement. He said the Korean negotiators were prepared to agree to the text of the paragraph as tabled by the U.S. negotiators, with the understanding that existing arrangements for the use of utilities and services and payment therefor by the U.S. armed forces will continue in effect unless otherwise agreed by the two governments, which was previously confirmed by general Fuller at the 35th session.

2. Mr. Habib replied that the U.S. negotiators confirmed that understanding and believed that it was implicit in the language of Agreed Minute #2 to the Utilities and Services provisions. He noted that the negotiators had now reached full agreement on the Accounting Procedures Article.

Local Procurement

3. Turning to the article on local procurement, Mr. Chang stated that Mr. Sin would present the views of the Korean negotiators. Mr. Sin stated that the

0088

Korean negotiators accepted the U.S. draft of paragraph 3 and Agreed Minute #3, with the provision that the U.S. negotiators agree to a new Agreed Minute #4 to read as follows:

"4. Regarding paragraph 3, it is understood that 'materials, supplies, equipment and services procured for official purposes' refers to direct procurement by the United States armed forces or their authorized procurement agencies from Korean suppliers. 'Materials, supplies, equipment and services procured for ultimate use' refers to procurement by contractors of the United States armed forces from Korean suppliers of items to be incorporated into or necessary for the production of the end product of their contracts with the United States Armed Forces."

4. In response to queries concerning his statement that the Korean negotiators accepted the text of Agreed Minute #3, Mr. Sin indicated that in subparagraph (b) the Korean negotiators wished to substitute the term "authorized representative of the United States armed forces" for the term "authorized agent of the United States armed forces."

5. He also stated that the agreement of the Korean negotiators to paragraph 3 was conditioned upon (a) U.S. acceptance of an understanding that the U.S. will be given exemption only in the last stages of procurement unless it is agreed in the Joint Committee that the tax/for which exemption is sought may be identified specifically and forms a significant part of the purchase price of the item, and (b) agreement by the U.S. negotiators to the insertion of the words "in advance" following the words "appropriate certification" in the first sentence of paragraph 3 of the U.S. draft. Further, the Korean agreement to the inclusion of the traffic tax in the list of exemptions was conditioned

0089

upon the explanation given by the U.S. negotiators at the 26th negotiating meeting that this exemption would apply only to bulk purchases of transportation by the U.S. armed forces and not to purchases by individual travellers. Mr. Habib replied that the U.S. negotiators would take these proposed understandings under consideration.

6. Mr. Sin stated that the Korean negotiators would accept the text of Agreed Minute #2, provided the phrase "appropriate persons" was changed to "appropriate representatives". He said if the U.S. negotiators accepted the Korean proposals, full agreement on this article would be achieved.

7. Mr. Habib replied that the U.S. negotiators would study the Korean proposals and respond to them as soon as possible.

Security Measures

8. Turning to the Security Measures Article, Mr. Chang stated that there were three points at issue, namely, (a) should invited contractors be covered by the provisions of this article?; (b) should language be included in this article to make it consistent with the Criminal Jurisdiction Article?; and (c) should individual persons and their property be covered by the provisions of this article? He said the Korean negotiators were prepared to make concessions with regard to the first two points. They would agree to the inclusion in the Korean draft respectively of the phrase "the persons who are present in the Republic of Korea pursuant to Article ____ "between the words 'the civilian component' and 'their dependents' and

0090

the phrase "consistent with Article____,",before the words "for the punishment of offenders" if the U.S. negotiators would agree to delete the phrase "of the persons referred to in this paragraph, and their property". Mr. Habib replied that the U.S. negotiators would study this proposal and respond at a subsequent meeting.

Labor Procurement

9. Turning to the Labor Procurement Article, Mr. Chang stated that he would discuss, paragraph by paragraph, the modifications proposed by the U.S. negotiators at the previous meeting. The Korean negotiators had no objection to the deletion of the phrase "who is an employee of the Government of Korea" from paragraph 1(b). However, the Korean negotiators saw no reason why the members of the Korean Service Corps should be exempted from the application of this article. They are ordinary laborers and their exclusion from the provisions of this article would be incompatible with the Korean laws and regulations of Labour and the spirit of the Constitution of the Republic of Korea. Article 29, paragraph 1 of the constitution states that workers shall have the right of independent association, collective bargaining and collective action for the purpose of improving their working conditions.

10. The U.S. negotiators had explained that the direct hire system in Japan was left over from an earlier period of military occupation, Mr. Chang continued. Although the situation in the Republic of Korea was not one of military occupation, the Korean authorities were seeking to avoid a situation in which surplus

0091

Korean labor could be hired under adverse conditions. Therefore, the Korean negotiators proposed the following alteration in paragraph 2 of the Korean draft of this article. In the first sentence after the word "satisfied", add the words "to the maximum extent practicable". Following the first sentence, a new sentence should be inserted, to read as follows:

> "In case the United States military authorities exercise direct recruitment and employment of laborers, they shall provide the Government of the Republic of Korea with the relevant information required for labor administration."

11. Mr. Chang stated that the Korean negotiators had been pleased by the statement of the U.S. negotiators that the United States Government accepted the principle of withholding taxes and social security contributions. However, this was provided for in paragraph 2 of the Korean draft. If the U.S. negotiators found the language in this draft to be unacceptable, the Korean negotiators were prepared to consider any alternative language which the U.S. negotiators might wish to propose.

12. Mr. Chang recalled that the U.S. negotiators had proposed transferring the final clause of paragraph 3 of the U.S. draft to be added to Agreed Minute #2. Inasmuch as this would not change the meaning of the provision in any way, the Korean negotiators did not find the proposal acceptable. Mr. Habib stated that in that case, the U.S. negotiators withdrew the proposal.

13. Mr. Chang then referred to the previous discussion by the U.S. negotiators of the meaning of "general conformity" with Korean labor laws, customs, and practices. He said the Korean negotiators wished to have labor

0092

disputes settled in accordance with the existing Korean laws and regulations. The U.S. negotiators, however, appeared to be trying to create new regulations. They had said that it was not proper for one sovereign power to hail another sovereign power into its courts. The Korean negotiators proposed that this entire question be discussed in an informal meeting away from the negotiating table.

14. Mr. Habib replied that the U.S. negotiators were not prepared to discuss important matters of principle such as this outside of the formal negotiations. They wanted the record to show clearly that the United States Government will not submit itself to Korean courts, arbitration panels, or similar bodies. This was a logical position, taken in accordance with international law.

15. Regarding "general conformity", Mr. Habib said that the United States armed forces intended to continue to act as a good employer and to conform voluntarily to Korean laws and practices to the same extent as other Korean employers. However, the U.S. armed forces could not promise to conform precisely because of the unforeseeable nature of certain personnel and management decisions which had to be made from time to time. An example would be the necessity of terminating exployment for security reasons. Questions of security could vitally affect the accomplishment by the U.S. armed forces of their mission in Korea, a mission which they had to accomplish under unique conditions. The U.S. armed forces were not prepared to submit cases involving

0093

security to ROK arbitration panels or courts. If the Korean authorities had any doubts or questions as to the manner in which the U.S. armed forces were conforming with Korean laws and regulations, they could always raise those questions in the Joint Committee.

16. Brig. General Fuller commented that agreement with the Korean position would prevent the U.S. armed forces from discharging employees for security reasons. In effect, the Korean negotiators were proposing that the U.S. armed forces be prevented from taking action which would prevent the impairment of the accomplishment of their mission in Korea.

17. Mr. Chang replied that the Korean negotiators had proposed an informal discussion for the purpose of asking questions and hearing explanations by the U.S. negotiators on the matters which had just been discussed. If the U.S. negotiators did not wish to hold an informal discussion, the Korean negotiators withdrew their proposal. With regard to the question of security cases, the U.S. negotiators misunderstood the Korean position. Mr. Chang pointed out that the Korean draft of this article fully covers the question of dismissals for security reasons.

18. In response to a question by General Fuller, Mr. Chang stated that the Korean negotiators objected to the phrase "would materially impair" in paragraph 3 of the U.S. draft. He said that interpretation of this phrase might well be controversial. There was no way of gauging the extent to which the U.S. armed forces might go in using this provision. It could be used as

0094

an excuse for any type of firing, including a reduction in force. Under the terms of the Korean draft, the U.S. armed forces could terminate employment for security reasons.

19. General Fuller stated that, it was necessary for the U.S. armed forces to have the authority to terminate employment which would materially affect the accomplishment of their mission, inasmuch as their mission was the only reason for their presence in the Republic of Korea.

20. Gmneral Fuller asked the Korean negotiators to explain what they meant by "relevant information required for labor administration". Mr. Chang replied that the reference was to the number of employees hired, the places of employment, the job classification of their positions, and similar information.

21. General Fuller commented that one reason why the U.S. armed forces have not made fuller use in the past of the ROK labor offices is that these offices have been able to provide only common labor, whereas the bulk of the requirements of the U.S. armed forces are for skilled and semi-skilled laborers, such as typists, clerks, plumbers, engineers, etc.

22. Mr. Chang stated that the Korean negotiators were puzzled by one comment made at the previous meeting by the U.S. negotiators. General Fuller had said that in Japan and Germany, the U.S. Government was not made the respondent in labor disputes which were taken to court. The Korean negotiators had noticed that the

language of the SOFA with Iceland was similar to the language of the Korean draft. Did this mean that the U.S. Government did go to court in Iceland?

23. General Fuller replied that in Iceland, as elsewhere, the U.S. Government did not act as respondent. He said the host government, as the employer, defended the cases in court. In Iceland, the Icelandic Government is the employer and the SOFA does not call for the United States Government to act as the defendant in such cases. General Fuller pointed out that this procedure is not that which is being proposed by the U.S. negotiators. He said the U.S. negotiators would draft a statement answering the questions of the Korean negotiators, which pertained to the Korean draft.

Criminal Jurisdiction

24. Turning to the Criminal Jurisdiction Article, Mr. Habib stated that the U.S. negotiators wished to respond to the statement made at the previous meeting by the Korean negotiators and to ask some questions regarding the Korean position.

25. Mr. Habib recalled that the Korean negotiators had objected to that provision of the U.S. draft which would exempt U.S. personnel from the jurisdiction of ROK military courts during time of martial law. He pointed out that in no other status of forces agreement has the U.S. Government agreed to give the host government such jurisdiction. It should not surprize the Korean negotiators, therefore, that the U.S. negotiators have no intention to agree to any such provision in the SOFA with the Republic of Korea. Although the Korean draft is silent on this point, the Korean negotiators had pointed out that U.S. personnel would be subject

0096

to Korean military courts unless the Agreement contains a provision such as that which is included in the U.S. draft. Therefore, the U.S. negotiators would like to hear the Korean negotiators state again their position on this point.

26. With regard to the official duty certificate, Mr. Habib recalled that the Korean negotiators had indicated that their reason for providing the procedures contained in paragraph 3(a)(ii) of their draft and for including a definition of official duty in the Agreed Minutes of their draft was to avoid disputes over the interpretation of "official duty". Far from avoiding disputes, the Korean provisions would foster disputes. In keeping with worldwide precedents, the U.S. negotiators believe that duty is best defined by those who assign the duty. In actual fact, the definition suggested by the Korean negotiators was illogical and contrary to reality.

27. As an example, Mr. Habib asked the Korean negotiators to consider the case of artillery firing practice on a firing range. Korean nationals wander onto the range while the firing is in progress and are hit. Under the Korean definition, firing of the shells which hit the Koreans would not be considered in line of duty, since wounding civilians is not a "normal function" of artillery practice firing. This definition is palpably unacceptable to the U.S. negotiators. Mr. Habib reminded the Korean negotiators that this article deals with criminal jurisdiction, not civil liability, which is provided for elsewhere in the

Agreement. If the Korean negotiators were concerned that U.S. officers might abuse their trust in executing duty certificates, the U.S. negotiators could assure the Korean negotiators that the execution of the duty certificates would be done in a responsible manner by responsible officers. This is the procedure followed elsewhere; there is no reason to establish an entirely new precedent which is inconsistent with normal world-wide practice. The U.S. negotiators, therefore, could not agree to the Korean draft.

28. Regarding pre-trial custody, Mr. Habib asked why the Korean authorities desired it when the U.S. armed forces were prepared to obligate themselves to produce defendants on request and to prevent them from escaping Korean jurisdiction. He pointed out that in actual practice, the Japanese authorities have shown no desire for pre-trial custody.

29. Regarding post-trial custody, Mr. Habib reiterated that the U.S. authorities had previously received from the ROK Government a suggestion that the U.S. authorities might take post-trial custody of defendants convicted under ROK jurisdiction. The U.S. negotiators had thought that they were responding to this suggestion. The U.S. draft would not obligate the Korean authorities in any way but would merely call on them to entertain a request for post-trial custody. Unless this provision were included in the Agreement, the U.S. authorities would not have the right to take post-trial custody, even if the Korean authorities wanted them to do so.

0098

30. With regard to dependents, Mr. Habib stated that the Korean negotiators apparently did not agree with the coverage given by the U.S. draft. He pointed out that the number of dependents who would be covered by the SOFA would be relatively small, since most of the military dependents in Korea were MAAG dependents who would not be covered by the SOFA. The Korean negotiators should consider the fact that dependents are covered by this article in every other status of forces agreement.

31. Mr. Habib commented that the provision of the U.S. draft which permitted waiver of exclusive jurisdiction by the ROK Government had been included as an attempt to assist the Korean authorities. It was thought desirable to provide for some procedure which would permit the ROK authorities to avoid the holding of a trial in cases over which they might not wish to exercise jurisdiction. In such cases, the U.S. authorities would take appropriate administrative action against the offenders.

32. Mr. Habib said the waiver of concurrent jurisdiction was another matter. Under other status of forces agreements, the rate of waiver had provedatoo be very high. The U.S. negotiators would like to hear the Korean negotiators state their position on this question, as well as on the other points which Mr. Habib had just discussed.

33. Mr. Chang stated that with regard to the questions of U.S. personnel being subject to ROK military courts and the coverage of dependents, the

0099

Korean negotiators had already stated that they found it difficult to accept the U.S. position in principle because of conflict with the ROK Constitution. However, the Korean negotiators were not adamant on these questions and there was room for further negotiation.

34. In response to a question by Mr. Habib as to what provision on the Constitution was relevant, Mr. Chang stated that the U.S. proposals on these two subjects were not in keeping with the spirit of the ROK constitution. Mr. Habib replied that the SOFA was being negotiated in connection with existing Korean laws, not just with regard to spirit.

35. Mr. Chang asked whether the U.S. negotiators had any further comments to make regarding the Korean position. Mr. Habib replied that the Korean negotiators had expressed some concern over the fact that the U.S. draft used the term "authorities of the United States" rather than "military authorities of the United States". He said this was a matter of internal concern for the United States and should not worry the Koreans. The language had been made broad enough to provide for any possible exercise of jurisdiction by U.S. authorities.

36. Mr. Habib referred to the Korean comments regarding the U.S. proposal for the recognition of a combat zone. The Korean negotiators had said that the ROKG could not sacrifice the right of a citizen of the Republic of Korea to seek redress in Korean courts simply because he lived in a certain geographical area. Mr. Habib reminded the Korean negotiators that when a U.S. soldier is prosecuted in a court of the Republic

0100

of Korea, the citizen who has been injured by the soldier obtains no redress. The punishment is by the sovereign, the Republic of Korea, and is punishment for a violation of the sovereign's laws. The criminal jurisdiction article of the SOFA, therefore, grants no Korean citizen the right of redress. He must seek redress in the civil courts, not the criminal courts. The existence of a combat zone in which the U.S. authorities would exercise exclusive jurisdiction would not mean that U.S. personnel would not be amenable to civil jurisdiction within that area. The liability of a U.S. soldier to an individual ROK citizen for a wrong committed against the latter is not within the purview of the criminal jurisdiction article but falls elsewhere in the Agreement.

37. Finally, Mr. Habib referred to the Korean proposal that U.S. soldiers should be subject to trial by ROK civilian courts, even though they were accused of committing offenses for which Korean soldiers were tried by Korean courts-martial. He said the U.S. negotiators could not understand why the Korean negotiators could not agree that if a Korean soldier is tried by a Korean court-martial, a U.S. soldier should be tried by a U.S. court-martial for the same type of offense.

38. Mr. Chang stated that the Korean negotiators would respond at the next meeting to the views expressed by the U.S. negotiators at this meeting. It was agreed to hold the next meeting on March 20 at 2:00 p.m.

0101

3. 제47차 회의, 3.20

0102

외 무 부 문 서 보 존 실

0103

형사재판 관할권에 관한 우리측 대안 및 최종안 (64.3.17)

외 무 부 문 서 보 존 실

0104

內容	韓國側案	美國側案	NATO-北大西洋聯邦加盟國 協定		
1. 管轄權의 適用範圍					
1) 美軍当局의 管轄權에 服하는 者	美軍人 및 軍屬	美軍人, 軍屬 및 家族	派遣國法에 服하는 모든 者의 刑事的 및 懲戒的 犯罪	미군법에 복하는 자 (합의의사록에서 그 범위를 미군당국이 한국당국에 통고해야 한다고 규정)	미국측 안을 수락한다.
2) 行使機關					
(1) 美國	(1) 美國軍事当局	(1) 美國当局	(1) 派遣國 軍当局	미국군사당국	(1)미국군사당국
(2) 韓國	(2) 大韓民國当局	(2) 大韓民國 民事当局	(2) 接受國 当局	대한민국당국	(2) 대한민국당국 (단, 군법회의에 회부하지 않는다.
3) 適用地域	大韓民國 全領域	(1) 戰斗地域; 美國当局이 專屬管轄權을 行使한다. 合同委員会에서 決定. 休戰線으로부터 美軍团 및 韓國野戰軍이 配置된 後方境界線까지)		(1) 미국측의 전투지역의 개념을 철회케 하고 그 대신 미군사당국으로 하여금 공무집행중 범죄 여부를 증명케 한다. (2) 상기 1안이 관철되지 않을 경우 귀농선까지로 한정시킨다.	(1) 전투지역의 한계를 합동위원회에서 결정한다.

內容	韓國側 案	美國側 案	NATO-獨逸聯邦共和國 協定		
		(2) 戒厳令宣布地域 ; 美國当局이 專屬管轄权을 行使한다. (3) 韓國領域外 犯罪 ; 韓國의 管轄权이 미치지 못한다.		비상계엄 하에서는 미군당국이 전속관할권을 갖인다. 단 경비계엄에서는 미군당국의 관할권 포기 요청에 동정적 고려를 한다. 불가.	미국측 안 수락. 불가.
2. 專屬管轄权 1) 韓國의 管轄权 行使	1) 韓國에 対한 安全을 包含한 犯罪로서 美國法에 依하여 處罰될수 없는 犯罪에 対하여 專屬的管轄权을 行使한다	1) 懲戒的 및 行政的 制裁 : 美國当局의 管轄权 抛棄要請에 対해서 韓國当局이 好意的 考慮를 한다.	1) 接受国에 対한 安全에 関한 罪를 包含해서 接受国法에 依하여서는 處罰되지만 派遣国法에 依하여서는 處罰되지 않는 犯罪	한국이 전속적관할권을 행사하지 않기로 결정하였을 경우에는 가능한한 속히 미군당국에 통고한다.	미군의 포기요청이 있을 경우 동정적 고려를 한다.
3. 管轄权의 競合 1) 韓國의 第一次的 管轄权 行使	1) 美軍当局의 第一次的 管轄权에 属하지 않는 犯罪에 対하여 第一次的 管轄权 行使	1) 韓國当局은 美國当局에 秩序와 規律維持의 責任이 있음을 是認하며 管轄权行使의 权利	第19條 1) 接受国은 派遣国의 要請에 따라 管轄权에 対한 行使权을 抛棄한다	(1) 특정사건에 있어서 미군당국이 관할권행사를 요청하는 경우 한국당국은 동 관할권 행사가 한국의 사법상 중대한 이익을 침해하지 않는한 제1차적 관할권을 포기 한다. (2) 미군당국은 개별적 사건을 한국당국에 통고해야 한다.	

~2~

0106

內容	韓國側案	美國側案	NATO-獨逸聯邦共和國協定		
		를 無條件 最終的으로 拋棄한다. 但, 特定事件에 있어 特定事情으로 特히 重要하다고 認定할 때는 韓國當局이 通知받은 後 15日以內에 合同委員會에서 協議 2) 韓國軍人이 犯하여 軍法裁判에 回附된 犯罪에 關聯된 美軍人에 對해서 第一次管轄權 行使	2) 獨逸國은 特定事件에 있어 必要한 境遇, 通告받은 後 21日以內에 通告하여 權利拋棄를 撤回할 수 있다. 3) 同事件에 關한 關係當局間의 諒解가 成立되지 않는 境遇, 派遣國의 外交使節은 獨逸政府에 陳情할 수 있으며, 獨逸政府는 解決하여야 한다	한국당국은 한국에 중대한 법익이 침해된다는 의견을 갖일 경우 그 구체적이유를 제시하여 미군당국에 15일 이내에 통고하여야 하며 상기 기간이 경과한 경우 한국당국은 제 1차적관할권을 포기한 것으로 인정한다. 불가.	불가.
2) 公務執行中犯罪 (1) 決定權	(1) 管轄檢事 (2) 不服時 指揮官의 申請으로 法務長官이 最終決定	(1) 所屬美軍指揮官이 確定的으로 證明	第18條 (1) 派遣國의 最高關係當局이 派遣國法律에 따라 決定 但, 獨逸當局의 要請에 따라 獨逸政府와 派遣國의 外交	(1) 관할 지방법원이 최종적으로 결정.	(1) 미군당국의 최고군사령관이 미국법에 따라 결정하되 반증이 있을 경우에는 합동위원회에서 결정한다.

內容	韓國側案	美國側案	NATO 獨逸聯邦共和國 協定		
(2) 定義	(1) 公務執行中에 犯한 作爲 및 不作爲로서 그行爲가 公務와 直接 關聯된 犯罪 (2) 公務執行中의 모든 行爲가 아니다. 特定公務의 正常的機能으로서 正当히 要求되는 行爲로부터 벗어난 것은 公務상의 行爲이다	(1) 公務執行中에 犯한 作爲 및 不作爲에 依한 犯罪	使節間의 討議를 通해 再審될수 있다.		(1) 미국측안을 수락한다. 단, 한국측안의 제 2항은 양해사항으로 기록에 남긴다.
4. 韓國에 通常居住者	美軍当局은 管轄权 없음	美國当局은 美國軍人 以外는 管轄权 없음	派遣國当局은 管轄权 없음		미국측 안 수락.
5. 犯人의 引渡 1) 美國当局 手中에 있을 때	1) 法官의 令狀提示와 同時, 韓國当局에 引渡	1) 司法節次가 끝나고 韓國当局이 要請할 때까지 美國当局이 保護한다	1) 接受國에 依하여 起訴될 때까지 派遣國当局이 拘禁	(1)	(2) 기소되고 한국당국이 요청할 때 까지 미국당국이 구금한다.

内容	韓国側 案	美國側 案	NATO-独逸聯邦共和国 協定		
			第22條 2) 接受國은 派遣国当局의 要請이 있으면 犯人을 引渡 3) 独逸当局이 釋放 또는 無罪放免하거나 刑의 宣告를 할 때까지 派遣国当局이 拘禁 4) 派遣国当局은 独逸当局에 拘禁을 移讓할 수 있으며, 独逸当局의 移讓要請에 好意的 考慮 5) 独逸国의 安全에 대한 犯罪에 関한 拘禁은 独逸当局이 行한다 6) 派遣国当局은 捜査및 刑事訴訟을 為하여 独逸当局으로 하여금 拘禁된 者를 利用케 하며, 証據湮滅의		

~ 4 ~

0109

事項	韓國側 案	美國側 案	NATO-獨逸聯邦共和國 協定		
			危險防止를 爲하여 措置한다. 7) 暫定逮捕 (第20條) (1) 派遣國當局은 逮捕令狀없이 다음의 境遇 暫定逮捕할 수 있다. (派遣國管轄에 服하지 않는 者로서) ① 身分不明者 ② 逃亡의 憂慮가 있는 者 ③ 獨逸當局의 要請이 있는 時 ④ 急기 獨逸의 檢事나 警官의 支援을 要請하는 것이 不可한 時, 派遣國施設內에서 現逆犯이거나 可罰性있는 未遂犯行中에 있는 者		

~4~

0110

容	韓國側 案	美國側 案	NATO-獨逸聯邦共和國 協定		
			(2) 上記者의 證據物의 押收 등 (3) 遲滯없이 最隣近의 獨逸檢事, 警官 또는 法官에 引渡하여야 한다.		

內容	韓國側 案	美國側 案	NATO-獨逸聯邦共和國 協定		
2) 韓國当局 手中에 있을 때	1) 正当한 事由가 없으면 美國当局에 保護를 引渡. 2) 起訴되면 美國当局은 申請에 依하여, 犯人의 保護를 韓國当局에 引渡	1) 直時 美國当局에 引渡하며 司法節次가 完了되고 韓國当局이 要請할때까지 美國当局이 保護 2) 韓國当局의 嫌疑者에 対한 捜査 및 裁判을 為하여 要請할때는 応한다. 3) 犯人을 拘禁할 때 韓國施設 使用을 要請할수 있다.			(1) 한국안 대로 주장하되 정당한 사유 유무에 대하여는 합동위원회에서 결정한다. (2) 미국측안 2항 및 3항을 수락한다.
6. 犯罪捜査 1) 証人 및 犯人의 召喚	1) 証人으로 召喚되면 出頭하여야 한다. 2) 出頭할수 없을 時는 韓國当局은 法에 따라 必要한 措置를 取한다	1) 韓國法에서 強制되는 때에만 召喚이 応한다 (但 軍事上의 非常事態 時는 除外) 2) 美國当局의 韓國國民이나 居住人을 証人이나 專門家로 必要한	第37條 1) 派遣軍当局은 独逸法律上 強制的인 것은 條件으로 証人 및 犯人이 召還되면 出頭토록 한다 但 軍事上의 非常事態時에는 除外된다. 2) 家族은 独逸法律에 定하는 바에따라 召還 3) 派遣軍当局에 依하여서는 出頭토록 할수 없는	(1)	(1) 피고를 대상에서 삭제한다. (2) 비상사태기간이 종료하면 즉시 출도하여야 한다. (3) 가족은 예외이다. 이상 조건을 유보하고 미측안을 수락한다.

~5~

0112

內容	韓國側案	美國側案	NATO-独逸駐屯外國協定		
	3) 美軍当局은 韓国法官發行 令狀이 提示되면 令狀執行에 必要한 모든 措置를 取한다	將는 韓國檢察總長 또는 韓國政府当局이 指定하는 其他機関을 通하여 出頭토록 한다. 3) 証人에 対한 費用 및 報酬는 合同委員会에서 定한다.	者가 軍当局에서 必要한 境遇 独逸当局은 이들이 出頭토록 해야 한다. 4) 公務上機密이나 安全을 害할 情報의 說露가 招来될 憂慮가 있는 時, 法廷이나 当局은 関係当局의 書面上의 同意를 求하여야 한다. 第38條		
7. 刑의 執行(服役) 1) 美國当局이 言渡한 刑의 執行	1) 美軍当局이 協力을 要請하면 韓國当局이 好意的인 考慮를 한다.	1) 美國当局이 協力을 要請하면 韓國当局이 好意的인 考慮를 한다.	1) 派遣國当局이 協力을 要請하면 接受国은 好意的인 考慮를 한다.		(1) 쌍방안이 동일함.
2) 韓國当局이 言渡한 刑의 執行		1) 美國当局이 保護의 引渡를 要求하면 韓国当局이 好意的인 考慮를 한다.		(1) 미국측 안을 수락한다. 단, 장기형을 받은 자에 대하여는 일정한 기간을 복역한 자에 대하여서만 호의적 고려를 한다. 단기형을 받은자에 대하여는 호의적인 고려를 한다.	(1) 미국측 안을 기록상에 남기고 본문으로부터 삭제한다.
3) 行刑施設 視察		1) 美國政府代表者는 行刑施設을 視察할 수 있다			(1) 미국측 안대로 수락한다.

0113

內容	韓國側案	美國側案	NATO 独逸聯邦共和国 協定		
[illegible]		1) 韓國当局은 收監者를 保護하기 爲한 모든 措置를 取한다. 2) 美國当局의 保護引渡要請에 対하여 韓國当局은 好意的인 考慮를 하여야 한다			(1) 미측안 수락.
5) 行刑施設의 水準		1) 行刑施設은 合同委員会에서 合意한 最低水準을 充足시켜야 한다			(1) 법무부와 협의 결정.
6) 私物의 給與		1) 美國当局은 私食, 私物의 差入, 医療의 便宜를 提供할수 있다.			(1) 법무부와 협의 결정.
8. 二重處罰	不可	不可	不可		양측안 동일.
9. 被疑者의 权利	1) 直時 迅速한 裁判을 받을 权利	1) 直時 迅速한 裁判을 받을 权利 (1) 修習期间을 畢한 法官으로 構成된 公平한 裁判部의	1) 直時 迅速한 裁判을 받을 权利		(1) 미측안 수락.

0114

內容	韓国側案	美國側案	NATO·独逸聯邦共和国 協定		
		公開裁判을 받을 权利			
	2) 裁判前에 嫌疑事実을 通知받을 权利	2) 裁判前에 嫌疑事実을 通知받을 权利 (1) 相当한 事由가 없으면 遲滞없이 釋放한다 (2) 嫌疑事実을 被疑者가 解得하는 言語로 通知받을 权利 (3) 辯護人이 裁判前에 証人의 陳述에 接近할 权利	2) 裁判前에 嫌疑事実을 通知받을 权利		미측안 수락
	3) 証人審問의 权利 4) 被疑者에게 有利한 証人의 陳述을 聽取할 权利	3) 証人審問의 权利 4) 被疑者에게 有利한 証人의 陳述을 聽取할 权利	3) 証人審問의 权利 4) 被疑者에게 有利한 証人의 陳述을 聽取할 权利		

內容	韓國側 案	美國側 案	NATO 및 獨逸聯邦共和國 協定		
	5) 辯護人의 助力을 받은 權利	5) 辯護人의 助力을 받은 權利 (1) 逮捕, 拘禁 直時부터 存在 (2) 모든 訴訟節次에 參與하는 權利	5) 辯護人의 助力을 받은 權利		(1) 미국안 수락.
	6) 有能한 通譯의 助力을 받은 權利	6) 有能한 通譯의 助力을 받은 權利 (1) 逮捕, 拘禁 直時부터 存在	6) 有能한 通譯의 助力을 받은 權利		(1) 미국안 수락.
	7) 自國政府代表者와 接見할 權利 但, 非公開裁判의 境遇에는 此限에 不在	7) 自國政府代表者와 接見할 權利 (1) 逮捕, 拘禁 直時부터 存在 (2) 開廷時의 被疑者의 陳述은 有罪의 證據로 採証할수 없다. (3) 모든 節次에 參與할 權利 包含	第23條, 第24條 7) 自國政府代表者와 接見할 權利		(1) 법무부와 협의 결정.

0116

內容	韓國側案	美國側案	NATO-独逸聯邦共和國 協定		
10. 土地施設 [illegible] 1) 土地施設 [illegible]	1) 美軍当局은 軍構成員 및 軍屬만 逮捕할수 있다. 2) 韓國当局은 美軍当局이 同意하는 境遇 및 現行犯 追跡 境遇 모든 者를 逮捕할수 있다. 3) 韓國当局은 美國軍隊 및 構成員의 財產에 対한 押收, 搜索 또는 檢証은 行하지 않는다. 但, 韓國当局의 要請이 있으면 美軍当局이 이를 行하고, 美軍当局의 同意를 얻어 韓國当局도 行할수 있다.	1) 美國当局은 原則的으로 모든者를 逮捕할수 있다. 2) 韓國当局은 原則的으로 美國軍隊 및 構成員의 財產에 対한 押收, 搜索 또는 檢証을 行할수 없다. 但, 美國当局이 同意한 境遇 이를 行할수 있다.	1) 派遣國은 警察权을 行使할 权利를 가진다.		(1) 미국당국은 군인, 군속 및 가족을 체포할 수 있다. 단, 한국인 현행범을 체포할 수 있다. (1) 한국측 원안대로 주장. (1) 한국측 원안대로 주장.

~10~

0117

內 容	韓 國 側 案	美 國 側 案	獨逸聯邦共和國 協定		
2) 土地施設 周辺	1) 美軍当局은 正当한 法節次에 따라 施設의 安全에 関하여 現行犯을 逮捕할수 있다. 2) 美軍当局의 管轄权에 属하지 않는 者를 直時 韓国当局에 引渡한다.	1) 美国当局은 既遂 또는 未遂 現行犯을 逮捕 또는 拘禁할수 있다. 2) 美軍構成員, 軍属 및 家族이 아닌 者를 直時 韓国当局에 引渡한다	2) 派遣國은 接受國当局과의 合意下에 軍隊構成員間의 軍紀維持를 為하여 必要한 限度內에서 警察权을 行使할수 있다		(1) 한국측 안대로 주장.
11. 戰爭勃發時		刑事裁判管轄权規定을 直接 停止하고, 美国当局이 専属的 管轄权을 行使한다.			(1) 미국측안 수락.
12. 協定発効 以前의 犯罪		協定発効 以前의 犯罪에는 適用되지않으며 大田協定에 依據 處理한다			(1) 미국측안 수락.

~~[illegible] (1971. 12. 31.)~~

SOFA NEGOTIATION

Agenda for the 47th Session

14:00 March 20, 1964

1. Continuation of Discussions on:

   a. Criminal Jurisdiction Article

2. Other Business

3. Agenda and Date of the Next Meeting

4. Press Release

0119

기 안 용 지

자체 통제	외무부 4국 관 김영식	기안처	미주과 이근팔	전화번호	근거서류접수일자
	과장	국장	차관	장관	
관계관 서명	38				
기안 년월일	1964. 3. 27.	시행 년월일	검열 1964.3.30 통제관	보존 년한	정서기장
분류 기호	외구미 722.2	전체 통제			
경유 수신 참조	대통령 (참조: 비서실장) 국무총리			발신	장관
제목	제 47 차 주둔군지위협정 체결 교섭 실무자회의 보고				

1964. 3. 20. 하오 3 시부터 동 5 시 까지 외무부 제 1 회의실에서 개최된 제 47 차 주둔군지위협정 체결 교섭 실무자회의에서 토의된 내용을 별첨과 같이 보고합니다.

유 첨: 제 47 차 교섭회의 보고서 1부. 끝.

발송 No 194 1964. 3 30 외무부

1966.12.31 에 예고문에 의거 일반문서로 재분류됨

승인서식 1—1—3 (11 00900—03) (195mm×265mm16절지)

0120

제 47차

한·미간 주둔군지위협정 체결 교섭 실무자회의

보 고 서

1. 일 시: 1964년 3월 20일 하오 3시부터 동 5시 까지.
2. 장 소: 외무부 제 1 회의실.
3. 토의사항:

가. 형사재판관할권

1) 우리측은 미측이 제 46차 회의에서 주장한 사항에 대하여 우리측 입장을 다음과 같이 제시하였다.

(1) 한국의 재판권 행사기관: 우리 나라 헌법과 법률은 일반법원이 원칙적으로 재판을 할 수 있으며 예외적으로 4가지 경우에 군법재판에 회부하게 되어 있다.

(2) 계엄령 선포: 계엄령 선포 하의 군법재판에서도 3심제를 포함한 사법절차는 일반재판에 있어서와 동일하게 하여 인권옹호를 기하고 있다.

(3) 공무집행중 범죄: 우리 나라 사법상 검사는 수사의 주체로서 범죄의 수사에 착수하기 위하여서는 우선 검사가 재판권 유무를 판단할 필요가 있으며 우리측 규정은 분쟁의 여지를 남기지 않기 위함이다.

(4) 가족: 가족은 군인, 군속과는 그 성격이 판이하여 반듯이 군기에 복할 필요가 없으며, 따라서 가족은 한국재판 관할권에 복하여야 할 것으로 믿는다. 그러나 우리의 입장은 교섭상 융통성이 전혀 없는 것은 않이다.

(5) 전속관할권의 포기 요청: 미측의 포기 요청은 우리측에게 의무를 부과하려는 것으로 보며 호의적 고려를 하고 않하고는 한국측에 달려 있는 것이다.

(6) 관할권의 경합: 각국이 상당히 많은 경우 재판관할권을 포기하고 있다는 점을 인정하나 미측안은 기타 협정에서 볼 수 없을 정도로 제한을 가하고 있다.

(7) 군법회의: 미측 주장은 기타 협정에서 그 선례를 찾아 볼 수 없으며 우리측에 일단 관할권이 인정되면 미군은 민사법원 또는 군법재판에 복하여야 할 것이다.

0121

64-3-62

미국.문 109-112

0122

(8) 미측의 관할권 행사기관: 양측은 주한미군의 지위를 규정할 것을 교섭중에 있는 것으로서 미측의 관할권의 행사기관은 막연하게 미국당국이라고 할 것이 않이라 미군당국으로 규정하여야 한다.

(9) 전투지역: 관할권의 행사를 무조건 지역적으로 제한하려는 것은 부당하다. 미군의 전투태세를 위한 특수사정은 인정하는 바이나 전투지역의 개념을 본문으로 부터 삭제하고 관할권 행사의 포기등으로 운영면에서 해결을 모색하여야 할 문제이다.

(10) 피의자의 권리: 우리 헌법과 법률상 충분히 보장되고 있다. 미측이 협정에서 규정할 것을 기필 원한다면 반대는 않겠다.

2) 미측은 한국헌법 제 106 조의 규정이 반듯이 군법재판에서 4 가지 예외적인 경우가 취급되어야 한다고 규정한 것은 않임으로 미측이 한국의 군법재판에 복하지 않겠다는 주장은 한국헌법에 위배되는 것으로 보지 않으며 한국측의 피의자에 대한 권리 및 가족에 대한 주장은 신축성이 있는 것으로 본다고 미측 견해를 밝혔다.

3) 양측은 양측초안의 1 항 부터 3 항 까지 축조적으로 차의점을 지적 검토하였다.

4. 기타 사항: 차기 회의 일자: 1964 년 3 월 27 일 하오 2 시. 끝.

64-3-67

Criminal Jurisdiction

1. In opening the meeting, Mr. Chang said that he would like to respond to the questions and statements made by the chief U. S. negotiator at the previous meetings.

2. With regard to the phrase "authorities of the Republic of Korea", Mr. Chang said the Korean negotiators do not want to limit Korean authority to the civil side. As he had mentioned at the previous meeting, a member of the American forces, their civilian component, or [one of] their dependents may have to be subject to trial by the Korean military tribunals in cases where ordinary Korean civilians would be triable by the Korean military courts. The Korean Constitution, in Article 106, states that in cases of espionage on military affairs, offenses against sentinels and sentry-posts, distribution of harmful food to armed forces, and offenses against prisoners of war, civilians and soldiers alike would be subject to the military tribunal in accordance with provisions of law. If the Korean negotiators accepted the U. S. version of "civil authorities of the Republic of Korea", the Korean authorities would have to initiate criminal proceedings against such offenses only in a civil court. It is the understanding of the Korean negotiators that espionage or violation of any law relating to official secrets of the state may be tried by the civil court. However, ~~we feel~~ [they believe that] offenses involving espionage on military affairs should be dealt with by the military court rather than the civil court for security reasons.

0125

3. As for the problem of trying American servicemen by Korean military courts under Martial Law, the U. S. negotiators had stated that the U. S. armed forces could not allow their personnel to be tried by the summary procedures of ROK military courts. The existing code of criminal procedures applicable in the case of civil courts is also applied at military courts even under martial law. The Korean negotiators understand that the concern of the U. S. negotiators, indicated by the reference to summary procedures, may be over the composition of the Korean military tribunal, which the Korean negotiators believe to be more or less universal. If that understanding is correct, Mr. Chang continued, the Korean negotiators would further like to know what are the other elements of concern to the U. S. negotiators, as expressed in their reference to summary procedures.

4. Regarding the official duty certificate, the Korean negotiators do not challenge the contention of the U. S. negotiators that the local commander may well determine whether one of his soldiers is or is not on duty. However, determination of whether an (offense arising out of an) act or omission committed on duty has a genuine link with the performance of official duty should not be made by a field commander but by a judicial officer who has the sole authority to take up criminal cases under Korean laws. The example given by the U. S. negotiators of artillery firing practice on a firing range is irrelevant to the criminal case under discussion and not to the point. The Korean negotiators would like to

0126

give an example, said Mr. Chang, which would justify their concern on this point. Suppose a soldier was ordered to proceed from Seoul to Suwon on official business. He had to park his car on the street somewhere along the Yongdongpo main street and unfortunately became involved in a quarrel with a Korean and committed assault and battery or serious injury. Even though this example sounds like a hypothetical case, we cannot rule out the possibility of such unfortunate cases occurring. What the Korean negotiators contend in such a case is that a local commander may well certify that the offense was committed during the hours of the soldier's duty, but he is not empowered to determine whether the offense arose out of an act or omission directly related to the official order he issued.

5. Further, Mr. Chang said, the U. S. draft has not attempted to formulate any concise explanation of when an offense does arise out of an act or omission done in the performance of official duty. This is why the Korean negotiators had prepared in their draft the exact meaning of "official duty". If the U. S. negotiators don't like some of the wording in the Korean draft, the Korean negotiators would propose to modify it in line with a circular of the United States Army, Far East, which was published in January, 1956. The Korean negotiators believe that the U. S. authorities could have no objection to accepting the Korean proposal, because such definition of "official duty" is their own interpretation.

0127

6. With regard to dependents, Mr. Chang continued, the status of the dependents is substantially different from that of the members of the U. S. armed forces and civilian component. Dependents of members of the U. S. armed forces in Korea are not in the same position as members of the forces and the civilian component. Moreover, they are not subject to the same strict discipline as are members of the armed forces. However, as the Korean negotiators had indicated at the last meeting, they are not trying to be inflexible in their approach to this problem.

7. With regard to the problem of waiving exclusive jurisdiction by the Korean Government, Mr. Chang continued, the U. S. side had stated that its request for sympathetic consideration was nothing but a humanitarian statement. However, the Korean negotiators feel that the problem under discussion is something more than a humanitarian affair. In brief, inasmuch as the right of exclusive jurisdiction is inalienable, the Korean authorities do not desire to obligate themselves to the extent that they have to give sympathetic consideration to the request for waiver. Furthermore, the U. S. side had stated that the provision as indicated in the U. S. draft is an attempt to assist the Korean authorities. The U. S. negotiators are offering the Korean authorities assistance for which the latter do not ask.

8. With respect to waiver of concurrent jurisdiction, Mr. Chang

0128

continued, the Korean negotiators are well aware that the rate of waiver in other countries had proved to be very high. As he had mentioned before, the Korean authorities are prepared to waive in as many cases as in the precedents referred to by the U. S. negotiators. However, the Korean negotiators are unable to understand why the provision in this agreement should be differently worded ~~from those of others~~ (than similar provisions in other agreements.) The U. S. negotiators had said further that the provision as stated in the U. S. draft is a standard provision in most Status of Forces Agreements, but so far as the Korean negotiators know, there is no such provision in any of the existing Status of Forces Agreements, particularly the last paragraph of the U. S. draft, barring the host country and its nationals from instituting criminal proceedings in case the Joint Committee fails to come to an agreement on the question of waiver.

9. The U. S. negotiators insist, continued Mr. Chang, that if an offense committed by a member of the ROK armed forces would have been tried by court-martial, then such an offense committed by a member of the United States armed forces would also be subject to trial by American court-martial. The Korean negotiators recalled that at previous meetings, the U. S. negotiators time and again had pointed out that the Korean draft should be discussed in line with precedents in other SOFA's. Since the Korean negotiators believe that most of the receiving countries in the precedents have military law and military courts, the Korean negotiators expected to find

0129

provisions similar to those the U. S. negotiators have proposed in this regard. Therefore, they wished to ask the U. S. negotiators in what Status of Forces Agreement and with what country they have made identical provisions.

~~10.~~ Mr. Chang stated that the Korean negotiators are really at a loss to find the real intention of the U. S. negotiators in proposing this provision. Unless the U. S. negotiators withdrew this proposition, the Korean authorities would have to give up entirely their right to exercise criminal jurisdiction over members of the U. S. military forces.

10. With regard to the term "authorities of the United States", Mr. Chang continued, the U. S. negotiators had stated that the language had been made broad enough to provide for any possible exercise of jurisdiction by U. S. authorities. He said the Korean negotiators would like to emphasize that the subject and matters of discussion throughout this SOFA negotiation is the military status of the U. S. armed forces but not any other U. S. authority in Korea. It is utterly inconceivable that any United States authority other than the U. S. military authorities would have jurisdiction in Korea. Moreover, the Korean negotiators could not find any similar provision in any other SOFA. In this respect, they would appreciate an explanation of any possible difficulty envisaged by the U. S. negotiators in case the word "military" is inserted.

0130

11. ~~12~~. Regarding so-called "combat zone", as the Korean negotiators repeatedly had made clear, criminal jurisdiction and the military operation are totally different concepts, which cannot be confounded. The imposition of a geographical limitation on the exercise of jurisdiction is incompatible with the sovereign judicial right to be exercised throughout the territory of the Republic of Korea and is not acceptable to the Korean negotiators. They hope the difficulties indicated by the U. S. negotiators with regard to the so-called "combat zone" may be dealt with and solved by an agreeable and effective exercise of waiver of the right of jurisdiction.

12. ~~13~~. Regarding trial safeguards, Mr. Chang continued, the U. S. negotiators had said that as a result of study of Korean criminal procedures, laws and practices, it was necessary to list trial safeguards. However, the Korean negotiators found the provisions provided in the U. S. draft article are more or less the same as those provided in the Korean Constitution and the Code of Criminal Procedures. That is the reason why the Korean negotiators had not enumerated such provisions in their draft. If the U. S. negotiators desire to insert these provisions in the SOFA, in principle, the Korean negotiators have no objection to it.

0131

13. ~~14.~~ Mr. Habib reminded the Korean negotiators that the question of pre-trial custody was also a matter of concern to the U.S. negotiators. Noting that Mr. Chang had not discussed this question in his just-concluded remarks, Mr. Habib asked for a statement of the Korean position regarding pre-trial custody. Mr. Chang replied that pre-trial custody was closely connected with the question of post-trial custody. The Korean negotiators wished to withhold comment on both subjects until a later meeting.

14. ~~15.~~ Regarding Korean military courts, Mr. Habib inquired whether it was not the case that Article 106 of the ROK Constitution stated that military tribunals "may", not "must", exercise jurisdiction over civilians during periods of martial law. Mr. Chang acknowledged this to be the case. In effect, Mr. Habib continued, it would not be a violation of the Constitution if that right of jurisdiction were not exercised. The people who drafted the Constitution had recognized that the exercise of jurisdiction over criminal cases by military tribunals was not necessarily the best way of handling those cases. The U.S. negotiators, Mr. Habib said, did not believe that the Korean negotiators were seriously concerned with Korean military jurisdiction over Americans. They would reserve further comment on this point until later discussion of specific sections of this article.

15. ~~16.~~ Mr. Habib pointed out that the U.S. negotiators had not claimed that the provision in the U.S. draft providing for waiver of concurrent jurisdiction was a standard provision in all status of forces agreements. What he had said previously was that the reference to waiver in the text of both the U.S. and Korean drafts of this article was standard language. The Agreed Minutes, of course, were another matter. The language in the U.S. draft of the Agreed Minutes was not the standard language.

16. ~~17.~~ Mr. Habib stated that Mr. Chang had made two statements indicating willingness on the part of the Korean negotiators to consider the U.S. point of view. The

0132

first of these was Mr. Chang's statement that the enumeration of trial safeguards was consistent with ROK law and that if the U.S. negotiators wished to include such an enumeration in this article, the Korean negotiators would not object in principle. The second was Mr. Chang's statement that the Korean negotiators were not inflexible on the subject of dependents. Mr. Habib said the U.S. negotiators would defer discussion on these points until the Korean position had been somewhat refined.

17. In other respects, Mr. Habib continued, there appeared to be no recognition on the part of the Korean negotiators of other problems existing with regard to this article or of the explanations given by the U.S. negotiators. In particular, the Korean negotiators' discussion of the duty certificate was difficult to accept. He pointed out that there was a profound difference between the example given by the U.S. negotiators and that given by the Korean negotiators. In the Korean negotiators' example, the offense was clearly not an on-duty offense. But in the example given by the U.S. negotiators, an on-duty offense would be construed as an off-duty offense, according to the definition of off-duty offenses which the Korean negotiators wished to include in the Agreement. Mr. Habib again pointed out that in no status of forces agreement is there any such definition, the reason being that only the commander who assigns the duty is able to determine whether or not an offense was committed in the line of that duty. In some status of forces agreements, there is provision for a review system. Where such a system has been used, the finding has always been that only the commander is competent to determine what constitutes duty.

18. Pointing out that there was a great similarity in the two drafts, Mr. Habib suggested that the negotiators, having exchanged views in general terms, now proceed with a paragraph by paragraph discussion of the drafts in order to identify the specific differences existing in the texts.

19. Mr. Chang agreed but said that before proceeding to paragraph by paragraph discussion, the Korean negotiators wished to make a few further comments. With regard to enumeration of trial safeguards, they agreed to the idea of an enumeration

0133

but they did not necessarily accept the entire enumeration in the U.S. draft. With regard to the subject of dependents as a whole, the U.S. negotiators could accept the statement of the Korean negotiators at face value but detailed discussion should be deferred until a later meeting. With regard to the duty certificate question, the U.S. negotiators should not have any difficulty in accepting the definition published in the January, 1956 circular of the U.S. Army, Far East, either as part of the text or as an understanding in the negotiating record.

20. The negotiators then began paragraph by paragraph discussion and in paragraph 1(a) noted that the Korean draft contained the word "military" in front of the word "authorities" while the U.S.draft contained the phrase "and their dependents" and referred to "all" criminal and disciplinary jurisdiction.

21. Mr. Habib stated that if the Korean negotiators were unwilling to include the phrase "and their dependents" in this subparagraph, their position was not very flexible. He pointed out that if dependents were to be subject to U.S. jurisdiction, they would have to be mentioned in this subparagraph.

22. Mr. Chang replied that inclusion or exclusion of the word "all" was not an important matter and could be discussed later. On the other hand, the question of whether to refer to "authorities" or "military authorities" was a very important question which was not just simply a matter of wording but a question which affects the judicial rights of the Korean people as a whole. With regard to dependents, the Korean negotiators believed that measures could be worked out to include them in this article without specifically referring to them in this subparagraph. He pointed out that the U.S. negotiators had not made any definite explanation as to how far the U.S. military courts have jurisdiction over dependents. The Korean negotiators wished to know what the U.S. authorities would do regarding those persons over whom the armed forces would have no jurisdiction.

23. Mr. Habib replied that the U.S. armed forces would have disciplinary jurisdiction over such persons. It was also possible that in future, jurisdiction

0134

will be provided that does not exist at present. In wartime, the armed forces would have jurisdiction over dependents under the provisions of the "hostilities" paragraph in the U.S. draft. In this connection, Mr. Habib urged the Korean negotiators to study carefully the provisions of paragraph 2(b), which provides that the Republic of Korea will have exclusive jurisdiction over offenses not punishable by U.S. law.

24. In reply to Mr. Chang's query whether paragraph 2(b) included or excluded disciplinary action, Mr. Habib stated that an offense could be handled either by criminal jurisdiction or by disciplinary jurisdiction. If the offense were not punishable by U.S. law, and was punishable by ROK law, paragraph 2(b) provides that the ROK authorities could exercise jurisdiction, if they decided to do so. It gives them the right to exercise jurisdiction but they do not have to do so if they do not wish to.

25. In response to a further query by Mr. Chang whether the U.S. authorities would take disciplinary action or turn the defendant over to the Korean authorities, in the case of an offense punishable by Korean law but not by U.S. law, Mr. Habib stated that paragraph 2(b) would give the ROK Government the right to exercise jurisdiction. As an example, Mr. Habib asked the Korean negotiators to consider the case of a dependent who commits murder. He is not punishable by U.S. law but is punishable by Korean law. Therefore, the ROK authorities would have jurisdiction. However, there might be cases in which the Korean authorities would not wish to exercise their jurisdiction. In those cases, they could waive their jurisdiction, either concurrent or exclusive, according to the provisions of the U.S. draft.

26. In paragraph 1(b), Mr. Habib identified the key difference as being the use of "civil authorities" in the U.S. draft, compared with "authorities" in the Korean draft. Also, the U.S. draft states that the Korean authorities "shall have the right to exercise jurisdiction" whereas the Korean draft says they "shall have jurisdiction". This is not a substantial point, Mr. Habib said, but the language of the U.S. draft is similar to the language of paragraph 1(a) in both drafts.

0135

27. Pointing out that the Korean negotiators had previously said that all Korean soldiers are tried by courts-martial, Mr. Habib asked if the language of the Korean draft meant that all U.S. soldiers would be tried by Korean courts-martial. Mr. Chang replied that all members of the ROK armed forces are subject to trial by court-martial. However, the "authorities" referred to in the Korean draft could be either civilian or military. Mr. Habib asked why all members of the ROK armed forces are subject to trial by court-martial. Could it have any connection with the fact that they are serving in a combat zone? Mr. Chang said he would answer that question at a subsequent meeting.

28. Mr. Chang also suggested deferring discussion of "shall have the right to exercise jurisdiction" versus "shall have jurisdiction" until a subsequent meeting. The Korean negotiators believed the difference in language could be easily reconciled.

29. Turning to paragraph 2, Mr. Habib pointed out that the use of the term "military authorities" in the Korean draft and the inclusion of the phrase "and their dependents" in the U.S. draft had already been discussed. Subparagraphs (b) and (c) were identical in both drafts.

30. In paragraph 3(a), Mr. Habib noted the same differences in language regarding the use of the term "military authorities" and the phrase "and their dependents" in the Korean and U.S. drafts, respectively. Subparagraph (a)(i) in both drafts was identical. In subparagraph (a)(ii) of the Korean draft appeared the definition of on-duty offenses which the Korean negotiators had just indicated need not necessarily be included in the text of the Agreement.

31. Mr. Chang stated that if agreement could be reached by the negotiators on the definition contained in the U.S. Army Far East circular which he had mentioned, it need not be included in the text. Mr. Habib replied that the U.S. negotiators would not agree on a definition of duty. There is no such definition in any status of forces agreement

0136

By definition, duty is what the commander calls duty. This is a universally accepted principle.

32. Mr. Chang replied that if the U.S. negotiators would accept the second and third sentences of subparagraph (a)(ii) of the Korean draft, the Korean negotiators would be willing to delete the first sentence, which constituted the definition of duty. Mr. Habib replied that this proposal was unacceptable to the U.S. negotiators. He said the U.S. negotiators were prepared to discuss how the commanding officer could responsibly fulfill his function of defining duty but they were unable to agree to any proposal which would vest that function in some person not connected with the duty.

33. Mr. Chang stated that the Korean negotiators were not insisting that agreement on the definition of duty contained in the U.S. Army Far East circular be included in the text of the article or even in an Agreed Minute. If the negotiators could just reach agreement on that definition, there would be no problem in solving this question.

34. At this point, the negotiators broke off substantive discussion to spend the last few minutes of the meeting in bidding farewell to General Fuller and to Mr. Kang, each of whom was attending his last negotiating session prior to departure on another assignment.

36. The next meeting was scheduled for March 27 at 2:00 p.m.

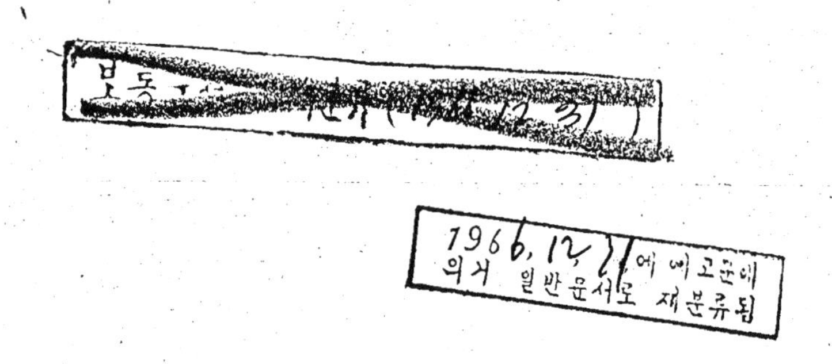

0137

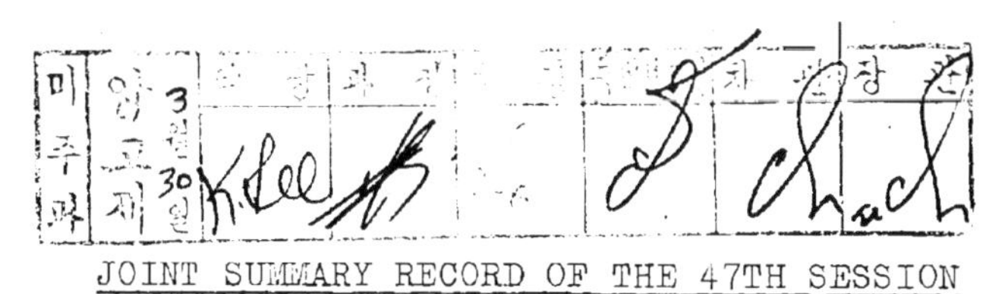

JOINT SUMMARY RECORD OF THE 47TH SESSION

1. Time and Place: 3:00-5:00 P.M. March 20, 1964
   at the Foreign Ministry's Conference
   Room (No.1)

2. Attendants:

ROK Side:

Mr. Chang, Sang Moon	Director European and American Affairs Bureau
Mr. Yoon, Doo Sik	Director Prosecutor's Bureau Ministry of Justice
Mr. Koo, Choong Whay	Chief, American Section Ministry of Foreign Affairs
Mr. Chung, Tai Kyun	Chief Prosecutor's Section Prosecutor's Bureau Ministry of Justice
Col. Kim, Won Kil	Chief, Military Affairs Section Ministry of National Defense
Mr. Kang Suk Jae	2nd Secretary Ministry of Foreign Affairs
Mr. Lee, Chung Bin	3rd Secretary Ministry of Foreign Affairs
Mr. Chung, Woo Young (Rapporteur and Interpreter)	3rd Secretary Ministry of Foreign Affairs
Mr. Lee, Keun Pal	3rd Secretary Ministry of Foreign Affairs
Mr. Kim, Nai Sung	Staff Officer Europe Section Ministry of Foreign Affairs

U.S. Side:

Mr. Philip C. Habib	Counselor American Embassy
Brig. Gen. G.G. O'Connor	Deputy Chief of Staff 8th U.S. Army
Brig. Gen. L.J. Fuller	Staff Judge Advocate United Nations Command

0138

Col. Howard Smigelow	Deputy Chief of Staff 8th U.S. Army
Col. Kenneth C. Crawford	Staff Judge Advocates Office 8th U.S. Army
Capt. John Wayne	Assistant Chief of Staff USN/K
Mr. Benjamin A. Fleck (Rapporteur and Press Officer)	First Secretary American Embassy
Mr. James Sartorius	2nd Secretary American Embassy
Maj. Robert D. Peckham	Staff Officer JAG 8th U.S. Army
Mr. Robert A. Kinney	J-5 8th U.S. Army
Mr. Kenneth Campen	Interpreter

Criminal Jurisdiction

1. In opening the meeting, Mr. Chang said that he would like to respond to the questions and statements made by the chief U.S. negotiator at the previous meetings.

2. With regard to the phrase "authorities of the Republic of Korea", Mr. Chang said the Korean negotiators do not want to limit Korean authority to the civil side. As he had mentioned at the previous meeting, a member of the American forces, their civilian component, or one of their dependents may have to be subject to trial by the Korean military tribunals in cases where ordinary Korean civilians would be triable by the Korean military courts. The Korean Constitution, in Article 106, states that in cases of espionage on military affairs, offenses against sentinels and sentry-posts, distribution of harmful food to armed forces, and offenses against prisoners of war, civilians and soldiers alike would be subject to the military tribunal in accordance with provisions of law. If the Korean negotiators accepted

0139

the U.S. version of "civil authorities of the Republic of Korea", the Korean authorities would have to initiate criminal proceedings against such offenses only in a civil court. It is the understanding of the Korean negotiators that espionage or violation of any law relating to official secrets of the state may be tried by the civil court. However, they believe that offenses involving espionage on military affairs should be dealt with by the military court rather than the civil court for security reasons.

3. As for the problem of trying American servicemen by Korean military courts under Martial Law, the U.S. negotiators had stated that the U.S. armed forces could not allow their personnel to be tried by the summary procedures of ROK military courts. The existing code of criminal procedures applicable in the case of civil courts is also applied at military courts even under martial law. The Korean negotiators understand that the concern of the U.S. negotiators, indicated by the reference to summary procedures, may be over the composition of the Korean military tribunal, which the Korean negotiators believe to be more or less universal. If that understanding is correct, Mr. Chang continued, the Korean negotiators would further like to know what are the other elements of concern to the U.S. negotiators, as expressed in their reference to summary procedures.

4. Regarding the official duty certificate, the Korean negotiators do not challenge the contention of the U.S. negotiators that the local commander may well determine whether one of his soldiers is or is not on duty.

0140

However, determination of whether an offense arising out of an act or omission committed on duty has a genuine link with the performance of official duty should not be made by a field commander but by a judicial officer who has the sole authority to take up criminal cases under Korean laws. The example given by the U.S. negotiators of artillery firing practice on a firing range is irrelevant to the criminal case under discussion and not to the point. The Korean negotiators would like to give an example, said Mr. Chang, which would justify their concern on this point. Suppose a soldier was ordered to proceed from Seoul to Suwon on official business. He had to park his car on the street somewhere along the Yongdongpo main street and unfortunately became involved in a quarrel with a Korean and committed assault and battery or serious injury. Even though this example sounds like a hypothetical case, we cannot rule out the possibility of such unfortunate cases occurring. What the Korean negotiators contend in such a case is that a local commander may well certify that the offense was committed during the hours of the soldier's duty, but he is not empowered to determine whether the offense arose out of an act or omission directly related to the official order he issued.

5. Further, Mr. Chang said, the U.S. draft has not attempted to formulate any concise explanation of when an offense does arise out of an act or omission done in the performance of official duty. This is why the Korean negotiators had prepared in their draft the

0141

exact meaning of "official duty". If the U.S. negotiators don't like some of the wording in the Korean draft, the Korean negotiators would propose to modify it in line with a circular of the United States Army, Far East, which was published in January, 1956. The Korean negotiators believe that the U.S. authorities could have no objection to accepting the Korean proposal, because such definition of "official duty" is their own interpretation.

6. With regard to dependents, Mr. Chang continued, the status of the dependents is substantially different from that of the members of the U.S. armed forces and civilian component. Dependents of members of the U.S. armed forces in Korea are not in the same position as members of the forces and the civilian component. Moreover, they are not subject to the same strict discipline as are members of the armed forces. However, as the Korean negotiators had indicated at the last meeting, they are not trying to be inflexible in their approach to this problem.

7. With regard to the problem of waiving exclusive jurisdiction by the Korean Government, Mr. Chang continued, the U.S. side had stated that its request for sympathetic consideration was nothing but a humanitarian statement. However, the Korean negotiators feel that the problem under discussion is something more than a humanitarian affair. In brief, inasmuch as the right of exclusive jurisdiction is inalienable, the Korean authorities do not desire to obligate themselves to the extent that they have to give sympathetic consideration to the request for waiver. Furthermore, the U.S. side had stated that the provision as indicated in the U.S. draft is an attempt

0142

to assist the Korean authorities. The U.S. negotiators are offering the Korean authorities assistance for which the latter do not ask.

8. With respect to waiver of concurrent jurisdiction, Mr. Chang continued, the Korean negotiators are well aware that the rate of waiver in other countries had proved to be very high. As he had mentioned before, the Korean authorities are prepared to waive in as many cases as in the precedents referred to by the U.S. negotiators. However, the Korean negotiators are unable to understand why the provision in this agreement should be differently worded than similar provisions in other agreements. The U.S. negotiators had said further that the provision as stated in the U.S. draft is a standard provision in most Status of Forces Agreements, but so far as the Korean negotiators know, there is no such provision in any of the existing Status of Forces Agreements, particularly the last paragraph of the U.S. draft, barring the host country and its nationals from instituting criminal proceedings in case the Joint Committee fails to come to an agreement on the question of waiver.

9. The U.S. negotiators insist, continued Mr. Chang, that if an offense committed by a member of the ROK armed forces would have been tried by court-martial, then such an offense committed by a member of the United States armed forces would also be subject to trial by American court-martial. The Korean negotiators recalled that at previous meetings, the U.S. negotiators time and again had pointed out that the Korean draft should be discussed in line with precedents in other SOFA's. Since the Korean negotiators believe that most of the

receiving countries in the precedents have military law and military courts, the Korean negotiators expected to find provisionn similar to those the U.S. negotiators have proposed in this regard. Therefore, they wished to ask the U.S. negotiators in what Status of Forces Agreement and with what country they have made identical provisions. Mr. Chang stated that the Koraan negotiators are really at a loss to find the real intention of the U.S. negotiators in proposing this provision. Unless the U.S. negotiators withdrew this proposition, the Korean authorities would have to give up entirely their right to exercise criminal jurisdiction over members of the U.S. military forces.

10. With regard to the term "authorities of the United States", Mr. Chang continued, the U.S. negotiators had stated that the language had been made broad enough to provide for any possible exercise of jurisdiction by U.S. authorities. He said the Korean negotiators would like to emphasize that the subject and matters of discussion throughout this SOFA negotiation is the military status of the U.S. armed forces but not any other U.S. authority in Korea. It is utterly inconceivable that any United States authority other than the U.S. military authorities would have jurisdiction in Korea. Moreover, the Korean negotiators could not find any similar provision in any other SOFA. In this respect, they would appreciate an explanation of any possible difficulty envisaged by the U.S. negotiators in case the word "military" is inserted.

0144

11. Regarding so-called "combat zone", as the Korean negotiators repeatedly had made clear, criminal jurisdiction and the military operation are totally different concepts, which cannot be confounded. The imposition of a geographical limitation on the exercise of jurisdiction is incompatible with the sovereign judicial right to be exercised throughout the territory of the Republic of Korea and is not acceptable to the Korean negotiators. They hope the difficulties indicated by the U.S. negotiators with regard to the so-called "combat zone" may be dealt with and solved by an agreeable and effective exercise of waiver of the right of jurisdiction.

12. Regarding trial safeguards, Mr. Chang continued, the U.S. negotiators had said that as a result of study of Korean criminal procedures, laws and practices, it was necessary to list trial safeguards. However, the Korean negotiators found the provisions provided in the U.S. draft article are more or less the same as those provided in the Korean Constitution and the Code of Criminal Procedures. That is the reason why the Korean negotiators had not enumerated such provisions in their draft. If the U.S. negotiators desire to insert these provisions in the SOFA, in principle, the Korean negotiators have no objection to it.

13. Mr. Habib reminded the Korean negotiators that the question of pre-trial custody was also a matter of concern to the U.S. negotiators. Noting that Mr. Chang had not discussed this question in his just-concluded remarks, Mr. Habib asked for a statement of the Korean position regarding pre-trial custody. Mr. Chang replied that pre-trial custody was closely connected with the question of post-trial custody. The Korean negotiators

0145

wished to withhold comment on both subjects until a later meeting.

14. Regarding Korean military courts, Mr. Habib inquired whether it was not the case that Article 106 of the ROK Constitution stated that military tribunals "may", not "must", exercise jurisdiction over civilians during periods of martial law. Mr. Chang acknowledged this to be the case. In effect, Mr. Habib continued, it would not be a violation of the Constitution if that right of jurisdiction were not exercised. The people who drafted the Constitution had recognized that the exercise of jurisdiction over criminal cases by military tribunals was not necessarily the best way of handling those cases. The U.S. negotiators, Mr. Habib said, did not believe that the Korean negotiators were seriously concerned with Korean military jurisdiction over Americans. They would reserve further comment on this point until later discussion of specific sections of this article.

15. Mr. Habib pointed out that the U.S. negotiators had not claimed that the provision in the U.S. draft providing for waiver of concurrent jurisdiction was a standard provision in all status of forces agreements. What he had said previously was that the reference to waiver in the text of both the U.S. and Korean drafts of this article was standard language. The Agreed Minutes, of course, were another matter. The language in the U.S. draft of the Agreed Minutes was not the standard language.

16. Mr. Habib stated that Mr. Chang had made two statements indicating willingness on the part of the Korean negotiators to consider the U.S. point of view.

0146

The first of these was Mr. Chang's statement that the enumeration of trial safeguards was consistent with ROK law and that if the U.S. negotiators wished to include such an enumeration in this article, the Korean negotiators would not object in principle. The second was Mr. Chang's statement that the Korean negotiators were not inflexible on the subject of dependents. Mr. Habib said the U.S. negotiators would defer discussion on these points until the Korean position had been somewhat refined.

17. In other respects, Mr. Habib continued, there appeared to be no recognition on the part of the Korean negotiators of other problems existing with regard to this article or of the explanations given by the U.S. negotiators. In particular, the Korean negotiator's discussion of the duty certificate was difficult to accept. He pointed out that there was a profound difference between the example given by the U.S. negotiators and that given by the Korean negotiators. In the Korean negotiators' example, the offense was clearly not an on-duty offense. But in the example given by the U.S. negotiators, an on-duty offense would be construed as an off-duty offense, according to the definition of off-duty offenses which the Korean negotiators wished to include in the Agreement. Mr. Habib again pointed out that in no status of forces agreement is there any such definition, the reason being that only the commander who assigns the duty is able to determine whether or not an offense was committed in the line of that duty. In some status of forces agreements, there is provision for a review system. Where such a system has been used, the finding has always been that only the commander is competent to determine what constitutes duty.

0147

18. Pointing out that there was a great similarity in the two drafts, Mr. Habib suggested that the negotiators, having exchanged views in general terms, now proceed with a paragraph by paragraph discussion of the drafts in order to identify the specific differences existing in the texts.

19. Mr. Chang agreed but said that before proceeding to paragraph by paragraph discussion, the Korean negotiators wished to make a few further comments. With regard to enumeration of trial safeguards, they agredd to the idea of an enumeration but they did not necessarily accept the entire enumeration in the U.S. draft. With regard to the subject of dependents as a whole, the U.S. negotiators could accept the statement of the Korean negotiators at face value but detailed discussion should be deferred until a later meeting. With regard to the duty certificate question, the U.S. negotiators should not have any difficulty in accepting the definition published in the January, 1956 circular of the U.S. Army, Far East, either as part of the text or as an understanding in the negotiating record.

20. The negotiators then began paragraph by paragraph discussion and in paragraph 1(a) noted that the Korean draft contained the word "military" in front of the word "authorities" while the U.S. draft contained the phrase "and their dependents" and referred to "all" criminal and disciplinary jurisdiction.

21. Mr. Habib stated that if the Korean negotiators were unwilling to include the phrase "and their dependents" in this subparagraph, their position was not very flexible. He pointed out that if dependents were to be subject to U.S. jurisdiction, they would have to be mentioned in this subparagraph.

0148

22. Mr. Chang replied that inclusion or exclusion of the word "all" was not an important matter and could be discussed later. On the other hand, the question of whether to refer to "authorities" or "military authorities" was a very important question which was not just simply a matter of wording but a question which affects the judicial rights of the Korean people as a whole. With regard to dependents, the Korean negotiators believed that measures could be worked out to include them in this article without specifically referring to them in this subparagraph. He pointed out that the U.S. negotiators had not made any definite explanation as to how far the U.S. military courts have jurisdiction over dependents. The Korean negotiators wished to know what the U.S. authorities would do regarding those persons over whom the armed forces would have no jurisdiction.

23. Mr. Habib replied that the U.S. armed forces would have disciplinary jurisdiction over such persons. It was also possible that in future, jurisdiction will be provided that does not exist at present. In wartime, the armed forces would have jurisdiction over dependents under the provisions of the "hostilities" paragraph in the U.S. draft. In this connection, Mr. Habib urged the Korean negotiators to study carefully the provisions of paragraph 2(b), which provides that the Republic of Korea will have exclusive jurisdiction over offenses not punishable by U.S. law.

24. In reply to Mr. Chang's query whether paragraph 2(b) included or excluded disciplinary action, Mr. Habib stated that an offense could be handled either by criminal jurisdiction or by disciplinary jurisdiction. If the

offense were not punishable by U.S. law, and was punishable by ROK law, paragraph 2(b) provides that the ROK authorities could exercise jurisdiction, if they decided to do so. It gives them the right to exercise jurisdiction but they do not have to do so if they do not wish to.

25. In response to a further query by Mr. Chang whether the U.S. authorities would take disciplinary action or turn the defendant over to the Korean authorities, in the case of an offense punishable by Korean law but not by U.S. law, Mr. Habib stated that paragraph 2(b) would give the ROK Government the right to exercise jurisdiction. As an example, Mr. Habib asked the Korean negotiators to consider the case of a dependent who commits murder. He is not punishable by U.S. law but is punishable by Korean law. Therefore, the ROK authorities would have jurisdiction. However, there might be cases in which the Korean authorities would not wish to exercise their jurisdiction. In those cases, they could waive their jurisdiction, either concurrent or exclusive, according to the provisions of the U.S. draft.

26. In paragraph 1(b), Mr. Habib identified the key difference as being the use of "civil authorities" in the U.S. draft, compared with "authorities" in the Korean draft. Also, the U.S. draft states that the Korean authorities "shall have the right to exercise jurisdiction" whereas the Korean draft says they "shall have jurisdiction". This is not a substantial point, Mr. Habib said, but the language of the U.S. draft is similar to the language of paragraph 1(a) in both drafts.

27. Pointing out that the Korean negotiators had previously said that all Korean soldiers are tried by

0150

courts-martial, Mr. Habib asked if the language of the Korean draft meant that all U.S. soldiers would be tried by Korean courts-martial. Mr. Chang replied that all members of the ROK armed forces are subject to trial by court-martial. However, the "authorities" referred to in the Korean draft could be either civilian or military. Mr. Habib asked why all members of the ROK armed forces are subject to trial by court-martial. Could it have any connection with the fact that they are serving in a combat zone? Mr. Chang said he would answer that question at a subsequent meeting.

28. Mr. Chang also suggested deferring discussion of "shall have the right to exercise jurisdiction" versus "shall have jurisdiction" until a subsequent meeting. The Korean negotiators believed the difference in language could be easily reconciled.

29. Turning to paragraph 2, Mr. Habib pointed out that the use of the term "military authorities" in the Korean draft and the inclusion of the phrase "and their dependents" in the U.S. draft had already been discussed. Subparagraphs (b) and (c) were identical in both drafts.

30. In paragraph 3(a), Mr. Habib noted the same differences in language regarding the use of the term "military authorities" and the phrase "and their dependents" in the Korean and U.S. drafts, respectively. Subparagraph (a) (i) in both drafts was identical. In subparagraph (a) (ii) of the Korean draft appeared the definition of on-duty offenses which the Korean negotiators had just indicated need not necessarily be included in the text of the Agreement.

31. Mr. Chang stated that if agreement could be reached by the negotiators on the definition contained in the U.S. Army Far East circular which he had mentioned, it need not be included in the text. Mr. Habib replied that the U.S. negotiators would not agree on a definition of duty. There is no such definition in any status of forces agreement. By definition, duty is what the commander calls duty. This is a universally accepted principle.

32. Mr. Chang replied that if the U.S. negotiators would accept the second and third sentences of sub-paragraph (a) (ii) of the Korean draft, the Korean negotiators would be willing to delete the first sentence, which constituted the definition of duty. Mr. Habib replied that this proposal was unacceptable to the U.S. negotiators. He said the U.S. negotiators were prepared to discuss how the commanding officer could responsibly fulfill his function of defining duty but they were unable to agree to any proposal which would vest that function in some person not connected with the duty.

33. Mr. Chang stated that the Korean negotiators were not insisting that agreement on the definition of duty contained in the U.S. Army Far East circular be included in the text of the article or even in an Agreed Minute. If the negotiators could just reach agreement on that definition, there would be no problem in solving this question.

34. At this point, the negotiators broke off substantive discussion to spend the last few minutes of the meeting in bidding farewell to General Fuller and to Mr. Kang, each of whom was attending his last negotiating session prior to departure on another assignment.

0152

35. The next meeting was scheduled for March 27, at 2:00 p.m.

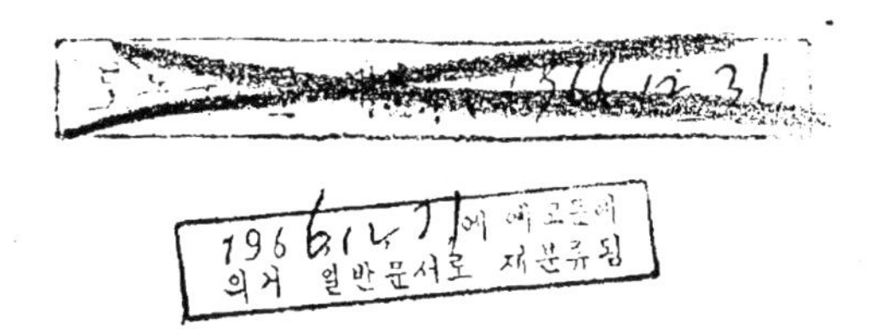

0153

4. 제48차 회의, 4. 3

0154

기 안 용 지

자체 통제		기안처	미주과 이근팔	전화번호	근거서류접수일자
	과장	국장	차관	장관	
관계관 서명					
기안 년월일	1964.4.1.	시행 년월일		보존 년한	정서기장
분류 기호	외구미 722.2	전체 통제		종결	
경유 수신 참조	건의		발신		
제목	제 48 차 주둔군지위협정 체결 교섭회의에 임할 우리측 입장				

4 월 3 일 개최될 제 48 차 주둔군지위협정 체결을 위한 한.미간 교섭회의에서는 노무조달, 군계약자 및 보호조치에 관한 조항을 토의하도록 예정하고 있는 바 이에 대하여 우리측 교섭실무자는 3 월 24 일 회합을 갖고 제 48 차 회의에서 취할 태도를 별첨과 같이 결정하였아오니 재가하여 주시기 바랍니다.

유 첨: 제 48 차 주둔군지위협정 체결교섭회의에 임할 우리측 태도. 끝.

1964.4.1 (48차)

1966.12.31.에 예고문에 의거 일반문서로 재분류됨

승인서식 1-1-3 (11 00900-03) (195mm×265mm16절지)

0155

가. 노무조달

(1) 노무자의 고용주의 정의를 규정한 미측초안 1(a)항은 수락한다.

(2) 노무자의 정의를 규정한 1(b)항중 except 이하를 삭제할 것을 주장하고 그 대신 " provided that the Korean nationals shall be employed to the maximum extent "용어의 삽입을 제의한다.

(3) K.S.C.에 관하여서는 관계부처와 별도로 협의하기로 하고 본 협정으로 부터 제외한다.

(4) 가사사용인은 한국의 노동법의 적용을 받지 않기로 되어 있음으로 삭제할 것을 주장한다.

(5) 노무관리에 관한 미측초안 2항은 우리초안 2항의 규정과 동일한 내용임으로 우리측안을 수락할 것을 주장한다.

(6) 미측초안 3항중 "in general conformity"에 대하여서는 각국의 협정에서 규정한 바와 같이 "shall be laid down by the legislation" 용어로 대치할 것을 주장한다.

(7) 노무분재 해결에 관한 독일, 아이스랜드, 일본등 각국에 있어서의 현황에 대한 미측의 설명을 청취한다.

(8) 미측 초안 4항은 수락할 수 없다.

(9) 노무조달에 있어서 미군에게 우선순위를 인정하려는 미초안 5(a)항에 대하여서는 의의가 없으며 5(b)항의 병역으로 부터의 노무자의 보류는 수락할 수 없으며 노무동원으로 부터의 면제는 합동위원회에서 그 인정범위를 결정토록 한다.

(10) 합의의사록 1항(수정안)에 대하여 미측의 견해를 청취한다.

나. 군계약자

(1) 우리측의 군계약자의 정의를 미측이 수락한다면 가족에 관한 제 22 차 회의에서의 우리측의 발언을 반영시켜"and the dependents of such persons "용어를 삽입할 것을 제의한다.

0156

(2) 우리측 합의의사록 1 항 및 2 항을 철회하고 미측 합의의사록 2 항을 수락한다. 단, 미측이 말한 바와 같이 미군은 점차적으로 제 3 국인을 한국인으로 대치하고 있으며 본 협정 발효 이후에는 제 3 국인을 고용할 의도가 없다는 것을 양해사항으로 유보한다.

(3) 우리초안 8항 전단을 수정하여 " and the dependents of such persons "용어를 삽입한다.

(4) 미측이 원한다면 " terms and conditions of employment " 용어를 우리초안 3(i)항에 삽입하여 준다.

(5) 미측 합의의사록 제 1 항을 수락한다.

(6) 우리측 합의의사록 제 3항의 " private vehicles "이라함은 "passenger car and wagon type car either for pleasure or business "를 뜻한다.

다. 보호조치

(1) 우리측이 제 46 차 회의에서 (ㄱ) 안전보호의 대상에 군계약자 및 그들의 가족을 포함하고 (ㄴ) 미국정부 재산의 보호를 위한 입법조치는 우리안 대로 주장할 것 (ㄷ) 형사재판관할권과 관련하여 범법자를 처벌하는 것은 미측 주장을 수락하여 우리 초안 후단을 수정 제안한 바 있음으로 상기 제 점에 대한 미측 견해를 청취한다. 끝.

0157

기 안 용 지

자체통제		기안처	미주과 이근팔	전화번호	근거서류접수일자

	과장	국장	차관	장관		
				대		

관계관 서명	
기안 년월일	1964. 3. 20.
시행 년월일	
보존 년한	
분류 기호	외구미722.2
전체 통제	
종결	
경유 수신 참조	건의
발신	
정서	
기장	
제목	제 47차 주둔군지위협정 체결교섭회의에 임할 우리측 입장

3월 20일 개최될 제 47차 주둔군지위협정 체결을 위한 한.미간 교섭회의에서는 형사재판관할권에 관한 조항을 토의하도록 예정하고 있는바 이에 대하여 우리측 교섭실무자는 3월 17일 회합을 갖고 제 47차 회의에서 취할 태도를 별첨과 같이 결정 하였아오니 재가하여 주시기 바랍니다.

유 첨: 제 47차 주둔군지위협정 체결교섭회의에 임할 우리측 입장. 끝

승인서식 1-1-3 (11 00900-03) (195mm×265mm16절지)

1966, 12, 31 에 예고문에 의거 일반문서로 재분류됨

0158

가. 형사재판관할권

미측이 제 46 차 회의에서 주장한 사항에 대하여 우리측은 다음과 같이 우리측 입장을 주장한다.

(1) 한국의 재판권 행사기관: 미측은 한국의 민사당국 만이 관할권을 행사할 수 있다고 주장하고 있는바 한국의 헌법과 법률은 일반 법원이 원칙적으로 재판을 할 수 있으며 예외적으로 간첩죄, 유해음식물에 관한 죄, 초소 초병에 관한 죄, 포로에 관한 죄, 등 4 가지 범죄에 한하여 군법회의에 회부하게 되어 있다. 군사기밀에 관한 간첩죄, 포로에 관한 죄등은 그 성질상 일반법원 보다 군법재판에 회부함이 적절한 것인바 미측 주장대로 하면 그렇게 할 수 없는 곤난점이 있다.

(2) 계엄령 선포: 계엄령 선포 하 군법재판에서도 법관 구성에 있어서 약간의 차의점이 있을 뿐 3 심제를 포함한 사법절차는 일반재판에 있어서와 동일하게 하여 인권옹호를 기하고 있다.

(3) 공무집행중 범죄: 우리 나라 사법상 검사는 수사의 주체로서 범죄의 수사에 착수하기 위하여서는 우선 검사가 관할권 유무를 판단할 필요가 있으며 우리측 규정은 분쟁의 여지를 남기지 않기 위함이다. 물론 최종적으로 법관이 재판에서 특정 범죄가 공무집행중 발생하였는가에 대하여 결정하게 될 것이다. 우리측은 군지휘관이 누구 보다도 군인의 공무집행여부를 잘 알 수 있다는 것은 인정하며 미측 주장에 대한 교섭상 고려의 여지는 없는 것은 않이다.

(4) 가족: 가족은 군사명 수행을 그 주된 목적으로 하는 군인, 군속과는 그 성격이 판의하며 또한 가족은 군기에 반듯이 복종해야 하는 것도 않인 만큼 우리 나라 관할권에 복함이 옳다. 그러나 가족에 대한 우리의 입장은 교섭상 융통성이 전혀 없는 것은 않이다.

(5) 전속관할권의 포기 요청: 전속관할권의 포기 요청에 대하여 호의적 고려를 해야 한다는 미측의 주장은 인도적인 점 만이 않인 의무를 부과하려는 것으로 보며 우리가 문제시하고 있는

0159

것은 인도적 문제보다 법적인 문제이며 호의적 고려를 하고 않하고는 전적으로 한국측에 달려 있는 것이다.

(6) 관할권의 경합: 우리는 각국이 상당히 많은 경우 관할권을 포기 하고 있다는 점을 인정하는 바이지만 미측안은 타국과의 협정에서 볼 수 없는 정도의 제한을 가하여 한국정부 뿐만 아니라 국민의 재판을 받을 권리까지도 포기시키려는 것은 수락할 수 없다.

(7) 군법회의: 미측의 주장은 각 협정에 그 선례를 찾아 볼 수 없으며 우리측에 일단 관할권이 인정된다면 미군은 민사법원 또는 군법재판에 복하여야 할 것임에도 불구하고 미군법재판에 회부하려는 것은 우리 나라 재판관할권을 전적으로 인정하지 않겠다고 하는것 인가를 문의한다.

(8) 미측의 관할권 행사기관: 양측은 주한미군대의 지위를 규정할 것을 교섭중에 있는 것으로서 관할권의 행사기관은 미군당국으로 규정 되어야 한다. 미군당국으로 규정함으로서 야기될 미군측의 곤난점은 무엇인가?

(9) 전투지역: 재판관할권의 행사를 무조건 지역적으로 제한하려는 것은 모순이다. 미군의 전투태세를 위한 특수사정은 인정하는 바 이나 전투지역의 개념을 본문으로 부터 삭제하고 관할권의 행사의 실지 운영면에서 해결을 모색하여야 할 문제이다.

(10) 피의자의 권리: 우리 헌법과 법률상 충분히 보장되고 있다. 미측이 협정에서 규정할 것을 기필 원한다면 반대는 않겠다.

(11) 재판전 및 재판 후 신병 인도: 양측의 견해차의가 그리 큰 것은 않이라고 보며 앞으로 교섭에서 해결될 것으로 믿는다. 끝.

0160

SOFA NEGOTIATION

Agenda for the 48th Session

15:30 April 3, 1964

1. Continuation of Discussions on:

    a. Labor Article

    b. Contractors Article

    c. Security Measures Article

2. Other Business

3. Agenda and Date of the Next Meeting

4. Press Release

0161

Submitted on April 3. 64

STATEMENT
소견진술
MR. OGDEN C. REED
CIVILIAN PERSONNEL DIRECTOR
오그든 씨.리이드
민간인 인사처장

I am glad to be here and to present pertinent information on USFK's direct hire personnel system for the Korean workforce. We have translated presentation for ease of communication.

이자리에서 한국인 종업원을 위한 주한미군의 직속고용인사제도를 말씀드리게 되었음을 영광으로 생각 합니다. 이해하시기 쉽게 설명을 번역해 보았읍니다.

First, some background information:

먼저 기초적인 자료를 말씀드리겠읍니다.

USFK employs almost 20,000 appropriated fund Korean employees under definitive policy controls. In addition, over 11,000 non-appropriated fund employees and 3,000 invited contractor employees are administered under personnel policy parallel to appropriated fund personnel policy. We, thus, are referring to around 34,000 direct-hire employees.

주한 미군은 결정적인 방침통제하에서 거의 20,000명에 달하는 영달자금 한국인 종업원을 고용하고 있읍니다. 그뿐만아니라 11,000명 이상의 비영달자금종업원과 약 3,000명의 초청청부업자 종업원이 있는데 이들도 영달자금 종업원의 인사방침에 못지않은 인사방침하에서 행정됩니다. 그래서 우리는 약 34,000명의 직속종업원에 대해서 말씀드리고 있는것입니다.

USFK has 10 area civilian personnel offices located throughout ROK, in areas of military concentration. These offices employ and administer Korean and other civilian personnel for USFK organizations in the area. Area personnel offices classify jobs and establish pay grades, recruit, appoint, establish step rates, promote, reassign, effect disciplinary actions, complete retirement and other separation actions, provide training services and assistance on improved line supervision and employment-management relations.

주한미군은 10개의 지구인사처를 한국안에 가지고 있는데 주로 군사시설이 집중된곳에 위치하고 있읍니다. 이 인사처는 각지구에있는 주한미군예하부대을 위하여 한국인과 기타 민간인직원을 고용하고 행정합니다. 직무분류를 하고, 급여등급을 결정하고, 모집을하고, 임명을하고, 년공가봉을 설정하며 승급을 시키고, 재배치를하고, 징계, 정년퇴직및 기타해직조치를 취하고, 교육을 실시하며 개선된 각층에서의 감독관습을위하ㄴ 도움을주고 또한 노사관계도 취급합니다.

As General O'Connor has stated, USFK personnel practices and standards parallel or exceed Laborur Standard Act of May 15, 1953, as supplemented by executive orders. The Laborur Standard Act, Act No. 286, covers a large number of articles and all pertinent articles are clearly met in personnel policy and procedures applicable to USFK Korean employees. In

"오커너어" 준장께서 말씀한바와 같이 주한미군의 인사관례와 기준은 1953년5월15일 발포된 근로기준법과 그시행령에 부합하거나 혹은능가하는 것입니다. 법령 286호인 근로기준법은 다수한 조항을 망라하였는데 그중의 모든 적절한 조항이 주한미군 한국인 종업원에게 적용되는 인사방침과 절차에 의해 분명히 합치되고 있읍니다.

0162

addition, certain special advantages of a civil service type are found in Korean personnel management.

그뿐만 아니라 한국인 인사관리에는 공무원근무형태의 특전도 있읍니다.

I will cover 11 basic elements of Korean personnel administration, with appropriate tie-in to certain articles of the Labour Standards Act and local practices and to US-style civil service concepts, if relevant.

이제 관련된 근로기준법과 지방관습및 미식 공무원 개념에 결부시키면서 한국인종업원행정의 11가지 기본요소를 소개코저 합니다.

1. JOB CLASSIFICATION AND COMPENSATION.

1. 직무분류와 보수

a. Korean employment is based upon job classifications and job ranking by grade levels. These are reflected in a Manual of Standard Job Definitions. There are three grade schedules, with pay rates associated with each grade level. One schedule is for administrative, custodial, and professional-type jobs, the non-Manual Schedule: the second schedule is for industrial-type jobs, the Wage Board Schedule; the third is for marine jobs.

ㄱ. 한국인 종업원의 고용은 직무분류와 등급별 직무배열에 기초를 둡니다. 이것은 기준업무정의편람에 반영되어 있읍니다. 세가지의 등급 "스케쥴"이 있는데 각 등급마다 알맞는 급여율이 딸려있읍니다. 첫번 "스케쥴"은 행정, 관리, 및 전문직용인데 "제네랄 스케쥴" (사무계통)이라 부릅니다. 둘째 "스케쥴"은 공원직용인데 "외이지 보오드" (기술계통)라 부릅니다. 셋째번은 해상직원용 입니다.

b. Basic pay rates are commensurate with that of prevailing pay practices in reputable and responsible Korean businees firms. These rates are kept up-to-date by means of periodic locality wage surveys. Currently, our average monthly wage is over 9,000 won and our rates are fully competitive.

ㄴ. 기본급여율은 저명하고 확고한 한국기업체에서 지불하는 현행급여와 맞먹습니다. 이 급여율은 정기적으로 실시하는 지방노임조사에 의해서 뒤떠러지지않게 하고 있읍니다. 현재 평균 급여는 월 9,000원 이상이 되는데 이것은 과히 손색없는 것이라고 봅니다.

c. A year-end bonus of one full month's pay is paid on or about 15 December, providing the employee has six month's continuous service. We do not pay summer bonuses; however, locality pay credit for these bonuses and other allowances are incorporated in the basic rate schedule.

ㄷ. 6개월 근속을하면 12월15일경에 한달분급여에상당하는 년말상여를 지불합니다. 하기상여금은 없으나 시중에서 주고있는 하기상여금과 기타 수당은 기본급여율에 포함되어 있읍니다.

d. The regularly scheduled work week in most organizations is established as eight hours a day and 40 hours a week; some organizations also provide Saturday work. Overtime pay is provided for all required hours of

ㄹ. 대개의 부서에서는 하로 8시간에 주40시간근무가 정상근무주로 설정되어있는데 어떤부서에선 토요일 근무도합니다. 특근수당은 근로기준법 제46조에따라 하로 8시간에 주48시간을 초과근무한것에 대해서 1.5배로 지불

work in excess of eight hours a day or 48 hours per week at time and a half, in line with Article 46 of the Laborur Standards Act. This is strictly enforced and equitably administered.

합니다. 이것은 엄격히 실시되며 공정하게 행정됩니다.

e. Consistent with Article 三 of ROK law, rates for work regularly scheduled and performed between 2200 and 0600 hours is increased by 50% of the straight time rate, as a night differential.

ㅁ. 한국근로기준법 46조에 의거해서, 2200시부터 0600시 사이에 정규적으로 계획되어 근무한것에 대해서는 야간수당으로 50%가 통상인금에 가산 지불됩니다.

2. SEVERANCE PAY, ACCIDENT COMPENSATION AND RELATED SOCIAL INSURANCE ASPECTS.

2. 해(퇴)직금, 장해보상및관계사회보장:

a. Consistent with ROK practice and exceeding ROK law (Article 28), severance pay is provided eligible employees with long term services retroactively to 30 April 1956 at which time USFK personnel and leave records were authenticated. Severance payments are not granted if an employee is separated for felony or grave misconduct including theft.

ㄱ. 유자격장기근무종업원은 주한미군의 인사및 휴가기록이 확증되었던 1956년 4월30일을 기준하여 해(퇴)직금을 받게되어있읍니다. 이것은 한국의 관례에 일치하며 한국기준법 제28조를 능가하는것입니다. 중죄또는 중대한 비행으로 해직되는 종업원에겐 해(퇴)직금은 지불되지 않습니다.

b. Upon reaching age 61, Korean employees normally are retired if 8 continuous years of severance credits have been earned. Management may elect to retain employees posessing special skills in short supply for an additional period. Mandatory retirement age is 65. Age provisions of our retirement plan are consistent with local practice.

ㄴ. 61세에 달하였을때 8년근속의 해(퇴)직금이 수득되었으면 한국인 종업원은 대개 퇴직하게 됩니다. 그러나 관리당국은 얻기 어려운 특수기술을 가진 종업원을 계속근무 시킬수 있읍니다. 65세가 되면 전부 정년퇴직하게 됩니다. 정년퇴직계획의 년령규정은 시중관례와 일치하는것입니다.

c. Employees injured on the job, disabled for work, or suffering death (including diseases caused by employment) are eligible for accident and death benefits. These benefits are based upon rules of the Bureau of Employees Compensation, U. S. Department of Labor and include emergency and first-aid type treatment of the post dispensary or hospital; continued treatment at the Army designated hospital in the area; compensation for injuries

ㄷ. 공상, 장해 또는 사망한 종업원은 (직업병을 포함하여) 사고 및 사망 보상을 받습니다. 이 보상은 미노동성 장해보상국규정에 의거하는 것인데 미군병원에서의 응급치료, 군지정의 시중병원에서의 가료, 급여정지 3일이 초과하는 경우의 부상에대한 장해보상등인데 장해보상신청건에 종업원의 자의로 병가나 년가의 사용으로 대체할수도 있읍니다. 사망시에는 미망인, 년소자제 또는 기타가족의

3

0164

resulting in disability for work beyond three workdays after stoppage of pay, following use of any sick and/or annual leave which an employee may elect to use prior to accepting disability compensation. If the injury results in death, compensation is payable to the widow, minor children, or certain other dependents as appropriate. These benefits are effectively administered and meet requirements of Articles 78-83 of the Laborur Standards Act.

순위로 유족에대한 보상이 지급됩니다. 이 보상은 효율적으로 행정되며 근로기준법 제 78부터 83조까지의 조항요건에 합치합니다.

3. MEDICAL SERVICES AND SICK LEAVE.

3. 의료와 병가

a. All Korean personnel, as well as other employees, receive medical examinations and participate in annual X-ray check-ups and immunization programs.

ㄱ. 다른모든 미국인과같이 한국인 종업원은 신체검사를 받고 년차 X광선과 예방주사 "프로그램"에 참가합니다. 이러한 써어비스는 한국인종업원에게 부여되는 특혜조치입니다.

b. In case the employee or a military dispensary determines that employees have a contagious or other disabling disease (such as tuberculosis) employees are placed on an extended leave status (sick, annual or leave without pay) for a period of up to one year. If the illness continues more than a year, employees who later recover have priority reemployment rights.

ㄴ. 본인자신이나 미군 병원이 전염병 또는 기타 근로불능질병 (폐병같은것)에 걸렸다고 판정하면 그종업원은 최고 1년의 장기휴가 (병가, 년가 또는 무급휴가)를 받게됩니다. 질병이 1년이상에 걸치면 회복되었을 때 종업원은 우선직장복귀권이 부여됩니다.

c. In addition to annual leave, employees accrue eight hours of sick leave upon completion of each 28-day pay period. This is a special, civil-service type benefit. Sick leave accumulates from year to year so long as it is unused and employees remain in service. Most employees have large amounts of sick leave to their credit, to help in case of tuberculosis or other illness.

ㄷ. 년가이외에 28일급여기간마다 8시간의 병가를 수득합니다. 이것은 특별한 것이며 공무원근무형의 특면인것입니다. 병가는 사용하지않고 현직에 머물러 있는한 매년 누적할수 있읍니다. 대부분의 종업원이 폐병 또는 기타 질병에 대비해서 많은 시간의 병가를 가지고 있읍니다.

4. LEAVE AND HOLIDAYS.

4. 휴가와 공휴일:

a. One day of annual or vacation leave with pay is accrued each 28-day pay period. This is consistent with Article 47 of the Laborur Standards Act.

ㄱ. 28일 급여기간마다 년가 (휴양)을 수득하는데 이것은 근로기준법 47조에 해당합니다.

0165

b. Employees [illegible] granted in line with Article 60, a total of 60 calendar days with pay in connection with childbirth: however, at least 30 calendar days of such maternity leave must be used after childbirth.

ㄴ. 법제 6[illegible]에 의해서 60일간의 산전휴가가 허용되는데 최소한 30일간은 산후에 사용도록 하고 있읍니다.

c. Other types of leave are provided, such as leave without pay (LWOP), excused absence for voting, etc.

ㄷ. 기타 무급휴가, 투표시출타등의 휴가가 있읍니다.

d. In most cases employees receive time-off with pay on American holidays. On Korean legal holidays, employees may be excused without charge to leave or loss of pay. If employees are required to work they receive double-time. In effect, holiday time-off meets Korean law (Articles 45-46 and Article 23-3 of the Executive Decree). Use of both types of holidays exceeds Korean practice.

ㄹ. 대개의 경우 미국공휴일에는 유급으로 쉬게됩니다. 한국법정공휴일에는 휴가중당이나 소득감소없이 쉬게됩니다. 근무를 한다면 배액지불이됩니다. 사실인즉 공휴일휴게는 한국법령에 맞는것이고 (제45·46조와 시행령 23—3)양국의 휴인 시중관습보다는 더좋은것이라고봅니다.

5. DISCIPLINARY AND SEPARATION ACTIONS.

5. 징계와 해직조치

a. It is policy of the Department of the Army to afford protection to its employees against arbitrary or inequitable action on disciplinary procedures. Employees have the right to answer a written letter to charges and to explain their point of view. Supervisors cannot take arbitrary action against employees. Efforts are made by supervisors and civilian personnel officer to solve problems before disciplinary measures are required.

ㄱ. 일방적인 또는 부당한 징계절차 모부터 종업원을 보호하자는것이 미육군성의 방침인것입니다. 종업원은 서면으로 항변을할권리를 갖었고 자신을 변론할수도 있읍니다. 감독자들은 일방적인 조처를 취하지못하도록 되어있읍니다. 징계조치가 필요하게 되기전에 감독자와 인사관은 문제를 해결하도록 노력하는것입니다.

b. Employees cannot be separated without a 30-day notice in pay status, consistent with Article 27-2 of ROK law.

ㄴ. 근로기준법 제 27—2조의거하여 30일간의 유급상태 통고기간없이는 해직될수 없읍니다.

c. Reduction in force procedures have been established on a Korea-wide basis which give preferred retention rights to employees with longer service and with Korean War service.

ㄷ. 장기근무와 전시제대자에게 강력한 잔류권을 줄수있는 감원절차가 한국전역별로 설정되있읍니다.

5

0166

6. GRIEVANCE AND APPEALS PROCEDURES. Grievance and appeals procedures through management channels have been established for employee use. Procedures include:

a. Grievance procedure for less significant complaints not concerned with removal actions. These actions, upon employee grievance, are subject to two levels of management review.

b. The formal appeals procedures is used only for removals and involves both field review and a formal appellate review by a top-level Board. Determinations and the EUSA Chief of Staff.

c. General problems of a group nature may also be presented by Employee-Management Councils. In addition, FOEU may represent employees on individual grievances where employees so request, as well as being interested in group grievances.

7. PERFORMANCE APPRAISAL.

a. Employee's performance is expected to be reviewed at least annually, as a means of improved employee-communication and to improve work quality.

b. Formal written performance appraisals are used to award superior employees with cash payments or to support changes to lower grade (and occasionally separations) when performance is marginal or unsatisfactory.

c. This approach to employee productivity and on-job communications, we believe, represents a useful innovation.

8. INCENTIVE AWARDS.

a. Korean employees partici-

6. 불평진정절차

관리당국계통을 통하는 불평진정절차가 마련되었읍니다. 그절차는:

ㄱ. 파면조치와는 관계없는 덜중대한 불평을 위한것인데 불평이 자기된다음 2단계의 관리당국의 심사를 받습니다.

ㄴ. 정식불평진정절차는 파면에 한해서 사용되는데 지구별의 심사와 그 위사령부 위원회의 정직심사를 받습니다. 미8군 참모장의 결정이 최종적인것입니다.

ㄷ. 다수 종업원이 관계되는 일반적인 문제는 또한 종업원—관리위원회에 제출됩니다. 종업원의 요청으로 외기노조는 개인적 불평에서 대변을 할수있고 집단적 불평에 관심이 있는것은 물론입니다.

7. 근무성적평정

ㄱ. 종업원 의사소통을 원활이하고 작업의 질적인 향상을 도모코저 최소한 1년에 한번은 종업원의 근무성적이 평정됩니다.

ㄴ. 탁월한 종업원에대한 상금부여 또는 근무성적이 저조하거나 원만하지 못함때 얕은 등급으로의 변경이 필요하면 (때로는해직) 정식서면근평이 실시됩니다.

ㄷ. 이종업원 생산성과 직무상의 의사소통을 유창케하는 방법은 유익한 혁신을 나타내는것이라고 믿습니다.

8. 장려보상

ㄱ. 한국종업원은 작업개선을하고 좋은 인사방침과 복지향상을 위해서 많은 "아이디어"를 제출하므로서 제안 "프로그램"에 참가합니다.

pate in the suggestion program by submitting many ideas for work improvements and to promote better personnel policies and employee services. Use of employee suggestions is an American procedure, designed to stimulate employee initiative and interest.

종업원 제안제도의 활용은 미식제도인것이며 종업원의 창의성과 관심을 북돋는데 목적이 있읍니다.

b. Employees receive cash or honorary awards, or both for the following:

ㄴ. 다음과같은 경우에는 상금 또는 명예상 또는 두개 도두 수여받습니다.

(1) Adopted suggestion.

(1) 채택된 제안.

(2) Sustained superior performance of assigned duties, performance of special acts or services, or long service.

(2) 맡겨진 임무의 탁월한 수행, 특별공로, 또는 장기근무.

(3) Any meritorious personal effort which contributes to the efficiency, economy, or other improvement of the Army operations.

(3) 군작전의 효율적, 경제적 또는기타 개선에 이바지하는 개인적인 공적

c. We correctly are conducting "Operation Teamwork," a suggestion drive to improve joint US-ROK activities.

ㄷ. 한 미유대강화를 보기위해 "오파레이숀 팀웍" 라는 제안운동을 현재 전개중에 있읍니다. 나누어 드란것을 참조해 주시길 바랍니다.

9. EMPLOYEE-MANAGEMENT RELATIONS.

9. 노사관계

a. When the Army establishes a new policy in the administration of Korean employees or revises the current policy, efforts are made to keep employees informed of these changes. We are passing out one example of our [illegible] ean newsletter.

ㄱ. 한국인 종업원 행정에 관한 새로운 방침을 수립하거나 현존방침을 변경할 때에는 이러한 개정을 모든 종업원이 알도록 노력을 합니다. 최근에 나온 종업원신문을 나누어 드리겠읍니다.

b. Employee-Management Councils are established in major organizations as one means of providing direct communications between representatives of employees and the commander of the activity.

ㄴ. 큰 단위부대에는 종업원— 관리 위원회가 설립되있는데 종업원의 대표와 부대장과의 직접적인 의사소통을 하자는데 목적이 있읍니다.

c. EUSA's policy on union activities provides that employees are free to join a union if they so desire, or to refrain from joining a union if they do not desire to join. Currently, the only employee union with

ㄷ. 노조활동에관한 미8군의 방침에 의하면 종업원은 자의대로 자유로히 노조에 가입할수있고 또않할수도 있읍니다. 현재 미8군이 공식적인 협의를 갖는 유일한 노동조합은 외국기관 노동조합인데 9개의 지부를 갖이고 있읍니다. 이협의는 1961년에 교환된서한에 입각하는것이며

7

0168

which EUSA has formal consultation is the Foreign Organizations Employees' Union, with nine USFK sub-chapters. This consultation is based upon an exchange of letters in 1961 which established the basic framework for management-union consultations. Consultations occur in most cases at least once a week at the field chapter local and national headquarters level on a wide variety of personnel matters.

노사협의의 기본적인 체제를 규정하고 있읍니다. 지부에서는 최소한 매주 1번, 본부에서는 수시로 협의를 개최합니다.

10. TRAINING PROGRAM.

a. The U. S. Government has a great interest in self-development and in skills and supervisory training for the Korean workforce. This supports the USFK objective to obtain full Korean utilization and the eventual replacement of third-state nationals.

b. The Army has approved Korean employees to enroll in U. S. Army extension courses provided by AG School, Signal School, Engineer School, and others in the States.

c. Last year 2,081 Koreans completed supervisory training, involving 16,840 manhours, and 50,610 manhours were spent in skills training.

10. 교육 프로그램

ㄱ. 미국정부는 한국인 종업원의 자기계발 기술 및 감독자교육에 깊은 관심을 갖이고 있읍니다. 이것은 철저한 한국인활용을 달성하고 제 3국인 종업원을 점차적으로 대치한다는 주한미군의 목적을 뒷밭침하는것입니다.

ㄴ. 미국본토에 있는 부관학교, 통신학교, 공병학교, 기타 학교가 제공하는 통신강좌에 한국인 종업원이 입학할수 있도록 미육군은 허락을 했읍니다.

ㄷ. 작년동안에 연 16,840 시간이 소비된 감독자교육을 2,081 명의 한국인이 수강했읍니다. 기술교육에 50,610시간이 소요됐읍니다.

11. SAFETY.

a. USFK has an active accident prevention program and is consistently on the look-out for hazards. Our record here, we believe, is superior.

b. It may be of interest to note that safety inspections are largely conducted by Korean specialists and that EUSA has established a career program for Korean safety personnel.

11. 안전

ㄱ. 주한미군은 적극적인 사고미연방지 "프로그램"을 갖었고 위험에 대한 감시를 항상 게을리하지않고 있읍니다. 안전기록은 월등히 좋은것이라고 자부합니다.

ㄴ. 흥미있는 사실은 안전검열의 거의전부가 한국인 전문관에 의해서 실시된다는것인데, 미8군은 한국인 안전관계 직원의 양성계획에 나섰읍니다.

CONCLUDING COMMENTS:

In line with the foregoing review, Korean personnel administration in USFK fully meets pertinent requirements of the Labour Standards Act and has also a number of other advantages of a civil-service type. The eleven elements of the Korean personnel program described above show, we believe, a progressive and business - like approach to the management of the Korean workforce. Our direct-hire system has met the manpower needs of USFK and working conditions are favorable. We believe that the ROK Office of Labor Affairs and other interested officials are aware of this.

Thank you.

결론

이상말씀드린바와같이 주한미군의 한국인 인사행정은 적절한 지시사항에 충분히 맞는것이며 공무원근무형의 특전도 여러가지 갖었다고 봅니다. 이제 7가지 말씀드린 한국인 인사 "프로그램"의 11가지요소는 한국인 종업원의 관리에대한 진보적이며 질서있는 방법을 나타내는 것이라 믿습니다. 당사령부의 직속고용 제도는 주한미군의 인력필요성을 충족 시키고있고 종업원의 근모조건은 양호한 것으로 보고 있읍니다. 한국노동청 당국과 기타 관계기관 여러분이 이것을 알고 계실것으로 믿습니다.

고맙습니다.

9

0170

Submitted on April 3, 64

"ORIENTATION TO YOUR NEW JOB"

새로운 직무에대한 인사관리지침

PREPARED AND ISSUED

BY

OFFICE OF THE CIVILIAN PERSONNEL DIRECTOR

EIGHTH UNITED STATES ARMY

30 MARCH 1964

0171

HEADQUARTERS EIGHTH UNITED STATES ARMY
Office of the Civilian Personnel Director
APO 301, San Francisco, California

F O R E W O R D

This "Orientation to Your New Job" is for you. This pamphlet deals mainly with your rights, privileges and obligations as a civilian employee of the United States Army in Korea. Your understanding of the contents of this pamphlet will be of benefit to both you and your supervisor.

This orientation pamphlet also describes a number of personnel policies and procedures, some of which were recently installed. Your supervisor or a representative of the civilian personnel office will explain any points which may not be clear to you.

The pamphlet was translated and printed bilingually to help you become fully acquainted with it. However, in case of any conflict or ambiguity between the English text and the Korean translation, the English text is applicable.

This summary of governing personnel policies and employee rights and obligations should assist in your orientation to United States Army employment and provide an appreciation of management concepts underlying the employment and utilization of the Korean workforce.

Ogden C. Reed
OGDEN C. REED
Civilian Personnel Director

0172

미제 8군 사령부
민간인 인사처
군우 301

머 릿 말

이 "새 직무와 인사관리지침" 은 여러분을 위해 마련되었읍니다. 이 책자는 주한 미육군의 한 민간인 종업원으로서의 권리, 특전, 및 책임을 주로 다룹니다. 이 책자의 내용을 이해한다는것은 여러분과 여러분 감독자에게 큰 이익이 될것입니다.

또한 이 책자는 최근에 설정된것을 포함하는 여러가지 인사방침과 절차를 설명합 니다. 미심한점은 여러분의 감독자나 인사처 직원이 설명해 드립니다.

완전한 이해를 얻고저 한미양국어로 번역출판했는데 상치되는 점 또는 분명치못한 점이 있다면 그것은 영문판이 옳은것으로합니다.

주한미육군의 고용관계를 소상히 알게하고 한국인작업군의 고용과 활용 및에 스며있는 관리개념을 파악하는데 이 현행인사방침과 종업원권리와 책임에 관한 개요가 크게 도움이 될것으로 봅니다.

Ogden C. Reed
오그든 씨. 리이드
민 간 인 인 사처장

0173

TO: KOREAN EMPLOYEES OF THE UNITED STATES ARMY

1. INTRODUCTION: a. You are an employee of the U. S. Army in Korea and as such are welcome to the ranks of those who make this work their means of livelihood. If you are a new employee, the U. S. Army is interested in orienting you to governing policies and procedures and to assisting in you rapid adjustment to the new job. If you are an old employee but assigned to a new job, we wish to reacquaint you with governing policies or procedures and to facilitate your orientation to the new job.

b. Our overall aim is to be provide good personnel conditions, to help develop Korean employee skills wherever appropriate, and to effectively utilize the Korean workforce in support of joint U. S. - ROK security objectives.

c. EUSA wage and labor practices are now considered to parallel or exceed all Korean labor standards. In addition, EUSA is providing other personnel management advantages: Performance appraisal based on performance requirements; a fair adverse action procedure, tied to a specific table of standard penalties for disciplinary offenses; provision of employee facilities and services; mutual communication and personnel problem-solving through employee-management councils and labor-management consultation; effective procedures for employee complaints and grievances; emphasis on skills and supervisory training; stress on employee safety; and incentive awards.

d. Being an employee of the United States Government, you have certain rights. You also have responsibilities and there are some things you must always remember. These rights and responsibilities are outlined for your guidance.

2. EMPLOYMENT PROCESSING: a. You have just received your proof of employment or personnel change (SF 50). Keep it in your own personal file for future reference. You will receive one of these forms for each change in your job classification or personnel status.

b. You also received an EA Form 469 "Personnel Service Record," which you are to give to your supervisor. Your supervisor will record on this form all changes in your pay status, appraisal of your work performance, commendations, and where necessary disciplinary actions.

c. During processing, you answered questions on previous employment and educational background. This information is recorded on an Application for Employment form. Complete and accurate information on this form may help you obtain a better position in the future at a higher rate of pay. Your application and other completed papers are enclosed in a file with your name and date of birth on it. This is known as your 201 file and is kept by the civilian personnel office. This file will be a record of your service with the United States Government.

d. Changes of position and change of pay status will be included

알: 주한 미육군 한국인 종업원 제위

1. 서론: ㄱ. 당신은 주한 미육군의 한 종업원이며 이 직업으로 생계를 함께하는 여러사람의 대열에 참가하게 되었음을 충심으로 환영하는바입니다. 당신이 신규종업원이라면 현행 인사방침과 절차에 익숙해지고 새로운 직무에 하루속히 순응되도록 도와드리는데 주한 미육군은 적지않은 관심을 가지고 있읍니다. 당신이 새로운 직무에 전직한 구면이라면 그 직무에 쉽게 맞어드러가게 하기위해 현 방침과 절차를 되풀이하여 자세히 알게됨을 바라 마지않습니다.

ㄴ. 전반적인 목적은 우수한 인사관리조건을 제공하고 어디서든지 한국인 종업원의 기술을 계발하도록 도웁고 한미공동방위목표를 지원하는데 한국인 작업군을 효과적으로 활용하려는데 있읍니다.

ㄷ. 주한미육군의 임금이나 고용조건은 이제 한국의 재반근로기준에 못지않거나 또는 능가하는것으로 사려됩니다. 그뿐더러 주한 미육군은 다음과같은 인사관리상의 이점을 가지고 있는데 즉: 업무수행요건을 밑바탕으로하는 근무평정; 규율범칙에대한 기준벌칙에 상부하는 공평한 불리조치절차; 종업원 후생과 복지에관한 규정; 종업원—관리위원회와 노사협의를 통한 의사소통과 인사문제 해결; 효과적인 종업원 불평진정절차; 기술과 감독자교육의 강조; 종업원 안전업무 증강; 장려보상계획등 입니다.

ㄹ. 미국정부의 한 종업원으로서 당신은 확고한 권리를 가졌고 한편 항상 기억해두어야할 책임과 기타사항이 있는것입니다.

2. 고용수속: ㄱ. 방금 고용 또는 인사이동에대한증거서류를 받았는데 (기준양식 50) 장차에 소용될것이니 잘 간직해두시오. 직무분류 또는 기타 신분사항에 변경이 있을때마다 이런 서류를 받습니다.

ㄴ. 미8군양식 469인 "인사기록표" 도 받았을것인데 그것은 당신의 감독자에게 전하십시오. 당신의 감독자는 이 양식에 당신의 인금사항변경, 근무평정, 표창사항, 때로는 징계조치등을 기록합니다.

ㄷ. 수속중에 경력과 교육에 관계되는 질문에 답변하였는대

in your 201 file as they occur. Copy of any letters of appreciation and/or other awards that you may receive in recognition for outstanding performance of your duties or other achievements will be placed in your 201 file. Any formal disciplinary action taken against you will also be filed in this 201 file. A short time after separation from employment, your 201 file is forwarded to the Federal Records Center, Missouri in the United States. If, at a future date, however, you again desire employment with the U. S. Army, the file will be referred to and your past employment record reviewed. Any detrimental information in your file may prevent re-hire. Favorable comments will help assure your reemployment.

3. JOB CLASSIFICATION AND COMPENSATION: a. Your employment is based upon job classification and job ranking by grade levels. These are reflected in a Manual of Job Definitions for Korean Employees, EUSA Pamphlet 620-5. There are three grade schedules, with pay rates associated with each grade level. One schedule is for administrative, custodial, and professional-type jobs, the Non-Manual Schedule; the second schedule is for industrial type jobs, the Manual Schedule; the third is for Marine jobs.

b. Your basic pay rate is commensurate with that of prevailing pay practices in reputable and responsible Korean business firms. Rates are kept up-to-date by means of periodic locality wage surveys.

c. You are assured that you will receive equal pay treatment to that of your fellow employees whose type and level of duties and responsibilities are similar to yours. Permanent changes in your duties and responsibilities of work are the basis for new job classifications and for promotion or change to lower grade in compliance with the Army's policy of consistent and equitable wage administration. The Position and Pay Management program is designed to insure like pay for like work, to determine level of responsibility and difficulty of jobs, and to obtain an economical and efficient job and grade structure.

d. Periodic increases in pay will be given to you automatically if your supervisor considers your services satisfactory. These are called "periodic step increases." However, periods of unpaid absence (absence without pay, suspension, etc.) in excess of 40 hours for a 26 week waiting period or 80 hours for a 52 week waiting period must be offset by an amount of creditable service equal to the excess before your step increases can be effected. Following is the regular requirement for advancement in each step:

Steps "a" to "b", "b" to "c", and "c" to "d" --- 26 weeks

Steps "d" to "e", "e" to "f", and "f" to "g" --- 52 weeks

e. You will be paid a year-end bonus of one full month's pay on or about 15 December, provided you have six months continuous service. The rate used in the computation will be the scheduled rate applicable to the last pay period worked exclusive of overtime or holiday pay or night differential.

f. The regularly scheduled work week in most organizations is established as eight hours a day and 40 hours a week; some organizations also

3

0176

이러한 자료는 구직신청서에 모두 기록됩니다. 이 서류에 기재된 완전하고 정확한 자료는 후일에 높은 직위로 승급하는데 참고로 합니다. 구직신청서를 비롯한 기타서류는 당신의 성명과 생일을 표시하는 인사철에 간직해 둡니다. 이 인사철은 소위 201철 이라는것인데 인사처가 보관합니다. 이 인사철이 당신의 미국정부근무의 기록이 되는것입니다.

ㄹ. 직위와 인금사항에 변경이 있을때마다 당신의 201철에 증거서류가 들어갑니다. 맡은일을 월등히 잘했거나 기타 공적에 대해서 주는 감사장이나 표창장의 사본도 201철에 넣게됩니다. 해직이 있은 잠시후 이 201철은 미국 미조리주에 있는 연방기록 보관소로 송부합니다. 그러나 장래에 당신이 또 다시 주한미육군에 취직할때에는 조회를 해서 과거고용기록을 검토하는것입니다. 기록이 좋지못하면 다시 취직하는것이 어렵게 될수있고 좋은 기록사항은 재취직을 수월하게 할것입니다.

3. 직위분류와 보수: ㄱ. 당신의 고용은 직무분류와 등급배열에 입각합니다. 이것이 주한미육군 "팜프렛" 620—5 인 한국인 종업원 업무정의 편람에 반영되어있읍니다. 세가지의 등급일람표가 있는데 등급마다 알맞는 인금률이 있읍니다. 서무계통 일람표는 행정, 관리 및 전문직을 나타내고 다음것은 기술계통 일람표로서 공원직에 해당하며 셋째번은 해사직원에 적용되는것입니다.

ㄴ. 당신의 기본인금률은 평판높고 확고한 한국 기업체에서 주는 현행인금과 맞먹는것입니다. 정기적인 지방노임조사를 하여서 이 인금률이 뒤떠러지지않게 하고 있읍니다.

ㄷ. 당신은 당신과 비슷한 임무와 책임의 종류와정도의 직무를 수행하는 동료종업원들의 인금과 같은대우를 받도록 보장되어 있읍니다. 모순성없고 균형잡힌 미육군의 인금행정방침에 준거해서 당신의 임무와 책임에 항구적인변경이 생기면 새롭게 직무분류를 하게되며 승급도 되고 알은 등급으로 변경되기도 합니다. 직위및인금관리 "프로그램" 은 같은 업무에 대해서 같은 인금을 지불하고 책임과 어려운 정도를 결정짓고, 경제적이고도 효율적인 직무와 등급구조를 획득하기위하여 짜여진것입니다.

ㄹ. 당신의감독자가 당신이 직무를 원만히 수행했다고 간주하면 자동적으로 정기가봉을 받읍니다. 이것을 정기년공가봉이라고 부릅니다. 그러나 26주 적격기간에서 40시간 또는 52주 적격기간에서 80시간을 초과하여 무급결근기간 (무급휴가, 정직등) 이 있었을때는 정기년공가봉을 받기위해 그것을 상쇄할수있을만큼 같은기간을 더 근무를해야만합니다. 다음표는 각급에서 가봉을 받는데 필요한 통상적격기간입니다.

provide Saturday work. You will get overtime pay at time and a half for all required hours of work in excess of eight hours a day or 48 hours per week. Rates for work regularly scheduled and performed between 2200 and 0600 hours is increased by 50% of the straight time rate, as a night differential.

4. SEVERANCE PAY, ACCIDENT COMPENSATION AND RELATED SOCIAL INSURANCE ASPECTS: a. When you are separated from U. S. Army employment, you will receive one full month's pay (exclusive of overtime, holiday and night differential pay) for each full year of continuous service completed. For severance pay purpose, service credits for eligible employees with long term services will be granted retroactively to 30 April 1956 at which time USFK personnel and leave records were authenticated. Severance payments are not granted if you are separated for felony or grave misconduct including theft. They apply to all other involuntary separations, including resignations.

b. Upon reaching age 61, Korean employees normally are retired if eight continuous years of severance credits have been earned. Management may elect to retain employees possessing special skills in short supply for an additional period. Mandatory retirement age is 65.

c. If you are injured while in the performance of your official duties, you must immediately report your injury to your supervisor regardless of how minor it is. Employees injured on the job, disabled for work, or suffering death (including disease caused by employment) are eligible for accident and death benefits. These benefits are based upon rules of the Bureau of Employees Compensation, U. S. Department of Labor and include emergency and first-aid type treatment at the post dispensary or hospital; continued treatment at the Army-designated hospital in the area; compensation for injuries resulting in disability for work beyond three workdays after stoppage of pay, following use of any sick and/or annual leave which an employee may elect to use prior to accepting disability compensation. If the injury results in death, compensation is payable to the widow, minor children, or certain other dependents as appropriate.

5. MEDICAL SERVICES AND SICK LEAVE: a. All Korean personnel, as well as other employees, receive medical examinations and participate in annual X-ray check-ups and immunization programs.

b. If you or a military dispensary determine that you have a contagious or other disabling disease (such as tuberculosis), you are placed on an extended leave status (sick, annual or leave without pay) for a period of up to one year. If the illness continues more than a year, employees who later recover have priority reemployment rights.

c. In addition to annual leave, you accrue eight hours of sick leave upon completion of each 28-day pay period. Sick leave accumulates from year to year so long as it is unused and you remain in service. The following will be your guide in the utilization of your sick leave privileges:

(1) It will usually be impossible for you to request sick leave in advance except for medical, dental or optical appointment. However, you will make every effort to send word to your supervisor as early as

급수 a 로부터b, b 로부터 c, c 로부터d——26주일
급수 d 로부터e, e 로부터 f, f 로부터g——52주일

ㅁ. 만6개월근속을 하면 12월15일경에 년말상여를 타는데 한달치의 인금에 해당합니다. 상여금계산에 사용되는 인금율은 특근, 휴일근무 또는 야간근무수당을 제외한 최종인금기간에 적용된 정규인금율인것입니다.

ㅂ. 일8시간과 주40시간근무가 대개의 근무처의 정규근무시간입니다. 어떤 근무처에서는 토요일에도 근무를 합니다. 일8시간 또는 주40시간을 초과해서 지시한대로 근무한 시간은 1.5 배로특근수당을 지급잘습니다. 2200—0600 시 사이에 근무하면 150% 의 야간수당이 나옵니다.

4. 해(퇴)직금, 장해보상 및 사회보장관계: ㄱ. 주한미육군고용에서 해직할때는 1년근속에 한달치인금 (특근, 휴일 및 야간수당제외) 씩을 받습니다 해 (퇴) 직금에 있어서는 장기근무를 한 유자격종업원의 근속년수가 주한미군의 인사및휴가기록이 확증될수있는 1956년 4월30일에 소급하여서 인정됩니다. 절도행위를 포함하는 중죄나 중대한 비행때문에 해직될때엔 해 (퇴)직금은 지불되지 않습니다. 기타 모든 자원이아닌 해직이나 사직시에는 지불됩니다.

ㄴ. 61세가되고 8년근속의 해 (퇴)직금소득이 되었다면 일반적으로 정년퇴직을 합니다. 구득하기어려운특별한 기술을 가진 종업원은 관리측이 연장근무를 시킬수있읍니다. 65세가되면 무조건 정년퇴직을 합니다.

ㄷ. 공무수행중에 부상을 당했으면 정도의 경중을 막론하고 감독자에게 즉각 보고를 해야합니다. 공상, 상해 또는 사망한 종업원(직업병포함)은 장해보상을 받습니다. 이 장해보상은 미노동성 장해보상국 규정에 입각하며 기지병원에서의 응급치료, 주한미육군의 지정한 시내병원에서의 가료, 인금지급이 정지된지 3일이 지나도록 근무부능한 공상에대한 장해보상등이 포함됩니다. 병가나 년가는 종업원의 자의대로 장해보상을 받지않고 이용할수도 있읍니다. 공상으로 사망시에는 미망인, 년소자녀 또는 기타 가족순위로 보상금이 지불됩니다.

5. 의료와병가: ㄱ. 한국인직원을 포함하는모든직원은 건강진단을 받어야하고 년차 X 광선과 예방주사 "프로그램" 에 참가해야합니다.

ㄴ. 당신자신 또는 기지병원당국이 전염병이나 기타 지장을주는 병(폐병등)에 걸렸다고 단정하면 당신은 최고1년간의 장기휴가상태 (병가, 년가 또는 무급휴가)에 놓이게됩니다. 질병이 1년이상에 걸치게되면 완치된후 우선적인 재고용권으로 직장복귀합니다.

ㄷ. 년가와 더불어 당신은 28일 인금기간마다 8시간의 병가를 수득합니다. 사용하지않은채로 계속근무를 하면 병가는 무제한으로 해마다 축적됩니다. 병가특전을 사용하는데는 다음과같은 주의사항에 유의해야 합니다.

0179

possible on the first day of absence due to illness.

(2) Remember that a major purpose of sick leave is to accumulate sick leave credits to help you in case of a long sickness.

(3) If you are sick for more than three days you will be required to present a medical certificate issued by a licensed doctor establishing that you are incapacitated to report to work.

(4) If there is reason to believe that sick leave is being abused, your supervisor may require a medical certificate for periods of less than three days.

(5) You are not to abuse the use of this sick leave privilege. Your supervisor and the civilian personnel office are responsible for making necessary checks to make sure that sick leave is used properly.

d. Employees are granted a total of 60 calendar days with pay in connection with childbirth; However, at least 30 calendar days of such maternity leave must be used after childbirth. To be eligible for maternity leave, employee must have completed 10 months continuous service immediately preceding the period of maternity leave.

6. LEAVE AND HOLIDAYS: a. You accrue one day of annual (vacation) leave with pay per 28 day period. You may elect to accumulate such leave; however, any annual leave accumulated in excess of 240 hours must be used during the current year or forfeited at the beginning of the new leave year. You are expected to cooperate with your supervisor in scheduling the use of vacation or annual leave. When you resign, or are separated from employment, you will receive a lump sum payment for all accumulated annual leave remaining to your credit.

b. There are other types of leave such as leave without pay (LWOP), excused absence for voting, etc.

c. Three categories of holidays are identified:

U. S. Legal Holidays*	Korean Legal Holidays*	Traditional Holidays
1 January	1 January	Lunar New Year
22 February	1 March	Chusuk
30 May	17 July	
4 July	15 August	
1st Monday-September	3 October	
11 November	25 December	
4th Thursday-November		
25 December		

*And any other calendar day designated as a U. S. holiday by U. S. Law or Executive Order of the President or any other calendar day designated as a Korean holiday by the Republic of Korea.

(1) 냇과, 칫과 또는 안과의 지정일치료를 제외하고 병가를 사전에 신청한다는것은 대체적으로 불가능한것입니다. 그러나, 병때문에 출근을 못하게된 바로 그날에 되도록 빨리 당신의 감독자에게 병고결근을 통지하도록 온갖 노력을 하시오.

(2) 병가의목적은 장기에걸친 병에 대비해서 병가일수를 축적해두는데 있음을 명심해 둡시다.

(3) 3일이상의 병고결근시에는 면허있는의사의 진단서를 제출해야하며 출근을 할수없었다는것이 실증되어야합니다.

(4) 병가가 남용됐다는 믿을만한 이유가 있을때에는 3일이하의 병고결근시에도 당신의 감독자는 진단서제출을 지시할수 있읍니다.

(5) 병가특전을 남용하지 마시오. 당신의 감독자와 인사처는 병가가 정당하게 사용됐나를 굳게 알기위해 필요한 조사를 하는 책임을 가졌읍니다.

ㄹ. 60일간의 유급산전후 휴가가 허용됩니다. 그러나 적어도 30일간은 산후에 사용하도록 해야합니다. 산전후 휴가는 만 10개월 근속을 해야 특전을 누릴수 있읍니다.

6. 휴가와 공휴일: ㄱ. 28일 임금기간마다 1일간의 년가 (휴양)를 수득하는데 축적해 둘수도 있읍니다. 그러나 240시간을 초과하여 축적된 년가는 당해휴가년도중에서 사용해야하며 그렇지않으면 다음휴가년도초에 상실됩니다. 휴양 또는 년가의 사용계획을 짤때에는 당신의 감독자와 협조해주길 바랍니다. 사직할때 또는 해직될때에는 그당시에 남은 년가는 현금으로 환산해서 지불합니다.

ㄴ. 무급휴가 (LWOP), 투표비근등의 기타휴가제도도 있읍니다.

ㄷ. 다음과같은 공휴일이 인정됩니다:

미국법정공휴일*	한국법정공휴일*	풍속적공휴일
1 월 1일	1월 1일	구정
2 월 22일	3월 1일	추석
5 월 30일	7월 17일	
7 월 4일	8월15일	
9 월 제 1 목요일	10월3일	
11월11일	12월25일	
11월 제4 목요일		
12월25일		

* 미국법령 또는 대통령령으로 미국공휴일로 공포된 날 또는 한국법령 또는 대통령령으로 한국공휴일로 공포된날.

d. When you are prevented from working on U. S. legal holidays because of the closing of your office or installation, you may be excused from working on such holidays, that day is treated as a normal workday; thus straight time will be paid for work performed during regularly scheduled working hours with leave charged for any absence during such holidays.

e. You may be excused on the Korean legal holidays listed above without charge to leave or loss of pay. However, when, by order of a responsible supervisor, you are required to work and fail to do so, you cannot ask for excused absence and such absence will be charged as absence without leave. When you are required to work on Korean legal holidays, you will be paid double or 200% of regular straight time pay.

7. PERSONNEL ACTIONS: a. A review of comparative qualifications of candidates is the basis for promotions. Under the merit promotion program for Korean employees, you can compete for open vacancies; your supervisor's recommendation is important in your competition with other candidates for promotion. You may be promoted without competition if the position you currently occupy is reclassified to a higher grade, provided you are qualified for the reclassified position.

b. Reassignment actions involving no change in grade may be taken either at your request or at the convenience of your supervisor. However, you have to present a firm reason for requesting reassignment. If he can release you, he will give you a written statement of release for transfer. If he cannot release you at that time, you must give him at least a two weeks notice. If there is a vacancy for which you qualify at your choice of location, a transfer will be arranged by the civilian personnel office.

c. You may be changed to lower grade if you are not qualified or capable of performing duties of your position after you have been given an opportunity to correct your deficiencies. In addition, administrative reorganizations may lead to a reduction in the level of assigned duties or a reclassification of your position to a lower grade. In addition, reduction in force actions sometimes require changes to lower grade.

d. Eighth Army policy permits salary retention in all situations (such as RIF and management-imposed changes to lower grade) except when based on your own request, or when resulting from your inefficiency or disciplinary offense. The one provision is that you have served continuously for a period of two years or longer in a position of the same or higher grade or salary. The saved pay will be retained by you for a period of two years unless earlier otherwise terminated or covered by a wage adjustment.

e. When you desire to resign your position, it is requested that you give your supervisor at least a two weeks notice. This will give him an opportunity to obtain a replacement to fill the position you are leaving without loss of production. If you want to leave your job because you desire to move to another position, do not resign. Request a reassignment instead, as discussed in an earlier paragraph.

8. DISCIPLINARY ACTIONS: a. It is policy of the Department of the Army to afford protection to its employees against arbitrary or inequitable disci-

ㄹ. 당신직장이 쉬기때문에 미국법정공휴일에 근무를 못하게되면 휴가를 충당하거나 소득에 감소를보지않고서 놀게됩니다. 그렇지 않으면 그날은 보통 출근일과 같게 출근해서 근무를하고 통상인금이 지불되며 그러한 공휴일에 출근을 않했으면 휴가가 충당됩니다.

ㅁ. 위에있는 한국법정공휴일에는 휴가를 충당하거나 소득에 감소됨이 없이 놀게합니다. 그러나 책임감독자의 지시로서 출근을 지지받고 그날에 결근을 하면 휴가는 인정되지않고 무단결근으로 취급됩니다. 한국법정공휴일에 지시를 받고 근무를하면 통상인금의 배액을 지불합니다.

7. <u>인사조치:</u> ㄱ. 후보자의 비교자격의 검토로서 승급의 토대를 삼습니다. 실적승급 "프로그램" 에 의해서 당신은 승급 공개경쟁에 참가할수 있읍니다. 여러후보자와의 승급공개경쟁에서 감독자의 소견은 중요한 의의를 가집니다. 당신이 현재 점하고 있는 직위가 높은등급으로 재조정될때에는 경쟁없이 승급합니다. 다만 재조정된 직위에 자격이 있다고 인정은 받어야합니다.

ㄴ. 등급에 변경이없는 재배치조치는 당신의 요청으로또는 관리측의 형편으로 취해질수있읍니다. 그러나 재배치를 요청하는 확고한 이유가 제시되어야합니다. 감독자의 전출승인은 서면으로 해줍니다. 당시에 전출승인을 해주지못할 형편이면 당신은 최소한 2주일간의 사전전출통고를 감독자에게 해야합니다. 맞당한곳에 알맞는 자리가 생기면 인사처가 전출조치를 취해줍니다.

ㄷ. 결함을 시정할 일정기간이 주어진 다음에도 자격이 맞지않거나 또는 당신의 직위에 맡겨진 임무를 수행할 능력이 없을때는 얕은 등급으로 변경될수있읍니다. 또한 행정적재편결과로서 맡겨진 임무정도의 저하나 현직위를 얕은 등급으로 변경시키는 재조정이 있기쉬운것입니다. 감원시에도 얕은 등급으로의 변경을 때때로 초래할것입니다.

ㄹ. 자진요청했을때 또는 무능력이나 규율범칙때문인것을 제외하고 주한미8군은 모든경우 (감원,관리측이 지시하는 얕은급수로의 변경등) 에 현인금 보규권을 부여합니다. 한가지조건은 같은직위 또는 그상급에서 2년이상 근속을 했을때 한해서 그렇게 현인금을 그대로 갖고있게 해줍니다. 다른 변경사항이 또는 봉급인상이 발생되지않는이상 이 현인금보류는 2년간 유효합니다.

ㅁ. 사직을 할때는 최소한 2주일간의 사전통고를감독자에게 해야합니다. 그래야 그는 후임자를 지체없이 선정하고 생산에 지장을 없게할수있읍니다. 다른직위로 가기위해서라면 사직하지말고 전출을 신청하시오.

8. <u>징계조치:</u> ㄱ. 일방적이고 부당한 징계조치로부터 종업원을 보호해주려는것이 미육군성의 방침인것입니다. 그러나 설정된 절차에 의하면 중대한

plinary action. However, established procedures allow you to be discharged from employment for serious misconduct, failure to perform your duties in a satisfactory manner or repeated absence from work without permission. You have the right to answer a written letter of charges and to explain your point of view and to receive a written decision. Efforts will be made by your supervisor and the civilian personnel officer to solve problems before disciplinary measures are required. In return, you, as an employee, are expected to:

(1) Maintain an attitude of respect for administrative authority and toward supervisors, charged with responsibility for the direction of your work;

(2) Observe the spirit as well as the letter of law and regulations issued to govern official and off-duty conduct and to protect property;

(3) Conduct your on-the-job duties according to ethical standards;

(4) Refrain from passing on information or spreading rumors regarding operations, plans, equipment or personnel which might endanger U. S. - ROK security or discredit the interests of your employer, the U. S. Army;

b. The following are disciplinary penalties: (1) Oral reprimand; (2) Written reprimand; (3) Suspension without pay; (4) and Removal from employment. Prior to suspension without pay or removal, you will be advised in writing of proposed action and given an opportunity to reply. If you fail to reply or furnish irrelevant information, the proposed action will be implemented as scheduled.

9. GRIEVANCE AND APPEAL PROCEDURES: a. Grievance and appeal procedures have been established for your use if you feel you have been unfairly treated or if you are reasonably sure you do not deserve removal.

b. Procedures include:

(1) Grievance procedure for less significant complaints not concerned with removal actions. These complaints, upon initiation of an employee grievance, are subject to two levels of management review.

(2) The formal appeal procedure is used only for removals and involves both field review and a formal appellate review by a top-level Board. Determinations are final and are approved by the EUSA Chief of Staff.

c. General problems of a group nature may also be presented to the Employee-Management Council in your organization which has been established to obtain effective and constructive communications up and down, and between employees and management.

d. In addition, Foreign Organizations Employees Union may assist in individual grievances where employees request their representation, as well as group grievances.

비행, 맡겨진 직무를 원만히 수행치못할때 또는 무단결근을 연거퍼 할때는 당신을 해직시킬수있게 되어있읍니다. 한편 당신은 서면으로서 자신을 변호하고 의견을 진술할 권리를 가졌으며 서면결정을 받습니다. 당신의 감독자와 인사관은 징계조치가 필요하게되기전에 문제해결을 위한 노력을 아끼지 않을것입니다. 동시에 다음과같은 사항에 깊이 유의해주길 바랍니다.

(1) 당신의 직무지시를 하는 책임을 가진감독자와 행정당국에 공손한 태도를 갖도록 합시다.

(2) 업무상과 일과외 행동을 다스리고 재산보호를 목적으로 발포된 제반규정을 진지하게 지켜야합니다.

(3) 윤리적인 기준에 따라서 집무중의 행동을 단정히가집시다.

(4) 작전, 계획, 장비 또는 인사에관한 정보를 제공한다거나 또는 소문을 퍼뜨리지않도록 유의합시다. 이것은 한미공동방위를 위태롭게 하고 당신의 고용주로서의 주한미육군의 권익을 손상시키는행위입니다.

ㄴ. 다음과같은 징계조치가 있읍니다. 즉 (1) 구두징계, (2) 서면징계 (3) 무급정직, (4) 파면이 그것입니다. 무급정직 또는 파면시는 조치를 취하기전에 서면으로 예정된조치에 관한 통지를 받고 이에대한 항변을 할수있읍니다. 항변을 하지않거나 가당치않은 설명을 할때는 예정된조치는 그대로 실시됩니다.

9. <u>불평진정절차</u> : ㄱ. 부당하게 대우됐다고 느끼든지 파면되지않을만한것이였다는사유가 있을때는 설정된불평진정절차에 호소할수 있읍니다.

ㄴ. 절차는 다음과 같습니다.

(1) 파면경우가아닌 덜 중요한 불평에대한 진정절차. 종업원이 이러한 불평을 제시하면 2단계에걸친 관리측의 검토와 심의를 받습니다.

(2) 정식진정절차는 파면사건만을 다루는데 지역별심사와 검토를 받고 다음에 상부심의위원회의 정식공소심사를 받습니다. 미8군 참모장의 결재가 최정결정으로 됩니다.

ㄷ. 또한 여러사람에 관계되는 일반적인 문제거리는 종업원—관리 위원회에 회부될수있는데 당신의 근무처에설치된 이 위원회는 상부와 하부 그리고 종업원과 관리측 사이의 유울적이고 선설적인 의사소통을 원활히 하고저있는것입니다.

ㄹ. 다른한편 외기노조는 종업원의 요청으로 개인진정이나 집단적인 진정에서 대변을 할수있읍니다.

10. PERFORMANCE APPRAISAL: a. Your performance is expected to be reviewed at least annually, as a means of improved employee-communication and to improve work quality.

b. Formal written performance appraisals are used to award superior employees with cash payments or to support changes to lower grade and, occasionally, separations when performance is marginal or unsatisfactory.

c. If you are a new employee, your supervisor will be advised by the civilian personnel office after you have completed approximately nine months service that you are nearing completion of your trial period. He will summarize his observation on your job performance and behavior and then recommend your be either retained as a permanent employee or dismissed. Completion of the trial period will assure you greater job security.

11. REDUCTION IN FORCE: a. Because of limitations of personnel authorizations, money, workload, or reorganization, the Army sometimes conducts a reduction in force, after various counter measures are undertaken.

b. Reduction-in-force procedures have been established which give retention rights to employees with longer service with the U. S. Army and to wartime veteran employees. Employees who are serving a trial period cannot compete with employees who have completed their trial period, and are separated before them.

c. Reduction-in-force is effected on a commuting area and also on a Korea-wide basis.

d. In addition to the above RIF protection, an employee in a higher graded position and fully qualified for the position has retreat rights to jobs which can broadly be considered as entrance into the line of work. When more than one employee is competing for the position, displacement will be made by seniority basis within retention groupings.

12. INCENTIVE AWARDS: a. You are encouraged to participate in the suggestion program by submitting ideas for work improvements and to promote better personnel policies and employee services.

b. You may receive cash or honorary awards, or both for the following:

(1) Adopted suggestion;

(2) Sustained superior performance of assigned duties, performance of special acts or services, or long service; or

(3) Any meritorious personal effort which contributes to the efficiency, economy, or other improvement of Army operations.

13. EMPLOYEE-MANAGEMENT RELATIONS: a. When the Army establishes a new policy in the administration of Korean employees or revises the current policy, efforts are made to keep you informed of these changes and to obtain your comments on item.

10. 근무성적평정: ㄱ. 의사소통을 유창히하고 근무의 질적인 향상을 도모하기위한 방법으로 1년에 최소한 한번은 당신의 근무성적이 평정됩니다.

ㄴ. 정식서면근무평정은 우수한 종업원의 상금수여나 얕은 등급으로의 변경을 위한 입증에 사용되고 때로는 근무성적이 저조하거나 좋지못한 종업원의 해직의 해직시에도 사용합니다.

ㄷ. 당신이 신규종업원이라면 만 9개월근무가 끝날무렵에 시용평가를 하게됐음을 인사처가 당신의 감독자에게 통지합니다. 감독자는 그간의 직무성적과 태도에 관해 관찰한바를 요약해서 당신을 정식종업원으로 계속 근무시키든지 또는 해직하는 천거를 하는것입니다. 시용기간이 종료되면 직업보장이 더 확고해집니다.

11. 감 원: ㄱ. 인사정원제한, 자금사정, 작업량 감소 또는 부서재편성등의 이유로 때때로 감원을 실시하게 됩니다. 구제수단이 강구됨은 물론이죠.

ㄴ. 감원절차에 의하면 주한미육군에 장기근무한 종업원과 전시제대자에게 우선권을 줍니다. 시용기간근무를 하는 종업원은 시용기간을 종료한 종업원과 감원순위에서 대항할수없으며 먼저 감원됩니다.

ㄷ. 감원은 통근가능지역과 전한국지역별로 실시합니다.

ㄹ. 상기한 감원잔류권에 더하여 높은 등급직위에 있고 그 직위에 충분한 자격이있는 종업원은 그직종취업시의 선행조건이라고 광범하게 해석할수있는 직무로 되도라가는 우선권이 있읍니다.

12. 장려보상: ㄱ. 작업개선에관한 "아이디어"를 제출하여 제안 "프로그램" 에 적극참가하고 좋은 인사방침과 종업원복지향상에 이바지하기를 바랍니다.

ㄴ. 다음과같은 사항에대해서는 상금 또는 명예상부여를 받습니다.

(1) 채택된제안

(2) 맡겨진 임무를 탁월하게 수행한것, 특별공로, 또는

(3) 군임무수행에 효과적이고 경제적이고 기타 개선에 공헌이된 개인적인 공적.

13. 종업원-관리관계: ㄱ. 한국인종업원행정방침을 새로 설정할때 또는 현방침을 개정할때는 이러한 변경을 당신이 잘 알고있도록 모든 노력을 합니다.

b. If you do not understand your supervisor's instructions, be sure to tell him you do not understand. If you have problems, discuss them with your supervisor. In addition to this type of communication with management, Employee-Management Councils are established in your organization as a means of providing direct communications between representatives of employees and the commander of the activity.

c. Also, Employee-Management Councils may be utilized as an important means of improving and developing favorable community relations and as a means of informing the local community of organizational missions which contribute to joint US-ROK security objectives.

d. EUSA's policy on union activities is expressed in Section XIX of EUSA Pamphlet on Personnel Policies and Procedures for Korean Employees. This policy provides that employees are free to join a union if they so desire, or to refrain from joining a union if they do not desire to join. Currently, the only employee union with which EUSA has formal consultation is the Foreign Organizations Employees Union. This consultation is based upon an exchange of letters in 1961 which establishes the basic framework for management-union consultation.

14. TRAINING PROGRAM: a. In most cases, your employer will provide some type of training to make you a better employee. You may be given training on the job as a whole or on some phase of it. It also may be your privilege to receive training which will enable you to do a more difficult job than the one to which you are now assigned, thus preparing the way for your advancement. Your interest in taking part in an expanded training program is solicited. Supervisor and managerial development, typing, correspondence, logistics management, conference leadership and other skills training courses are offered.

b. The United States Government wants you to develop your skills and to qualify for promotion. To earn an opportunity for promotion you must do your work well and through study prepare yourself for higher positions. If you want to become a supervisor in addition to learning your basic work and obtaining technical skills, you should read pertinent books, observe other supervisors, and ask to attend classes on supervisor development.

c. The Army authorizes Korean employees to enroll in U. S. Army extension courses provided by stateside Army agencies. Please check with your supervisor or the civilian personnel office. Direct contact of employees with the schools is prohibited for administrative purposes; enrollment in available courses may be arranged through the area civilian personnel office.

15. SAFETY: a. Although the Command and your supervisor is definitely interested in and will assist you in avoiding accidents, each individual employee has the responsibility to take care of himself and to follow safety rules and regulations. Be sure you report any safety hazard you notice to your supervisor or submit suggestions.

b. Your supervisor will give appropriate emphasis to safe working practices in your shop or office. Listen carefully to him, and do not hesitate

ㄴ. 당신의 감독자의 작업지시를 잘 이해하지못하겠으면 잘 모르겠다고 반드시 일러주사오. 무슨 문제거리라가 생기면 우선 감독자와 상의하시오. 이러한 관리측과의 의사소통과 더불어 종업원대표와 직장의 책임자간에 직접적인 의견교환을 할수있도록 당신직장에는 종업원―관리 위원회가 설정되어있읍니다.

ㄷ. 종업원―관리위원회는 또한 지역사회와의 우호적관계를 개선 및 개발하고 한미공동방위임무에 공헌하는 당신직장의 임무를 지역사회 주민에게 알려주게하는 좋은 방법으로서도 활용됩니다.

ㄹ. 한국인종업원인사방침 및 절차에관한 주한미8군의 "팜프레트"의 제 19장에 노조활동에 관계되는 방침이 설명되어있읍니다. 이 방침에 의하면 종업원은 자의대로 노조에 자유로히 가입할수있고 또 안할수도 있읍니다. 현재 주한미8군과 정식으로 협의를 갖는 노동조합은 전국외국기관노동조합뿐입니다. 이러한 협의는 노사협의의 기초적체제를 규정하는 1961년도의 서신교환에 입각하는것입니다.

14. 교육 "프로그램" : ㄱ. 대개의 경우 주한미육군은 당신이 훌륭한 종업원이 되도록 여러가지 교육을 실시합니다. 전반적으로 업무상 교육이 될수도 있고 또는 일부만이 그렇게 될수도있읍니다. 교육에 참가하는것은 당신의 특권이며 현재 맡겨진것보다 더 어려운 직무를 수행할수있게하고 따라서 승진의길을 여는것입니다. 당신이 교육 "프로그램" 에 적극 참가하는것을 권유하는바입니다. 감독자와 관리층개발, 타자, 공문작성, 병참관리, 회의지도법, 기타 여러가지 기술교육이 있읍니다.

ㄴ. 미국정부는 당신이 기술을 습득하고 승급을 할자격을 갖추도록 희망합니다. 당신이 승급의 기회를 얻을려면 맡은직무를 잘해야하고 연구를 통해서 높은자리로 승진할 능력을 자신이 길러야합니다. 기본직무와 특기습득이외에 감독자가 되어보자고 한다면 적절한 책을 읽고 다른 감독자가하는일을 관찰하고 또 감독자계발교육에 참가를 신청해야합니다.

ㄷ. 한국인종업원도 미국본토에있는 육군학교가 제공하는 미육군 통신강좌에 입학이 허용됩니다. 자세한것은 감독자나 인사처에 문의해 보십시오. 행정형편상 각개 종업원이 학교당국과 직접교섭을 하는것은 금지되어있읍니다. 입학절차는 민간인 인사처가 밟어 드립니다.

15. 안 전: ㄱ. 당사령부와 당신의 감독자는 사고미연방지에 큰 관심을 기우리고 또 당신을 도웁지만 각자가 자신을 돌보는 책임이있고 제반 안전수칙을 지킬 의무가 있읍니다. 위험사실을 발견하는대로 감독자에게 연락하거나 또는 제안으로 해서 제출하시오.

to raise any question in regard to safety practices.

16. CONCLUSION: a. Your work is considered by the United States Army as essential to its mission. You will have the opportunity to develop your skills and receive special training. This will make you a more productive worker and open up opportunities for promotion. In turn, this will promote the efficiency of the operations of the U. S. Army in Korea.

b. Make new friends and enjoy your work. At the same time, be sure to follow regulations and the instructions of your supervisor.

c. We hope that you will fit in your new organization quickly and that you rapidly learn the duties of your job. We are sure that you will make a real contribution to the activities of your organization.

d. We welcome you as an employee of the United States Government.

ㄴ. 당신의 감독자는 사무실이나 현장에서의 안전업무에 대해서 적절한 강조를 게을리하지 않을것입니다. 안전 업무관례에 관한 의문이 있으면 서슴치말고 언제나 물어봅시다.

16. 결 론: ㄱ. 당신의 직무는 주한미육군임무수행에 불가결한것입니다. 기술을 연마할 기회가 많이있고 교육도 받을수 있읍니다. 이것은 당신이 생산성높은 종업원이 되게하고 승급의 문을 열어주는것입니다. 동시에 주한미육군의 작업효율성을 향상시켜줍니다.

ㄴ. 새 친구도 사귀고 자미있게 일합시다. 잊지말것은 모든 규정이나 감독자의 지시에 잘 따르도록 해야한다는것입니다.

ㄷ. 새로운 직장에 재빨리 익숙해 들어가고 맡은바 임무를 조속히 익히게됨을 바랍니다. 당신의 직장에 힘껏 공헌하심을 믿어마지 않습니다.

ㄹ. 다시한번 미국정부직원의 일원이 되었음을 충심으로 환영하는 바입니다.

Submitted on April 3 '64

VEHICLES OF INVITED CONTRACTORS-US FORCES, KOREA

MARCH 1964

TYPE	US GOVT OWNED	CONTRACTOR-OWNED	PRIVATELY OWNED	TOTAL	PERCENT OF TOTAL
Trucks	435	4	1	440	61%
Jeeps	35	3	2	40	6%
Sedans	17	16	10	43	6%
Trailers	72	14	-	86	12%
Station Wagons	10	11	7	28	4%
Bus	3	19	-	22	3%
Motor Cycles	-	25	-	25	3%
Industrial Equipment	31	5	-	36	5%
TOTAL	603	97	20	720	100%

0192

기 안 용 지

관리번호 1464

자체통제	외무사무관 김성	기안처	미주과 이근팔	전화번호	근거서류접수일자
	과장	국장	차관	장관	
관계관 서명					
기안년월일	1964. 4. 7.	시행년월일		보존년한	정서기장
분류기호	외구미 722.2	전체통제			
경유 수신 참조	대통령 (참조: 비서실장) 국무총리			발신	장관
제목	제 48 차 주둔군지위협정 체결 교섭 실무자회의 보고				

검열 1964. 4. 10 통제관

1964. 4. 3. 하오 3 시 30분 부터 동 5 시 까지 외무부 제 1 회의실에서 개최된 제 48 차 주둔군지위협정 체결 교섭 실무자회의에서 토의된 내용을 별첨과 같이 보고합니다.

유 첨: 제 48 차 교섭회의 보고서 1 부. 끝.

발송 No. 20 1964. 4. 10 외무부

보통문서로 재분류 (1966. 12. 31.)

1966, 12. 31 예고문에 의거 일반문서로 재분류됨

승인서식 1-1-3 (11 00900-03) (195mm×265mm16절지)

0193

제 48 차

한·미간 주둔군지위협정 체결 교섭 실무자회의

보 고 서

1. 일 시: 1964 년 4 월 3 일 하오 3 시 30 분 부터 동 5 시 까지.

2. 장 소: 외무부제 1 회의실

3. 토의사항:

가. 노무조달

(1) 미측은 K.S.C.가 한국정부와 유엔군사령부와의 협정에 의하여 조직된 준군대적인 체제를 갖고 있음으로 일반노무자와는 동일시할 수 없다고 말하였으며 우리측은 1955 년 9 월 이후 자유모집을 원칙으로 함에 따라 일반노무자와 별다른 차의가 없게 되었다고 지적하고 미측이 원한다면 주둔군지위협정의 테두리 밖에서 별도로 해결할 것을 제의하였다.

(2) 미측에서는 미군의 노무관리현황에 관하여 설명하여 미군의 노무관리가 대체적으로 한국의 법령과 관례에 따라 운영되고 있다고 주장하였다. 우리측은 미군의 노무관리중 특히 노무자에 대한 제재 및 해고현황은 수락할 수 없는 문제라는 태도를 취하고 전적으로 우리 나라 법령에 의거 운영할 것을 요구하였다.

(3) 양측대표는 노무조달에 관한 주장의 차의점을 검토 조정하기 위하여 가까운 시일내에 비공식적인 실무자회의를 개최할 것에 합의하였다.

나. 군계약자

(1) 우리측은 미측이 "미국법에 따라 조직된 법인체를 포함한 사람과 고용자로서 통상 미국에서 거주하는 자"라고 규정한 우리 초안의 군계약자의 정의를 수락한다면 그들의 가족을 포함시킬 용의가 있음을 밝혔다.

(2) 양측은 쌍방의 주장이 상당히 접근하였음을 시인하고 군계약자의 개인용 차량등록에 관하여 의견을 교환하고 다음 기회에 토의하기로 하였다.

다. 보호조치

(1) 우리측은 제 46 차회의에서 우리측이 제시한 대안이 미측의 요구를 충족시킬 수 있을 것으로 본다고 말하고 미측이 한국의 입법 조치 의무를 완화하는 대안을 제시한데 대하여 약간의 자구수정을 하였다.

4. 기타 사항: 차기 회의일자: 1964 년 4 월 10 일 하오 2 시. 끝.

April 3, 1964

Labor Procurement

1. General O'Connor opened the meeting by referring to the information sheet on the Korean Service Corps which had been passed to the Korean negotiators prior to the meeting. He stated that Lt. Colonel Mulkey was present to answer any questions which the Korean negotiators might wish to ask concerning the KSC. He pointed out that one of the unique features of the KSC is its mobility. Because of the necessity for moving components of the KSC from place to place as the situation requires, members are paid more than ordinary laborers of the same category. The KSC, General O'Connor continued, is a para-military organization, which has its own distinctive uniform, operates its own messes, and is commanded by military officers. Therefore, its personnel do not logically fit under the category of "employee" as defined in the U.S. draft of the Labor Procurement Article.

2. Mr. Chang thanked the U.S. negotiators for the information which they had furnished concerning the KSC. He remarked that the Korean negotiators had been unable, however, to identify or find any traces of the agreement between the United Nations Command and the Government of the Republic of Korea, ~~to which the U.S. negotiators had alluded.~~ referred to in information sheet provided by the U.S. side.

3. Lt. Colonel Mulkey stated that the signed documents were on file with the Staff Judge Advocate. He pointed out that, among other provisions, the agreement stipulated that not more than 7,000 persons were to be enrolled in the KSC at any one time. General O'Connor stated that the U.S. negotiators would furnish a copy of the pertinent documents to the Korean negotiators.

4. Mr. Chang stated that the records available to the Korean negotiators showed that on March 8, 1955, at the 8th session of the 24th National Assembly, it was agreed that recruitment to the KSC should be suspended. From September, 1955, Mr. Chang added, the records showed that KSC members were supplied from the free labor market. Mr. Chang pointed out that this matter had already been discussed at three or four negotiating meetings and that a few more such discussions appeared to be necessary ~~before the~~

0195

mention of the KSC be deleted from the Status of Forces Agreement and

agreements cited by the U.S. negotiators have been produced. The Korean negotiators suggested, therefore, that the entire question of the Korean Service Corps be taken up as a separate matter of discussion outside of the framework of the status of forces negotiations.

5. Mr. Habib replied that the U.S. negotiators would study this proposal carefully to see whether it was feasible.

6. Mr. Chang went on to say that the Korean negotiators were not concerned about the benefits or amenities made available to KSC members. What they were concerned about was that the conditions under which KSC members are recruited should conform to the Korean labor laws. Mr.Habib pointed out that under the existing arrangements, the KSC members are recruited for the U.S. armed forces by the Korean authorities. The conditions under which they were recruited were, therefore, the responsibility of the Korean authorities. He asked whether the Korean negotiators believed that KSC members should have the right to strike. Mr. Chang replied in the affirmative. Mr. Habib poihted out that KSC members are under military discipline and that the Korean officers under whom they serve would probably take a very dim view of giving them the right to strike. Mr. Habib commented that it appeared that the Korean negotiators wished to modify the nature of the KSC or even eliminate it entirely. Mr.Chang stated that there was no intention on the part of the Korean negotiators to eliminate the KSC and indicated that the Korean Government would continue to provide the KSC labors upon request by the U.S armed forces. He emphasized that the Korean negotiators believed that the KSC labors, while they are supplied for employment by U.S. military forces, are entitled to all the privileges and rights provided in the Korean labor laws.

~~Mr. Habib then remarked that this matter was not within the scope of the status of forces negotiations. The U.S. negotiators would take under consideration the Korean negotiators' suggestion that it be discussed outside of the negotiations.~~

7. General O'Connor remarked that in response to questions asked by the Korean negotiators at the 46th meeting on March 13, the U.S. negotiators had passed to the Korean negotiators a fact sheet regarding the provisions in certain other status of forces agreements for legal representation by the host government of the U.S. armed forces in their capacity as employer.

0196

8. Mr. Chang thanked the U.S. negotiators for the information which had been provided but indicated that the Korean negotiators wished to ask some questions. First, the second paragraph of the fact sheet referred to countries where a system of indirect hire is in effect. Does this mean that in those countries where direct hire is in effect, the U.S. Government would be a party to legal suits under the provisions of the Labor Procurement Article? Major Peckham replied that General Fuller had already answered that question at an earlier meeting. Major Peckham said he wished to reiterate the position of the U.S. Government. That position, an accepted principle of international law, is that the U.S. Government consents to be sued only in its own courts and not in the courts of any other nation.

9. Mr. Chang then asked the U.S. negotiators to explain the difference between a system of direct hire and a system of indirect hire. General O'Connor explained that the U.S. armed forces in Korea operate a system of direct hire. They recruit their Korean personnel directly from the labor market in conformity with the local labor laws, with the assistance of the host government if necessary or desirable. He pointed out that a system of indirect hire is much more cumbersome to operate.

10. General O'Connor pointed out that paragraph 3 of the U.S. draft states that the conditions of employment, compensation, and the labor-management practices established by the U.S. armed forces for their employees shall be in general conformity with the labor laws, customs and practices of the Republic of Korea. The U.S. armed forces in Korea have as their objective to be a good employer. In achieving that objective, they aim to provide favorable conditions for their Korean personnel to help develop employee skills and to utilize the Korean employees as effectively as possible in support of joint U.S.-ROK security objectives. He said that Mr. Reed, Director of the Office of Civilian Personnel, was present at the meeting in order to discuss the direct hire personnel system operated by the U.S. armed forces for their Korean work force. General O'Connor remarked that the U.S. negotiators believed that the wage and labor practices to be discussed by Mr. Reed are in general conformity with ROK labor laws and compare favorably with the practices

0197

of other employers of Korean personnel.

10. Mr. Reed then read the statement attached to this Agreed Summary as Appendix I.

11. General O'Connor stated that the purpose of Mr. Reed's explanation had been to demonstrate to the Korean negotiators that the U.S. armed forces, as an employer, act in general conformity with Korean laws and practices, as stated in paragraph 3 of the U.S. draft. The U.S. negotiators believed their draft should be satisfactory to both sides, while the Korean draft, based as it was on the Japanese system of indirect hire, was not applicable to the situation in Korea.

12. Mr. Chang stated that Mr. Reed's presentation had been very informative and enlightening. The Korean negotiators did not dispute the fact that the present treatment of Korean employees by the U.S. armed forces is fair and meets the standards of the Korean labor laws. However, the Korean negotiators had to insist that Korean employees should not be treated under the provisions of any other law than Korean law. To apply the provisions of some other country's laws to Korean employees would be an infringement of the sovereignty of the Republic of Korea. This was particularly the case with regard to the matters covered under Sections 5 and 6 of Mr. Reed's statement.

13. Mr. Habib replied that the negotiators were not negotiating the labor practices mentioned by Mr. Reed. They were negotiating paragraph 3 of this article. The U.S. draft of this paragraph stated that the Korean employees ofthe U.S. armed forces would be treated "in general conformity with the labor laws, customs and practices of the Republic of Korea". Obviously, at any time the Korean authorities believed that the practices of the U.S. armed forces were not in conformity with Korean laws and practices,

0198

the Korean authorities could raise the question in the Joint Committee. In the process of negotiation, each side will have exercised its sovereignty in agreeing to the provisions of this article. It was the impression of the U.S. negotiators that the ROK Labor Office was quite satisfied with the labor practices of the U.S. armed forces. Mr. Reed confirmed this statement by Mr. Habib. In fact, said Mr. Reed, the ROK Labor Office had been particularly satisfied during the past year. Mr. Habib remarked that it was obvious that the U.S. armed forces must respect, and have been respecting, the desire of the Korean authorities to protect the interests of the Korean employees of the U.S. armed forces. Paragraph 3 of the U.S. draft will allow the Korean authorities to take issue with any apparent disparity at any time, in keeping with the process of constant consultation in the Joint Committee.

14. Mr. Chang stated that as a matter of principle, any specific aspect of administration in a sovereign state should be regulated by the laws of that state and not by the laws of another state. Since the U.S. negotiators had indicated that the labor practices of the U.S. armed forces would conform to Korean labor laws, why could the U.S. negotiators not accept the Korean draft of this paragraph? The Korean negotiators did not understand the insistence of the U.S. negotiators on including the phrase "general conformity".

15. General O'Connor stated that the Korean draft was addressed to an entirely different type of labor system than the one that was currently in effect in Korea. He suggested that informal discussion of this article might facilitate agreement. He also asked whether the Korean negotiators wished to state any views concerning paragraphs 4, 5, and 6 of the U.S. draft, which had no equivalents in the Korean draft. Mr. Chang stated that the views of the Korean negotiators regarding those paragraphs would depend upon the wording ultimately agreed upon for paragraph 3.

0199

Invited Contractors

16. Turning to the Invited Contractors Article, Mr. Chang stated that the Korean negotiators had not changed their intention to limit the application of this article, insofar as corporations are concerned, to corporations organized under the laws of the United States. The Korean negotiators were still prepared, as had been stated by the Korean Chief Negotiator at the 22nd meeting, to consider favorably the inclusion of dependents if the U.S. negotiators were willing to agree to this limitation on corporations. If the U.S. negotiators would so agree, the Korean negotiators were prepared to agree to the following:

a. In paragraph 1, Insertion of the words "and the dependents of such persons" following the words "United States";

b. Acceptance of Agreed Minute #2 of the U.S. draft and withdrawal of Agreed Minutes #1 and #2 of the Korean draft;

c. Modification of paragraph 8 of the Korean draft to read as follows: "The Korean authorities shall have the primary right to exercise jurisdiction over the contractors, their employees, and the dependents of such persons referred to in paragraph 1 ......"

d. Acceptance of Agreed Minute #1 of the U.S. draft, in order further to accommodate the desires of the U.S. negotiators.

Mr. Chang stated that in accepting Agreed Minute #2 of the U.S. draft, the Korean negotiators had taken note of the statement by the U.S. negotiators that the U.S. armed forces are gradually replacing third-country contractor employees with Korean nationals and have no intention to bring in any additional third-country nationals after the Agreement comes into force.

17. Mr. Habib remarked that it appeared that the negotiators had come a long way toward agreement on this article. He said the U.S. negotiators would study the

0200

Korean proposals and give their views at a later meeting.

18. ~~19~~. Mr. Habib noted that the Korean negotiators had not referred to paragraph 3. Recalling that agreement had been reached on the subparagraphs of paragraph 3 from (a) through (h), he wondered why the Korean negotiators wished to omit subparagraph (i), dealing with driving permits and vehicle registration. Believing that the Korean position might be the result of lack of sufficient details concerning the types and numbers of vehicles used by the invited contractors, the U.S. negotiators were prepared to supply that information. Mr. Habib thereupon passed to the Korean negotiators a table containing this information. This table is attached to this Joint Summary as Appendix II. Mr. Habib asked whether the concern of the Korean negotiators was centered upon vehicles owned by the employees of the contractors.

19. ~~20~~. Mr. Chang replied that the Korean negotiators were concerned about vehicles owned by both the employees and the contractors. Mr. Habib then pointed out that employee-owned vehicles numbered only 20 out of a total of 720. He also pointed out that 85% of all the vehicles used by the contractors were owned by the U.S. Government, with only 13% owned by the contractors. In reply to Mr. Chang's question regarding the difference between government-owned and contractor-owned vehicles, Mr. Habib replied that there were certain special types of vehicles required by the contractors for certain kinds of work. These vehicles were not normally available in Korea from armed forces sources and therefore were brought in by the contractors themselves. Mr. Chang thanked Mr. Habib for the tabulation, which he said would be helpful. Mr. Chang indicated it was not the ROK Government's intention to tax U.S. government-owned vehicles, and that the ROK side would examine the tabulation of invited contractors vehicles and present the ROK views later.

Security Measures

20 ~~21~~. Turning the the Security Measures Article, Mr. Habib noted that the U.S. negotiators had informally discussed with the Korean negotiators certain proposed alternative language which would remove from the text of this article the specific reference to legislation. The U.S. negotiators did not believe that a commitment to legislation was necessary in the article but they did want the negotiating record to show that "such actions" would include legislation, when appropriate; for example, to ensure the security of U.S. Government property.

0201

21 ~~22~~. Mr. Chang stated that the alternative language suggested by the U.S. negotia-

tors was not acceptable. He suggested certain changes in language which would make the alternative language read as follows:

> "The Republic of Korea will take such actions as it deems necessary, with the cooperation of the United States where appropriate, to ensure the adequate security and protection of the United States Armed Forces, the members thereof, the civilian component, the persons present in the Republic of Korea pursuant to Article ______, their dependents and their property, and the installations, equipment, property, records and official information of the United States, and, as consistent with Article _____, for the punishment of offenders under the applicable laws of the Republic of Korea."

22. Mr. Habib said the U.S. negotiators would study the Korean proposal. However, the language which they had proposed did not appear to impose any obligation on the Republic of Korea to take adequate measures to ensure the security of the U.S. armed forces.

23. It was agreed to hold the next meeting on April 10 at 2:00 p.m.

1966, 12, 31 에 예고문에 의거 일반문서로 재분류됨

0202

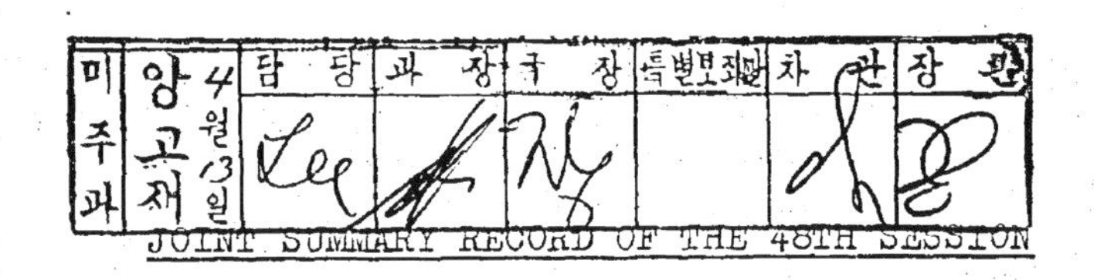

JOINT SUMMARY RECORD OF THE 48TH SESSION

관리번호 7463

1/3

1. Time and Place: 3:30-5:00 P.M. April 3, 1964 at the Foreign Ministry's Conference Room (No.1)

2. Attendants:

ROK Side:

Mr. Chang, Sang Moon	Director European and American Affairs Bureau
Mr. Yoon, Doo Sik	Director Prosecutor's Bureau Ministry of Justice
Mr. Shin Kwan Sup	Director Customs Bureau Ministry of Finance
Mr. Koo, Choong Whay	Chief, American Section Ministry of Foreign Affairs
Mr. Chung, Tai Kyun	Chief Prosecutor's Section Prosecutor's Bureau Ministry of Justice
Col. Kim, Won Kil	Chief, Military Affairs Section Ministry of National Defense
Mr. Lee, Chung Bin	3rd Secretary Ministry of Foreign Affairs
Mr. Chung, Woo Young (Rapporteur and Interpreter)	3rd Secretary Ministry of Foreign Affairs
Mr. Lee, Keun Pal	3rd Secretary Ministry of Foreign Affairs
Mr. Kim, Nai Sung	Staff Officer Europe Section Ministry of Foreign Affairs

U.S. Side:

Mr. Philip C. Habib	Counselor American Embassy
Brig. Gen. G.G. O'Connor	Deputy Chief of Staff 8th U.S. Army
Col. Howard Smigelow	Deputy Chief of Staff 8th U.S. Army

0203

Col. Kenneth C. Crawford	Staff Judge Advocates Office 8th U.S. Army
Capt. John Wayne	Assistant Chief of Staff USN/K
Mr. Benjamin A. Fleck (Rapporteur and Press Officer)	First Secretary American Embassy
Mr. Robert A. Lewis	2nd Secretary American Embassy
Maj. Robert D. Peckham	Staff Officer JAG 8th U.S. Army
Mr. Robert A. Kinney	J-5 8th U.S. Army
Mr. Kenneth Campen	Interpreter
Mr. Ogden C. Reed	Civilian Personnel Director 8th U.S. Army

Labor Procurement

1. General O'Connor opened the meeting by referring to the information sheet on the Korean Service Corps which had been passed to the Korean negotiators prior to the meeting. He stated that Lt. Colonel Mulkey was present to answer any questions which the Korean negotiators might wish to ask concerning the KSC. He pointed out that one of the unique features of the KSC is its mobility. Because of the necessity for moving components of the KSC from place to place as the situation requires, members are paid more than ordinary laborers of the same category. The KSC, General O'Connor continued, is a para-military organization, which has its own distinctive uniform, operates its own messes, and is commanded by military officers. Therefore, its personnel do not logically fit under the category of "employee" as defined in the U.S. draft of the Labor Procurement Article.

2. Mr. Chang thanked the U.S. negotiators for the information which they had furnished concerning the KSC.

0204

He remarked that the Korean negotiators had been unable, however, to identify or find any traces of the agreement between the United Nations Command and the Government of the Republic of Korea, referred to in information sheet provided by the U.S. side.

3. Lt. Colonel Mulkey stated that the signed documents were on file with the Staff Judge Advocate. He pointed out that, among other provisions, the agreement stipulated that not more than 7,000 persons were to be enrolled in the KSC at any one time. General O'Connor stated that the U.S. negotiators would furnish a copy of the pertinent documents to the Korean negotiators.

4. Mr. Chang stated that the records available to the Korean negotiators showed that on March 8, 1955, at the 8th session of the 24th National Assembly, it was agreed that recruitment to the KSC should be suspended. Mr. Chang added that the records showed that from September, 1955, KSC members were supplied from the free labor market. Mr. Chang pointed out that this matter had already been discussed at three or four negotiating meetings and that a few more such discussions appeared to be necessary even after the agreements cited by the U.S. negotiators have been produced. The Korean negotiators suggested, therefore, that mention of the KSC be deleted from the Status of Forces Agreement and the entire question of the Korean Service Corps be taken up as a separate matter of discussion outside of the framework of the status of forces negotiations.

5. Mr. Habib replied that the U.S. negotiators would study this proposal carefully to see whether it was feasible.

0205

6. Mr. Chang went on to say that the Korean negotiators were not concerned about the benefits or amenities made available to KSC members. What they were concerned about was that the conditions under which KSC members are recruited should conform to the Korean labor laws. Mr. Habib pointed out that under the existing arrangements, the KSC members are recruited for the U.S. armed forces by the Korean authorities. The conditions under which they were recruited were, therefore, the responsibility of the Korean authorities. He asked whether the Korean negotiators believed that KSC members should have the right to strike. Mr. Chang replied in the affirmative. Mr. Habib pointed out that KSC members are under military discipline and that the Korean officers under whom they serve would probably take a very dim view of giving them the right to strike. Mr. Habib commented that it appeared that the Korean negotiators wished to modify the nature of the KSC or even eliminate it entirely. Mr. Chang stated that there was no intention on the part of the Korean negotiators to eliminate the KSC, and indicated that the Korean Government would continue to provide the KSC labors upon request by the U.S. armed forces. He emphasised that the Korean negotiators believed that the KSC labors, while they are supplied for employment by U.S. military forces, are entitled to all the priveleges and rights provided in the Korean labor laws.

7. General O'Connor remarked that in response to questions asked by the Korean negotiators at the 46th meeting on March 13, the U.S. negotiators had passed to the Korean negotiators a fact sheet regarding the provisions in certain other status of forces agreements

0206

for legal representation by the host government of the U.S. armed forces in their capacity as employer.

8. Mr. Chang thanked the U.S. negotiators for the information which had been provided but indicated that the Korean negotiators wished to ask some questions. First, the second paragraph of the fact sheet referred to countries where a system of indirect hire is in effect. Does this mean that in those countries where direct hire is in effect, the U.S. Government would be a party to legal suits under the provisions of the Labor Procurement Article? Major Peckham replied that General Fuller had already answered that question at an earlier meeting. Major Peckham said he wished to reiterate the position of the U.S. Government. That position, an accepted principle of international law, is that the U.S. Government consents to be sued only in its own courts and not in the courts of any other nation.

9. General O'Connor pointed out that paragraph 3 of the U.S. draft states that the conditions of employment, compensation, and the labor-management practices established by the U.S. armed forces for their employees shall be in general confromity with the labor laws, customs and practices of the Republic of Korea. The U.S. armed forces in Korea have as their objective to be a good employer. In achieving that objective, they aim to provide favorable conditions for their Korean personnel to help develop employee skills and to utilize the Korean employees as effectively as possible in support of joint U.S.-ROK security objectives. He said that

0207

Mr. Reed, Director of the Office of Civilian Personnel, was present at the meeting in order to discuss the direct hire personnel system operated by the U.S. armed forces for their Korean work force. General O'Connor remarked that the U.S. negotiators believed that the wage and labor practices to be discussed by Mr. Reed are in general conformity with ROK labor laws and compare favorably with the practices of other employers of Korean personnel.

10. Mr. Reed then read the statement attached to this Agreed Summary as Appendix I.

11. General O'Connor stated that the purpose of Mr. Reed's explanation had been to demonstrate to the Korean negotiators that the U.S. armed forces, as an employer, act in general conformity with Korean laws and practices, as stated in paragraph 3 of the U.S. draft. The U.S. negotiators believed their draft should be satisfactory to both sides, while the Korean draft, based as it was on the Japanese system of indirect hire, was not applicable to the situation in Korea.

12. Mr. Chang stated that Mr. Reed's presentatinn had been very informative and enlightening. The Korean negotiators did not dispute the fact that the present treatment of Korean employees by the U.S. armed forces is fair and meets the standards of the Korean labor laws. However, the Korean negotiators had to insist that Korean employees should not be treated under the provisions of any other law than Korean law. To apply the provisions of some other country's laws to Korean employees would be an infringement of the sovereignty of the Republic of Korea. This was particularly the case with regard to the matters covered under Sections 5 and 6 of Mr. Reed's statement.

0208

13. Mr. Habib replied that the negotiators were not negotiating the labor practices mentioned by Mr. Reed. They were negotiating paragraph 3 of this article. The U.S. draft of this paragraph stated that the Korean employees of the U.S. armed forces would be treated "in general conformity with the labor laws, customs and practices of the Republic of Korea". Obviously, at any time the Korean authorities believed that the practices of the U.S. armed forces were not in conformity with Korean laws and practices, the Korean authorities could raise the question in the Joint Committee. In the process of negotiation, each side will have exercised its sovereignty in agreeing to the provisions of this article. It was the impression of the U.S. negotiators that the ROK Labor Office was quite satisfied with the labor practices of the U.S. armed forces. Mr. Reed confirmed this statement by Mr. Habib. In fact, said Mr. Reed, the ROK Labor Office had been particularly satisfied during the past year. Mr. Habib remarked that it was obvious that the U.S. armed forces must respect, and have been respecting, the desire of the Korean authorities to protect the interests of the Korean employees of the U.S. armed forces. Paragraph 3 of the U.S. draft will allow the Korean authorities to take issue with any apparent disparity at any time, in keeping with the process of constant consultation in the Joint Committee.

14. Mr. Chang stated that as a matter of principle, any specific aspect of administration in a sovereign state should be regulated by the laws of that state and not by the laws of another state. Since the U.S. negotiators had indicated that the labor practices of the U.S. armed forces would conform to Korean labor laws, why could the

0209

U.S. negotiators not accept the Korean draft of this paragraph? The Korean negotiators did not understand the insistence of the U.S. negotiators on including the phrase "general conformity".

15. General O'Connor stated that the Korean draft was addressed to an entirely different type of labor system than the one that was currently in effect in Korea. He suggested that informal discussion of this article might facilitate agreement. He also asked whether the Korean negotiators wished to state any views concerning paragraphs 4, 5 and 6 of the U.S. draft, which had no equivalents in the Korean draft. Mr. Chang stated that the views of the Korean negotiators regarding those paragraphs would depend upon the wording ultimately agreed upon for paragraph 3.

Invited Contractors

16. Turning to the Invited Contractors Article, Mr. Chang stated that the Korean negotiators had not changed their intention to limit the application of this article, insofar as corporations are concerned, to corporations organized under the laws of the United States. The Korean negotiators were still prepared, as had been statdd by the Korean Chief Negotiator at the 22nd meeting, to consider favorably the inclusion of dependents if the U.S. negotiators were willing to agree to this limitation on corporations. If the U.S. negotiators would so agree, the Korean negotiators were prepared to agree to the following:

0210

a. In paragraph 1, insertion of the words "and the dependents of such persons" following the words "United States";

b. Acceptance of Agreed Minute #2 of the U.S. draft and withdrawal of Agredd Minutes #1 and #2 of the Korean draft;

c. Modification of paragraph 8 of the Korean draft to read as follows: "The Korean authorities shall have the primary right to exercise jurisdiction over the contractors, their employees, and the dependents of such persons referred to in paragraph 1 ... "

d. Acceptance of Agreed Minute #1 of the U.S. draft, in order further to accommodate the desires of the U.S. negotiators.

Mr. Chang stated that in accepting Agreed Minute #2 of the U.S. draft, the Korean negotiators had taken note of the statement by the U.S. negotiators that the U.S. armed forces are gradually replacing third-country contractor employees with Korean nationals and have no intention to bring in any additional third-country nationals after the Agreement comes into force.

17. Mr. Habib remarked that it appeared that the negotiators had come a long way toward agreement on this article. He said the U.S. negotiators would study the Korean proposals and give their views at a later meeting.

18. Mr. Habib noted that the Korean negotiators had not referred to paragraph 3. Recalling that agreement had been reached on the subparagraphs of paragraph 3 from (a) through (h), he wondered why the Korean negotiators

wished to omit subparagraph (i), dealing with driving permits and vehicle registration. Believing that the Korean position might be the result of lack of sufficient details concerning the types and numbers of vehicles used by the invited contractors, the U.S. negotiators were prepared to supply that information. Mr. Habib thereupon passed to the Korean negotiators a table containing this information. This table is attached to this Joint Summary as Appendix II. Mr. Habib asked whether the concern of the Korean negotiators was centerdd upon vehicles owned by the employees of the contractors.

19. Mr. Chang replied that the Korean negotiators were concerned about vehicles owned by both the employees and the contractors. Mr. Habib then pointed out that employee-owned vehicles numbered only 20 out of a total of 720. He also pointed out that 85% of all the vehicles used by the contractors were owned by the U.S. Government, with only 13% owned by the contractors. In reply to Mr. Chang's question regarding the difference between government-owned and contractor-owned vehicles, Mr. Habib replied that there were certain special types of vehicles required by the contractors for certain kinds of work. These vehicles were not normally available in Korea from armed forces sources and therefore were brought in by the contractors themselves. Mr. Chang thanked Mr. Habib for the tabulation, which he said would be helpful. Mr. Chang indicated it was not the ROK Government's intention to tax U.S. government-owned vehicles, and that the ROK side would examine the tabulation of invited contractors vehicles and present the ROK views later.

0212

Security Measures

20. Turning to the Security Measures Article, Mr. Habib noted that the U.S. negotiators had informally discussed with the Korean negotiators certain proposed alternative language which would remove from the text of this article the specific reference to legislation. The U.S. negotiators did not believe that a commitment to legislation was necessary in the article but they did want the negotiating record to show that "such actions" would include legislation, when appropriate; for example, to ensure the security of U.S. Government property.

21. Mr. Chang stated that the alternative langugage suggested by the U.S. negotiators was not acceptable. He suggested certain changes in language which would make the alternative language read as follows:

> "The Republic of Korea will take such actions as it deems necessary, with the cooperation of the United States where appropriate, to ensure the adequate security and protection of the United States Armed Forces, the members thereof, the civilian component, the persons present in the Republic of Korea pursuant to Article_____, their dependents and their property, and the installations, equipment, property, records and official information of the United States, and, as consistent with Article ___, for the punishment of offenders under the applicable laws of the Republic of Korea."

22. Mr. Habib said the U.S. negotiators would study the Korean proposal. However, the language which they had proposed did not appear to impose any obligation on the Republic of Korea to take adequate measures to ensure the security of the U.S. armed forces.

23. It was agreed to hold the next meeting on April 10 at 2:00 p.m.

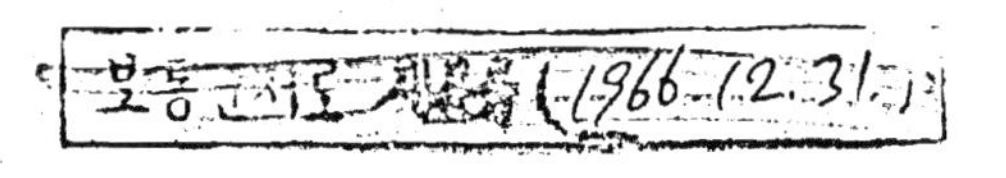

0213

STATEMENT
소견진술
MR. OGDEN C. REED
CIVILIAN PERSONNEL DIRECTOR
오그든 씨.리이드
민간인 인사처장

I am glad to be here and to present pertinent information on USFK's direct hire personnel system for the Korean workforce. We have translated presentation for ease of communication.

First, some background information:

USFK employs almost 20,000 appropriated fund Korean employees under definitive policy controls. In addition, over 11,000 non-appropriated fund employees and 3,000 invited contractor employees are administered under personnel policy parallel to appropriated fund personnel policy. We, thus, are referring to around 34,000 direct-hire employees.

USFK has 10 area civilian personnel offices located throughout ROK, in areas of military concentration. These offices employ and administer Korean and other civilian personnel for USFK organizations in the area. Area personnel offices classify jobs and establish pay grades, recruit, appoint, establish step rates, promote, reassign, effect disciplinary actions, complete retirement and other separation actions, provide training services and assistance on improved line supervision and employment-management relations.

As General O'Connor has stated, USFK personnel practices and standards parallel or exceed Laborur Standard Act of May 15, 1953, as supplemented by executive orders. The Laborur Standard Act, Act No. 286, covers a large number of articles and all pertinent articles are clearly met in personnel policy and procedures applicable to USFK Korean employees. In

이자리에서 한국인 종업원을 위한 주한미군의 직속고용인사제도를 말씀드리게 되었음을 영광으로 생각 합니다. 이해하시기 쉽게 설명을 번역해 보았읍니다.

먼저 기초적인 자료를 말씀드리겠읍니다.

주한 미군은 결정적인 방침통제하에서 거의 20,000명에 달하는 영달자금 한국인 종업원을 고용하고 있읍니다. 그뿐만아니라 11,000명 이상의 비영달자금종업원과 약 3,000명의 초청청부업자 종업원이 있는데 이들도 영달자금종업원의 인사방침에 못지않은 인사방침하에서 행정됩니다. 그래서 우리는 약 34,000명의 직속종업원에 대해서 말씀드리고 있는것입니다.

주한미군은 10개의 지구인사처를 한국안에 가지고 있는데 주로 군사시설이 집중된곳에 위치하고 있읍니다. 이 인사처는 각지구에있는 주한미군 예하부대을 위하여 한국인과 기타 민간인직원을 고용하고 행정합니다. 직무분류를 하고, 급여등급을 결정하고, 모집을하고, 임명을하고, 년공가봉을 설정하며 승급을 시키고, 재배치를하고, 징계, 정년퇴직및 기타해직조치를 취하고, 교육을 실시하며 개선된 각층에서의 감독관습을위한 도움을주고 또한 노사관계도 취급합니다.

"오커너어" 준장께서 말씀한바와 같이 주한미군의 인사관례와 기준은 1953년5월15일 발포된 근로기준법과 그시행령에 부합하거나 혹은능가하는 것입니다. 법령 286호인 근로기준법은 다수한 조항을 망라하였는데 그중의 모든 적절한 조항이 주한미군 한국인 종업원에게 적용되는 인사방침과 절차에 의해 분명히 합치되고 있읍니다.

0214

addition, certain special advantages of a civil service type are found in Korean personnel management.

I will cover 11 basic elements of Korean personnel administration, with appropriate tie-in to certain articles of the Labour Standards Act and local practices and to US-style civil service concepts, if relevant.

1. JOB CLASSIFICATION AND COMPENSATION.

a. Korean employment is based upon job classifications and job ranking by grade levels. These are reflected in a Manual of Standard Job Definitions. There are three grade schedules, with pay rates associated with each grade level. One schedule is for administrative, custodial, and professional-type jobs, the non-Manual Schedule: the second schedule is for industrial-type jobs, the Wage Board Schedule; the third is for marine jobs.

b. Basic pay rates are commensurate with that of prevailing pay practices in reputable and responsible Korean businees firms. These rates are kept up-to-date by means of periodic locality wage surveys. Currently, our average monthly wage is over 9,000 won and our rates are fully competitive.

c. A year-end bonus of one full month's pay is paid on or about 15 December, providing the employee has six month's continuous service. We do not pay summer bonuses; however, locality pay credit for these bonuses and other allowances are incorporated the basic rate schedule.

d. The regularly scheduled work week in most organizations is established as eight hours a day and 40 hours a week; some organizations also provide Saturday work. Overtime pay is provided for all required hours of

그뿐만 아니라 한국인 인사관리에는 공무원근무형태의 특전도 있읍니다.

이제 관련된 근로기준법과 지방 관습및 미식 공무원 개념에 결부시키 면서 한국인종업원행정의 11가지 기본 요소를 소개코저 합니다.

1. 직무분류와 보수

ㄱ. 한국인 종업원의 고용은 직무분류와 등급별 직무배열에 기초를 둡니다. 이것은 기준업무정의편람에 반영되어 있읍니다. 세가지의 등급 "스케쥴"이 있는데 각 등급마다 알맞는 급여율이 딸려있읍니다. 첫번 "스케쥴"은 행정, 관리, 및 전문직용인데 "제네랄 스케쥴" (사무계통)이라 부릅니다. 둘째 "스케쥴"은 공원직용인데 "와이지 보오드" (기술계통)라 부릅니다. 셋째번은 해상직원용 입니다.

ㄴ. 기본급여율은 저명하고 확고한 한국기업체에서 지불하는 현행급여와 맞먹습니다. 이 급여율은 정기적으로 실시하는 지방노임조사에 의해서, 뒤떨어지지않게 하고 있읍니다. 현재 평균 급여는 월 9,000원 이상이 되는데 이것은 과히 손색없는 것이라고 봅니다.

ㄷ. 6개월 근속을하면 12월15일경에 한달분급여에상당하는 년말상여를 지불합니다. 하기상여금은 없으나 시중에서 주고있는 하기상여금과 기타 수당은 기본급여율에 포함되어 있읍니다.

ㄹ. 대개의 부서에서는 하로 8시간에 주40시간근무가 정상근무주로 설정되어있는데 어떤부서에선 토요일 근무도합니다. 특근수당은 근로기준법 제46조에따라 하로 8시간에 주48시간을 초과근무한것에 대해서 15배로 지불

work in excess of eight hours a day or 48 hours per week at time and a half, in line with Article 46 of the Laborur Standards Act. This is strictly enforced and equitably administered.

합니다. 이것은 엄격히 실시되며 공정하게 행정됩니다.

e. Consistent with Article 46 of ROK law, rates for work regularly scheduled and performed between 2200 - 0600 hours is increased by 50% of the straight time rate, as a night differential.

ㅁ. 한국근로기준법 46조에 의거해서, 2200시부터 0600시 사이에 정규적으로 계획되어 근무한것에 대해서는 야간수당으로 50%가 통상인금에 가산 지불됩니다.

2. SEVERANCE PAY, ACCIDENT COMPENSATION AND RELATED SOCIAL INSURANCE ASPECTS.

2. 해(퇴)직금, 장해보상및관계 사회보장:

a. Consistent with ROK practice and exceeding ROK law (Article 28), severance pay is provided eligible employees with long term services retroactively to 30 April 1956 at which time USFK personnel and leave records were authenticated. Severance payments are not granted if an employee is separated for felony or grave misconduct including theft.

ㄱ. 유자격장기근무종업원은 주한미군의 인사및 휴가기록이 확증되었던 1956년 4월30일을 기준하여 해(퇴)직금을 받게되어있읍니다. 이것은 한국의 관례에 일치하며 한국기준법 제28조를 능가하는것입니다. 중죄또는 중대한 비행으로 해직되는 종업원에겐 해(퇴)직금은 지불되지 않습니다.

b. Upon reaching age 61, Korean employees normally are retired if 8 continuous years of severance credits have been earned. Management may elect to retain employees posessing special skills in short supply for an additional period. Mandatory retirement age is 65. Age provisions of our retirement plan are consistent with local practice.

ㄴ. 61세에 달하였을때 8년근속의 해(퇴)직금이 수득되었으면 한국인 종업원은 대개 퇴직하게 됩니다. 그러나 관리당국은 얻기 어려운 특수기술을 가진 종업원을 계속근무 시킬수 있읍니다. 65세가 되면 전부 정년퇴직하게 됩니다. 정년퇴직계획의 년령규정은 시중관례와 일치하는것입니다.

c. Employees injured on the job, disabled for work, or suffering death (including diseases caused by employment) are eligible for accident and death benefits. These benefits are based upon rules of the Bureau of Employees Compensation, U. S. Department of Labor and include emergency and first-aid type treatment of the post dispensary or hospital; continued treatment at the Army designated hospital in the area; compensation for injuries

ㄷ. 공상, 장해 또는 사망한 종업원은 (직업병을 포함하여) 사고 및 사망 보상을 받습니다. 이 보상은 미노동성 장해보상국규정에 의거하는 것인데 미군병원에서의 응급치료, 군지정의 시중병원에서의 가료, 급여정지 3일이 초과하는 경우의 부상에대한 장해보상등인데 장해보상신청전에 종업원의 자의로 병가나 년가의 사용으로 대체할수도 있읍니다. 사망시에는 미망인, 년소자제 또는 기타가족의

resulting in disability for work beyond three workdays after stoppage of pay, following use of any sick and/or annual leave which an employee may elect to use prior to accepting disability compensation. If the injury results in death, compensation is payable to the widow, minor children, or certain other dependents as appropriate. These benefits are effectively administered and meet requirements of Articles 78-83 of the Laborur Standards Act.

순위로 유족에대한 보상이 지급됩니다. 이 보상은 효율적으로 행정되며 근로기준법 제 78부터 83조까지의 조항요건에 합치합니다.

3. MEDICAL SERVICES AND SICK LEAVE.

a. All Korean personnel, as well as other employees, receive medical examinations and participate in annual X-ray check-ups and immunization programs.

b. In case the employee or a military dispensary determines that employees have a contagious or other disabling disease (such as tuberculosis) employees are placed on an extended leave status (sick, annual or leave without pay) for a period of up to one year. If the illness continues more than a year, employees who later recover have priority reemployment rights.

c. In addition to annual leave, employees accrue eight hours of sick leave upon completion of each 28-day pay period. This is a special, civil-service type benefit. Sick leave accumulates from year to year so long as it is unused and employees remain in service. Most employees have large amounts of sick leave to their credit, help in case of tuberculosis or other illness.

3. 의료와 병가

ㄱ. 다른모든 미국인과같이 한국인 종업원은 신체검사를 받고 년차 X광선과 예방주사 "프로그램"에 참가합니다. 이러한"써어비스"는 한국인종업원에게 부여되는 특혜조치입니다.

ㄴ. 본인자신이나 미군 병원이 전염병 또는 기타 근로불능질병 (폐병같은것)에 걸렸다고 단정하면 그종업원은 최고 1년의 장기휴가 (병가, 년가 또는 무급휴가)를 받게됩니다. 질병이 1년이상에 걸치면 회복되었을때 종업원은 우선직장복귀권이 부여됩니다.

ㄷ. 년가이외에 28일급여기간마다 8시간의 병가를 수득합니다. 이것은 특별한 것이며 공무원근무형의 특권인것입니다. 병가는 사용하지않고 현직에 머물러 있는한 매년 축적할수 있읍니다. 대부분의 종업원이 폐병 또는 기타 질병에 대비해서 많은 시간의 병가를 가지고 있읍니다.

4. LEAVE AND HOLIDAYS.

a. One day of annual or vacation leave with pay is accrued each 28-day pay period. This is consistent with Article 47 of the Laborur Standards Act.

4. 휴가와 공휴일:

ㄱ. 28일 급여기간마다 년가 (유양)을 수득하는데 이것은 근로기준법 47조에 해당합니다.

b. Employees are granted in line with Article 60, a total of 60 calendar days with pay in connection with childbirth; however, at least 30 calendar days of such maternity leave must be used after childbirth.

ㄴ. 법제 60조에 외해서 60일간의 산전유가가 허용되는데 최소한 30일간은 산후에 사용도록 하고 있읍니다.

c. Other types of leave are provided, such as leave without pay (LWOP), excused absence for voting, etc.

ㄷ. 기타 무급유가, 투표시출타등의 유가가 있읍니다.

d. In most cases employees receive time-off with pay on American holidays. On Korean legal holidays, employees may be excused without charge to leave or loss of pay. If employees are required to work they receive double-time. In effect, holiday time-off meets Korean law (Articles 45-46 and Article 23-3 of the Executive Decree). Use of both types of holidays exceeds Korean practice.

ㄹ. 대개의 경우 미국공휴일에는 유급으로 쉬게됩니다. 한국법정공휴일에는 유가충당이나 소득감소없이 쉬게됩니다. 근무를 한다면 배액지불이됩니다. 사실인즉 공휴일유게는 한국법령에 맞는것이고 (제45:46조와 시행령 23-3)양국의 유일 시중관습보다는 더좋은것이라고봅니다.

5. DISCIPLINARY AND SEPARATION ACTIONS.

5. 징계와 해직조치

a. It is policy of the Department of the Army to afford protection to its employees against arbitrary or inequitable action on disciplinary procedures. Employees have the right to answer a written letter to charges and to explain their point of view. Supervisors cannot take arbitrary action against employees. Efforts are made by supervisors and civilian personnel officer to solve problems before disciplinary measures are required.

ㄱ. 일방적안 또는 부당한 징계절차 모부터 종업원을 보호하자는것이 미육군성의 방침인것입니다. 종업원은 서면으로 항변을할권리를 갖었고 자신을 변론할수도 있읍니다. 감독자들은 일방적인 조치를 취하지못하도록 되어있읍니다. 징계조치가 필요하게 되기전에 감독자와 인사관은 문제를 해결하도록 노력하는것입니다.

b. Employees cannot be separated without a 30-day notice in pay status, consistent with Article 27-2 of ROK law.

ㄴ. 근로기준법 제 27-2조의거하여 30일간의 유급상태 동고기간없이는 해직될수 없읍니다.

c. Reduction in force procedures have been established on a Korea-wide basis which give preferred retention rights to employees with longer service and with Korean War service.

ㄷ. 장기근무와 전시제대자에게 강력한 잔류권을 줄수있는 감원절차가 한국전역별로 설정되있읍니다.

5

0218

6. GRIEVANCE AND APPEALS PROCEDURES. Grievance and appeals procedures through management channels have been established for employee use. Procedures include:

6. 불평진정절차

관리당국계통을 통하는 불평진정절차가 마련되있읍니다. 그절차는:

a. Grievance procedure for less significant complaints not concerned with removal actions. These actions, upon employee grievance, are subject to two levels of management review.

ㄱ. 파면조치와는 관계없는 덜중대한 불평을 위한것인데 불평이 자기된다음 2단계의 관리당국의 심사를 받습니다.

b. The formal appeals procedures is used only for removals and involves both field review and a formal appellate review by a top-level Board. Determinations and the EUSA Chief of Staff.

ㄴ. 정식불평진정절차는 파면에 한해서 사용되는데 지구별의 심사와 그 위사령부 위원회의 정직심사를 받습니다. 미8군 참모장의 결정이 최종적인것입니다.

c. General problems of a group nature may also be presented by Employee-Management Councils. In addition, FOEU may represent employees on individual grievances where employees so request, as well as being interested in group grievances.

ㄷ. 다수 종업원이 관계되는 일반적인 문제는 또한 종업원— 관리위원회에 제출됩니다. 종업원의 요청으로 외기노조는 개인적 불평에서 대변을 할수있고 집단적 불평에 관심이 있는것은 물론입니다.

7. PERFORMANCE APPRAISAL.

7. 근무성적평정

a. Employee's performance is expected to be reviewed at least annually, as a means of improved employee-communication and to improve work quality.

ㄱ. 종업원 의사소통을 원활이하고 작업의 질적인 향상을 도모코저 최소한 1년에 한번은 종업원의 근무성적이 평정됩니다.

b. Formal written performance appraisals are used to award superior employees with cash payments or to support changes to lower grade (and occasionally separations) when performance is marginal or unsatisfactory.

ㄴ. 탁월한 종업원에대한 상금부여 또는 근무성적이 저조하거나 원만하지 못할 때 얕은 등급으로의 변경이 필요하면 (때로는해직) 정식서면근평이 실시됩니다.

c. This approach to employee productivity and on-job communications, we believe, represents a useful innovation.

ㄷ. 이종업원 생산성과 직무상의 의사소통을 유창케하는 방법은 유익한 혁신을 나타내는것이라고 믿습니다.

8. INCENTIVE AWARDS.

8. 장려보상

a. Korean employees partici-

ㄱ. 한국종업원은 작업개선을하고 좋은 인사방침과 복지향상을 위해서 많은 "아이디어"를 제출하므로서 제안 "프로그램"에 참가합니다.

0219

pate in the suggestion program by submitting many ideas for work improvements and to promote better personnel policies and employee services. Use of employee suggestions is an American procedure, designed to stimulate employee initiative and interest.

b. Employees receive cash or honorary awards, or both for the following:

(1) Adopted suggestion.

(2) Sustained superior performance of assigned duties, performance of special acts or services, or long service.

(3) Any meritorious personal effort which contributes to the efficiency, economy, or other improvement of the Army operations.

c. We correctly are conducting "Operation Teamwork," a suggestion drive to improve joint US-ROK activities.

9. EMPLOYEE-MANAGEMENT RELATIONS.

a. When the Army establishes a new policy in the administration of Korean employees or revises the current policy, efforts are made to keep employees informed of these changes. We are passing out one example of our [illegible]an newsletter.

b. Employee-Management Councils are established in major organizations as one means of providing direct communications between representatives of employees and the commander of the activity.

c. EUSA's policy on union activities provides that employees are free to join a union if they so desire, or to refrain from joining a union if they do not desire to join. Currently, the only employee union with

종업원 제안제도의 활용은 미식제도인것이며 종업원의 창의성과 관심을 북돋는데 목적이 있읍니다.

ㄴ. 다음과같은 경우에는 상금 또는 명예상 또는 두개 도두 수여받습니다.

(1) 채택된 제안

(2) 맡겨진 임무의 탁월한수행, 특별공로, 또는 장기근무.

(3) 군작전의 효율적, 경제적 또는기타 개선에 이바지하는 개인적인 공적

ㄷ. 한 미유대강화를 보기위해 "오파레이숀 팀웍" 라는 제안운동을 현재 전개중에 있읍니다. 나누어 드린것을 참조해 주시길 바랍니다.

9. 노사관계

ㄱ. 한국인 종업원 행정에 관한 새로운 방침을 수립하거나 현존방침을 변경할 때에는 이러한 개정을 모든 종업원이 알도록 노력을 합니다. 최근에 나온 종업원신문을 나누어 드리겠읍니다.

ㄴ. 큰 단위부대에는 종업원— 관리 위원회가 설립되있는데 종업원의 대표와 부대장과의 직접적인 의사소통을 하자는데 목적이 있읍니다.

ㄷ. 노조활동에관한 미8군의 방침에 의하면 종업원은 자의대로 자유로히 노조에 가입할수있고 또않할수도 있읍니다. 현재 미8군이 공식적인 협의를 갖는 유일한 노동조합은 외국기관 노동조합인데 9개의 지부를 갖이고 있읍니다. 이협의는 1961년에 교환된서한에 입각하는것이며

which EUSA has formal consultation is the Foreign Organizations Employees' Union, with nine USFK sub-chapters. This consultation is based upon an exchange of letters in 1961 which established the basic framework for management-union consultations. Consultations occur in most cases at least once a week at the field chapter local and national headquarters level on a wide variety of personnel matters.

노사협의의 기본적인 체제를 규정하고 있읍니다. 지부에서는 최소한 매주 1번, 본부에서는 수시로 협의를 개최합니다.

10. TRAINING PROGRAM.

10. 교육 프로그램

a. The U. S. Government has a great interest in self-development and in skills and supervisory training for the Korean workforce. This supports the USFK objective to obtain full Korean utilization and the eventual replacement of third-state nationals.

ㄱ. 미국정부는 한국인 종업원의 자기계발 기술 및 감독자교육에 깊은 관심을 갖이고 있읍니다. 이것은 철저한 한국인활용을 달성하고 제 3국인 종업원을 점차적으로 대치한다는 주한미군의 목적을 뒷받침하는것입니다.

b. The Army has approved Korean employees to enroll in U. S. Army extension courses provided by AG School, Signal School, Engineer School, and others in the States.

ㄴ. 미국본토에 있는 부관학교, 통신학교, 공병학교, 기타 학교가 제공하는 통신강좌에 한국인 종업원이 입학할수 있도록 미육군은 허락을 했읍니다.

c. Last year 2,081 Koreans completed supervisory training, involving 16,840 manhours, and 50,610 manhours were spent in skills training.

ㄷ. 작년동안에 연 16,840 시간이 소비된 감독자교육을 2,081 명의 한국인이 수강했읍니다. 기술교육에 50,610시간이 소요됐읍니다.

11. SAFETY.

11. 안전

a. USFK has an active accident prevention program and is consistently on the look-out for hazards. Our record here, we believe, is superior.

ㄱ. 주한미군은 적극적인 사고미연방지 "프로그램"을 갖었고 위험에 대한 감시를 항상 게을리하지않고 있읍니다. 안전기록은 월등히 좋은것이라고 자부합니다.

b. It may be of interest to note that safety inspections are largely conducted by Korean specialists and that EUSA has established a career program for Korean safety personnel.

ㄴ. 흥미있는 사실은 안전검열의 거의전부가 한국인 전문관에 의해서 실시된다는것인데 미8군은 한국인 안전관계 직원의 양성계획에 나섰읍니다.

0221

CONCLUDING COMMENTS:

In line with the foregoing review, Korean personnel administration in USFK fully meets pertinent requirements of the Labour Standards Act and has also a number of other advantages of a civil-service type. The eleven elements of Korean personnel program described above show, we believe, a progressive and business - like approach to the management of the Korean workforce. Our direct-hire system has met the manpower needs of USFK and working conditions are favorable. We believe that the ROK Office of Labor Affairs and other interested officials are aware of this.

Thank you.

결론

이상말씀드린바와같이 주한미군의 한국인 인사행정은 적절한 지시사항에 충분히 맞는것이며 공무원근무형의 특전도 여러가지 갖었다고 봅니다. 이제 7가지 말씀드린 한국인 인사 "프로그램"의 11가지요소는 한국인 종업원의 관리에대한 진보적이며 질서있는 방법을 나타내는 것이라 믿습니다. 당사령부의 직속고용 제도는 주한미군의 인력필요성을 충족시키고있고 종업원의 근모조건은 양호한 것으로 보고 있읍니다. 한국노동청 당국과 기타 관계기관 여러분이 이것을 알고 계실것으로 믿습니다.

그맙습니다.

9

0222

5. 제49차 회의, 4.10

0223

SOFA NEGOTIATION

Agenda for the 49th Session

14:00 April 10, 1964

1. Continuation of Discussions on:

   a. Contractors Article

   b. Criminal Jurisdiction Article

2. Other Business

3. Agenda and Date of the Next Meeting

4. Press Release

0224

4/10

The term "official duty" as used in Article ______ and the Agreed Minutes is not meant to include all acts by members of the Armed Forces and the civilian component during periods when they are on duty, but is meant to apply only to acts which are required to be done as functions of those duties which the individuals are performing. Thus, a substantial departure from the acts a person is required to perform in a particular duty usually will indicate an act outside of his "official duty".

0225

AGREED MINUTE

2. The undertaking of the United States Government to conform to Korean labor laws, customs, and practices, does not imply any waiver by the United States Government of its immunities under international law. [Moreover, the United States Government may terminate employment whenever the continuation of such employment would materially impair the accomplishment of the mission of the United States armed forces].

0226

AGREED MINUTE

3. It is understood that the Government of the Republic of Korea shall be reimbursed for direct costs incurred in providing assistance requested pursuant to paragraph 2.

0227

기 안 용 지

관리 번호 74-66

자 체 통 제	외무부 김 성	기안처	미 주 과 이 근 팔	전화번호	근거서류접수일자
	과장	국장	차관	장관	
관계관 서 명					
기 안 년월일	1964. 4. 13.	시 행 년월일	검열 1964. 4. 15 통제관	보 존 년 한	정 서 기 장
분 류 기 호	외구미 722.2	전 체 통 제	결		
경 유 수 신 참 조	대 통 령 (참 조: 비 서 실 장) 국 무 총 리			발 신	장 관
제 목	제 49 차 주둔군지위협정 체결 교섭 실무자회의 보고				

1964. 4. 10. 하오 2 시 부터 동 4 시 까지 외무부 제 1 회의실에서 개최된 제 49 차 주둔군지위협정 체결 교섭 실무자회의에서 토의된 내용을 별첨과 같이 보고합니다.

유 첨: 제 49 차 주둔군지위협정 체결 교섭 실무자회의 보고서 1 부. 끝.

승인서식 1-1-3 (11-00900-03) (195mm×265mm16절지)

022

제 49 차

한·미간 주둔군지위협정 체결 교섭 실무자회의

보 고 서

1. 일 시: 1964 년 4 월 10 일 하오 2 시 부터 동 4 시 까지.

2. 장 소: 외무부 제 1 회의실

3. 토의사항:

가. 군계약자

(1) 한·미 양측은 군계약자 소유 차량의 등록 및 운전면허에 관하여 제 48 차 교섭회의에서 미측대표가 제시한 차량 소유 관계 일람표에 의하여 군계약자인 법인체 및 군계약자의 고용인이 소유하고 있는 차량의 소유식별방법을 검토하였으며,

(2) 우리측은 법인체인 군계약자의 소유 차량에 대하여서는 차량의 등록 및 운전면허에 관한 일정한 특권을 부여할 용의가 있으나 군계약자의 고용인이 소유하고 있는 차량에 대하여서는 일반외국인의 경우와 다를 것이 없음으로 특권을 인정할 수 없다고 주장하였다.

나. 형사재판관할권

(1) 양측대표는 형사재판관할권에 관한 양측 초안 본문 3 항부터 12 항까지 쌍방 초안의 차의점을 토의하였으며

(2) 우리측은 한·미 상호방위조약 제 2 조에 해당하는 전쟁상태가 발발하였을 경우 협정 전 조문의 효력 정지 여부 (또는 형사재판관할권에 국한시키는지의 여부)에 관하여 우리측 입장이 확정되는 대로 조문 초안을 제출할 것이라고 밝혔다.

(3) 미측은 공무 집행중 작위 또는 부작위에 기인하는 범죄의 정의에 관하여 본문의 정의에 첨가하여 양해사항으로서 우리 주장대로 "공무 집행중의 모든 행위를 포함하는 것이 아니고 특정공무의 정상적 기능으로서 요구되는 행위로 부터 이탈한 행위는 공무 밖의 행위"임을 규정할 것을 제의하였다.

4. 기타 사항: 차기 회의 일자: 1964. 4. 17. 하오 2 시 부터

0229

64-3-64

64-3-15(1) 미국.북 110-12(1)

0229-1

1. Mr. Chang opened the meeting by introducing the following new members of the Korean negotiating team: Mr. YUN Ki-an, just returned from a diplomatic assignment in New York, Mr. YI Kae-chol, just returned from an assignment to the ROK Consulate General in Cairo and newly assigned to the Foreign Ministry's Africa Section, and Mr. PAK Won-chul, the Treaty Section. Mr. Chang also announced that during the absence of Mr. Chung U-yong at a training course, the interpreter for the Korean negotiators would be Mr. YI Kun-pal. Mr. Habib welcomed the new Korean negotiators on behalf of the U.S. negotiators.

Invited Contractors

2. Discussion was begun on the Invited Contractors Article with a series of questions by the Korean negotiators with regard to the tabulation of contractor-used vehicles which the U.S. negotiators had tabled at the previous meeting. These questions elicited the following information from the U.S. negotiators. The vehicles listed in the tabulation as being "contractor-owned" are owned by the legal entity which has signed the contract with the U.S. armed forces. This legal entity is usually a corporation, although in one or two cases the legal entity may be an individual contractor. Those vehicles which are not owned by a legal entity are entered in the "privately-owned" column. The important criterion in this regard is whether the vehicle is used in the performance of the contract. Contractor-owned vehicles are registered in the name of the legal entity; privately-owned vehicles are registered in the name of the individual owner. Ownership can be verified by examination of the ownership certificate, registration certificate, or insurance papers.

3. Mr. Habib stated that the questions being raised by the Korean negotiators were matters of administration and that there would be procedures worked out so that the Joint Committee could readily obtain such information, should it so desire. The U.S. negotiators wondered why the Korean negotiators appeared to be so intent on distinguishing between contractor-owned and privately-owned vehicles. What did the Korean negotiators wish to propose regarding this subject?

0230

4. Mr. Chang replied that the Korean negotiators wished to know how to distinguish

privately-owned vehicles from the others because they intended to make the privately-owned vehicles subject to the same Korean laws and regulations as those owned by ordinary aliens, while according certain privileges only to the vehicles which were used by the contractors in the performance of their contracts.

5. Mr. Habib replied that the U.S. negotiators were prepared to listen to the proposal of the Korean negotiators. However, the U.S. negotiators wished to make clear that the owners of these privately-owned vehicles were not ordinary aliens. For the purposes of the Agreement, a contractor is in Korea solely to perform a contract for the U.S. armed forces. He can not, therefore, be considered to be in the same category as the ordinary foreign resident.

6. Mr. Chang replied that the Korean negotiators had already agreed to accord those privileges enumerated in Paragraph 3, except subparagraph (1) to the invited contractors as well as to members of the U.S. armed forces and the civilian component; they were not, therefore, equating the contractors with ordinary aliens. However, the taxes and fees connected with registration and licensing of vehicles were local assessments and a distinction should be made, therefore, between privately-owned vehicles and others. The privately-owned vehicles should be subject to the same fees and regulations as those owned by ordinary aliens.

7. Mr. Habib said the U.S. negotiators understood the Korean position. The Korean negotiators, however, should take into account the fact that 90% of the contracts are on a cost plus fixed fee basis. This means that if a contractor purchases a vehicle for use in fulfilling the contract, the U.S. Government bears the cost. Consequently, contractors are not permitted to have more vehicles than are necessary.

Criminal Jurisdiction

8. Turning to the Criminal Jurisdiction Article, Mr. Habib recalled that at the

0231

last previous meeting devoted to this article, discussion had not been completed on paragraph 3. He suggested, therefore, that discussion be resumed with subparagraph (a)(ii), which dealt with the question of duty offenses. During the previous discussion, the Korean negotiators had stated that they would not insist that the definition of duty, as contained in the circular published by the U.S. Army, Far East in January, 1956, be included in the text of the Agreement or in the Agreed Minutes. The Korean chief negotiator had stated that if agreement could be reached on that definition, there would be no problem in solving this matter. The U.S. negotiators had considered the Korean suggestion that the definition might be included in the negotiating record. They believed that this might offer a sound and satisfactory way of handling the problem. Therefore, if the Korean negotiators would accept the Agreed Minute #2 in the U.S. draft re paragraph 3(a), the U.S. negotiators agreed that the following definition could be placed in the negotiating record as the basis on which duty certificates would be issued:

> "The term 'official duty' as used in Article ____ and the Agreed Minutes is not meant to include all acts by members of the Armed Forces and the civilian component during periods when they are on duty, but is meant to apply only to acts which are required to be done as functions of those duties which the individuals are performing. Thus, a substantial departure from the acts a person is required to perform in a particular duty usually will indicate an act outside of his 'official duty'".

Mr. Habib called the attention of the Korean negotiators to the fact that the above definition was based on the full text of the definition which had appeared in the Army circular which they had cited, and not on the partial text suggested by the Korean negotiators.

9. Mr. Chang stated that the Korean negotiators would examine the U.S. proposal and give their views at a later meeting. He suggested that the negotiators resume their paragraph by paragraph consideration of this article.

10. Mr. Habib agreed to continue paragraph by paragraph discussion but stated that the U.S. negotiators would ~~like to deviate from~~ the exact sequence of

0232

the paragraphs in order to clarify the thinking of each side on specific points at issue. In order to enable the U.S. negotiators to expedite consideration of certain key issues, therefore, he wished to refer to paragraph 9 and its related Agreed Minutes. At the 47th negotiating meeting, the Korean negotiators had stated that they accepted the principle of enumerating trial safeguards in the Agreement but that they did not necessarily agree with the entire enumeration in the U.S. draft. The U.S. negotiators would like to know what specific portions of that enumeration were objectionable to the Korean negotiators.

11. Mr. Chang replied that there was no serious difference of opinion with regard to the text of paragraph 9. However, the enumeration in the related Agreed Minute caused the Korean negotiators some difficulties, which they would clarify in the near future. They wished to know whether the enumeration in the Agreed Minute could be converted into an understanding in the negotiating record.

12. Mr. Habib replied that this matter was of fundamental importance, so far as the United States Government was concerned. Trial safeguards lie at the heart of the question of jurisdiction. This matter was of such great concern to the U.S. authorities, including the Congress, that the U.S. negotiators must insist that the enumeration of trial safeguards be retained in the text of the Agreement and the Agreed Minutes, rather than placed in the negotiating record.

13. Mr. Chang stated that the Korean negotiators would make their specific views on this matter known at a later meeting. Briefly expressed, they were of the opinion that the enumeration in the Agreed Minute overlapped that contained in paragraph 9, which was extensive, and that the enumeration in the Agreed Minute could therefore be incorporated into the negotiating record.

0233

14. The negotiators then resumed paragraph by paragraph examination of the texts, beginning with paragraph 3(b). The use of the term "military authorities of the United States" in the Korean draft, as compared with "authorities of the United States" in the U.S. draft was found to occur in paragraphs 4, 5(a), 5(b),

6(a), 6(b), 7(a) and 7(b). It was agreed that when the question of usage was finally decided, the same usage would be used in all of these paragraphs.

15. Subparagraphs (b) and (c) of paragraph 3 were found to be identical. In paragraph 4, it was noted that the word "armed" had been omitted from the phrase "armed forces" in the Korean draft. Mr. Habib pointed out that the term "armed forces" is used throughout the Agreement and should be considered, therefore, to be the standard usage.

16. In paragraph 5(a), Mr. Habib pointed out that the U.S. draft uses the language "have custody" while the Korean draft uses "exercise jurisdiction". This difference arises out of the differing provisions in the two drafts with regard to custody. When the question of language relating to custody is settled, agreement on the language of paragraph 5 (a) will be almost automatic.

17. Mr. Habib noted that paragraph 5(b) of the Korean draft omitted the word "promptly". The U.S. negotiators believed that it was important that there should be prompt notification of arrest. Mr. Chang stated that the Korean negotiators believed this to be a reciprocal matter and that if the U.S. military authorities promptly notified the ROK authorities, as provided for in paragraph 5(c) of the Korean draft, the ROK authorities would reciprocate.

18. Mr. Habib replied that paragraph 5(c) of the Korean draft had no counterpart in the U.S. draft. Nor did it have any precedents in the NATO Agreement or the Agreement with Japan, the reason being that it imposes on the U.S. military forces an onerous requirement which serves no fundamental purpose. The absence of such a provision has created no problems in the countries mentioned but its inclusion in this Agreement would undoubtedly create problems. Why did the Korean negotiators wish to include it? Mr. Chang replied that he would give the Korean views on this question at a subsequent meeting.

19. Mr. Habib pointed out that the U.S. draft of paragraph 5(c) used the phrase "a dependent" instead of the phrase "their dependents" which appeared in the Korean draft. The U.S. negotiators considered "a dependent" to be standard usage and preferable.

0234

Mr. Chang said the Korean negotiators accepted usage of the phrase "a dependent".

20. With regard to paragraph 5(c) of the U.S. draft and its counterpart, 5(d) of the Korean draft, Mr. Habib stated that in these provisions the question of custody arises. Whereas, the U.S. language provides procedure for retention of custody by the U.S. authorities, the Korean language is a considerable revision of the similar paragraphs in the NATO and Japanese Agreements and provides for a handing over to Korean custody upon the issuance of a warrant. Mr. Habib added that the U.S. negotiators do not believe that retention of custody by the U.S. authorities will interfere with the course of justice. On the contrary, they believe that such a provision has much to commend it. This is a matter of major, substantial interest to the U.S. Government. The U.S. authorities have reservations about existing Korean facilities for both pre-trial and post-trial custody. He noted that the proposal for post-trial custody, contained in the last sentence of the U.S. draft of paragraph 5(c), was a response to indications given by earlier Korean negotiators that they would prefer that post-trial custody not be a Korean responsibility and that they would welcome a provision such as this one. The U.S. negotiators believed that neither pre-trial nor post-trial custody by the U.S. authorities would interfere with the judicial proceedings. Furthermore, they saw many advantages to the proposal.

21. Mr. Chang asked whether the phrase in the U.S. draft "pending completion of all judicial proceedings" was intended to include the duration of the sentence as well as the duration of the trial or trials. Mr. Habib replied that the phrase meant until all appellate proceedings have been completed.

22. It was noted that paragraph 6(a) and (b) and paragraph 7(a) were identical except for the aforementioned inclusion of the word "military" from before the word "authorities" in the Korean draft.

0235

23. In paragraph 7(b), Mr. Habib noted that there were two additional sentences in the U.S. draft, relating back to paragraph 5(c). If agreement were reached on post-trial custody, he explained, these two sentences would be essential, since without them

the U.S. authorities could not carry out post-trial custody. He also pointed out that these provisions did not indicate any intention on the part of the U.S. authorities to avoid just punishment of convicted offenders.

24. It was noted that the two drafts of paragraph 8 were identical, except for the inclusion of "military" and the omission of "armed" in the Korean draft and the addition in the U.S. draft of the words "his sentence has been remitted or suspended, or he". In this connection, Mr. Chang requested an explanation of the terms suspension, remission, and pardon, which was provided by Colonel Crawford. answer

25. It was noted that the two drafts of paragraph 9 were identical, except for some minor changes of wording in subparagraphs (e) and (f) of the Korean draft.

26. It was noted that the two drafts of paragraph 10(a) were identical. Mr. Habib noted that paragraph 10(b) of the Korean draft would not give the U.S. armed forces the authority to maintain discipline and order among other elements of the United Nations Command, such as the Thai and Turk contingents. Noting that the situation in this regard in Korea was perhaps unique, Mr. Habib pointed out that the U.S. draft was also not satisfactory. However, the U.S. draft did provide additional authority to the U.S. military police to ensure the security of members of the U.S. armed forces outside of their facilities and areas. He said the U.S. negotiators would consider this matter and submit suggested changes at a later date.

27. Mr. Habib pointed out that there was no counterpart in the Korean draft to paragraph 11 in the U.S. draft. Mr. Chang replied that the Korean negotiators had not yet decided whether to agree to the inclusion of this paragraph in the Criminal Jurisdiction Article or to make it a separate article. When they reached a decision, they would table their proposed draft.

0236

28. Mr. Habib pointed out that there also was no counterpart in the Korean

draft for paragraph 12 of the U.S. draft. He said that provisions such as those in paragraph 12 were normal in such agreements. Mr. Chang replied that the Korean negotiators agreed in principle with the provisions of paragraph 12.

29. Mr. Chang asked if it would be possible for the U.S. negotiators to provide the Korean negotiators with the texts of the arrangements, agreements, and practices referred to in the preamble to the Agreed Minutes in the U.S. draft. Mr. Habib replied that there was no (precise and complete) text which applied to current arrangements or practices. It was agreed that the Korean negotiators should meet informally with Colonel Crawford for an explanation of existing arrangements and practices. ~~documents~~

30. It was decided to leave paragraph by paragraph discussion of the Agreed Minutes until the next meeting, which was scheduled for April 17 at 2:00 p.m.

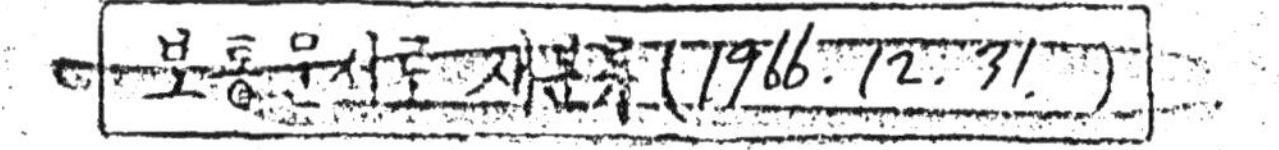

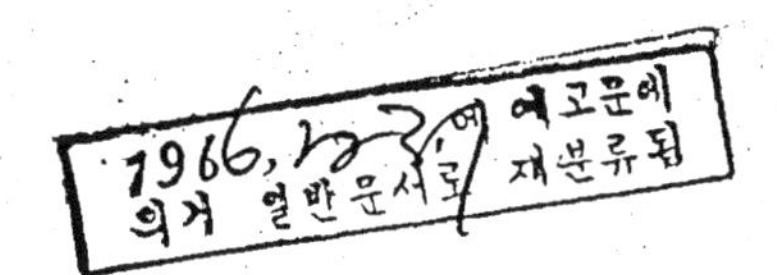

0237

JOINT SUMMARY RECORD OF THE 49TH SESSION

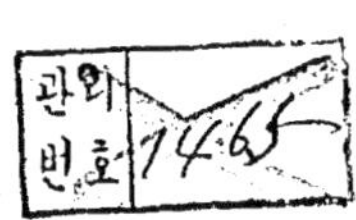

1. Time and Place: 2:00 - 4:00 P.M. April 10, 1964 at the Foreign Ministry's Conference Room (No.1)

1/3

2. Attendants:

ROK Side:

Mr. Chang, Sang Moon	Director European and American Affairs Bureau
Mr. Yoon, Doo Sik	Director Prosecutor's Bureau Ministry of Justice
Mr. Koo, Choong Whay	Chief, American Section Ministry of Foreign Affairs
Mr. Chung, Tai Kyun	Chief Prosecutor's Section Prosecutor's Bureau Ministry of Justice
Col. Kim, Won Kil	Chief, Military Affairs Section Ministry of National Defense
Mr. Lee, Keun Pal (Rapporteur and Interpreter)	3rd Secretary Ministry of Foreign Affairs
Mr. Ahn, Yun Ki	3rd Secretary Ministry of Foreign Affairs
Mr. Lee, Kae Chul	3rd Secretary Ministry of Foreign Affairs
Mr. Park, Won Chul	3rd Secretary Ministry of Foreign Affairs
Mr. Kim, Nai Sung	Staff Officer Europe Section Ministry of Foreign Affairs

U.S. Side:

Mr. Philip C. Habib	Counselor American Embassy
Brig. Gen. G.G. O'Connor	Deputy Chief of Staff 8th U.S. Army
Col. Howard Smigelow	Deputy Chief of Staff 8th U.S. Army

0238

Col. Kenneth C. Crawford	Staff Judge Advocates Office 8th U.S. Army
Capt. John Wayne	Assistant Chief of Staff USN/K
Mr. Benjamin A. Fleck (Rapporteur and Press Officer)	First Secretary American Embassy
Mr. Robert A. Lewis	2nd Secretary American Embassy
Maj. Robert D. Peckham	Staff Officer JAG 8th U.S. Army
Mr. Robert A. Kinney	J-5 8th U.S. Army
Mr. Kenneth Campnn	Interpreter

1. Mr. Chang opened the meeting by introducing the following new faces of the Korean negotiating team: Mr. Ahn Yun-ki, Mr. Lee Kae-chul, and Mr. Park Won-chul, all of the Foreign Ministry, Mr. Chang also annonnced that during the absence of Mr. Chung Woo Young at a training course, the interpreter for the Korean negotiators would be Mr. Lee Keun-pal. Mr. Habib welcomed the new Korean negotiators on behalf of the U.S. negotiators.

Invited Contractors

2. Discussion was begun on the Invited Contractors Article with a series of questions by the Korean negotiators with regard to the tabulation of contractor-used vehicles which the U.S. negotiators had tabled at the previous meeting. These questions elicited the following information from the U.S. negotiators. The vehicles listed in the tabulation as being "contractor-owned" are owned by the legal entity which has signed the contract with the U.S. armed forces. This legal entity is usually a corporation,

0239

although in one or two cases the legal entity may be an individual contractor. Those vehicles which are not owned by a legal entity are entered in the "privately-owned column. The important criterion in this regard is whether the vehicle is used in the performance of the contract. Contractor-owned vehicles are registered in the name of the legal entity; privately-owned vehicles are registered in the name of the individual owner. Ownership can be verified by examination of the ownership certificate, registration certificate, or insurance papers.

3. Mr. Habib stated that the questions being raised by the Korean negotiators were matters of administration and that there would be procedures worked out so that the Joint Committee could readily obtain such information, should it so desire. The U.S. negotiators wondered why the Korean negotiators appeared to be so intent on distinguishing between contractor-owned and privately-owned vehicles. What did the Korean negotiators wish to propose regarding this subject?

4. Mr. Chang replied that the Korean negotiators wished to know how to distinguish privately-owned vehicles from the others because they intended to make the privately-owned vehicles subject to the same Korean laws and regulations as those owned by ordinary aliens, while according certain privileges only to the vehicles which were used by the contractors in the performance of their contracts.

5. Mr. Habib replied that the U.S. negotiators were prepared to listen to the proposal of the Korean

negotiators. However, the U.S. negotiators wished to make clear that the owners of these privately-owned vehicles were not ordinary aliens. For the purposes of the Agreement, a contractor is in Korea solely to pefform a contract for the U.S. armed forces. He can not, therefore, be considerdd to be in the same category as the ordinary foreign resident.

6. Mr. Chang replied that the Korean negotiators had already agreed to accord those privileges enumerated in Paragraph 3, except subparagraph (i) to the invited contractors as well as to members of the U.S. armed forces and the civilian component; they were not, therefore, equating the contractors with ordinary aliens. However, the taxes and fees connected with registration and licensing of vehicles were local assessments and a distinction should be made, therefore, between privately-owned vehicles and others. The privately-owned vehicles should be subject to the same fees and regulations as those owned by ordinary aliens.

7. Mr. Habib said the U.S. ndgotiators understood the Korean position. The Korean negotiators, however, should take into account the fact that 90% of the contracts are on a cost plus fixed fee basis. This means that if a contractor purchases a vehicle for use in fulfilling the contract, the U.S. Government bears the cost. Consequently, contractors are not permitted to have more vehicles than are necessary.

Criminal Jurisdiction

8. Turning to the Criminal Jurisdiction Article, Mr. Habib recalled that at the last previous meeting

0241

devoted to this article, discussion had not been completed on paragraph 3. He suggested, therefore, that discussion be resumed with subparagraph (a)(ii), which dealt with the question of duty offenses. During the previous discussinn, the Korean negotiators had stated that they would not insist that the definition of duty, as contained in the circular published by the U.S. Army, Far East in January, 1956, be included in the text of the Agreement or in the Agreed Minutes. The Korean chief negotiator had stated that if agreement could be reached on that definition, there would be no problem in solving this matter. The U.S. negotiators had considered the Korean suggestion that the definition might be included in the negotiating record. They believed that this might offer a sound and satisfactory way of handling the problem. Therefore, if the Korean negotiators would accept the Agreed Minute #2 in the U.S. draft re paragraph 3(a), the U.S. negotiators agreed that the following definition could be placed in the negotiating record as the basis on which duty certificates would be issued:

> "The term 'official duty' as used in Article____ and the Agreed Minutes is not meant to include all acts by members of the Armed Forces and the civilian component during periods when they are on duty, but is meant to apply only to acts which are required to be done as functions of those duties which the individuals are performing. Thus, a substantial departure from the acts a person is required to perform in a particular duty usually will indicate an act outside of his 'official duty'".

Mr. Habib called the attention of the Korean negotiators to the fact that the above definition was based on the full text of the definition which had appeared in the Army circular which they had cited, and not on the partial text suggested by the Korean negotiators.

9. Mr. Chang stated that the Korean negotiators would examine the U.S. proposal and give their views at a later meeting. He suggested that the negotiators resume their paragraph by paragraph consideration of this article.

10. Mr. Habib agreed to continue paragraph by paragraph discussion but stated that the U.S. negotiators would like to deviate from the exact sequence of the paragraphs in order to clarify the thinking of each side on specific points at issue. In order to enable the U.S. negotiators to expedite consideration of certain key issues, therefore, he wished to refer to paragraph 9 and its related Agreed Minutes. At the 47th negotiating meeting, the Korean negotiators had stated that they accepted the principle of enumerating trial safeguards in the Agreement but that they did not necessarily agree with the ~~actual~~ entire enumeration in the U.S. draft. The U.S. negotiators would like to know what specific portions of that enumeration were objectionable to the Korean negotiators.

11. Mr. Chang replied that there was no serious difference of opinion with regard to the text of paragraph 9. However, the enumeration in the related Agreed Minute caused the Korean negotiators some difficulties, which they would clarify in the near future. They wished to know whether the enumeration in the Agreed Minute could be converted into an understanding in the negotiating record.

12. Mr. Habib replied that this matter was of fundamental importance, so far as the United States

0243

Government was concerned. Trial safeguards lie at the heart of the question of jurisdiction. This matter was of such great concern to the U.S. authorities, including the Congress, that the U.S. negotiators must insist that the enumeration of trial safeguards be retained in the text of the Agreement and the Agreed Minutes, rather than placed in the negotiating record.

13. Mr. Chang stated that the Korean negotiators would make their specific views on this matter known at a later meeting. Briefly expressed, they were of the opinion that the enumeration in the Agreed Minute overlapped that contained in paragraph 9, which was extensive, and that the enumeration in the Agreed Minute could therefore be incorporated into the negotiating record.

14. The negotiators then resumed paragraph by paragraph examination of the texts, beginning with paragraph 3(b). The use of the term "military authorities of the United States" in the Korean draft, as compared with "authorities of the United States" in the U.S. draft was found to occur in paragraphs 4, 5(a), 5(b), 6(a), 6(b), 7(a) and 7(b). It was agreed that when the question of usage was finally decided, the same usage would be used in all of these paragraphs.

15. Subparagraphs (b) and (c) of paragraph 3 were found to be identical. In paragraph 4, it was noted that the word "armed" had been omitted from the phrase "armed forces" in the Korean draft. Mr. Habib pointed out that the term "armed forces" is used throughout the Agreement and should be considered, therefore, to be the standard usage.

16. In paragraph 5(a), Mr. Habib pointed out that the U.S. draft uses the language "have custody" while the Korean draft uses "exercise jurisdiction". This difference arises out of the differing provisions in the two drafts with regard to custody. When the question of language relating to custody is settled, agreement on the language of paragraph 5(a) will be almost automatic.

17. Mr. Habib noted that paragraph 5(b) of the Korean draft omitted the word "promptly". The U.S. negotiators believed that it was important that there should be prompt notification of arrest. Mr. Chang stated that the Korean negotiators believed this to be a reciprocal matter and that if the U.S. military authorities promptly notified the ROK authorities, as provided for in paragraph 5(c) of the Korean draft, the ROK authorities would reciprocate.

18. Mr. Habib replied that paragraph 5(c) of the Korean draft had no counterpart in the U.S. draft. Nor did it have any precedents in the NATO Agreement or the Agreement with Japan, the reason being that it imposes on the U.S. military forces an onerous requirement which serves no fundamental purpose. The absence of such a provision has created no problems in the countries mentioned but its inclusion in this Agreement would undoubtedly create problems. Why did the Korean negotiators wish to include it? Mr. Chang replied that he would give the Korean views on this question at a subsequent meeting.

0245

19. Mr. Habib pointed out that the U.S. draft of paragraph 5(c) used the phrase "a dependent" instead of the phrase "their dependents" which appeared in the Korean draft. The U.S. negotiators considered "a dependent" to be standard usage and preferable. Mr. Chang said the Korean negotiators accepted usage of the phrase "a dependent".

20. With regard to paragraph 5(c) of the U.S. draft and its counterpart, 5(d) of the Korean draft, Mr. Habib stated that in these provisions the question of custody arises. Whereas, the U.S. language provides procedure for retention of custody by the U.S. authorities, the Korean language is a considerable revision of the similar paragraphs in the NATO and Japanese Agreements and provides for a handing over to Korean custody upon the issuance of a warrant. Mr. Habib added that the U.S. negotiators do not believe that retention of custody by the U.S. authorities will interfere with the course of justice. On the contrary, they believe that such a provision has much to commend it. This is a matter of major, substantial interest to the U.S. Government. The U.S. authorities have reservations about existing Korean facilities for both pre-trial and post-trial custody. He noted that the proposal for post-trial custody, contained in the last sentence of the U.S. draft of paragraph 5(c), was a response to indications given by earlier Korean negotiators that they would prefer that post-trial custody not be a Korean responsibility and that they would welcome a provision such as this one. The U.S. negotiators believed that

neither pre-trial nor post-trial custody by the U.S. authorities would interfere with the judicial proceedings. Furthermore, they saw many advantages to the proposal.

21. Mr. Chang asked whether the phrase in the U.S. draft "pending completion of all judicial proceedings" was intended to include all the proceedings of the trial or trials up to final sentencing. If that were the case, the phrase "until custody is requested by the authorities of the Republic of Korea " would have no meaning at all. Mr. Habib replied that the phrase meant until all appellate proceedings have been completed.

22. It was noted that paragraph 6(a) and (b) and paragraph 7(a) were identical except for the aforementioned inclusion of the word "military" from before the word "authorities" in the Korean draft.

23. In paragraph 7(b), Mr. Habib noted that there were two additional sentences in the U.S. draft, relating back to paragraph 5(c). If agreement were reached on post-trial custody, he explained, these two sentences would be essential, since without them the U.S. authorities could not carry out post-trial custody. He also pointed out that these provisions did not indicate any intention on the part of the U.S. authorities to avoid just punishment of convicted offenders.

24. It was noted that the two drafts of paragraph 8 were identical, except for the inclusinn of "military" and the omission of "armed" in the Korean draft and the addition in the U.S. draft of the words "his sentence has been remitted or suspended, or he". In this connection, Mr. Chang requested an explanation of the terms

0247

suspension, remission, and pardon, which was provided by Colonel Crawford.

25. It was noted that the two drafts of paragraph 9 were identical, except for some minor changes of wording in subparagraphs (e) and (f) of the Korean draft.

26. It was noted that the two drafts of paragraph 10(a) were identical. Mr. Habib noted that paragraph 10 (b) of the Korean draft would not give the U.S. armed forces the authority to maintain discipline and order among other elements of the United Nations Command, such as the Thai and Turk contingents. Noting that the situation in this regard in Korea was perhaps unique, Mr. Habib pointed out that the U.S. draft was also not satisfactory. However, the U.S. draft did provide additional authority to the U.S. military police to ensure the security of members of the U.S. armed forces outside of their facilities and areas. He said the U.S. negotiators would consider this matter and submit suggested changes at a later date.

27. Mr. Habib pointed out that there was no counterpart in the Korean draft to paragraph 11 in the U.S. draft. Mr. Chang replied that the Korean negotiators had not yet decided whether to agree to the inclusion of this paragraph in the Criminal Jurisdiction Article or to make it a separate article. When they reached a decision, they would table their proposed draft.

28. Mr. Habib pointed out that there also was no counterpart in the Korean draft for paragraph 12

of the U.S. draft. He said that provisions such as those in paragraph 12 were normal in such agreements. Mr. Chang replied that the Korean negotiators agreed in principle with the provisions of paragraph 12.

29. Mr. Chang asked if it would be possible for the U.S. negotiators to provide the Korean negotiators with the texts of the arrangements, agreements, and practices referred to in the preamble to the Agreed Minutes in the U.S. draft. Mr. Habib replied that there was no precise and complete text which applied to current arrangements or practices. It was agreed that the Korean negotiators should meet informally with Colonel Crawford for an explanation of existing arrangements and practices.

30. It was decided to leave paragraph by paragraph discussion of the Agreed Minutes until the next meeting, which was scheduled for April 17 at 2:00 p.m.

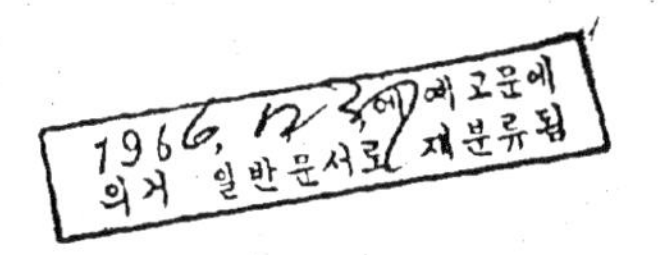

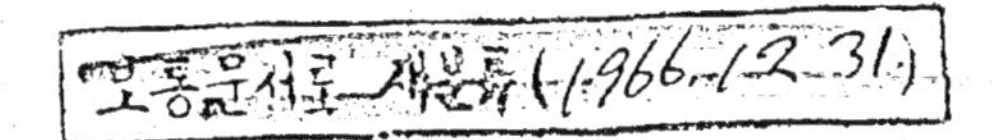

0249

6. 제50차 회의, 4.23

0250

SOFA NEGOTIATION

Agenda for the 50th Session

15:00 April 23,

1. Continuation of Discussions on:

   a. Criminal Jurisdiction Article

2. Other Business

3. Agenda and Date of the Next Meeting

4. Press Release

0251

기 안 용 지

자체 통제	외무사무관 김봉기	기안처	미주과 이근팔	전화번호	근거서류접수일자
	과장	국장	차관	장관	
관계관 서명					
기안 년월일	1964. 4. 24.	시행 년월일		보존 년한	정서기장
분류 기호	외구미 722.2	전체 통제			
경유 수신 참조	대통령 (참조: 비서실장) 국무총리			발신	장관
제목	제 50 차 주둔군지위협정 체결 교섭 실무자회의 보고				

1964. 4. 23. 하오 3 시 부터 동 4 시 45 분 까지 외무부 제 1 회의실에서 개최된 제 50 차 주둔군지위협정 체결 교섭 실무자회의에서 토의된 내용을 별첨과 같이 보고합니다.

유 첨: 제 50 차 주둔군지위협정 체결 교섭 실무자회의 보고서 1 부. 끝.

보통문서로 재분류(1966.12.31.)

1966,12.31에 예고문에 의거 일반문서로 재분류됨

발송 1964. 4. 28 외무부

승인서식 1—1—3 (11 00900—03) (195mm×265mm16절지)

0252

제 50 차

한.미간 주둔군지위협정 체결 교섭 실무자회의

보 고 서

1. 일 시: 1964년 4월 23일 하오 3시부터 동 4시 45분 까지.

2. 장 소: 외무부 제 1 회의실

3. 토의사항:

형사재판관할권

1.) 우리측은 미측이 주장하는 피의자의 권리 중 우리 나라 헌법과 관계 법령에 의하여 한국법정에서 재판을 받는 모든 자에게 이미 보장된 권리와의 중복을 피하기 위하여 중복되는 권리를 초안으로 부터 삭제할 것을 주장하고 기타 우리 나라 형사소송제도에 위배되는 권리는 수정 또는 삭제할 것을 제의하였는데 미측은 피의자의 권리는 한국의 헌법과 기타 법령에서 보장되었다 하여도 협정중에 열거하기를 요망하고 있으며 또한 형사소송제도에 위배되는 권리일지라도 교섭에 따라 합의되면 특례법 제정을 통하여서라도 보장하여 줄 것을 주장하고 우리측 제안을 검토하여 보겠다고 하였다.

2.) 미측이 제 49 차 회의에서 만약 한국측이 미군지휘관이 발행한 공무집행중 범죄 여부에 관한 증명서는 최종적인 증명력을 갖는다고 규정한 미측 규정을 수락한다면 우리측이 제안한 바에 따라 공무집행에 관한 정의를 미국동군이 규정한 원문 대로 합의의사록에 규정할 것을 제의한데 대하여 우리측은 정의와 결정권자에 관한 것은 별개의 문제임으로 정의에만 한정하여 미측제안 대로 회의록에서 규정할 것을 주장하였으나 미측은 한국측의 결정권자에 관한 대안 제시 때 까지 태도를 보류하겠다고 하였다.

3.) (1) 미측이 전투지역 내에서 발생하는 미군인 군속 및 가족에 관한 범죄에 대하여 전속적 관할권을 행사하겠다는 주장,

(2) 계엄령이 선포된 지역에서역시 미군인, 군속, 및 가족에 대하여 전속적 관할권을 행사하겠다는 주장, 및

(3) 한국외에서 발생한 범죄에 관하여 한국의 관할권이 미군인, 군속, 및 가족에 대하여 미칠 수 없다는 주장등에 대하여 우리측이 수락할 수 없음으로 대안을 제시할 것임을 밝혔다.

0253

64-3-16

64-3-16 (2)　　미국.오 110-11 (2)

0254

4.) 기타 양측은 쌍방 초안의 합의의사록 1항부터 9항까지 차의점을 대조 검토하였으며 다음 기회에 토의를 계속하기로 하였다.

4. 기타 사항: 차기 회의 일자: 1964년 5월 1일 하오 2시부터. 끝

보통문서로 재분류(1966.12.31.)

1966, 12, 31에 예고문에 의거 일반문서로 재분류됨

0255

(64-3-6)

0256

April 23, 1964

1. Mr. Chang opened the meeting by introducing Major YI Kae-hun, who was sitting in for Colonel Kim Won-kil.

2. ~~Turning to~~ Taking up the Criminal Jurisdiction Article, Mr. Chang stated that the Korean side was ready to respond to the remarks made by the United States negotiators at the previous meeting concerning trial safeguards. Mr. Chang then made the following statement:

0257

a. 1. The provision of Re paragraph 9(a) of the Korean draft in the agreed minutes guarantees to all persons on trial in the Korean courts not only those rights enumerated in paragraph 9 of the main text tabled by the United States negotiators, but also such other rights as are provided under the Constitution and laws of the Republic of Korea. Therefore, the Korean negotiators, with the view to eliminating the unnecessary and duplicate enumeration, propose the deletion of the following trial safeguards and rights enumerated in the Re paragraph 9 of the U.S. agreed minutes: the first sentence of Re paragraph 9(a), the latter part of the second subparagraph of Re paragraph 9(b), Re paragraph 9(c) and (d), Re paragraph 9(f), the preamble of Re paragraph 9, additional right of subparagraphs (b), (c), (d), (g), (h), (j) and the entire provisions except the second and third provisions of subparagraph (1) of the Re paragraph 9.

b. 2. The following provisions are either objectionable or questionable from the view point of relevant laws and regulations currently in effect and our views and counter-proposals on these provisions were presented.

(1) Re paragraph 9(a)

With respect to a military tribunal provided in the second sentence of paragraph 9(a), the Korean negotiators would like to withhold their views until such time as the matter would be taken up in connection with the text Paragraph (2) at a subsequent meeting.

(2) Re paragraph 9(b)

The Korean negotiators propose to delete the sentence with respect to the right to be informed a reasonable time prior to trial of the nature of the evidence that is to be used against the accused since there is no counterpart

0258

provision in the Korean code of criminal procedures and it is contrary to the spirit of the existing Law. However, in accordance with the provisions of articles 291, 292, 293, 296 and 307 of the Korean Code of Criminal Procedure, during the proceedings of a trial, the nature of the evidence is informed to the accused.

(3) Re Paragraph 9(e)

If the United States negotiators delete the word "confidentially" from the draft, the Korean negotiators will have no objection to the right to legal representation. The present Korean system requires ~~to put~~ placing the accused under surveillance of the competent officer during the interview. However, such presence of an officer shall not in any way interfere with the right of a counsel to communicate freely with the accused.

(4) Re Paragraph 9(g)

1) The Korean negotiators guarantee that a representative of the Government, a counsel, an interpreter, and the accused himself are all given the right to be present at all of the judicial proceedings. Therefore, it is entirely within the scope of discretion on the part of such a representative whether or not to exercise the already granted right. The Korean negotiators deem it extremely unfair that the absence of a representative of his own accord nullifies the statements of the accused, whereas the absence of a representative and the admissibility of statements as valid evidence are different matters. The Korean negotiators, therefore, propose to delete the sentence "and no statement of the accused taken in the absence of such a representative shall be admissible as evidence in support of the guilt of the accused."

0259

2) The second Agreed Minute re Paragraph 9 of the Korean draft regarding a public trial should be included as an additional sentence in the Agreed Minute re Paragraph 9(g) of the U.S. draft so that the provision of that Agreed Minute may not prejudice the provisions of article 105 of the Constitution and article 53 of the Court Organization Law. While these provisions guarantee that trials and decisions of the courts shall be open to the public, they also provide that trials may be closed to the public by a court decision when there is a possibility that open, trials may disturb the public safety and order or be harmful to decent customs.

(5) Additional right (a)

The Korean negotiators are prepared to accept the U.S. draft with the understanding that U.S. side would bear the expenses incurred in accordance with the provision of Article 56-2 of the Korean Code of Criminal Procedure.

(6) Additional right (e)

The Korean negotiators propose the deletion of the subparagraph with respect to the right that the accused shall not be subject to a heavier penalty than the one that was applicable at the time the alleged criminal offense was committed. The Korean negotiators have no objection to it; however, regarding the latter part of subparagraph (e), it would be contrary to the spirit of the judicial appeal system, if a prosecutor, defender of public interests, were not permitted to appeal to a higher court when he considers the amount of punishment or the judgement of facts are not proper. Consequently, a heavier penalty may be imposed by a higher court when appeal of a prosecutor is granted. Therefore, the Korean negotiators propose the U.S. draft be replaced by the following:

0260

"shall not be subject to a heavier penalty than the one that was applicable at the time the alleged criminal offense was committed or was adjudged by the court of the first instance as the original sentence when an appeal of a case is made by or on behalf of the accused."

(7) Additional right (f)

The Korean negotiators wish to hear the clarification of the meaning of the phraseology "requirement of proof."

(8) Additional right (i)

The Korean negotiators interpret the U.S. draft as implying merely that U.S. offenders should not be subject to punishment other than the decision of a judicial court. If the interpretation is correct, and concurred in the U.S. side, the Korean side may further consider the U.S. draft.

(9) Additional right (k)

With respect to the provision of subparagraph (k), the Korean negotiators propose the following alternative draft:

"shall be entitled to request the postponement of his presence at a trial if he is physically or mentally unfit to stand trial and participate in his defense;"

The U.S. version does not preclude a possibility of abuses of such right as provided in U.S. draft by the accused. Furthermore, the Korean negotiators deem it proper for the court to give consideration to the request of the accused and approve the postponement of trial. The above proposal is also compatible with the provision of article 306 of the Korean Code of Criminal Procedure regarding the suspension of procedure of public trial on the basis of mental or physical unfitness.

0261

(10) ~~Additional right (1)~~

1) Regarding the right provided in the ~~second~~ third paragraph of the Agreed Minute re Paragraph 9, ~~provision of subparagraph (1),~~ the Korean negotiators propose the deletion of the word "improper" from the U.S. draft to avoid the ambiguity of the meaning of the word.

2) With respect to the right provided in the fourth paragraph of the Agreed Minute re Paragraph 9, ~~third provision of subparagraph (1)~~, the Korean negotiators propose the deletion of the provision for the reasons explained in the clause of additional right (e) . Article 361 and 383 of the Korean Code of Criminal Procedure enumerate reasons of appeal to an appellate or the Supreme Court respectively.

0262

3. Mr. Habib thanked the Korean negotiators for their detailed presentation of their views on this subject. He said the U.S. negotiators would study Mr. Chang's remarks carefully before making a point-by-point response. However, they would like to clarify and reach agreement on certain basic principles underlying the matter of trial safeguards. The Korean negotiators had just stated the position that rights enumerated in the Constitution of the Republic of Korea need not be enumerated in the Status of Forces Agreement. The United States negotiators were of the opinion that if certain rights are enumerated in the ROK Constitution, there is no question but that they should also be enumerated in the SOFA. This should not be considered unnecessary duplication. The first principle, therefore, on which the U.S. negotiators sought agreement was the principle that a trial safeguard or other right can be included in the SOFA, regardless of whether it is or is not stated in the ROK Constitution. The U.S. negotiators believed that the Korean negotiators were willing to agree to this principle.

4. Mr. Habib pointed out that the question of including in the SOFA rights which were not included in the body of ROK law or mentioned in the ROK Constitution was a separate matter. The grant of jurisdiction by the U.S. Government does not imply that the U.S. Government is prepared to allow its people to be subject to trial procedures contrary to U.S. law, custom or practice. The U.S. negotiators presumed that this was a subject for negotiation and that the Korean negotiators were prepared to negotiate. He pointed out that if the negotiations resulted in agreement on inclusion in the SOFA of safeguards not found in the ROK penal code but deemed necessary for the protection of members of the U.S. armed forces, the ROK penal code could be adjusted to bring it into accord with the SOFA. He reminded the negotiators that they were not negotiating the treatment of Korean citizens. They were negotiating the treatment of American servicemen who were in Korea through no choice of their own under the terms of a treaty of mutual security. As an example of the type of question under discussion, Mr. Habib pointed out that confessions obtained illegally or improperly were admitted as evidence in trials in the Republic of Korea but not in the United States.

5. Summing up, Mr. Habib stated that the U.S. negotiators sought agreement to

0263

the following two principles:

a. Rights included in the ROK Constitution can be included in the Status of Forces Agreement; and

b. Rights not mentioned in the ROK Constitution or included in Korean laws can be included in the Status of Forces Agreement.

Mr. Habib emphasized that the U.S. negotiators were not seeking any violation of the ROK Constitution but were attempting to negotiate a SOFA which would provide the safeguards for members of the U.S. armed forces which the U.S. Government considers essential. The negotiation of such an agreement is in consonance with both the ROK Constitution and the U.S. Constitution and with accepted principles of international law. The U.S. negotiators would like to hear the views of the Korean negotiators regarding these principles.

6. Mr. Chang replied that the Korean negotiators believed that the major trial safeguards were listed in paragraph 9 of the Criminal Jurisdiction Article. They believed that rights already guaranteed in Korean laws and the ROK Constitution should not be enumerated in an Agreed Minute in addition to being enumerated in the text of the article. They also wished to point out that the Agreed Minute proposed by the U.S. negotiators contained provisions not found in other status of forces agreements. The Korean position was to minimize enumeration of such rights not found in Korean laws or the ROK Constitution, since the Korean negotiators considered such safeguards to be exceptional. In general, Mr. Chang continued, the Korean negotiators had no objection to the first principle referred to by Mr. Habib. Since the U.S. negotiators had emphasized the importance which they attached to this principle, the Korean negotiators had no reason to object to it.

7. With regard to the second principle stated by Mr. Habib, Mr. Chang said that inclusion of rights not mentioned in Korean law was subject to negotiation. Inasmuch inclusion of such rights in the SOFA would necessitate amendment of the Korean laws, the Korean negotiators wished to minimize the number of such rights.

0264

8. Mr. Habib expressed satisfaction with Mr. Chang's reply.

9. Mr. Chang said the Korean negotiators found the term "improper means" to be ambiguous. How did it differ from "illegal means"? Colonel Crawford replied that "illegal means" were means that were clearly against the law. "Improper means" referred to methods and procedures that were considered by a U.S. judge to be not up to an acceptable standard. He said that the two terms were synonymous for all practical purposes.

10. Mr. Habib stated that the negotiators had established two very helpful principles. The U.S. negotiators would study the statement made by Mr. Chang at the beginning of the meeting and would present their views at the next meeting. The U.S. negotiators had always assumed that whatever provisions were finally agreed to might require Korean legislation and that the ROK Government was prepared to seek such legislation.

11. It was then agreed to begin paragraph-by-paragraph discussion of the Agreed Minutes. Mr. Habib briefly reviewed the three Agreed Minutes re Paragraph 1(b), which have no counterparts in the Korean draft. The first of these would provide for the establishment of a "combat zone". This proposal and the Korean opposition to it constitute one of the fundamental differences in the two drafts.

12. Mr. Habib pointed out that the second Agreed Minute re Paragraph 1(b) would suspend the Criminal Jurisdiction Article during periods of martial law. He said that martial law would be relevant only to Korean citizens and that there was no reason to presume any requirement that the ROK Government should exercise martial law rights over U.S. personnel. Under the provisions of the ROK Constitution, the declaration of martial law is an extraordinary procedure.

13. As a practical matter, Mr. Habib continued, the third Agreed Minute re Paragraph 1(b), which would prevent the application of the SOFA to offenses committed outside Korea, is relatively unimportant. However, it is technically desirable because Korean law provides for the punishment of such offenses.

14. Mr. Chang replied that the Korean negotiators had already explained their opposition to the establishment of a combat zone. He asked how many duty and non-duty offenses had been committed during the past year in the area which the

0265

U.S. negotiators wished to designate as a combat zone. Mr. Habib said the U.S. negotiators would provide whatever data were available.

15. With regard to martial law, Mr. Chang pointed out that it was declared only in times of national emergency and that it applied to all persons resident in the Republic of Korea, not just to ROK citizens. With regard to offenses committed outside the Republic of Korea, Mr. Chang said that the third Agreed Minute proposed by the U.S. negotiators was incompatible with Article 5 of the ROK Criminal Code. Such a provision would prejudice the judicial rights of the ROK Government and would constitute a major infringement on ROK sovereignty. Therefore, it was unacceptable. Mr. Chang stated that Article 5 provides for the punishment of aliens who violate, while outside ROK territory, ROK laws dealing with insurrection, aggression, the national flag, currency, securities, documents and seals. He pointed out that there was in other status of forces agreements no provision similar to the proposed third Agreed Minute. He said the Korean negotiators would present at a later meeting, counter-proposals to the first and second Agreed Minutes re Paragraph 1(b) proposed by the U.S. negotiators.

16. Mr. Habib replied that it was clear that the U.S. negotiators have no intention of infringing on Korean sovereignty. He again explained that conclusion of the Status of Forces Agreement would be an act of Korean sovereignty, not an infringement on it.

17. Turning to the Agreed Minute re Paragraph 2, which also had no counterpart in the Korean draft, Mr. Habib stated that this Minute would provide for voluntary waiver of jurisdiction by the ROK Government in cases in which it enjoyed exclusive jurisdiction. He said the U.S. negotiators wished to emphasize the word voluntary in this connection. Unless this provision were included in the SOFA, the U.S. authorities would be unable to assume jurisdiction if the ROK authorities wished to waive.

18. Mr. Chang replied that the Korean negotiators had no difficulty in accepting the principle of voluntary waiver of exclusive jurisdiction. However, they believed that some arrangement could be worked out without spelling it out in an Agreed

0266

Minute. Mr. Habib replied that the U.S. negotiators would explore the legality of such an arrangement.

19. Mr. Habib pointed out that the U.S. and Korean drafts of the Agreed Minute re Paragraph 2(c) were identical in substance.

20. Mr. Habib stated that another basic difference in the two drafts lay in the Agreed Minute re Paragraph 3 proposed by the U.S. negotiators. He stated that the exercise of the waiver of jurisdiction has developed to a high degree in the countries where the United States has status of forces agreements. In Japan, for instance, over 90% of the cases are waived by the Japanese Government. The U.S. negotiators believe that the Korean authorities do not intend to try all cases and do intend to exercise the right of waiver. The U.S. Agreed Minute would provide that the ROK Government could seek a recall of waiver in those cases in which it wished to exercise jurisdiction. The presumption in the Korean draft is that in cases of particular importance to the ROK Government, it will not waive its jurisdiction. In the U.S. draft, the presumption is that in such cases, the ROK Government will recall its waiver. The ROK Government is interested in establishing its right to exercise jurisdiction; this would be spelled out in the text of the Article. The U.S. negotiators are interested in obtaining a maximum degree of waiver in order to maintain discipline and order among the U.S. armed forces.

21. Mr. Chang replied that the ROK authorities, as he had already indicated, were willing to waive in as many cases as other governments. The status of forces agreements with Japan and the NATO countries do not contain this provision; yet they waive jurisdiction in a high percentage of cases. There is no reason why the Korean authorities should not do the same. Furthermore, the Korean negotiators did not like this particular provision because it would not permit them to exercise the right of recall of waiver without going through the Joint Committee. The Korean negotiators would present a counter-proposal at the next meeting.

22. Turning to the Agreed Minutes re Paragraph 3(a), Mr. Habib stated that the first of these reflected the concern of the U.S. negotiators over the fact that the Korean draft of the Criminal Jurisdiction Article would provide that members of the

0267

U.S. armed forces would be subject to treatment different from that to which members of the ROK armed forces would be subject. Korean soldiers would be subject to trial by court martial for the same offenses for which U.S. soldiers would be subject to trial by Korean civil courts. He asked the Korean negotiators to consider the case of two friends, one an American soldier, the other a KATUSA soldier who were spending some off-duty time together and happened to get into a fight with some third party. The KATUSA soldier would be tried by court martial but the American would be haled before a Korean court, under the provisions of the Korean draft.

23. Regarding the second Agreed Minute re Paragraph 3(a), Mr. Habib reminded the Korean negotiators that the U.S. negotiators had made a proposal at the last meeting to agree to insert the definition of official duty into the negotiating record, provided the Korean negotiators would accept the second Agreed Minute re Paragraph 3(a) in the U.S. draft. He asked for the comments of the Korean negotiators regarding this proposal.

24. Mr. Chang replied that the Korean negotiators believed that the definition of official duty should be considered to be a separate matter from that of the issuance of a duty certificate. They did not agree, therefore, to the proposal of the U.S. negotiators. However, they had no objection to inclusion in the summary record of the definition of official duty tabled by the U.S. negotiators at the previous meeting without reffering to the issuance of a duty certificate. They would present a counter-proposal at the next meeting.

25. Mr. Habib stated that in principle, the U.S. negotiators had no objection to the Agreed Minute re Paragraph 4 in the Korean draft, to which there was no counterpart in the U.S. draft. However, the word "dependents" was missing. The U.S. negotiators would comment further on this matter after consulting Washington.

26. Mr. Habib stated that the Agreed Minute re Paragraph 5(b) in the Korean draft was related to the question of pre-trial custody. From the point of view of the U.S. negotiators, this Agreed Minute was not necessary. However, when a decision was finally reached on pre-trial custody, the fate of this Agreed Minute would be determined.

27. Turning to the Agreed Minutes re Paragraph 6, Mr. Habib stated that the first Minute of the Korean draft was much too broad in definition, for it would make officers of the United States subject to account before Korean courts for their conduct of the official business of the United States and could require them to bring

0268

official records of the United States into court in response to a summons. He said such a provision was not found in any other SOFA. The U.S. negotiators believed it to be an unreasonable requirement. Also, the second Agreed Minute of the Korean draft would place an obligation on witnesses somewhat similar to extradition proceedings. The U.S. negotiators did not believe that the Korean negotiators really intended that the U.S. armed forces would be obligated to return a serviceman from any place in the world if he were wanted as a witness in the course of an investigation or trial in Korea.

28. Mr. Habib pointed out that Agreed Minute #3 re Paragraph 6 in the U.S. draft has a precedent in the SOFA with the Federal Republic of Germany. The experience of the U.S. armed forces has shown that occasionally an official of either government may be summoned to testify and may be asked questions which affect the security of his government. The U.S. negotiators believe that the Korean negotiators would not want a Korean official to disclose such matters before a U.S. court-martial. Nor does the U.S. Government want its officials to be forced to disclose such matters before Korean courts.

29. Finally, Mr. Habib pointed out that while courts-martial in the United States have the authority to issue a summons, they cannot do so in Korea. Therefore, the U.S. negotiators, in the fifth paragraph of Agreed Minute #1 re Paragraph 6, were proposing language to make this possible through the offices of the ROK Government.

30. Mr. Chang the term "military exigency" used in Agreed Minute #1 re Paragraph 6 of the U.S. draft. requested an explanation of .

31. Mr. Habib replied that the certificate provided for by the U.S. draft would state why a witness could not appear at the exact time for which he had been summoned and how long he would be unavailable. The U.S. armed forces would not be arbitrary in this matter and would not avail themselves of this provision in a capricious manner. Under the circumstances in which the U.S. armed forces were present in Korea, it was quite possible that his military duties would prevent a soldier from appearing as a witness at the exact time or on the precise day specified

0269

in a summons. He said that this provision was intended to apply to individual cases and did not carry any connotation of general emergency conditions.

32. Mr. Chang remarked that the U.S. draft of this Agreed Minute referred to both witnesses and defendants. Mr. Habib replied that the U.S. armed forces would be bound by this provision to produce the defendant as well as witnesses. Mr. Chang replied that the Korean negotiators would give their views regarding this Agreed Minute at the next meeting. At this point, the meeting was adjourned.

33, It was agreed to hold the next meeting on May 1 at 2:00 p.m.

JOINT SUMMARY RECORD OF THE 50TH SESSION

1. Time and Place: 3:00 - 4:45 P.M. April 23, 1964
   at the Foreign Ministry's Conference Room (No.1)

2. Attendants:

ROK Side:

Mr. Chang, Sang Moon	Director European and American Affairs Bureau
Mr. Koo, Choong Whay	Chief, American Section Ministry of Foreign Affairs
Mr. Oh, Jae Hee	Chief, Treaty Section Ministry of Foreign Affairs
Mr. Chung, Tai Kyun	Chief Prosecutor's Section Prosecutor's Bureau Ministry of Justice
Mr. Lee, Myung Hi	Prosecutor Prosecutor's Bureau Ministry of Justice
Maj. Lee, Kye Hoon	Military Affairs Section Ministry of National Defense
Mr. Lee, Keun Pal (Rapporteur and Interpreter)	3rd Secretary Ministry of Foreign Affairs
Mr. Lee, Kae Chul	3rd Secretary Ministry of Foreign Affairs
Mr. Park, Won Chul	3rd Secretary Ministry of Foreign Affairs
Mr. Kim, Nai Sung	Staff Officer Europe Section Ministry of Foreign Affairs

U.S. Side:

Mr. Philip C. Habib	Counselor American Embassy
Brig. Gen. G.G. O'Connor	Deputy Chief of Staff 8th U.S. Army
Col. Howard Smigelow	Deputy Chief of Staff 8th U.S. Army

0271

Col. Kenneth C. Crawford	Staff Judge Advocates Office 8th U.S. Army
Capt. John Wayne	Assistant Chief of Staff USN/K
Mr. Benjamin A. Fleck (Rapporteur and Press Officer)	First Secretary American Embassy
Mr. Robert A. Lewis	2nd Secretary American Embassy
Mr. James Sartorius	2nd Secretary American Embassy
Maj. Robert D. Peckham	Staff Officer JAG 8th U.S. Army
Mr. Robert A. Kinney	J-5 8th U.S. Army
Mr. Kenneth Campen	Interpreter

1. Mr. Chang opened the meeting by introducing Major YI Kae-hun, who was sitting in for Colonel Kim Won-kil.

2. Taking up the Criminal Jurisdiction Article, Mr. Chang stated that the Korean side was ready to respond to the remarks made by the United States negotiators at the previous meeting concerning trial safeguards. Mr. Chang then made the following statement:

a. The provision of Agreed Minute #1 re Paragraph 9 of the Korean draft guarantees to all persons on trial in Korean courts not only those rights enumerated in paragraph 9 of the main text tabled by the United States negotiators, but also such other rights as are provided under the Constitution and laws of the Republic of Korea. Therefore, the Korean negotiators, with the view to eliminating unnecessary and duplicate enumeration, propose the deletion of the following trial safeguards and rights enumerated in the U.S. agreed minutes: the first sentence of the Agredd Minute re Paragraph 9(a), the latter part of the second paragraph of the Agreed Minute re Paragraph

9(b), the Agreed Minute re Paragraph 9(c) and (d), the Agreed Minute re Paragraph 9(f), the first paragraph of the Agreed Minute re Paragraph 9, the additional rights enumerated in subparagraphs (b), (c), (d), (g), (h), (j) and the remaining paragraphs of the Agreed Minute re Paragraph 9, except the third and fourth paragraphs.

b. The following provisions are either objectionable or questionable from the view point of relevant laws and regulations currently in effect and our views and counter-proposals on these provisions were presented.

(1) Re paragraph 9(a)

With respect to a military tribunal provided in the second sentence of the Agreed Minute re Paragraph 9(a), the Korean negotiators would like to withhold their views until such time as the matter would be taken up in connection with the text of Paragraph 2 at a subsequent meeting.

(2) Re paragraph 9(b)

The Korean negotiators propose to delete the sentence with respect to the right to be informed a reasonable time prior to trial of the nature of the evidence that is to be used against the accused since there is no counterpart provision in the Korean code of criminal procedures and it is contrary to the spirit of the existing Law. However, in accordance with the provisions of articles 291, 292, 293, 296 and 307 of the Korean Code of Criminal Procedure, during the proceedings of a trial, the nature of the evidence is informed to the accused.

(3) Re paragraph 9(e)

If the United States negotiators delete the word "confidentially" from the draft, the Korean

0273

negotiators will have no objection to the right to legal representation. The present Korean system requires placing the accused under surveillance of the competent officer during the interview. However, such presence of an officer shall not in any way interfere with the right of a counsel to communicate freely with the accused.

(4) Re paragraph 9(g)

1) The Korean negotiators guarantee that a representative of the Government, a counsel, an interpreter, and the accused himself are all given the right to be present at all of the judicial proceedings. Therefore, it is entirely within the scope of discretion on the part of such a representative whether or not to exercise the already granted right. The Korean negotiators deem it extremely unfair that the absence of a representative of his own accord nullifies the statements of the accused, whereas the absence of a representative and the admissibility of statements as valid evidence are different matters. The Korean negotiators, therefore, propose to delete the sentence "and no statement of the accused taken in the absence of such a representative shall be admissible as evidence in support of the guilt of the accused."

2) The second Agreed Minute re Paragraph 9 of the Korean draft regarding a public trial should be included as an additional sentence in the Agreed Minute re Paragraph 9(g) of the U.S. draft so that the provision of that Agreed Minute may not prejudice the provisions of article 105 of the Constitution and article 53 of the Court Organization Law. While these provisions guarantee that trials and decisions of the courts shall be open

0274

to the public, they also provide that trials may be closed to the public by a court decision when there is a possibility that open trials may disturb the public safety and order or be harmful to decent customs.

(5) Additional right (a)

The Korean negotiators are prepared to accept the U.S. draft with the understanding that U.S. side would bear the expenses incurred in accordance with the provision of Article 56-2 of the Korean Code of Criminal Procedure.

(6) Additional right (e)

The Korean negotiators propose the deletinn of the subparagraph with respect to the right that the accused shall not be subject to a heavier penalty than the one that was applicable at the time the alleged criminal offense was committed. The Korean negotiators have no objection to it; however, regarding the latter part of subparagraph (e), it would be contrary to the spirit of the judicial appeal system, if a prosecutor, defender of public interests, were not permitted to appeal to a higher court when he considers the amount of punishment or the judgement of facts are not proper. Consequently, a heavier penalty may be imposed by a higher court when appeal of a prosecutor is granted. Therefore, the Korean negotiators propose the U.S. draft be replaced by the following:

"shall not be subject to a heavier penalty than the one that was applicable at the time the alleged criminal offense was committed or was adjudged by the court of the first instance as the original sentence when an appeal of a case is made by or on behalf of the accused."

0275

(7) Additional right (f)

The Korean negotiators wish to hear clarification of the meaning of the phraseology "requirement of proof."

(8) Additional right (i)

The Korean negotiators interpret the U.S. draft as implying merely that U.S. offenders should not be subject to punishment other than the decision of a judicial court. If the interpretation is correct, and concurred in the by U.S. side, the Korean side may further consider the U.S. draft.

(9) Additional right (k)

With respect to the provision of sub-paragraph (k), the Korean negotiators propose the following alternative draft:

"shall be entitled to request the postponement of his presence at a trial if he is physically or mentally unfit to stand trial and participate in his defense;"

The U.S. version does not preclude a possibility of abuses of such right as provided in U.S. draft by the accused. Furthermore, the Korean negotiators deem it proper for the court to give consideration to the request of the accused and approve the postponement of trial. The above proposal is also compatible with the provision of article 306 of the Korean Code of Criminal Procedure regarding the suspension of procedure of public trial on the basis of mental or physical unfitness.

(10) 1) Regarding the right provided in the third paragraph of the Agreed Minute re Paragraph 9, the Korean negotiators propose the deletion of the word "improper" from the U.S. draft to avoid the ambiguity of the meaning of the word.

0276

2) With respect to the right provided in the fourth paragraph of the Agreed Minute re Paragraph 9, the Korean negotiators propose the deletion of the provision for the reason explained in the clause of additional right (e). Article 361 and 383 of the Korean Code of Criminal Procedure enumerate reasons of appeal to an appellate or the Supreme Court respectively.

3. Mr. Habib thanked the Korean negotiators for their detailed presentation of their views on this subject. He said the U.S. negotiators would study Mr. Chang's remarks carefully before making a point-by-point response. However, they would like to clarify and reach agreement on certain basic principles underlying the matter of trial safeguards. The Korean negotiators had just stated the position that rights enumerated in the Constitution of the Republic of Korea need not be enumerated in the Status of Forces Agreement. The United States negotiators were of the opinion that if certain rights are enumerated in the ROK Constitution, there is no question but that they should also be enumerated in the SOFA. This should not be considered unnecessary duplication. The first principle, therefore, on which the U.S. negotiators sought agreement was the principle that a trial safeguard or other right can be included in the SOFA, regardless of whether it is or is not stated in the ROK Constitution. The U.S. negotiators believed that the Korean negotiators were willing to agree to this principle.

4. Mr. Habib pointed out that the question of including in the SOFA rights which were not included in the body of ROK law or mentioned in the ROK Constitution was a separate matter. The grant of jurisdiction by the U.S. Government does not imply that the U.S. Government

0277

is prepared to allow its people to be subject to trial procedures contrary to U.S. law, custom or practice. The U.S. negotiators presumed that this was a subject for negotiation and that the Korean negotiators were prepared to negotiate. He pointed out that if the negotiations resulted in agreement on inclusion in the SOFA of safeguards not found in the ROK penal code but deemed necessary for the protection of members of the U.S. armed forces, the ROK penal code could be adjusted to bring it into accord with the SOFA. He reminded the negotiators that they were not negotiating the treatment of Korean citizens. They were negotiating the treatment of American servicemen who were in Korea through no choice of their own under the terms of a treaty of mutual security. As an example of the type of question under discussion, Mr. Habib pointed out that confessions obtained illegally or improperly were admitted as evidence in trials in the Republic of Korea but not in the United States.

5. Summing up, Mr. Habib stated that the U.S. negotiators sought agreement to the following two principles:

a. Rights included in the ROK Constitution can be included specifically in the Status of Forces Agreement; and

b. Rights not mentioned in the ROK Constitution or included in Korean laws can be included in the Status of Forces Agreement.

Mr. Habib emphasized that the U.S. negotiators were not seeking any violation of the ROK Constitution but were attempting to negotiate a SOFA which would provide the safeguards for members of the U.S. armed forces which the U.S. Government considers essential. The negotiation of such

0278

an agreement is in consonance with both the ROK Constitution and the U.S. Constitution and with accepted principles of international law. The U.S. ndgotiators would like to hear the views of the Korean negotiators regarding these principles.

6. Mr. Chang replied that the Korean negotiators believed that the major trial safeguards were listed in paragraph 9 of the Criminal Jurisdiction Article. They believed that rights already guaranteed in Korean laws and the ROK Constitution should not be enumerated in an Agreed Minute in addition to being enumerated in the text of the article and they considered it unnecessary duplication. They also wished to point out that the Agreed Minute proposed by the U.S. negotiators contained provisions not found in other status of forces agreements. Since the U.S. negotiators had emphasized the importance which they attached to the first principle mentioned by Mr. Habib, the Korean negotiators would take it into consideration to work out a mutually acceptable solution.

7. With regard to the second principle stated by Mr. Habib, Mr. Chang said that inclusion of rights not mentioned in Korean law was subject to negotiation. Inasmuch as inclusion of such rights in the SOFA would necessitate amendment of the Korean laws, the Korean negotiators wished to minimize the number of exceptional Laws.

8. Mr. Habib expressed satisfaction with Mr. Chang's reply.

9. Mr. Chang said the Korean negotiators found the term "improper means" to be ambiguous since they believe the meaning of the term "improper means" was included in the meaning of the term "illegal means". How did it differ from "illegal means". Colonel Crawford replied that "illegal means" were means that were clearly against

0279

the law. "Improper means" referred to methods and procedures that were considered by a U.S. judge to be not up to an acceptable standard. He said that the two terms were synonymous for all practical purposes.

10. Mr. Habib stated that the negotiators had established two very helpful principles. The U.S. negotiators would study the statement made by Mr. Chang at the beginning of the meeting and would present their views at the next meeting. The U.S. negotiators had always assumed that whatever provisions were finally agreed to might require Korean legislation and that the ROK Government was prepared to seek such legislation.

11. It was then agreed to begin paragraph-by-paragraph discussion of the Agreed Minutes. Mr. Habib briefly reviewed the three Agreed Minutes re Paragraph 1(b), which have no counterparts in the Korean draft. The first of these would provide for the establishment of a "combat zone". This proposal and the Korean opposition to it constitute one of the fundamental differences in the two drafts.

12. Mr. Habib pointed out that the second Agreed Minute re Paragraph 1(b) would suspend the Criminal Jurisdiction Article during periods of martial law. He said that martial law would be relevant only to Korean citizens and that there was no reason to presume any requirement that the ROK Government should exercise martial law rights over U.S. personnel. Under the provisions of the ROK Constitution, the declaration of martial law is an extraordinary procedure.

0280

13. As a practical matter, Mr. Habib continued, the third Agreed Minute re Paragraph 1(b), which would prevent the application of the SOFA to offenses committed outside Korea, is relatively unimportant. Howwver, it is techinically desirable because Korean law provides for the punishment of such offenses.

14. Mr. Chang replied that the Korean negotiators had already explained their opposition to the establishment of a combat zone. He asked how many duty and non-duty offenses had been committed during the past year in the area which the U.S. negotiators wished to designate as a combat zone. Mr. Habib said the U.S. negotiators would provide whatever data were available.

15. With regard to martial law, Mr. Chang pointed out that it was declared only in times of national emergency and that it applied to all persons resident in the Republic of Korea, not just to ROK citizens. With regard to offenses Committed outside the Republic of Korea, Mr. Chang said that the third Agreed Minute proposed by the U.S. negotiators was incompatible with Article 5 of the ROK Criminal Code. Such a provision would prejudice the judicial rights of the ROK Government and would constitute a major infringement on ROK sovereignty. Therefore it was unacceptable. Mr. Chang stated that Article 5 provides for the punishment of aliens who violate, while outside ROK territory, ROK laws dealing with insurrection, aggression, the national flag, currency, securities, documents and seals. He pointed out that there was in other status of forces agreements no provision similar to the proposed third Agreed Minute. He said the Korean negotiators would present at a later meeting counter-proposals to the first and second Agreed Minutes re Paragraph 1(b) proposed by the U.S. negotiators.

0281

16. Mr. Habib replied that it was clear that the U.S. negotiators have no intention of infringing on Korean sovereignty. He again explained that conclusion of the Status of Forces Agreement would be an act of Korean sovereignty, not an infringement on it.

17. Turnăng to the Agreed Minute re Paragraph 2, which also had no counterpart in the Korean draft, Mr. Hhbib stated that this Minute would provide for voluntary waiver of jurisdiction by the ROK Government in cases in which it enjoyed exclusive jurisdiction. He said the U.S. negotiators wished to emphasize the word voluntary in this connection. Unless this provision were included in the SOFA, the U.S. authorities would be unable to assume jurisdiction if the ROK authorities wished to waive.

18. Mr. Chang replied that the Korean negotiators had no difficulty in accepting the principle of voluntary waiver of exclusive jurisdiction. However, they believed that some arrangement could be worked out without spelling it out in an Agreed Minute. Mr. Habib replied that the U.S. negotiators would explore the legality of such an arrangement.

19. Mr. Habib pointed out that the U.S. and Korean drafts of the Agreed Minute re Paragraph 2(c) were identical in substance.

20. Mr. Habib stated that another basic difference in the two drafts lay in the Agreed Minute re Paragraph 3 proposed by the U.S. negotiators. He stated that the exercise of the waiver of jurisdiction has developed to a high degree in the countries where the United States has status of forces agreements. In Japan, for instance, over 90% of the cases are waivdd by the Japanese Government. The U.S. negotiators believe that the Korean authorities do not intend to try all cases and do intend to exercise

0283

the right of waiver. The U.S. Agreed Minute would provide that the ROK Government could seek a recall of waiver in those cases in which it wished to exercise jurisdiction. The presumption in the Korean draft is that in cases of particular importance to the ROK Government, it will not waive its jurisdiction. In the U.S. draft, the presumption is that in such cases, the ROK Government will recall its waiver. The ROK Government is interested in establishing its right to exercise jurisdiction; this would be spelled out in the text of the Article. The U.S. negotiators are interested in obtaining a maximum degree of waiver in order to maintain discipline and order among the U.S. armed forces.

21. Mr. Chang replied that the ROK authorities, as he had already indicated, were willing to waive in as many cases as other governments. The status of forces agreements with Japan and the NATO countries do not contain this provision; yet they waive jurisdiction in a high percentage of cases. There is no reason why the Korean authorities should not do the same. Furthermore, the Korean negotiators did not like this particular provision because it would not permit them to exercise the right of recall of waiver without going through the Joint Committee. The Korean negptiators would present a counter-proposal at the next meeting.

22. Turning to the Agreed Minutes re Paragraph 3(a), Mr. Habib stated that the first of these reflected the concern of the U.S. negotiators over the fact that the Korean draft of the Criminal Jurisdiction Article would provide that members of the U.S. armed forces would be subject to treatment different from that to which members of the ROK armed

0283

forces would be subject. Korean soldiers would be subject to trial by court martial for the same offenses for which U.S. soldiers would be subject to trial by Korean civil courts. He asked the Korean negotiators to consider the case of two friends, one an American soldier, the other a KATUSA soldier who were spending some off-duty time together and happened to get into a fight with some third party. The KATUSA soldier would be tried by court martial but the American would be haled before a Korean court, under the provisions of the Korean draft.

23. Regarding the second Agreed Minute re Paragraph 3 (a), Mr. Habib reminded the Korean negotiators that the U.S. negotiators had made a proposal at the last meeting to agree to insert the definition of official duty into the negotiating record, provided the Korean negotiators would accept the second Agreed Minute re Paragraph 3(a) in the U.S. draft. He asked for the comments of the Korean negotiators regarding this proposal.

24. Mr. Chang replied that the Korean negotiators believed that the definition of official duty should be considered to be a separate matter from that of the issuance of a duty certificate. They did not agree, therefore, to the proposal of the U.S. negotiators. However, they had no objection to inclusion in the summery record of the definition of official duty tabled by the U.S. negotiators at the previous meeting without refferring to the issuance of a duty certificate. They would present a counter-proposal at the next meeting.

25. Mr. Habib stated that in principle, the U.S. negotiators had no objection to the Agreed Minute re Paragraph 4 in the Korean draft, to which there was no

0284

counterpart in the U.S. draft. However, the word "dependents" was missing. The U.S. negotiators would comment further on this matter after consulting Washington.

26. Mr. Habib stated that the Agreed Minute re Paragraph 5(b) in the Korean draft was related to the question of pre-trial custody. From the point of view of the U.S. negotiators, this Agredd Minute was not necessary. However, when a decision was finally reached on pre-trial custody, the fate of this Agreed Minute would be determined.

27. Turning to the Agreed Minutes re Paragraph 6, Mr. Habib stated that the first Minute of the Korean draft was much too broad in definition, for it would make officers of the United States subject to account before Korean courts for their conduct of the official business of the United States and could require them to bring official records of the United States into court in response to a summons. He said such a provision was not found in any other SOFA. The U.S. negotiators believed it to be an unreasonable requirement. Also, the second Agreed Minute of the Korean draft would place an obligation on witnesses somewhat similar to extradition proceedings. The U.S. negotiators did not believe that the Korean negotiators really intended that the U.S. armed forces would be obligated to return a serviceman from any place in the world if he were wanted as a witness in the course of an investigation or trial in Korea.

28. Mr. Habib pointed out that Agreed Minute #3 re Paragraph 6 in the U.S. draft has a precedent in the SOFA with the Federal Republic of Germany. The experience of the U.S. armed forces has shown that occasionally an

0285

official of either government may be summoned to testify and may be asked questions which affect the security of his government. The U.S. negotiators believe that the Korean negotiators would not want a Korean official to disclose such matters before a U.S. court-martial. Nor does the U.S. Government want its officials to be forced to disclose such matters before Korean courts.

29. Finally, Mr. Habib pointed out that while courts-martial in the United States have the authority to issue a summons, they cannot do so in Korea. Therefore, the U.S. negotiators, in the fifth paragraph of Agreed Minute #1 re Paragraph 6, were proposing language to make this possible through the offices of the ROK Government.

30. Mr. Chang requested an explanation of the term "military exigency" used in Agreed Minute #1 re Paragraph 6 of the U.S. draft.

31. Mr. Habib replied that the certificate provided for by the U.S. draft would state why a witness could not appear at the exact time for which he had been summoned and how long he would be unavailable. The U.S. armed forces would not be arbitrary in this matter and would not avail themselves of this provision in a capricious manner. Under the circumstances in which the U.S. armed forces were present in Korea, it was quite possible that his military duties would prevent a soldier from appearing as a witness at the exact time or on the precise day specified in a summons. He said that this provision was intended to apply to individual cases and did not carry any connotation of general emergency conditions.

32. Mr. Chang remarked that the U.S. draft of this Agreed Minute referred to both witnesses and defendants.

Mr. Habib replied that the U.S. armed forces would be bound by this provision to produce the defendant as well as witnesses. Mr. Chang replied that the Korean negotiators would give their views regarding this Agreed Minute at the next meeting. At this point, the meeting was adjourned.

33. It was agreed to hold the next meeting on May 1 at 2:00 p.m.

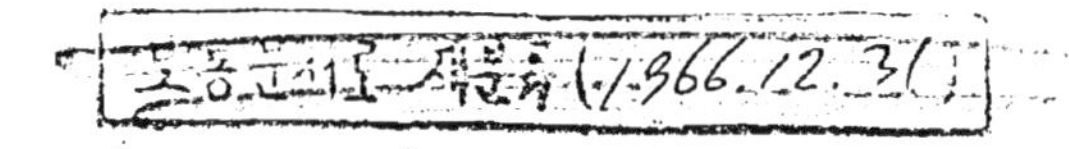

0287

정/리/보/존/문/서/목/록

<table>
<tr><td>기록물종류</td><td>문서-일반공문서철</td><td>등록번호</td><td>921
9594</td><td>등록일자</td><td>2006-07-27</td></tr>
<tr><td>분류번호</td><td>741.12</td><td>국가코드</td><td>US</td><td>주제</td><td></td></tr>
<tr><td>문서철명</td><td colspan="5">한.미국 간의 상호방위조약 제4조에 의한 시설과 구역 및 한국에서의 미국군대의 지위에 관한 협정 (SOFA) 전59권. 1966.7.9 서울에서 서명 : 1967.2.9 발효 (조약 232호) *원본</td></tr>
<tr><td>생산과</td><td>미주과/조약과</td><td>생산년도</td><td>1952 - 1967</td><td>보존기간</td><td>영구</td></tr>
<tr><td>담당과(그룹)</td><td>조약</td><td>조약</td><td>서가번호</td><td colspan="2">--</td></tr>
<tr><td>참조분류</td><td colspan="5"></td></tr>
<tr><td>권차명</td><td colspan="5">V.23 실무교섭회의, 제51-56차, 1964.5-6월</td></tr>
<tr><td>내용목차</td><td colspan="5">1. 제51차 회의, 5.5 (p.2~59)
2. 제52차 회의, 5.20 (p.60~105)
3. 제53차 회의, 5.28 (p.106~129)
4. 제54차 회의, 6.9 (p.130~161)
5. 제55차 회의, 6.19 (p.162~186)
6. 제56차 회의, 6.26 (p.187~207)

* 일지 :
1953.8.7 이승만 대통령-Dulles 미국 국무장관 공동성명
- 상호방위조약 발효 후 군대지위협정 교섭 약속
1954.12.2 정부, 주한 UN군의 관세업무협정 체결 제의
1955.1월, 5월 미국, 제의 거절
1955.4.28 정부, 군대지위협정 제의 (한국측 초안 제시)
1957.9.10 Hurter 미국 국무차관 방한 시 각서 수교 (한국측 제의 수락 요구)
1957.11.13, 26 정부, 개별 협정의 단계적 체결 제의
1958.9.18 Dawling 주한미국대사, 형사재판관할권 협정 제외 조건으로 행정협정 체결 의사 전달
1960.3.10 정부, 토지, 시설협정의 우선적 체결 강력 요구
1961.4.10 장면 국무총리-McConaughy 주한미국대사 공동성명으로 교섭 개시 합의
1961.4.15, 4.25 제1, 2차 한.미국 교섭회의 (서울)
1962.3.12 정부, 교섭 재개 촉구 공한 송부
1962.5.14 Burger 주한미국대사, 최규하 장관 면담 시 형사재판관할권 문제 제기 않는 조건으로 교섭 재개 통고
1962.9.6 한.미국 간 공동성명 발표 (9월 중 교섭 재개 합의)
1962.9.20~1965.6.7 제1-81차 실무 교섭회의 (서울)
1966.7.8 제82차 실무 교섭회의 (서울)
1966.7.9 서명
1967.2.9 발효 (조약 232호)</td></tr>
</table>

마/이/크/로/필/름/사/항

촬영연도	*롤 번호	화일 번호	후레임 번호	보관함 번호
2006-11-22	I-06-0068	08	1-207	

0001

1. 제51차 회의, 5.5

0002

공 란

공　　　란

공 란

공 란

공 란

공 란

공 란

공 란

공 란

공 란

공 란

공　란

공 란

공　　란

공 란

공 란

공 란

공 란

공 란

공 란

(HH. 4/23. 11:45. 接受.
共同部案)

再修正案

(1). 美側의 損害賠償分擔比率과 同意問題

i. 公務執行中의 不法行爲로 因한 損害賠償에 있어 賠償金의 分擔比率은 美側 75% 韓國側 25%로 한다.

ii. 賠償金이 決定되면 支給前에 美側에 通報하여 同意與否를 묻되 通報接受後 1月以內에 回報가 없으면 同意한것으로 보며 1月以內에 不同意回報가 있으면 이를 再審議한다.

再審議決定한것에 對하여는 다시 異議를 提起하지 못한다.

賠償金의 支拂은 美側에서 同意하거나 1月以內에 同意回報를 하지 아니하여 同意한것으로 看做되거나. 또는 不同意의 回報로 再審議決定하는대로 (再審議決定의 結果는 이를 美側에 通報는 하되 그同意를 받을 必要는 없음) 即時 이를 支拂한다.

0023

(2) 引受時期問題
本協定發效後 6月(또는 3月) 後에 大韓民國
法務部가 引受한다.

(3) KATUSA 와 勞務師團(KSC) 는 美側構
成員으로 본다.

(1966.12.31)

0024

US draft

Agreed Minute

With regard to any major dispute between employers except the contractors provided for in para 1 and any recognized employees or employee organization which cannot be settled through the use of existing under the provisions of this Agreement procedures of the United States armed forces, settlement shall be accomplished in the following manner:

a. The dispute shall be referred to the Office of Labor Affairs, Ministry of Health and Social Affairs, Republic of Korea, for conciliation.

b. In the event that the dispute is not settled by the procedure described in (a) above, the matter may be referred to a Special Committee appointed by the Office of Labor Affairs, Ministry of Health and Social Affairs, Republic of Korea for mediation. This committee shall be tri-partite in composition and shall consist of equal representation from the recognized employee organization, the Office of Labor Affairs, and United States Forces Korea.

c. In the event that the dispute is not settled by the procedures described in (a) and (b) above the dispute shall be referred to the Joint Committee, or such sub-committee as may be established thereunder for resolution of the dispute. (In resolving the dispute, the Joint Committee, or such sub-committee as may be established thereunder, shall give due consideration to the laws and regulations of the Republic of Korea.)

16-2

0025

R. U.S MAY/19

U.S. draft

d. During the period in which a dispute is being handled by the procedures mentioned in paras (a), (b) and (c) above recognized employee organizations and employees shall not indulge in any practices disruptive of normal work requirements.

e. Failure of any recognized employee organization or employee to abide by the decision of the Joint Committee or any sub-committees established thereunder on any dispute, or action in violation of para (d) above shall be considered just cause for the withdrawal of recognition of that organization and the discharge of that employee.

16-7

MAY, 19

0026

AGREED MINUTE

With regard to any major dispute between employers and any recognized employee organization, settlement shall be accomplished in the following manner:

a. The dispute shall first be referred to the United States armed forces for settlement through existing procedures of those forces.

b. In the event that the dispute is not settled by the procedure described in (a) above, the matter may be referred to the Office of Labor Affairs, Ministry of Health and Social Affairs, Republic of Korea. [The employers will consult and cooperate with the Office of Labor Affairs and will give due consideration to any recommendation of that office in the settlement of the dispute.]

c. In the event the dispute is not settled by the procedures described in (a) ~~and (b)~~ above [the dispute shall be referred to the Joint Committee, or such sub-committee as may be established thereunder, for resolution.] in conformity with the laws and regulations of the Republic of Korea.

0027

Acceptable with conditions

2. Employers will recruit employees to the maximum extent practicable with the assistance of the authorities of the Republic of Korea. In case employers exercise direct recruitment and employment of employees, employers will provide such relevant information as may be required for labor administration to the Office of Labor Affairs of the Republic of Korea.

0028

The ROK counter proposal on Labor problem

~~Re paragraph 2~~

The following paragraph is to be included in the Agreed Minutes: 4 Re paragraph 2 It is mutually agreed that if there arise any difficulties on the part of the United States Military authorities to be precisely conform with the labour laws of the Republic of Korea, the Joint Committee shall make its decisions in conformity with the laws and regulations of the Republic of Korea. ~~In case,~~ a decisions can not be made at the said Committee, the matter may be referred to the respective Governments for its final solution through diplomatic channel.

16-8

0029

duplication

AGREED MINUTE

Should the authorities of the Republic of Korea determine that in contravention of the obligation of the United States armed forces under paragraph 3 of this Article, a procedure of the United States armed forces does not conform with a provision of Korean labor law, practice or custom; or should any grievance arise between an employee and an employer, which grievance has not been settled under the grievance procedures of the United States armed forces, the matter shall be referred to the Joint Committee, or such sub-committee as may be established thereunder, for resolution.

16-9

0030

Unaccepted

번호 3089

3. To the extent not inconsistent with the provisions of this article, and the basic management needs of the United States armed forces, the conditions of employment, compensation, and labor-management practices established by the United States armed forces for their employees will conform with the labor laws, customs and practices of the Republic of Korea.

April 30. 64

0031

SOFA NEGOTIATION

Agenda for the 51st Session

14:00 May 5, 1964

1. Continuation of Discussions on:
    a. Customs Article
    b. Claims Article
    c. Local Procurement Article
2. Other Business
3. Agenda and Date of the Next Meeting
4. Press Release

0032

51차

한국제안

51차회의 (64.5.5) Agreed Minutes (Claims Article)

71차 M.S. replace

1. The amount to be paid to each claimant, under the provisions of paragraph 5(b) of this Article, except the cases being determined by adjudication, shall be communicated to the authorities of the United States before the payment is made.

In case any reply in favour of the decision is received from the U.S. side, or in default of a reply within one month of receipt of the communication envisaged above, the amount decided by the Korean Claims Authorities shall be regarded as agreed upon between the both Governments.

If, however, the authorities of the United States disagree to the amount decided by the Korean Claims Authorities and reply to this effect within the one-month period, the Korean Claims Authorities shall re-examine the case concerned. The amount decided as a result of the re-examination shall be final and conclusive. The Korean Claims Authorities shall notify the authorities of the United States of the result of re-examination as early as practicable.

The amount agreed upon between the both Governments or decided through the re-examination shall be paid to the claimant concerned without delay.

0033

2. The provisions of paragraph 5 of this Article will become effective after six months from the date of entry into force of this Agreement. Until such time the United States agrees to pay just and reasonable compensation in settlement of civil claims (other than contractual claims) arising out of acts or omissions of members of the United States armed forces done in the performance of official duty or out of any other act, omission or occurrence for which the United States armed forces are legally responsible. In making such payments United States authorities would exercise the authority provided under United States laws relating to Foreign Claims and regulations issued thereunder. In settling claims which are described as arising "..... out of any act, omission or occurrence for which the United States armed forces are legally responsible", United States authorities will take into consideration local law and practice.

0034

3. For the purpose of paragraph 5 of this Article, members of the Korean Augmentation to the United States Army (KATUSA) and members of the Korean Service Corps (KSC) shall be considered respectively as members and employees of the United States armed forces.

0035

美側非公式提議

(1) The costs under paragraph 5 to be borne by the United States shall not exceed 75% of the amounts (mutually agreed upon by claims authorities of both governments) as being properly payable under that paragraph.

0036

(B)

(2) The provisions of paragraph 5 of this article will become effective upon mutual agreement in the Joint Committee that the claims service of the Government of the Republic of Korea is prepared to undertake the procedures provided for in that paragraph. Until such time the United States agrees to pay just and reasonable compensation in settlement of civil claims (other than contractual claims) arising out of acts or omissions of members of the United States Forces done in the performance of official duty or out of any other act, omission or occurrence for which the United States Forces are legally responsible. In making such payments United States authorities would exercise the broad authority provided under United States laws relating to Foreign Claims and regulations issued thereunder. In settling claims which are described as arising ". . . . out of any act, omission or occurrence for which the United States Forces are legally responsible", United States authorities will take into consideration local law and practice.

0037

(D)

(3) For the purposes of paragraph 5 of this Article, members of the Korean Augmentation to the United States Army (KATUSA) shall be considered as members of the United States armed forces, and members of the Korean Service Corps (KSC) shall be considered as employees of the armed forces of the Republic of Korea.

0038

기 안 지

기 안 자	미주과 황영재	전화번호		공 보	필 요	불필요
	과장	국장	차관	장관		
협조자 서명					보존 년한	
기안 년월일	1964. 5. 6.	시행 년월일		통제관	정 서	기 장
분류기호 문서번호	외구미 722.2					
경유 수신 참조	대통령 (참조 : 비서실장) 국무총리 (참조 : 비서실장)	발 신	외무부 장관			
제 목	제 51 차 주둔군지위협정 체결 교섭 실무자회의 보고					

1964년 5월 5일 하오 2시부터 동 4시까지 외무부 제 1 회의실에서 개최된 제 51 차 주둔군지위협정 체결 교섭 실무자회의에서 토의된 내용을 별첨과 같이 보고합니다.

유첨 : 제 51 차 주둔군지위협정 체결 교섭 실무자회의 보고서 1 부, 끝

보통문서로 재분류 (1966.12.31)

공통서식 1—1 (갑) (16절지)

0039

제 51 차

한. 미 주둔군지위협정 체결교섭 실무자회의

보 고 서

1. 일 시: 1964 년 5 월 5 일 14:00 시 부터 16:00 시 까지

2. 장 소: 외무부 제 1 회의실

3. 토의 사항:

가. 현지조달 조항:

(1) 직접조달과 미군의 최종적인 사용을 위하여 계약자가 조달하는데 관한 정의를 규정하는 합의 의사록의 추가,

(2) 미군이 면세조치 증명을 사전에 발급토록하는 어구의 삽입,

(3) 기타 한. 미 양측의 교섭 및 증명발급당국에 대한 용어의 통일,

(4) 계약자를 통한 현지조달은 합동위원회에서 별도로 합의하지 않는한 최종적인 단계의 구매만을 의미 한다,

(5) 통행세의 면제는 집단 구매에만 해당 시킨다.

이상 한국측 제안에 대하여, 한. 미 양측은 (1), (2) 및 (3)에 완전합의 하였으며, (4) 및 (5)에 대하여 미국측은,

(1) 합동위원회에서 면세여부에 관하여 토의중에는 과세조치를 안하며,

(2) 민간 계약을 하고 개인이 일정한 절차에 따라 수송기관을 이용하는 경우는 집단구매로 인정하여 통행세를 면제 시킨다는 것을,

양해사항으로 한국측이 수락할것을 조건으로 합의할것임을 제의함.

이 문제에 대하여는 차기회의에서 토의하기로 하였으며, 한국측이 상기 미국측 제의를 수락하므로서 현지조달 조항은 완전합의에 이르게 되는 것임.

나. 관세 조항:

(1) 우리측은 비세출기관으로 수입되는 물자에 대한 세관검사권 유보에 대한 입장에는 변함이 없음을 재 천명하고 그 이유를 상세히 설명함.

0040

(2) 미국측은 비세출기관으로 수입되는 물자를 기타 군수물자와

0041

별도로 취급할수는 없으며 미군의 필요 불가결한 부분임을 역설 함.

(3) 양측 교섭 대표들은 비세출기관을 통한 불법적인 물자의 수입을 막자는 목적에는 의견의 차이가 없으며, 단지 그 방법에 차이가 있음을 시인하고 앞으로 상호 합의할수있는 방법에 관하여 더욱 연구 하기로 함.

다. 청구권 조항:

(1) 한국측은 미측대표들과의 비공식 회의 내용을 참고로 하여 한국측 청구권조항에 대한 합의 의사록으로서 요지 아래와 같이 제안함:

1) 공무집행중 제 3 자에 대한 청구 사정금액에 대하여는 미국측이 한국 송무당국에 재심을 요청할수있으며,

2) 상기 제 3 자에 대한 청구 규정은 협정 발표 6개월 후에 효력을 갖도록 할것과, KATUSA와 KSC 는 미군의 구성원 및 피고용자로 간주 할것.

(2) 미국측은 우리측 제안을 검토한후 회답하기로 함.

4. 기타 사항:

차기 회의 일자: 1964 년 5 월 12 일 14:00 시. 끝

0042

64-3-4/

64-3-17 (2) 미국.군 110-10 (2)

0043

1. Mr. Chang opened the meeting by introducing Mr. Cho, Choong Hoon, Chief of the Customs Section, Ministry of Finance, who was attending the meeting in place of Mr. Sin Kwan-sop; and Mr. Hwang, Young Chae of the America Section, Ministry of Foreign Affairs. Mr. Habib welcomed these gentlemen to the negotiations.

Local Procurement

2. Taking up the article on Local Procurement, Mr. Habib recalled that at the 66th negotiating meeting the Korean negotiators had made certain suggestions for revision of the U.S. draft. He said the U.S. negotiators were prepared to respond to those suggestions. The U.S. negotiators also wished to introduce some non-substantive changes in wording in Paragraph 1 in order to make the language of that paragraph consistent with the wording of Paragraphs 2 and 3 and with the new Agreed Minute #4 proposed by the Korean negotiators.

3. Mr. Habib then tabled a revised Paragraph 1, reading as follows:

> "1. The United States may contract for any materials, supplies, equipment and services (including construction work) to be furnished or undertaken in the Republic of Korea for purposes of, or authorized by, this Agreement, without restriction as to choice of contractor, supplier or person who provides such services. Such materials, supplies, equipment and services may, upon agreement between the appropriate authorities of the two Governments, also be procured through the Government of the Republic of Korea."

4. With regard to the revisions proposed by the Korean negotiators, Mr. Habib stated that, provided the Korean negotiators agreed to two understandings, the U.S. negotiators accepted the following changes in the U.S. draft:

a. Paragraph 3 - the words "in advance" to be added following the word "certification";

b. Agreed Minute #2 - the word "representatives" to be substituted for the word "persons";

c. Agreed Minute #3 - the word "representative" to be substituted for the word "agent";

d. Addition of the Agreed Minute #4 proposed by the Korean negotiators.

0044

5. Mr. Habib recalled that at the 46th negotiating meeting, the Korean negotiators had indicated their agreement to Paragraph 3 of the U.S.draft was conditioned upon: (a) "U.S. acceptance of an understanding that the U.S. will be given exemption only in the last stages of procurement unless it is agreed in the Joint Committee that the tax for which examption is sought may be identified specifically and forms a significant part of the purchase price of the item", and (b) agreement by the U.S. negotiators to the insertion of the words "in advance" following the words "appropriate certification" in the first sentence of Paragraph 3. Mr. Habib stated the U.S. negotiators agreed to these two conditions and to the other changes proposed by the Korean negotiators, provided the Korean negotiators would agree for the record that: (a) a tax for which exemption is sought will not be collected so long as it is under discussion in the Joint Committee, and (b) traffic tax exemptions will be continued on the basis of current practice, under which all U.S. armed forces personnel travelling on official Travel Requests obtain exemption.

6. Mr. Habib stated that the first understanding which he had mentioned was a logical corollary of the first condition stated by the Korean negotiators. With regard to the second understanding, he said the U.S. negotiators believed that the ROK Government had no intention to apply the traffic tax to bulk purchases of transportation for official travel. He said the term "bulk purchases" was a bit confusing. Actually, all official travel is performed on the basis of Travel Requests issued by the U.S. military authorities. The military authorities enter into annual contracts with the railroads and airlin for the purchase of transportation. The individual traveller who is travelling on official business presents a Travel Request to the ticket office and is issued a ticket which is charged to the annual contract. Mr. Habib stated that the U.S. negotiators were responding directly to the proposals made by the Korean negotiators and hoped that full agreement could now be reached on this article.

0045

7. Mr. Chang expressed the gratitude of the Korean negotiators for the response

made by the U.S. negotiators to the Korean proposals. He stated that he foresaw no difficulty in reaching agreement on the proposed revision of Paragraph 1 and on the other changes, including the understandings proposed by the U.S. negotiators. However, the Korean negotiators would study the statements made by the U.S. negotiators and ply at the next meeting.

Customs

8. Turning to the Customs Article, Mr. Cho recalled that the question of "members" or "units" in Paragraph 5(a) was still unresolved. He asked if the U.S. negotiators had any additional comments to make on this subject. Mr. Habib replied that the U.S. negotiators had no further comment to make at that time with regard to Paragraph 5(a).

9. Mr. Cho stated that the Korean negotiators wished to make some further remarks with regard to Agreed Minute #3 of the U.S. draft. As written, he said, the Agreed Minute would exempt from customs inspection cargo consigned to non-appropriated nd organizations as well as cargo consigned to the U.S. armed forces. Whereas the latter type of cargo consisted of goods under the control of the U.S. armed forces, cargo consigned to the non-appropriated fund organizations consisted of goods which would be sold for profit in post exchanges operated by civilian managers.

10. Mr. Habib interrupted at this point to say that to regard the post exchange as a business was to misconstrue the function and purpose of the post exchange. An army is not just guns and ammunition, he continued; it is all of the goods which are necessary to keep the soldier adequately equipped and trained, in good health, and to maintain his morale. Furthermore, the post exchanges are under the close and continuous control of the armed forces.

0046

11. Mr. Cho said that he did not mean to imply that the post exchanges were not controlled by the armed forces. However, in the past the Korean economy has been affected by the influx of PX goods. For example, in May, 1961, a Seventh Division post exchange

This is the very reason why Korean negotiators wish to make clear distinction between purely military cargo and PX goods.

had imported 10,000 yards of men's suiting. Inasmuch as the average monthly consumption of suiting by the Seventh Division was 90 yards, 10,000 yards was clearly an unreasonable quantity. In a second example, the First Ordnance Battalion at Uijongbu had imported 65 pairs of women's shoes from Hong Kong. As a result of an investigation by U.S. authorities, however, these shoes had been returned to HongKong. Because of cases like those which he had just cited, Mr. Cho continued, the Korean negotiators could not agree to exempt unconditionally from customs inspection all goods imported by non-appropriated fund organizations. The Korean negotiators were not questioning the existence of the post exchanges but they were concerned that there should be adequate safeguards against abuses by individuals. They realized that certain measures in this regard were enumerated in this and other articles of the Agreement and that U.S. and Korean agencies were co-operating to curb illegal activities. Nevertheless, such activities have been uncovered in the past and the Korean negotiators were convinced that customs inspections by Korean inspectors would check such undesirable activities in the future.

12. Although the U.S. negotiators had expressed the fear that inspection might [illegible] damage or delay the delivery of goods, Mr. Cho went on, the Korean negotiators could assure them that this would not be the case. They were prepared to discuss detailed measures which could be taken to insure that there would be no damage or delay. The Korean negotiators wished to point out that in Article 6 of the Mutual Security Treaty with Japan and in Article 11 of the SOFA with Japan, exemption from customs inspection was granted only to those unaccompanied goods shipped on a Government Bill of Lading. Goods accompanying units were exempted on the presentation of a certificate signed by the unit commander. It was quite clear to the Korean negotiators that in the SOFA with Japan cargo consigned to non-appropriated fund organizations was not considered to be a part of military cargo. There was no reason why the SOFA with the Republic of Korea should not have the same provision. Moreover, the economic situation in the Republic of Korea was different from that in Japan. The illegal disposal of PX goods has adversely affected the growth of certain elements of the Korean economy. It has been the practice to inspect goods con-

(Handwritten annotations: "would"; "of the U.S. side agrees to give the Korean Customs the right of inspection on goods consigned to non-appropriated fund organization"; "The Korean Negotiators")

0047

signed to the post exchanges through commercial channels from other countries than the United States. Currently, Korean customs officials were inspecting such goods, particularly watches, cameras, radios, etc. Therefore, there should be no difficulty in the future in having Korean customs officials inspect such goods. Military cargo is used solely for military purposes but goods consigned to the non-appropriated fund organizations are used for various purposes. Therefore, the proposal of the Korean negotiators would serve the purposes of the U.S. armed forces stationed in Korea. ~~Following Mr. Cho's remarks, Mr. Chang asked the U.S. negotiators to comment.~~

13. Mr. Habib remarked that the U.S. negotiators had already commented on innumerable occasions in the past in great detail on the arguments put forward by Mr. Cho. Nevertheless, he would refute them once again. In the first place, the non-appropriated fund organizations were an integral part of the U.S. military establishment and were regulated by military regulations. In this respect, there was no difference between a gallon of gasoline imported for use in an army jeep and a candy bar imported for consumption by a soldier. In the second place, the function of this Agreed Minute is to define military cargo. It is not concerned with illegal activities, which are covered elsewhere in this article and in other articles of the Agreement. There is no connection between a definition of military cargo and the illegal disposal of goods. In the third place, the U.S. negotiators had already explained that a definition referring to a Government Bill of Lading is no longer feasible because Government Bills of Lading are no longer used for all shipments. The text of the SOFA with Japan is no longer applicable in practice and the Japanese authorities do not inspect.

14. Mr. Habib said the examples of violations cited by the Korean negotiators were irrelevant to the question of defining military cargo. In any case, most of the violations of this type known to the Korean authorities had been originally discovered by U.S. armed forces investigators, not Korean customs officials. Stating that the legitimate concern of the Korean authorities was with the quantity of goods imported, not with the fact of importation itself, Mr. Habib pointed out that Agreed Minute #1 states explicitly that the importation of goods

0048

by non-appropriated fund organizations "shall be limited to the extent reasonably required for such use".

15. Mr. Habib then called the attention of the Korean negotiators to the various provisions of the article designed to deal with the prevention of abuses - Agreed Minute #4, which calls for "every practicable measure" to ensure that there will be no violation of Korean customs laws and regulations; Agreed Minute #5, which authorizes the Korean customs authorities to raise abuses or infringements with the appropriate authorities of the U.S. armed forces; Paragraph 9, which provides that each side will assist the other in conducting inquiries and collecting evidence; Paragraph 6, which prohibits illegal disposal of such goods; and Paragraph 8, which calls upon the U.S. armed forces to take all necessary steps to prevent abuses. Mr. Habib reiterated that all of these provisions regarding the prevention of abuses have nothing to do with the question of defining military cargo. The U.S. negotiators expect that the Joint Committee will set up procedures to carry out all of the provisions which he had just cited. Furthermore, the U.S. negotiators had proposed, at the 40th negotiating meeting on January 24, 1964, that an additional sentence be added to Agreed Minute #3, providing that pertinent information concerning cargo consigned to non-appropriated fund organizations would be furnished to the Korean authorities on request. The implementation of this provision would be up to the Joint Committee.

16. Mr. Habib stated that the U.S. armed forces were not in the business of black-marketing. Individuals, both American and Korean, were responsible for the existence of the black market. The U.S. authorities were just as concerned over this problem as the Korean authorities. There existed just as much opportunity for the diversion of goods such as tires as for the diversion of goods such as radios. The way to control diversions was to achieve better policing and greater cooperation between the law enforcement agencies of the two governments.

0049

17. Mr. Cho replied that the Korean negotiators were seeking to establish preventive measures rather than improve investigative procedures after violations have occurred. Although the actual implementation of the SOFA with Japan might differ from the language of the SOFA itself, still the definition in the SOFA with the Republic Korea should be equivalent to that in the SOFA with Japan. Although the additional sentence proposed by the U.S. negotiators for Agreed Minute #3 would provide that information be furnished to the Joint Committee, there would be no way in which to verify the information so provided. Furthermore, there would be no way to confirm that the importation of goods was being restricted to a "reasonable quantity".

18. Mr. Habib replied that documentation of shipments should be adequate verification. The Joint Committee could decide what type of documentation would be required. The U.S. armed forces were prepared to provide all necessary information to live up to the provisions of the Agreement. The whole purpose of this article and the Agreement as a whole was to give the Joint Committee a framework in which to function. The text proposed by the U.S. negotiators was sufficient to prevent illegal activities.

19. Mr. Chang remarked that the objective of both sides was the same but the methods proposed for achieving that objective were different. The Korean negotiators wanted to provide for customs inspection; the U.S. negotiators did not. The Korean negotiators would study the matter further.

20. Mr. Habib stated that the procedures proposed by the U.S. negotiators were more efficient and less cumbersome than those proposed by the Korean negotiators. He reminded the Korean negotiators that the U.S. negotiators were determined to uphold the principle that official cargo should not be subject to customs inspection.

Claims

21. Turning to the Claims Article, Mr. Chu tabled proposed Agreed Minutes which the U.S. negotiators agreed to study and comment on at a later meeting.

22. It was agreed to hold the next meeting on May 12 at 2:00 p.m.

1966, 12, 31.에 예고문에 의거 일반문서로 재분류됨

0050

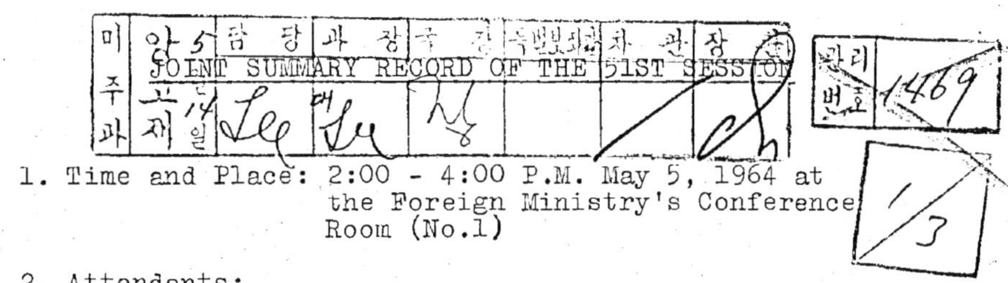

JOINT SUMMARY RECORD OF THE 51ST SESSION

1. Time and Place: 2:00 - 4:00 P.M. May 5, 1964 at the Foreign Ministry's Conference Room (No.1)

2. Attendants:

ROK Side:

Mr. Chang, Sang Moon	Director European and American Affairs Bureau
Mr. Koo, Choong Whay	Chief, American Section Ministry of Foreign Affairs
Mr. Oh, Jae Hee	Chief, Treaty Section Ministry of Foreign Affairs
Mr. Choo, Moon Ki	Chief Legal Affairs Section Ministry of Justice
Mr. Cho, Choong Hoon	Chief Customs Section Ministry of Finance
Maj. Lee, Kye Hoon	Military Affairs Section Ministry of National Defense
Mr. Chung, Woo Young (Rapporteur and Interpreter)	3rd Secretary Ministry of Foreign Affairs
Mr. Lee, Kae Chul	3rd Secretary Ministry of Foreign Affairs
Mr. Whang, Young Chae	3rd Secretary Ministry of Foreign Affairs
Mr. Park, Won Chul	3rd Secretary Ministry of Foreign Affairs

U.S. Side:

Mr. Philip C. Habib	Counselor American Embassy
Brig. Gen. G.G. O'Connor	Deputy Chief of Staff 8th U.S. Army
Col. Howard Smigelow	Deputy Chief of Staff 8th U.S. Army

0051

Col. Kenneth C. Crawford	Staff Judge Advocates Office 8th U.S. Army
Capt. John Wayne	Assistant Chief of Staff USN/K
Mr. Benjamin A. Fleck (Rapporteur and Press Officer)	First Secretary American Embassy
Mr. Robert A. Lewis	2nd Secretary American Embassy
Mr. James Sartorius	2nd Secretary American Embassy
Maj. Robert D. Peckham	Staff Officer JAG 8th U.S. Army
Mr. Robert A. Kinney	J-5 8th U.S. Army

1. Mr. Chang opened the meeting by introducing Mr. Cho, Choong Hoon, Chief of the Customs Section, Ministry of Finance, who was attending the meeting in place of Mr. Sin Kwan-sop; and Mr. Hwang, Young Chae of the America Section, Ministry of Foreign Affairs. Mr. Habib welcomed these gentlemen to the negotiations.

Local Procurement

2. Taking up the article on Local Procurement, Mr. Habib recalled that at the 46th negotiating meeting the Korean negotiators had made certain suggestions for revision of the U.S. draft. He said the U.S. negotiators were prepared to respond to those suggestions. The U.S. negotiators also wished to introduce some non-substantive changes in wording in paragraph 1 in order to make the language of that paragraph consistent with the wording of paragraphs 2 and 3 and with the new Agreed Minute #4 proposed by the Korean negotiators.

0052

3. Mr. Habib then tabled a revised paragraph 1, reading as follows:

> "1. The United States may contract for any materials, supplies, equipment and services (including construction work) to be furnished or undertaken in the Republic of Korea for purposes of, or authorized by, this Agreement, without restriction as to choice of contractor, supplier or person who provides such services. Such materials, supplies, equipment and services may, upon agreement between the appropriate authorities of the two Governments, also be procured through the Government of the Republic of Korea."

4. With regard to the revisions proposed by the Korean negotiators, Mr. Habib stated that provided the Korean negotiators agreed to two understandings, the U.S. negotiators accepted the following changes in the U.S. draft:

a. Paragraph 3 - the words "in advance" to be added following the word "certification";

b. Agreed Minute #2 - the word "representatives" to be substituted for the word "persons";

c. Agreed Minute #3 - the word "representative" to be substituted for the word "agent";

d. Addition of the Agreed Minute #4 proposed by the Korean negotiators.

5. Mr. Habib recalled that at the 46th negotiating meeting, the Korean negotiators had indicated their agreement to Paragraph 3 of the U.S. draft was conditioned upon: (a) "U.S. acceptance of an understanding that the U.S. will be given exemption only in the last stages of procurement unless it is agreed in the Joint Committee that the tax for which examption is sought may be identified specifically and forms a significant part of the purchase price of the item", and (b) agreement by the U.S. negotiators to the insertion of the words "in advance" following the words "appropriate certification" in the first sentence

0053

of Paragraph 3. Mr. Habib stated the U.S. negotiators agreed to these two conditions and to the other changes proposed by the Korean negotiators, provided the Korean negotiators would agree for the record that: (a) a tax for which exemption is sought will not be collected so long as it is under discussion in the Joint Committee, and (b) traffic tax exemptions will be continued on the basis of current practice, under which all U.S. armed forces personnel travelling on official Travel Requests obtain exemption.

6. Mr. Habib stated that the first understanding which he had mentioned was a logical corollary of the first condition stated by the Korean negotiators. With regard to the second understanding, he said the U.S. negotiators believed that the ROK Government had no intention to apply the traffic tax to bulk purchases of transportation for official travel. He said the term "bulk purchases" was a bit confusing. Actually, all official travel is performed on the basis of Travel Requests issued by the U.S. military authorities. The military authorities enter into annual contracts with the railroads and air lines for the purchase of transportation. The individual traveller who is travelling on official business presents a Travel Request to the ticket office and is issued a ticket which is charged to the annual contract. Mr. Habib stated that the U.S. negotiators were responding directly to the proposals made by the Korean negotiators and hoped that full agreement could now be reached on this article.

7. Mr. Chang expressed the gratitude of the Korean negotiators for the response made by the U.S. negotiators

0054

to the Korean proposals. He stated that he foresaw no difficulty in reaching agreement on the proposed revision of Paragraph 1 and on the other changes, including the understandings proposed by the U.S. negotiators. However, the Korean negotiators would study the statements made by the U.S. negotiators and reply at the next meeting.

Customs

8. Turning to the Customs Article, Mr. Cho recalled that the question of "members" or "units" in Paragraph 5 (a) was still unresolved. He asked if the U.S. negotiators had any additional comments to make on this subject. Mr. Habib replied that the U.S. negotiators had no further comment to make at that time with regard to Paragraph 5(a).

9. Mr. Cho stated that the Korean negotiators wished to make some further remarks with regard to Agreed Minute #3 of the U.S. draft. As written, he said, the Agreed Minute would exempt from customs inspection cargo consigned to non-appropriated fund organizations as well as cargo consigned to the U.S. armed forces. Whereas the latter type of cargo consisted of goods under the control of the U.S. armed forces, cargo consigned to the non-appropriated fund organizations consisted of goods which would be sold for profit in post exchanges operated by civilian managers.

10. Mr. Habib interrupted at this point to say that to regard the post exchange as a business was to misconstrue the function and purpose of the post exchange. An army is not just guns and ammunition, he continued; it is all of the goods which are necessary to keep the soldier adequately equipped and trained, in good health, and to maintain his morale. Furthermore, the post exchanges are under the close and continous control of the armed forces.

11. Mr. Cho said that he did not mean to imply that the post exchanges were not controlled by the armed forces. However, in the past the Korean economy has been affected by the influx of PX goods. This is the very reason why the Korean negotiators wish to make clear distinction between purly military cargo and PX goods. For example, in May, 1961, a Seventh Division post exchange had imported 10,000 yards of men's suiting. Inasmuch as the average monthly consumption of suiting by the Seventh Division was 90 yards, 10,000 yards was clearly an unreasonable quantity. In a second example, the First Ordnance Battalion at Uijongbu had imported 65 pairs of women's shoes from Hong Kong. As a result of an investigation by U.S. authorities, however, these shoes had been returned to Hong Kong. Because of cases like those which he had just cited, Mr. Cho continued, the Korean negotiators could not agree to exempt unconditionally from customs inspection all goods imported by non-appropriated fund organizations. The Korean negotiators were not questioning the existence of the post exchanges but they were concerned that there should be adequate safeguards against abuses by individuals. They realized that certain measures in this regard were enumerated in this and other articles of the Agreement and that U.S. and Korean agencies were cooperating to curb illegal activities. Nevertheless, such activities have been uncovered in the past and the Korean negotiators were convinced that customs inspections by Korean inspectors would check such undesirable activities in the future.

12. Although the U.S. negotiators had expressed the

0056

fear that inspection might damage or delay the delivery of goods, Mr. Cho went on, the Korean negotiators could assure them that this would not be the case. If the U.S. side would consent to give the Korean Customs the right of inspection on goods consigned to non-appropriated fund organization, the Korean negotiators were prepared to discuss detailed measures which could be taken to insure that there would be no damage or delay. The Korean negotiators wished to point out that in Article 6 of the Mutual Security Treaty with Japan and in Article 11 of the SOFA with Japan, exemption from customs inspection was granted only to those unaccompanied goods shipped on a Government Bill of Lading. Goods accompanying units were exempted on the presentation of a certificate signed by the unit commander. It was quite clear to the Korean negotiators that in the SOFA with Japan cargo consigned to non-appropriated fund organizations was not considered to be a part of military cargo. There was no reason why the SOFA with the Republic of Korea should not have the same provision.. Moreover, the economic situation in the Republic of Korea was different from that in Japan. The illegal disposal of PX goods has adversely affected the growth of certain elements of the Korean economy. It has been the practice to inspect goods consigned to the post exchanges through commercial channels from other countries than the United States. Currently, Korean customs officials were inspecting such goods, particularly watches, cameras, radios, etc. Therefore, there should be no difficulty in the future in having Korean customs officials inspect such goods. Military cargo is used solely for military purposes but goods consigned to the non-appropriated fund organizations are used for various

0057

purposes. Therefore, the proposal of the Korean negotiators would serve the purposes of the U,S. armed forces stationed in Korea.

13. Mr. Habib remarked that the U.S. negotiators had already commented on innumerable occasions in the past in great detail on the arguments put forward by Mr. Cho. Nevertheless, he would refute them once again. In the first place, the non-appropriated fund organizations were an integral part of the U.S. military establishment and were regulated by military regulations. In this respect, there was no difference between a gallon of gasoline imported for use in an army jeep and a candy bar imported for consumption by a soldier. In the second place, the function of this Agreed Minute is to define military cargo. It is not concerned with illegal activities, which are covered elsewhere in this article and in other articles of the Agreement. There is no connection between a definition of military cargo and the illegal disposal of goods. In the third place, the U.S. negotiators had already explained that a definition referring to a Government Bill of Lading is no longer feasible because Government Bills of Lading are no longer used for all shipments. The text of the SOFA with Japan is no longer applicable in practice and the Japanese authorities do not inspect.

14. Mr. Habib said the examples of violations cited by the Korean negotiators were irrelevant to the question of defining military cargo. In any case, most of the violations of this type known to the Korean authorities had been originally discoverdd by U.S. armed forces investigators, not Korean customs officials. Stating

0058

that the legitimate concern of the Korean authorities was with the quantity of goods imported, not with the fact of importation itself, Mr. Habib pointed out that Agreed Minute #1 states explicitly that the importation of goods by non-appropriated fund organizations "shall be limited to the extent reasonably required for such use."

15. Mr. Habib then called the attention of the Korean negotiators to the various provisions of the article designed to deal with the prevention of abuses - Agreed Minute #4, which calls for "every practicable measure" to ensure that there will be no violation of Korean customs laws and regulations; Agreed Minute #5, which authorizes the Korean customs authorities to raise abuses or infringements with the appropriate authorities of the U.S. armed forces; Paragraph 9, which provides that each side will assist the other in conducting inquiries and collecting evidence; Paragraph 6, which prohibits illegal disposal of such goods; and Paragraph 8, which calls upon the U.S. armed forces to take all necessary steps to prevent abuses. Mr. Habib reiterated that all of these provisions regarding the prevention of abuses have nothing to do with the question of defining military cargo. The U.S. negotiators expect that the Joint Committee will set up procedures to carry out all of the provisions which he had just cited. Furthermore, the U.S. negotiators had proposed, at the 40th negotiating meeting on January 24, 1964, that an additional sentence be added to Agreed Minute #3, providing that pertinent information concerning cargo consigned to non-appropriated fund organizations would be furnished to the Korean authorities on request. The

implementation of this provision would be up to the Joint Committee.

16. Mr. Habib stated that the U.S. armed forces were not in the business of black-marketing. Individuals, both American and Korean, were responsible for the existence of the black market. The U.S. authorities were just as concerned over this problem as the Korean authorities. There existed just as much opportunity for the diversion of goods such as tires as for the diversion of goods such as radios. The way to control diversions was to achieve better policing and greater cooperation between the law enforcement agencies of the two governments.

17. Mr. Cho replied that the Korean negotiators were seeking to establish preventive measures rather than improve investigative procedures after violations have occurred. Although the actual implementation of the SOFA with Japan might differ from the language of the SOFA itself, still the definition in the SOFA with the Republic of Koraa should be equivalent to that in the SOFA with Japan. Although the additional sentence proposed by the U.S. negotiators for Agreed Minute #3 would provide that information be furnished to the Joint Committee, there would be no way to confirm that the importation of goods was being restricted to a "reasonable quantity".

18. Mr. Habib replied that documentation of shipments should be adequate verification. The Joint Committee could decide what type of documentation would be required. The U.S. armed forces were prepared to provide all necessary information to live up to the provisions of the Agreement. The whole purpose of this article and the

0060

Agreement as a whole was to give the Joint Committee a framework in which to function. The text proposed by the U.S. negotiators was sufficient to prevent illegal activities.

19. Mr. Chang remarked that the objective of both sides was the same but the methods proposed for achieving that objective were different. The Korean negotiators wanted to provide for customs inspection; the U.S. negotiators did not. The Korean negotiators would study the matter further.

20. Mr. Habib stated that the procedures proposed by the U.S. negotiators were more efficient and less cumbersome than those proposed by the Korean negotiators. He reminded the Korean negotiators that the U.S. negotiators were determined to uphold the principle that official cargo should not be subject to customs inspection.

Claims

21. Turning to the Claims Article, Mr. Chu tabled proposed Agreed Minutes which the U.S. negotiators agreed to study and comment on at a later meeting.

22. It was agreed to hold the next meeting on May 12 at 2:00 p.m.

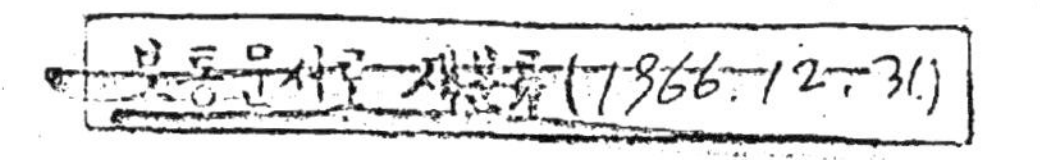

0061

2. 제52차 회의, 5.20

0062

재 무 부

재세지 134.2—1640 1964. 5. 5

수신 외무부장관 귀하

제목 주둔군지위협정체결실무자 경질

한미간 실무자 회의 당부 대표로 위촉된 세관국장 신 관섭(申寬燮)은 금번 정부 인사발령에 의거 기획관리실장으로 전임하게 됨으로 후임 실무자를 세관국 관세과장 재경서기관 조 충 훈(趙忠勳)으로 경질코저 하여니 조치하여 주시기 바랍니다. 끝

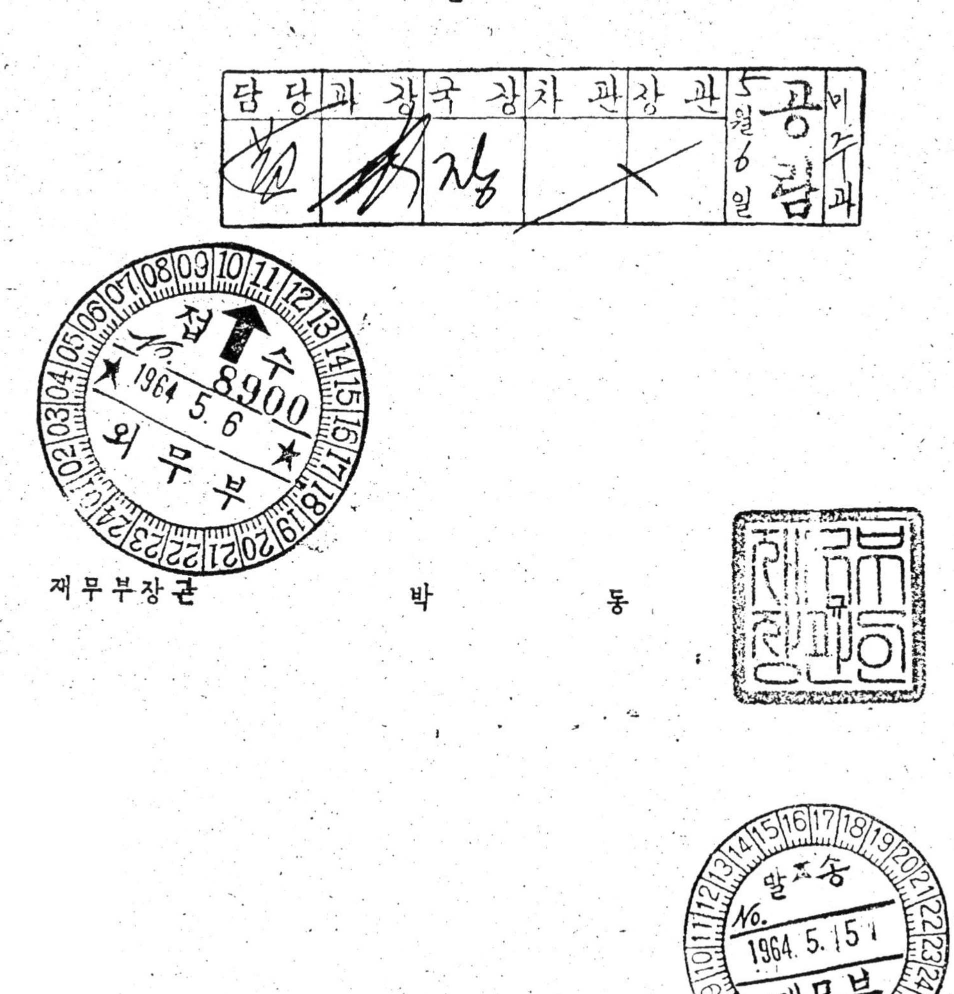

재무부장관 박 동

0063

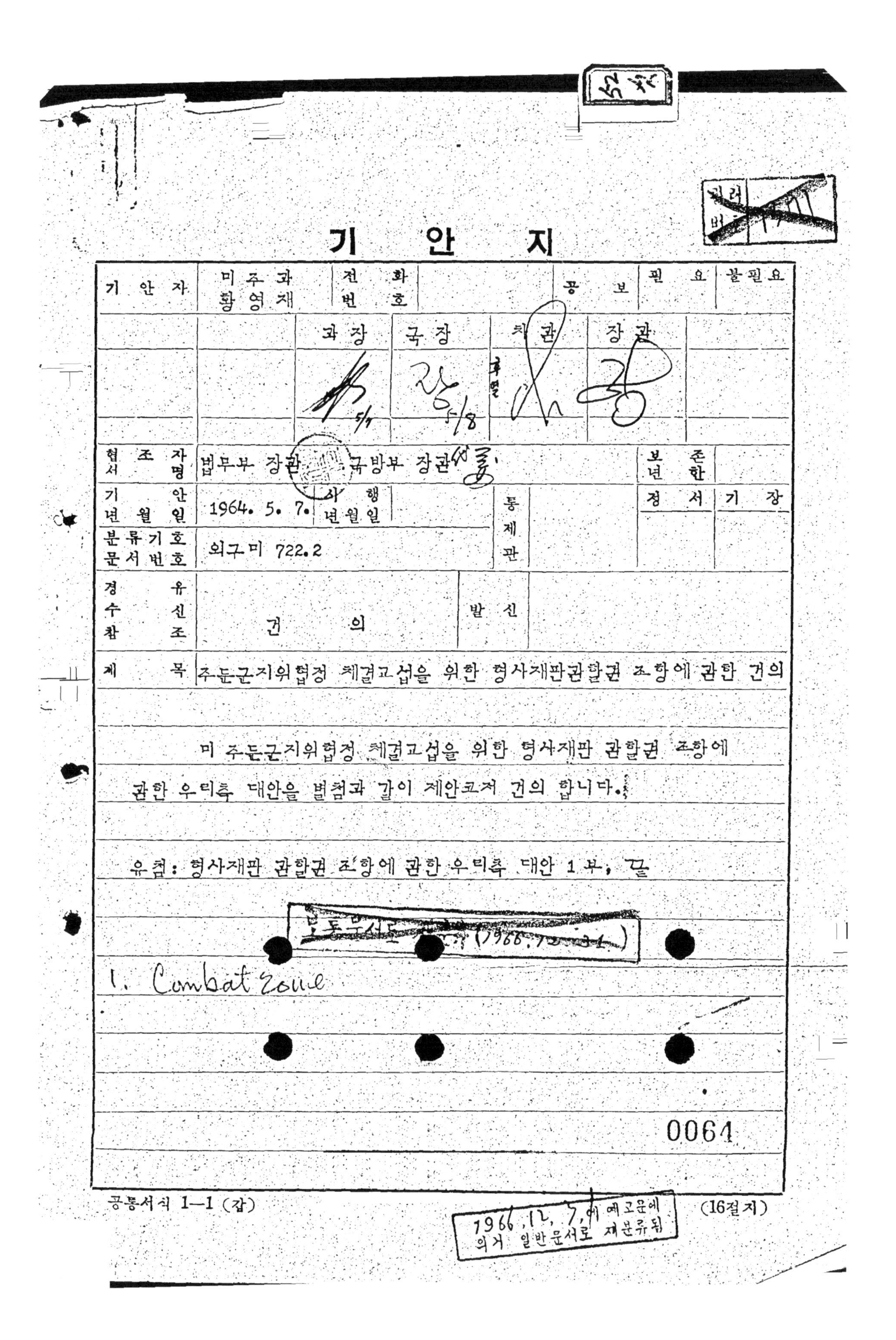

기 안 지

기 안 자	미주과 황영재	전화번호		공보	필요	불필요
		과장	국장	차관	장관	
협조자 서명	법무부 장관 국방부 장관				보존년한	
기안 년월일	1964. 5. 7.	시행 년월일		통제관	정서기장	
분류기호 문서번호	외구미 722.2					
경유 수신 참조	건의		발신			
제목	주둔군지위협정 체결교섭을 위한 형사재판관할권 조항에 관한 건의					

미 주둔군지위협정 체결교섭을 위한 형사재판 관할권 조항에 관한 우리측 대안을 별첨과 같이 제안코저 건의 합니다.

유첨: 형사재판 관할권 조항에 관한 우리측 대안 1부, 끝

1. Combat zone

0061

공통서식 1—1 (갑) (16절지)

1966.12.31. 에 예고문에 의거 일반문서로 재분류됨

内 容	第52次会議에 提出한 韓國側案	提 案 理 由
1. 管轄权行使 当局		
① 美國側行使 当局	美軍当局	美国案은 過去 國際的協定에서 그 例가 稀少할 뿐아니라, 美軍法会議 以外의 法廷을 設置할 可能性이 있어 이를 絶対로 排除한다.
② 韓國側行使 当局	大韓民國 当局 (諒解事項 ; 美軍犯法者는 原則的으로 韓國軍法会議에는 廻附되지않으며, 軍法会議에서 取扱될 犯罪를 犯하였을 時 民間裁判에 廻附할것을 要請하면 同情的으로 考慮를 한다)	接受國의 司法权行使機関은 接受國이 任意로 決定할 問題이지 美國側이 関與할 바 아니다. 韓國은 一般的 國際慣例를 尊重할것이다.

0065

內 容	第52次会議에 提出한 韓国側案	提 案 理 由
2. 適用範囲	美軍法에 服하는 모든 者	美国大審院의 最近判例에 依하면 美軍事当局은 家族에 対한 裁判管轄权을 가지지 못한다. 美軍法会議 以外의 法廷의 設置를 不許하는 韓国側 立場에 비추어 美軍事当局이 家族에 対한 裁判管轄权을 갖이게 되는 境遇에는 韓国側는 家族을 包含시키는데 反対하지 않을것이다. Uniform Code of Military Justice

0066

內容	第52次會議에 提出한 韓側案	提案理由
3. 適用地域 ① 戰斗地域	戰斗地域의 槪念을 管轄權의 適用地域問題에서 排除하고 競合管轄權의 抛棄條項에서 取扱하되, 公務執行中 與否에 關한 決定權 各項에서 解決策을 模索토록 美側에 要求한다.	戰斗地域의 制定은 全然 先例를 찾아볼수 없으며, 裁判管轄權과 軍作戰을 連關시킴은 不當할뿐만 아니라 大韓民國全域에 미쳐야 할 主權國家로서의 裁判管轄權을 地域的으로 制限함은 認定할수 없다.
② 戒嚴令 宣布地域	非常戒嚴令이 宣布된 地域內에서만 美軍當局이 專屬的 管轄權을 갖는다. 但, 警備戒嚴이 宣布된 地域內에서는 美軍當局의 管轄權 抛棄要請에 對하여 韓國當局은 同情的인 考慮를 한다.	戒嚴令은 憲法第75條2項에 依據, 非常戒嚴과 警備戒嚴으로 區分되고있으며, 戒嚴法 第10條에 依據 警備戒嚴下에서는 軍當局이 民事에 關한 行政및 司法權을 行使할수 없으므로 警備戒嚴下에서는 裁判管轄權은 韓國當局이 原則的으로 保有함이 妥當한것이다.

0067

內容	第52次會議에 提出한 韓國側 案	提案理由
4. 韓國의 重要的管轄權	韓國當局은 重要的管轄權을 行使하지 아니하기로 決定하였을 時에는 可及的 速히 美軍當局에 通告한다.	美國側은 美國當局의 重要的管轄權의 抛棄要請에 對해서 韓國當局이 好意的 考慮를 하여야 한다는 規定이 없으면, 韓國當局이 自發的으로 重要管轄權을 抛棄하려고 하여도 할수없기 때문에 同規定을 挿入하자고 主張하고 있는바, 韓國當局은 美國側의 抛棄要請이 없드라도 自由裁量에 依하여 抛棄할수있는 協定上의 根據를 마련함으로서 韓國當局의 主体性을 維持하는 一方, 美國側 提案에 符合하도록 試圖한 것이다.

0068

内容	第52次会議에 提出한 韓国側 案	提案理由
5. 管轄权의 競合 (韓國側의 第一次的 管轄权 行使)	1. 美軍当局이 权利抛棄가 (特히) 重大하다고 認定되는 境遇에는 权利抛棄에 該当하는 個別的 事件을 通告한다.	
	2. 韓国当局은 이 要請에 対하여 司法上의 重大한 利益을 侵害치 않는 限度内에서 抛棄한다. 韓国当局은 重大한 司法上의 利益을 侵害한다는 意見을 가지는 境遇에는 그 理由를 通告한다.	日本을 爲始한 大多数國家의 SOFA協定의 先例에 따라 第一次的 管轄权 抛棄要請 規定을 두되, 그 抛棄는 韓國当局의 重大한 司法上의 利益을 侵害치 않는 限度内에서만 可能하도록 制限을 加하고저 하는 것임. NATO 補充協定 第19條 2項 乃至 3項의 規定에 類似한 規定이기는 하나, 韓國側에 有利하도록 設定하고 있음.
	3. 美軍当局은 이 通告에 対하여 異議가 있는 境遇에는, 15日以内에 合同委員会에 回附한다. 異議가 없이 上記期間이 至過한 때에는 抛棄要請을 撤回한 것으로 看做한다.	
	4. 韓國当局이 管轄权을 抛棄한 境遇 美軍当局은 当該事件의 處理를 通告한다.	Greece 協定 第11條 2項의 先例에 따름과 아울러, 美軍当局이 当該事件의 處理에 愼重을 期하도록 間接的인 強制規範을 設定하려는데 있음.

0069

內容	第52次会議에 提出할 韓國側案	提案理由
6. 公務執行中의 犯罪.		公務執行中의 犯罪에 関한 ① 決定权者, ② 証據의 証明力 및 ③ 反証이 있는 境遇의 解決條項에 関한 韓國側案은 美國側이 "戰斗地域"에 関한 案을 撤回한다는 條件下에 提出하는 것임.
① 決定权者	美軍最高当局을 代身하여 美軍法務官이 証明한다.	各國先例를 보면 派遣國의 軍指揮官이 公務執行中 犯罪証明을 發行하는 것이 通例로 되어 있음에 勘案하여 決定权者가 "管轄地方檢察庁 檢事"이여야 된다는 本來의 韓国案을 撤回하고 左記 新案을 提出함으로서 美側案을 大体的으로 받아드리는 代身, "反証" 條項을 新設하여 우리 立場을 補充하려는 것임.

0070

內容	第52次会議에 提出할 韓國側案	提案理由
② 証據의 証明力	前記 美軍法務官의 証明은 充分한 証明力을 가진다.	美軍指揮官의 証明은 最終的이라는 美側提案은 West Indies의 境遇를 除外하고는 거의 그 先例가 없으며, 最終的인 証明力을 認定하므로서 反証을 들수있는 权利를 完全히 排除함은 不当할뿐만 아니라, 일단 充分한 証明力을 認定하되 反証을 들수있는 것이 先進各國 通例이므로 左記案을 提出하는 것임.
③ 反証이 있는 境遇의 解決	韓國檢察總長은 公務執行中 犯罪証明에 対한 反証이 있다고 認定할 境遇에는 問題를 合同委員会에 回付하여 決定토록 한다.	美側이 反証問題에 対하여 全혀 言及이 없음은 反証을 들을수있는 韓國側 权利를 完全히 排除하는 것으로서 不当한것이며, 各國의 先例를 보아도 合同委員会 또는 外交交涉을 通하여 解決을 模索하고 있음. 同証明의 適否에 関한 論難이 있을 可能性이 있으므로 合同委員会에서 解決토록 하려는 것임.

0071

內容	第52次会議에 提出한 韓國側案	提案理由
7. 犯人의 引渡 裁判系 拘禁		
① 美國当局의 手中에 있을 때	美國案에 다음事項을 追加한다. ① 美軍当局은 韓國当局에 拘禁을 移讓할수 있으며, 特定事件에 있어 韓國当局의 移讓要請에 好意的 考慮를 한다. ② 韓國의 安全에 対한 犯罪에 関한 拘禁은 韓國当局이 行한다.	独逸協定의 先例에 따르고, 韓國当局이 特定事件에 있어서는 犯人을 拘禁할수 있는 方便을 마련하였음.
② 韓國当局의 手中에 있을 때	(韓國案대로 主張하되) 正当한 事由有無에 対하여는 双方이 合同委員会에서 協議	正当한 事由有無의 判断은 合同委員会에서 協議하도록 함으로서, 美國側案에 一層 接近하는 提案임.
刑의 服務中拘禁		
① 美國当局이 言渡한 刑의 執行	双方案 同一	
② 韓國当局이 言渡한 刑의 執行	美國側을 受諾하되 記錄上에만 남기고, 本文으로 부터는 削除를 主張한다.	他國協定에는 全無한 規定인바, 本條項을 合意議事錄에 挿入하게되면 國民의 感情을 誘発할 憂慮가 있음.

0072

內容	第52次会議에 提出한 韓國側案	提案理由
8. 証人의 召喚	1. 美軍人 및 軍屬이 証人으로 召喚될 時, 美軍事当局은 韓國法에 依하여 強制되는 때에는 該人을 出頭토록 措置한다. 但, 軍事上의 非常事態時는 除外된다. 軍事上의 非常事態가 出頭를 阻害할 境遇에는, 韓國当局은 美軍事当局에서 提示한 狀況을 考慮하여 召喚을 適切히 延期토록 할수 있다. 家族은 軍事上의 非常事態에 不拘하고 韓國法에 따라 召喚된다. 2. 韓國国民이나 居住人이 美軍当局의 要請으로 証人 또는 專門家로 出頭하여야 한다는 美國側案을 受諾한다.	最初의 韓國側案과 같은 規定은 他協定에서 찾어볼수 없으며. 모든 協定에서는 本文에 相互協調의 原則을 規定하고 있을 뿐, 会意議事錄에 細部事項을 規定하고 있는 것은 独逸과의 協定以外에는 없음. 独逸과의 協定을 參照하였으며 全体的으로 보아 韓國側의 立場이 보다 強한 案임.

Wording change

check 日?

1966, 12, 31에 예고문에 의거 일반문서로 재분류됨

0073

SOFA NEGOTIATION

Agenda for the 52nd Session

14:00 May 20, 1964

1. Continuation of Discussions on:
   a. Local Procurement Article
   b. Criminal Jurisdiction Article
2. Other Business
3. Agenda and Date of the Next Meeting
4. Press Release

0074

관리번호 1472

기 안 지

기 안 자	미주과 이근팔	전화번호		공보	필요	불필요
	과장	국장	차관	장관		
협조자 서명					보존 년한	
기안 년월일	1964.5.21.	시행 년월일		통제관	정서	기장
분류기호 문서번호	외구미 722.2—					
경유 수신 참조	대통령: 참조 비서실장 국무총리: 참조: 비서실장 법무부장관	발신	장관			
제목	제 52 차 주둔군지위협정 체결 교섭 실무자회의 보고					

1964. 5. 20. 하오 3 시부터 동 4 시 15 분 가지 외무부 제 1 회의실에서 개최된 제 52 차 주둔군지위협정 체결 교섭 실무자회의에서 토의된 내용을 별첨과 같이 보고합니다.

유 첨: 제 52 차 주둔군지위협정 체결 교섭 실무자회의 보고서 1부. 끝

1966. 12. 22에 예고문에 의거 일반문서로 재분류됨

첨부물에서 분리되면 보통문서로 재분류

검열 1964. 5. 22 통제관

발송 No. 235 1964. 5. 22 외무부

공통서식 1—1 (갑) (16절지)

0075

제 52 차

한.미간 주둔군지위협정 체결 교섭 실무자회의

보 고 서

1. 일 시: 1964 년 5 월 20 일 하오 3 시 — 4 시 15 분.

2. 장 소: 외무부 제 1 회의실

3. 토의사항:

가. 형사재판관할권

1) 우리측은 42 차 회의에서 양측이 형사재판관할권에 관한 초안을 교환한 이래 미측의 초안내용과 그후의 주장을 검토하여 온 결과 협정의 조속한 체결을 위하여 다음과 같은 새로운 대안을 제시하게 되었다는 취지를 강조하고 미측에게 호양적인 입장에서 미측의 원래의 주장을 대폭 양보하는 대안을 하루 바삐 제시할 것을 촉구하였다.

(1) 미측의 관할권에 복하는 인적범위: 우리 안에 규정된 미군당국의 형사재판관할권의 인적 적용범위가 "미군대구성원 및 군속"으로 한정하였던 것을 "미군법에 복하는 모든 자"로 수정하여 가족이 포함될 수 있는 여지를 마련하였다.

(2) 미측의 행사기관: 미측이 미측의 관할권 행사기관을 "미국당국"으로 할 것을 주장하는데 대하여 우리측은 주한미군의 지위를 구정할 것을 논의하고 있는 만큼 "미군당국" 이 아닌 기타 여하한 미국당국의 관할권 행사를 인정할 수 없다는 우리측 주장을 강조하였다.

(3) 한국의 행사기관: 미측이 한국의 행사당국을 "민간당국"이라고 규정한데 대하여 우리측은 한국은 여하한 경우에도 미군인을 군법회의에 회부하지 않을 것을 기록에 유보하는 대신 한국의 행사기관을 민간당국으로 한정하려는 미측 주장을 철회할 것을 요구하였다.

(4) 전투지역: 미측이 주한미군의 전투태세의 완비를 위하여 소위 "전투지역" 내에서 전속적 관할권을 행사하겠다고 주장하는데 대하여 우리측은 우리가 대안을 제시하는 경합적관할권 및 피의자의 신병 인도 규정을 효과적으로 운영함으로서 미측의 요구를 충족시킬 수 있을 것임으로 전투지역의 개념을 철회할 것을 요구하였다.

0076

64-3-10

64-3-18 (3)

번호 1109 (3)

0077

(5) 경합적관할권: 경합적관할권의 대폭적인 포기를 주장하는 미측 입장에 대하여 우리측은 다음과 같은 요령으로 우리초안을 수정할 것을 제안하였다.

(ㄱ) 한국당국의 중대한 사법상의 이익을 침해하지 않는 한도내에서만 관할권 행사를 미측에 포기한다.

(ㄴ) 한.미 양국은 경미한 범죄의 신속한 처리를 위하여 그 방도를 강구한다.

(6) 재판전 피의자의 신병 보호: 미측의 주장을 대체적으로 참작하여 다음과 같이 우리측에 유리한 요점을 포함한 대안을 제시하였다.

(ㄱ) 미측 수중에 있는 미군인 및 군속의 신병은 모든 사법 절차가 끝나고 한국당국이 요청할 때까지 미측 수중에 둔다(1)그러나 미측은 언제던지 그신병을 한국당국에 인도 할 수 있으며 (2) 특정사건에 있어서 한국당국이 신병의 인도를 요청하면 미측은 동정적 고려를 하여야 한다.

(ㄴ) 국가의 안전에 관련된 범죄를 범한 자의 신병은 한국당국의 수중에 둔다.

(ㄷ) 피의자의 신병이 한국당국의 수중에 있을 때에는 정당한 이유와 필요성이 있는 경우외에는 미측의 인도요청에 대하여 동정적인 고려를 한다.

(7) 공무집행중의 범죄: 한국측은 국제선례를 참작하여 공무집행중 범죄 여부에 관한 우리초안을 철회하고 다음과 같은 대안을 제시하였다.

(ㄱ) 공무집행중 범죄 여부에 관한 증명서는 미군법무관이 지휘관을 대신하여 발급하며 그 증명서는 반증이 없는 한 충분한 증명력을 갖는다.

(ㄴ) 반증이 있는 경우에는 한국의 검찰총장은 합동위원회에 회부하여 결정토록 한다.

(ㄷ) 그러나 법관의 자유심증주의에 관한 우리 나라 형사소송법 제 308 조를 저해하는 것은 않이다.

0078

64-3-11

64- 3-18

미.오 1109 (3)

0079

(8) 계엄령 선포: 계엄령 선포 하에서 범법한 미군인은 한국의 군법회의에 회부하지 않을 것이라는 양해사항을 조건으로 미측의 계엄령에 관한 규정을 철회할 것을 주장하였다.

2) 미측은 우리측의 제안에 대하여 매우 광범하고도 건설적인 대안을 제시한데 대하여 감사하게 여기는 바이며 미측도 한국측 태도에 호응하여 호혜적인 입장에서 한국측 제안을 검토하여 조속한 시일내에 미측의 입장을 밝힐 것을 다짐하였다.

3) 양측대표는 우리측이 50차회의에서 제시한 피의자의 권리문제에 관하여 논의하였으며 미측은 다음과 같이 주장하였다.

(ㄱ) 한국의 헌법과 법률이 보장하고 있는 권리일지라도 미측이 필요하다고 인정하는 권리는 열거규정하기를 바라며

(ㄴ) 한국의 헌법과 법률에서 보장되지 않는 권리는 교섭에 따라 특별법을 제정하여 보장하기를 바란다

이에 대하여 우리측은 원칙적으로 동의하는 바이나 헌법과 법률이 이미 보장하고 있는 권리는 중복규정하지 않는 것이 체제상 좋을 것이며 여의치 못한 경우에 따도 열거의 범위를 최소한도로 축소하여 중복을 피하려는 것이 우리측 입장임을 밝혔다.

나. 현지조달

양측은 미군인이 공무여행차 우리 나라의 철도 또는 항공기등 교통시설을 이용하는 경우에 교통세를 면제하는데 관한 현존제도를 조사하여 다음 회의에서 토의하기로 하였다.

4. 기타 사항: 다음 회의일자: 1964년 5월 28일(목요일) 하오 2시. 끝

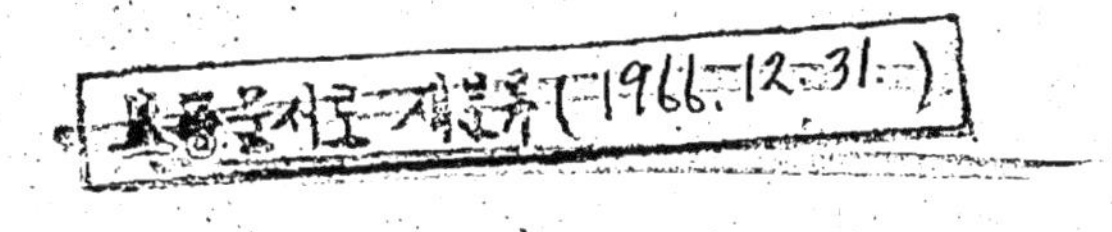

64-3-42

14-3-18(3)

0081

Agreed Joint Summary
D-52
May 20, 1964

STATUS OF FORCES NEGOTIATIONS: 52nd Meeting

SUBJECTS: 1. Criminal Jurisdiction
2. Local Procurement

PLACE: Ministry of Foreign Affairs

DATE: May 20, 1964

PARTICIPANTS:

Republic of Korea	United States
Chang	Philip C. Habib
Koo	Colonel Howard Smigelow, USA
Oh	Captain John Wayner, USN
Lee K.P	Colonel Kenneth C. Crawford, USA
Lee K.C.	Benjamin A. Fleck
Hur Hyung Koo	Robert A. Kinney
Cho Chung Hoon	Lt. Colonel Charles Wright, USA
Chung	Major Robert D. Peckham, USA
Park	James Sartorius
Maj. Lee, K.H	Kenneth Campen (Interpreter)

0082

1. Mr. Chang opened the meeting by introducing a new member of the ROK negotiating team, Mr. Hur, Hyung Koo, Chief of the Prosecutors Section, Ministry of Justice. Mr. Habib responded by introducing Lt. Colonel Charles Wright, of the Staff Judge Advocate's Office, Eighth United States Army, who will be succeeding Major Peckham as a member of the U.S. negotiating team. Both gentlemen were warmly welcomed to the negotiations.

Criminal Jurisdiction

2. Taking up the Criminal Jurisdiction Article, Mr. Chang made the following statement:

3. At the conclusion of Mr. Chang's statement, Mr. Habib said he wished to ask a few questions. First, did Mr. Chang's final comment, regarding the desire of the Korean negotiators to eliminate the reference in the U.S. draft to martial law, relate only to military personnel? Mr. Chang replied that the U.S. military personnel which he referred to in his statement included members of the U.S. armed forces and civilian components.

4. Mr. Habib then referred to Mr. Chang's statement that members of the U.S. armed forces would not be subject to trial by ROK court-martial under any circumstances. He asked if he had correctly understood Mr. Chang to say that this assurance would be read into the Agreed Joint Summary and not placed in the Agreed Minutes. Mr. Chang replied that this was a correct interpretation of the Korean negotiators' proposal.

5. Mr. Habib asked whether the Korean negotiators' position regarding U.S. jurisdiction over dependents was limited to the provisions of Paragraph 1. Mr. Chang replied that it was not limited to Paragraph 1, but would apply to the relevant paragraphs. However, the rights and privileges of dependents to be covered by the rest of the article should be dealt with through further negotiation.

6. Mr. Habib then stated that the U.S. negotiators believed that the Korean

negotiators had presented some constructive proposals. The U.S. negotiators welcomed the spirit in which those proposals had been made. The U.S. negotiators would study the Korean proposals carefully and would consult with Washington in detail. They would then try to present an equally comprehensive exposition of the U.S. views.

7. Mr. Habib noted that Mr. Chang had not mentioned the question of trial safeguards. He asked if the Korean position on this question remained unchanged. Mr. Chang replied affirmatively.

8. Mr. Habib recalled that the negotiators had previously discussed the question of including in the SOFA specific reference to certain safeguards which were enumerated in the ROK Constitution. He said it was not clear whether the Korean negotiators agreed or disagreed that specific reference should be made in the SOFA to such safeguards. The U.S. negotiators assumed that if a safeguard were mentioned in the Constitution the Korean negotiators could not object to its inclusion in the SOFA.

9. In reply, Mr. Chang said he would reiterate the Korean position. He said the Korean negotiators could not object if the U.S. negotiators wished to include in the SOFA items which are enumerated in the ROK Constitution and laws. However, it was a matter of style. If such safeguards are enumerated in the SOFA, the enumeration would have to include all the items listed in the Constitution. The Korean negotiators had included some safeguards in their proposed text but the U.S. negotiators wanted to include additional items. The Korean negotiators would study this matter and respond at a later meeting.

10. Mr. Habib recalled that he had proposed two principles during the course of the 50th meeting, namely, that items included in the ROK Constitution could be included in the SOFA and that items not included in the ROK Constitution could be included in the SOFA. Once these two principles were established, he continued, the negotiators could decide which items to include to make the SOFA more easily acceptable to both sides.

11. As an example of the U.S. negotiators' concern, Mr. Habib referred to the

0084

Agreed Minute re Paragraph 9(b) in the U.S. draft. He said that the ROK negotiators apparently agreed with the first paragraph of this Agreed Minute but had proposed deletion of the second paragraph, claiming that there is no counterpart in the Korean criminal procedures and that it is contrary to the spirit of the existing law. This paragraph guarantees the counsel of an accused the right to examine and copy the statements of witnesses prior to trial when these statements are contained in the file of the case. The Korean negotiators had argued that under the ROK code of criminal procedure, the accused is given the opportunity to know the nature of the evidence against him and that this would suffice. The U.S. negotiators, however, believed that the right sought for the accused in the second paragraph of this Agreed Minute was a common sense right which would not be incompatible with ROK law. Mr. Habib then quoted Article 273 of the ROK criminal code, which reads (in part) as follows: "(1) The court may, upon application, permit the prosecutor or the accused or his counsel to examine the accused or other witnesses and to inspect evidence before the date fixed for trial..." He pointed out that the right sought by the U.S. negotiators for incorporation in the SOFA was comparable in spirit to this provision of the ROK code, although not worded exactly the same.

12. As another example of a safeguard deemed necessary by the U.S. negotiators, Mr. Habib referred to the proposed Agreed Minute Re Paragraph 9(e). The Korean negotiators had argued that the Korean legal system requires that the accused be kept under surveillance by a competent Korean officer during any interview held by the accused with his counsel. They had therefore argued in favor of deleting the word "confidentially" from the proposed Agreed Minute. The U.S. negotiators believed that if a counsel is to perform effectively, he must be able to have his client confide in him without fear of being overheard. This could be accomplished by having the interview between the accused and his counsel take place in a locked room with a Korean guard posted outside.

13. As a further example of the variance between the positions of the two

0085

sides regarding trial safeguards, Mr. Habib referred to the Korean proposal to incorporate the second Agreed Minute Re Paragraph 9 of the Korean draft into the Agreed Minute re Paragraph 9(g) of the U.S. draft. This was undoubtedly an effort by the Korean negotiators to retain in force the provisions of Article 105 of the ROK Constitution, which reads as follows: "Trials and decisions of the courts shall be open to the public; however, trials may be closed to the public by a court when there is a possibility that such trials may disturb the public safety and order or be harmful to decent customs." Mr. Habib pointed out that the provisions of the Agreed Minute re Paragraph 9(g) of the U.S. draft were not intended to apply to the general public in all circumstances but were intended only to ensure that a representative of the U.S. Government would be able to attend all the proceedings connected with a trial, including any in camera proceedings.

14. Summing up, Mr. Habib pointed out that differences exist in both law and procedure between the U.S. legal system and that of the Republic of Korea. In some cases, these differences can be met by interpretation of the Korean laws. In other cases, the Korean laws may have to be amended to make them compatible with the terms of the SOFA. Such amendment of local law has taken place in connection with almost every SOFA which has been negotiated.

15. Mr. Chang stated that the Korean negotiators were in general agreement with the explanation given by the U.S. negotiators of the latter's position with regard to trial safeguards. The Korean negotiators were ready to settle through negotiation those items not presently covered by the ROK Constitution and laws. However, it did not seem necessary to them to include in the SOFA items which are already included in the Constitution and laws.

16. Mr. Habib pointed out that basic principles should be clearly stated in the SOFA, inasmuch as laws can be changed. The negotiators should bear in mind the fact that the passage of ex post facto laws has been a feature of recent Korean history.

0086

17. Mr. Chang said the Korean negotiators understood the concern of the U.S.

negotiators. However, if the laws were changed, the changes would be in the directio of more protection of human rights rather than less. Mr. Habib expressed the hope of the U.S. negotiators that this would be true but their lack of conviction, based on experience, that any changes in current laws would necessarily be for the better.

Local Procurement

18. Mr. Chang stated that the Korean negotiators wished to make their final comment regarding the Local Procurement Article. Before doing so, however, they wished to clear up one remaining question. The U.S. negotiators had said that under the present system, any individual travelling on official orders was issued transportation tax free under the terms of existing contracts with the U.S. armed forces. However, the Korean negotiators had been informed by transportation officials that this was not the case. According to these officials, tax exemption was granted only to individuals travelling in the U.N. car on railroad trains or in other chartered vehicles. Major Peckham replied that the current procedures were as the U.S. negotiators had described them. An individual travelling on official orders was granted tax exemption. An individual travelling without official orders was not granted tax exemption. It was then agreed that Mr. Ku and Mr. Fleck would conduct a joint inquiry and inform the negotiators of their findings.

18. It was agreed to hold the next meeting on May 28 at 2:00 p.m.

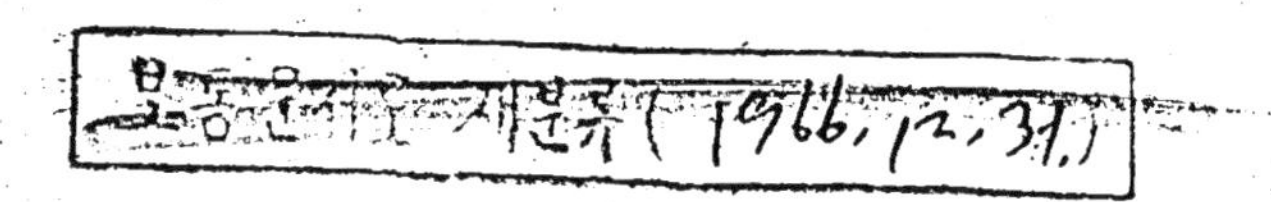

Since the drafts on the subject of Criminal Jurisdiction were exchanged at the 42nd meeting, the positions of both sides have become quite clear through a number of meetings over three months. During the period, both sides have had considerable time to study each others' positions as well as their major concerns. We believe past sessions have been productive in this sense.

However, we still face a wide gap between the two positions and the Korean negotiators believe it is high time for both sides to endeavor to narrow down the differences which exist between the two drafts and readjust their positions based on the spirit of friendly understanding and mutual cooperation.

On our part, we have carefully studied and reviewed the concerns and difficulties of the U.S. side as indicated through the meetings and have decided to make a voluntary concession in order to accommodate the U.S. side's desire as far as we can go. As you will notice, the new proposal which the Korean negotiators are going to table at today's meeting is indeed a great concession. We sincerely hope that the U.S. negotiators would give due consideration on our new proposals and would convey your views at a later meeting.

Now I would like to explain our new proposals item by item. First, in paragraph 1(a) of our draft, we offer to replace the phrase "the members of the United States armed forces and the civilian components" with a new phrase reading "all persons subject to the military law of the United States."

Our new proposal may not sound to you like a very new idea. However, by proposing this phrase, we are prepared to recognize the jurisdiction of U.S. military authorities in Korea over the dependents to the extent they are subject to U.S. military law. Whether the dependents are covered by the uniform code of military justice or not is an internal matter on your side.

0088

With regard to "authorities of the United States," to exercise criminal jurisdiction in Korea, we have designated the U.S. military authorities as sole authorities to exercise criminal jurisdiction since it is inconceivable for us that authorities other than U.S. military authorities would exercise jurisdiction within the Republic of Korea.

The chief U.S. negotiator stated at the 46th session that this is a matter of internal concern for the U.S. and that the language had been made broad enough to provide for any possible exercise of jurisdiction by U.S. authority. However, we are of the opinion that it is not the internal concern solely for the U.S. We believe that the exercise of criminal jurisdiction in Korea by the authorities of the United States, whether they be military authorities or other than military authorities, has to be mutually agreed upon. We have serious concern over the statement which implies the possibility of U.S. authorities in Korea other than military authorities exercising judicial power in Korea.

As for the authorities of the Republic of Korea exercising criminal jurisdiction, we understand your intention of limiting our authorities to the civil side is motivated from apprehensions that the U.S. military personnel might be tried by Korean court-martial. We are prepared to assure you that we would not exercise jurisdiction over U.S. military personnel by military tribunal under any circumstances. Accordingly we propose to record this assurance in the joint minutes and we believe you would accept our version. We are sure that our new proposal will certainly meet your requirements.

Turning to the so-called "combat zone", basically, our position of not recognizing the concept of combat zone remains as before. We understand that the U.S. side's primary objective

0089

to establish combat zone is to ensure combat readiness of the U.S. troops by having exclusive criminal jurisdiction in that area. Our view is that a workable arrangement in the custody clause and waiver clause could be agreed upon to satisfy your concern without resorting to the concept of a combat zone. Accordingly, we would suggest revision in our draft of the two respective clauses on the condition that the U.S. side will withdraw the concept of a combat zone.

With respect to the Agreed Minute re paragraph 3(c) of our draft concerning the problem of waiver of primary right to exercise jurisdiction, we offer to add the following paragraph as the first paragraph "the authorities of the Republic of Korea will, upon the notification of individual cases falling under the waiver provided in Article ___ paragraph 3(c) from the military authorities of the United States, waive its primary right to exercise jurisdiction under Article ___ except where they determine that it is of particular importance that jurisdiction be exercised by the authorities of the Republic of Korea."

Further, we propose to add the words "In addition to the foregoing provisions" before the second paragraph which has been placed as the first paragraph in our original draft. We are also prepared to consider the U.S. paragraph which reads "To facilitate the expeditious disposal of offenses of minor importance, arrangements may be made between United States authorities and the competent authorities of the Republic of Korea to dispense with notification".

As you may notice in our proposal, we are greatly binding ourselves by this paragraph, because under this clause we have to waive most of the cases by simple notification from the U.S. side. Under this clause, our ground for retaining primary right despite the waiver request is extremely limited due to the key phrase "particular importance". We would like to recall that

0090

at the previous meeting your side stated that the U.S. intention is to obtain maximum waiver. We believe that our new proposal would effectively meet your requirements.

As to the procedure for mutual waiver, we would prefer to settle the detailed arrangements through the Joint Committee. However, in accordance with the principle set forth above, we could conceive the following detailed procedures for future reference: "When the Korean authorities hold the view that by reason of special circumstances in a specific case, major interests of the Korean administration of justice make imperative the exercise of the Korean jurisdiction, they will notify the military authorities of the United States of that opinion within a reasonable period. In case an understanding cannot be reached in discussion between the both sides, the U.S. military authorities will seek agreement of the Joint Committee within fifteen days from the date of receipt of such notification.

If the U.S. authorities do not reply within fifteen days, the request for waiver will be deemed to have recalled." We have mentioned the above procedures as an example. We would propose that the final procedures would be negotiated at the Joint Committee.

With respect to the provisions of paragraph 5(d) of the Korean draft regarding the pre-trial custody of the accused, we wish to propose the following revision and an additional paragraph 5(e):

"Paragraph 5(d) An accused member of the United States Armed Forces or civilian component over whom the Republic of Korea is to exercise jurisdiction will, if he is in the hands of the United States, be under the custody of the United States during all judicial proceedings and until custody is requested by the authorities of the Republic of Korea.

0091

"The military authorities of the United States may transfer custody to the Korean authorities at any time and shall give sympathetic consideration to any request for the transfer of custody which may be made by the Korean authorities in specific cases."

"Paragraph 5(e) In respect of offenses solely against the security of the Republic of Korea provided in Paragraph 2(c), custody shall remain with the authorities of the Republic of Korea."

In order to meet the desires of the U.S. negotiators to the maximum extent, we propose to provide some additional provisions to facilitate expeiditious investigation and trial on the part of the authorities of the Republic of Korea.

With respect to the provisions regarding the custody in the hands of the Republic of Korea, we are assuring you that custody will be turned over to the hands of the United States unless there is any specific reason and if there arises any question as to the existence of adequate cause and necessity to retain such accused, it will be determined at the Joint Committee.

With respect to pre-trial custody of the security offenses, we would like to emphasize that the custody of such offender should rest with the authorities of the Republic of Korea since an offender of the security offenses against the Republic of Korea, while he is in the hands of the authorities other than Korean, could disclose security information to others. Accordingly the Korean negotiators find no reason why the military authorities of the United States should take custody of such an offender.

0092

~~Re Issuance of a Duty Certificate~~

The Korean negotiators would like to delete from the provision of paragraph 3(a) (ii) of the Korean draft the following ~~sentence~~ language "provided that such act or omission is directly related to the duty. The question as to whether offenses were committed in the performance of official duty shall be decided by a competent district public prosecutor of the Republic of Korea. In case the offender's commanding officer finds otherwise, he may appeal from the prosecutor's decision to the Ministry of Justice within ten days from the receipt of the decision of the prosecutor, and the decision of the Minister of Justice shall be final". ~~and~~ We propose the following alternative draft as Agreed Minute re Paragraph 3(a) (ii). If the U.S. negotiators accept the proposed alternative draft, the Korean negotiators would give favorable consideration to the U.S. proposal made at the previous meeting to record in the Joint Summary the definition of official duty modified after the FEAF version of 1956:

Re Paragraph 3(a) (ii), ~~propose the following~~:

"Where a member of the United States armed forces or civilian component is charged with an offense, a certificate issued by a staff judge advocate on behalf of his commanding officer stating that the alleged offense, if committed by him, arose out of an act or omission done in the performance of official duty, shall be sufficient evidence of the fact for the purpose of determining primary jurisdiction, unless the contrary is proved.

If the chief prosecutor of the Republic of Korea considers that there is proof contrary to the certificate of official duty, he will refer the matter to the Joint Committee for decision.

0093

The above statements shall not be interpreted to prejudice in any way Article 308 of the Korean Code of Criminal Procedure.

The Korean negotiators ~~propose~~ believe the alternative draft would meet the desires expressed by the United States negotiators with respect to the issuance of a duty certificate for determining primary jurisdiction over offenses arising out of an act done in the performance of official duty.

However, the Korean negotiators, taking into account the highly legal affairs involved, deem it proper that a Staff Judge Advocate should exercise the right to make such determination on behalf of the commanding officer at divisional level.

With respect to the validity of a duty certificate, the Korean draft provides that a certificate shall be sufficient evidence of the fact for the purpose of determining primary jurisdiction, unless the contrary is proved, whereas the U.S. draft provides that it shall be conclusive. The Korean negotiators believe that the Korean authorities should be accorded the opportunity to express their views as to the validity of a certificate in the event they find evidence contrary to the certificate.

The Korean draft provides the Joint Committee as the reviewing system of disputes to work out a mutually acceptable solution.

Further, The Korean negotiators reserve to the court the power to make determination of fact by referring to Article 308 of the Korean Code of Criminal Procedure.

With respect to the martial law clause, we have already mentioned our intention of giving assurance that the U.S. military personnel would not be subject to Korean courts-martial. As we understand your major interest in this clause is not to subject U.S. military personnel to our military tribunal which

0094

would be established under martial law, we believe that with this assurance your major requirement is satisfied and we hope your side would withdraw the provisions with regard to martial law.

~~[illegible] the exclusive jurisdiction, at the previous meeting, your side stated that you would [illegible] the local aspects of [illegible] involved. [illegible] U.S. response in this regard.~~

보통문서로 재분류(1966.12.31.)

19 에 예고문에 의거 일반문서로 재분류됨

0095

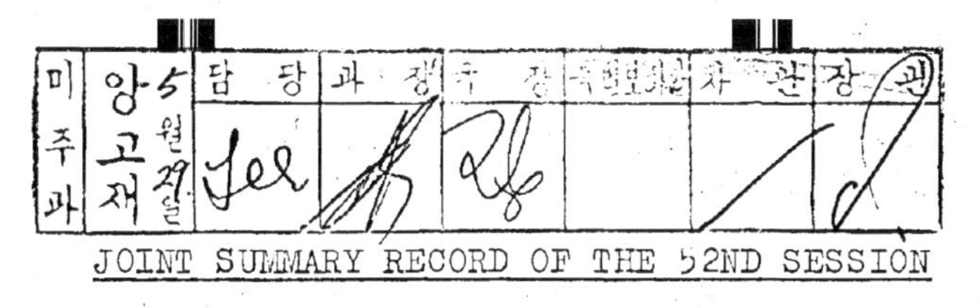

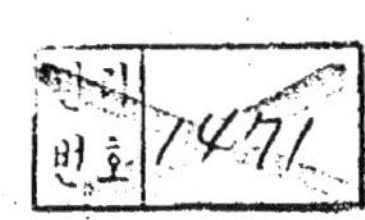

JOINT SUMMARY RECORD OF THE 52ND SESSION

1. Time and Place: 3:00 - 4:15 P.M. May 20, 1964 at the Foreign Ministry's Conference Room (No.1)

2. Attendants:

ROK Side:

Mr. Chang, Sang Moon	Director European and American Affairs Bureau
Mr. Koo, Choong Whay	Chief, American Section Ministry of Foreign Affairs
Mr. Oh, Jae Hee	Chief, Treaty Section Ministry of Foreign Affairs
Mr. Hur, Hyong Koo	Chief Prosecutors Section, Ministry of Justice
Mr. Cho, Choong Hoon	Chief Customs Section Ministry of Finance
Maj. Lee, Kye Hoon	Military Affairs Section Ministry of National Defense
Mr. Chung, Woo Young (Rapporteur and Interpreter)	3rd Secretary Ministry of Foreign Affairs
Mr. Lee, Kae Chul	3rd Secretary Ministry of Foreign Affairs
Mr. Lee, Keun Pal	3rd Secretary Ministry of Foreign Affairs
Mr. Park, Won Chul	3rd Secretary Ministry of Foreign Affairs

U.S. Side:

Mr. Philip C. Habib	Counselor American Embassy
Col. Howard Smigelow	Deputy Chief of Staff 8th U.S. Army
Capt. John Wayne	Assistant Chief of Staff USN/K
Col. Kenneth C. Crawford	Staff Judge Advocates Office 8th U.S. Army

0096

Mr. Benjamin A. Fleck (Rapporteur and Press Officer)	First Secretary American Embassy
Mr. Robert A. Kinney	J-5 8th U.S. Army
Lt. Col. Charles Wright	Staff Judge Advocate's Office Eighth United States Army
Maj. Robert D. Peckham	Staff Officer JAG 8th U.S. Army
Mr. James Sartorius	2nd Secretary American Embassy
Mr. Kenneth Campen	Interpreter

1. Mr. Chang opened the meeting by introducing a new member of the ROK negotiating team, Mr. Hur, Hyong Koo, Chief of the Prosecutors Section, Ministry of Justice. Mr. Habib responded by introducing Lt. Colonel Charles Wright, of the Staff Judge Advocate's Office, Eighth United States Army, who will be succeeding Major Peckham as a member of the U.S. negotiating team. Both gentlemen were warmly welcomed to the negotiations.

Criminal Jurisdiction

2. Taking up the Criminal Jurisdiction Article, Mr. Chang made the following statement:

Since the drafts on the subject of Criminal Jurisdiction were exchanged at the 42nd meeting, the positions of both sides have become quite clear through a number of meetings over three months. During the period, both sides have had considerable time to study each others' positions as well as their major concerns. We believe past sessions have been productive in this sense.

However, we still face a wide gap betwenn the two positions and the Korean negotiators believe it is high time for both sides to endeavor to narrow down the differences which exist between the two drafts and readjust their positions based on the spirit of friendly understanding and mutual cooperation.

On our part, we have carefully studied and reviewed the concerns and difficulties of the U.S. side as indicated through the meetings and have decided to make a voluntary concession in order to accommodate the U.S. side's desire as far as we can go. As you will notice, the new propoaal which the Korean negotiators are going to table at today's meeting is indeed a great concession. We sincerely hope that the U.S. negotiators would give due consideration on our new proposals and would convey your views at a later meeting.

Now I would like to explain our new proposals item by item. First, in paragraph 1(a) of our draft, we offer to replace the phrase "the members of the United States armed forces and the civilian components" with a new phrase reading "all persons subject to the military law of the United States."

Our new proposal may not sound to you like a very new idea. However, by proposing this phrase, we are prepared to recognize the jurisdiction of U.S. military authorities in Korea over the dependents to the extent they are subject to U.S. military law. Whether the dependents are covered by the uniform code of military justice or not is an internal matter on your side.

With regard to "authorities of the United States" to exercise criminal jurisdiction in Korea, we have designated the U.S. military authorities as sole authorities to exercise criminal jurisdiction since it is inconceivable for us that authorities other than U.S. military authorities would exercise jurisdiction within the Republic of Korea.

The chief U.S. negotiator stated at the 46th session that this is a matter of internal concern for the U.S. and that the language had been made broad enough to provide

0038

for any possible exercise of jurisdictinn by U.S. authority. However, we are of the opinion that it is not the internal concern solely for the U.S. We believe that the exercise of Criminal Jurisdiction in Korea by the authorities of the United States, whether they be military authorities or other than military authorities, has to be mutually agreed upon. We have serious concern over the statement which implies the possibility of U.S. authorities in Korea other than military authorities exercising judicial power in Korea.

As for the authorities of the Republic of Korea exercising criminal jurisdiction, we understand your intention of limiting our authorities to the civil side is motivated from apprehension that the U.S. military personnel might be tried by Korean court-martial. We are prepared to assure you that we would not exercise jurisdiction over U.S. military personnel by military tribunal under any circumstances. Accordingly we propose to record this assurance in the joint minutes and we believe you would accept our version. We are sure that our new proposal will certainly meet your requirements.

Turning to the so-called "combat zone", basically, our position of not recognizing the concept of combat zone remains as before. We understand that the U.S. side's primary objective to establish a combat zone is to ensure combat readiness of the U.S. troops by having exclusive criminal jurisdiction in that area. Our view is that a workable arrangement in the custody clause and waiver clause could be agreed upon to satisfy your concern without resorting to the concept of a combat zone. Accordingly,

0099

we would suggest revision in our draft of the two respective clauses on the condition that the U.S. side will withdraw the concept of a combat zone.

With respect to the Agreed Minute re Paragraph 3(c) of our draft concerning the problem of waiver of primary right to exercise jurisdiction, we offer to add the following paragraph as the first paragraph "the authorities of the Republic of Korea will, upon the notification of individual cases falling under the waiver provided in Article ____ paragraph 3(c) from the military authorities of the United States, waive its primary right to exercise jurisdiction under Article ____ except where they determine that it is of particular importance that jurisdiction be exercised by the authorities of the Republic of Korea."

Further, we propose to add the words "In addition to the foregoing provisions" before the second paragraph which has been placed as the first paragraph in our original draft. We are also prepared to consider the U.S. paragraph which reads "To facilitate the expeditious disposal of offenses of minor importance, arrangements may be made between United States authorities and the competent authorities of the Republic of Korea to dispense with notification".

As you may notice in our proposal, we are greatly binding ourselves by this paragraph, because under this clause we have to waive most of the cases by simple notification from the U.S. side. Under this clause, our ground for retaining primary right despite the waiver request is extremely limited due to the key phrase "particular importance". We would like to recall that at the previous meeting ypur side stated that the U.S. intention is to obtain maximum waiver. We believe that our new proposal would effectively meet your requirements.

0100

As to the procedure for mutual waiver, we would prefer to settle the detailed arrangements through the Joint Committee. However, in accordance with the principle set forth above, we could conceive the following detailed procedures for future reference: "When the Korean authorities hold the view that by reason of special circumstances in a specific case, major interests of the Korean administration of justice make imperative the exercise of the Korean jurisdiction, They will notify the military authorities of the United States of that opinion within a reasonable period. In case an understanding cannot be reached in discussion between the both sides, the U.S. military authorities will seek agreement of the Joint Committee within fifteen days from the date of receipt of such notification. If the U.S. authorities do not reply within fifteen days, the request for waiver will be deemed to have recalled." We have mentioned the above procedures as an example. We would propose that the final procedures would be negotiated at the Joint Committee.

With respect to the provisions of paragraph 5(d) of the Korean draft regarding the pre-trial custody of the accused, we wish to propose the following revision and an additional paragraph 5(e):

"Paragraph 5(d) An accused member of the United States Armed Forces or civilian component over whom the Republic of Korea is to exercise jurisdiction will, if he is in the hands of the United States, be under the custody of the United States during all judicial proceedings and until custody is requested by the authorities of the Republic of Korea.

0101

"The military authorities of the United States may transfer custody to the Korean authorities at any time and shall give sympathetic consideration to any request for the transfer of custody which may be made by the Korean authorities in specific cases."

"Paragraph 5(e) In respect of offenses solely against the security of the Republic of Korea provided in Paragraph 2(c), custody shall remain with the authorities of the Republic of Korea."

In order to meet the desires of the U.S. negotiators to the maximum extent, we propose to provide some additional provisions to facilitate expeditious investigation and trial on the part of the authorities of the Republic of Korea.

With respect to the provisions regarding the custody in the hands of the Republic of Korea, we are assuring you that custody will be turned over to the hands pf the United States unless there is any specific reason and if there arises any question as to the existence of adequate cause and necessity to retain such accused, it will be determined at the Joint Committee.

With respect to pre-trial custody of the security offenses, we would like to emphasize that the custody of such offender should rest with the authorities of the Republic of Korea since an offender of the security offenses against the Republic of Korea could disclose security information to others, while he is in the hands of the authorities other than Korea. Accordingly the Korean negotiators find no reason why the military authorities of the United States should take custody of such

0102

an offender.

The Korean negotiators would like to delete from the provision of paragraph 3(a) (ii) of the Korean draft the following language "provided that such act or omission is directly related to the duty. The question as to whether offenses were committed in the performance of official duty shall be decided by a competent district public prosecutor of the Republic of Korea. In case the offender's commanding officer finds otherwise, he may appeal from the prosecutor's decision to the Ministry of Justice within ten days from the receipt of the decision of the prosecutor, and the decision of the Minister of Justice shall be final." We propose the following alternative draft as Agreed Minute re Paragraph 3(a) (ii). If the U.S. negotiators accept the proposed alternative draft, the Korean negotiators would give favorable consideration to the U.S. proposal made at the previous meeting to record in the Joint Summary the definition of official duty modified after the FEAF version of 1956:

"Re Paragraph 3(a) (ii)

"Where a member of the United States armed forces or civilian component is charged with an offense, a certificate issued by a staff judge advocate on behalf of his commanding officer stating that the alleged offense, if committed by him, arose out of an act or omission done in the performance of official duty, shall be sufficient evidence of the fact for the purpose of determining primary jurisdiction, unless the contrary is proved.

"If the chief prosecutor of the Republic of Korea considers that there is proof contrary to the certificate of official duty, he will refer the matter to the Joint Committee for decision.

"The above statements shall not be interpreted to prejudice in any way Article 308 of the Korean Code of Criminal Procedure."

The Korean negotiators believe the alternative draft would meet the desires expressed by the United States negotiators with respect to the issuance of a duty certificate for determining primary jurisdiction over offenses arising out of an act done in the performance of official duty.

However, the Korean negotiators, taking into account the highly legal affairs involved, deem it proper that a Staff Judge Advocate should exercise the right to make such determination on behalf of the commanding officer at divisional level.

With respect to the validity of a duty certificate, the Korean draft provides that a certificate shall be sufficient evidence of the fact for the purpose of determining primary jurisdiction, unless the contrary is proved, whereas the U.S. draft provides that it shall be conclusive. The Korean negotiators believe that the Korean authorities should be accorded the opportunity to express their views as to the validity of a certificate in the event they find evidence contrary to the certificate.

The Korean draft provides the Joint Committe as the reviewing system of disputes to work out a mutually acceptable solution.

Further, the Korean negotiators reserve to the court the power to make determination of fact by referring to Article 308 of the Korean Code of Criminal Procedure.

0104

With respect to the martial law clause, we have already mentioned our intention of giving assurance that the U.S. military personnel would not be subject to Korean courts-martial. As we understand your major interest in this clause is not to subject U.S. military personnel to our military tribunal which would be established under martial law, we believe that with this assurance your major requirement is satisfied and we hope your side would withdraw the provisions with regard to martial law.

3. At the conclusinn of Mr. Chang's statement, Mr. Habib said he wished to ask a few questions. First, did Mr. Chang's final comment, regarding the desire of the Korean negotiators to eliminate the reference in the U.S. draft to martial law, relate only to military personnel? Mr. Chang replied that the U.S. military personnel to which he referred in his statement included members of the U.S. armed forces and civilian components.

4. Mr. Habib then referred to Mr. Chang's statement that members of the U.S. armed forces would not be subject to trial by ROK court-martial under any circumstances. He asked if he had correctly understood Mr. Chang to say that this assurance would be read into the Agreed Joint Summary and not placed in the Agreed Minutes. Mr. Chang replied that this was a correct interpretation of the Korean negotiators' proposal.

5. Mr. Habib asked whether the Korean negotiators' position regarding U.S. jurisdiction over dependents was limited to the provisions of Paragraph 1. Mr. Chang replied that it was not limited to Paragraph 1, but would apply to the relevant paragraphs. However, the rights and privileges of dependents to be covered by the rest of the

0105

article should be dealt with through further negotiation.

6. Mr. Habib then stated that the U.S. negotiators believed that the Korean negotiators had presented some constructive proposals. The U.S. negotiators welcomed the spirit in which those proposals had been made. The U.S. negotiators would study the Korean proposals carefully and would consult with Washington in detail. They would then try to present an equally comprehensive exposition of the U.S. views.

7. Mr. Habib noted that Mr. Chang had not mentinned the question of trial safeguards. He asked if the Korean position on this question remained unchanged. Mr. Chang replied affirmatively.

8. Mr. Habib recalled that the negotiators had previously discussed the question of including in the SOFA specific reference to certain safeguards which were enumerated in the ROK Constitution. He said it was not clear whether the Korean negotiators agreed or disagreed that specific referance should be made in the SOFA to such safeguards. The U.S. negotiators assumed that if a safeguard were mentioned in the Constitution the Korean negotiators could not object to its inclusion in the SOFA.

9/ In reply, Mr. Chang said he would reiterate the Korean position. He said the Korean negotiators could not object if the U.S. negotiators wished to include in the SOFA items which are enumerated in the ROK Constitution and laws. However, it was a matter of style. If such safeguards are enumerated in the SOFA, the enumeration would have to include all the items listed in the Constitution. The Korean negotiators had included some safeguards in their proposed text but the U.S. negotiators wanted to include additional items. The Korean negotiators would study

0106

this matter and respond at a later meeting.

10. Mr. Habib recalled that he hdd proposed two principle during the course of the 50th meeting, namely, that items included in the ROK Constitution could be included in the SOFA and that items not included in the ROK Constitttion could be included in the SOFA. Once these two principles were established, he continued, negotiators could decide which items to include to make the SOFA more easily to both sides.

11. As an example of the U.S. negotiators' concern, Mr. Habib referred to the Agreed Minute re Paragraph 9(b) in the U.S. draft. He said that the ROK negotiators apparently agreed with the first paragraph of this Agreed Minute but had proposed deletion of the second paragraph, claiming that there is no counterpart in the Korean criminal procedures and that it is contrary to the spirit of the existing law. This paragraph guarantees the couhsel of an accused the right to examine and copy the statements of witnesses prior to trial when these statements are contained in the file of the case. The Korean negotiators had argued that under the ROK code of criminal procedure, the accused is given the opportunity to know the nature of the evidence against him and that this would suffice. The U.S. negotiators, however, believed that the right sought for the accused in the second paragraph of this Agreed Minute was a common sense right which would not be incompatible with ROK law. Mr. Habib then quoted Article 273 of the ROK criminal code, which reads in part as follows: "(1) The court may, upon application, permit the prosecutor or the accused or his counsel to

0107

examine the accused or other witnesses and to inspect evidence before the date fixed for trial ..." He pointed out that the right sought by the U.S. negotiators for incorporation in the SOFA was comparable in spirit to this provision of the ROK code, although not worded exactly the same.

12. As another example of a safeguard deemed necessary by the U.S. negotiators, Mr. Habib referred to the proposed Agreed Minute Re Paragraph 9(e). The Korean negotiators had argued that the Korean legal system requires that the accused be kept under surveillance by a competent Korean officer during any interview held by the accused with his counsel. They had therefore argued in favor of deleting the word "confidentially" from the proposed Agreed Minute. The U.S. negotiators believed that if a counsel is to perform effectively, he must be able to have his client confide in him without fear of being overheard. This could be accomplished by having the interview between the accused and his counsel take place in a locked room with a Korean guard posted outside.

13. As a further example of the variance betwean the positions of the two sides regarding trial safeguards, Mr. Habib referred to the Korean proposal to incorporate the second Agreed Minute Re Paragraph 9 of the Korean draft into the Agreed Minute re Paragraph 9(g) of the U.S. draft. This was undoubtedly an effort by the Korean negotiators to retain in force the provisions of Article 105 of the ROK Constitution, which reads as follows: "Trials and decisions of the courts shall be open to the public; however, trials may be closed to the public by a court when there is a possibility that such trials

0108

may disturb the public safety and order or be harmful to decent customs." Mr. Habib pointed out that the provisions of the Agreed Minute re Paragraph 9(g) of the U.S. draft were not intended to apply to the general public in all circumstances but were intended only to ensure that a representative of the U.S. Government would be able to attend all the proceedings connected with a trial, including any *in camera* proceedings.

14. Summing up, Mr. Habib pointed out that differences exist in both law and procedure between the U.S. legal system and that of the Republic of Korea. In some cases, these differences can be met by interpretation of the Korean laws. In other cases, the Korean laws may have to be amended to make them compatible with the terms of the SOFA. Such amendment of local law has taken place in connection with almost every SOFA which has been negotiated.

15. Mr. Chang stated that the Korean negotiators were in general agreement with the explanation given by the U.S. negotiators of the latter's position with regard to trial safeguards. The Korean negotiators were ready to settle through negotiation those items not presently covered by the ROK Constitutinn and laws. However, it did not seem necessary to them to include in the SOFA items which are alrady included in the Constitution and laws.

16. Mr. Habib pointed out that basic principles should be clearly stated in the SOFA, inasmuch as laws can be changed. The negotiators should bear in mind the fact that the passage of *ex post facto* laws has been a feature of recent Korean history.

17. Mr. Chang said the Korean negotiators understood

0109

the concern of the U.S. negotiators. However, if the laws were changed, the changes would be in the direction of more protection of human rights rather than less. Mr. Habib expressed the hope of the U.S. negotiators that this would be true but their lack of conviction, based on experience, that any changes in current laws would necessarily be for the better.

18. It was agreed to hold the next meeting on May 28 at 2:00 p.m.

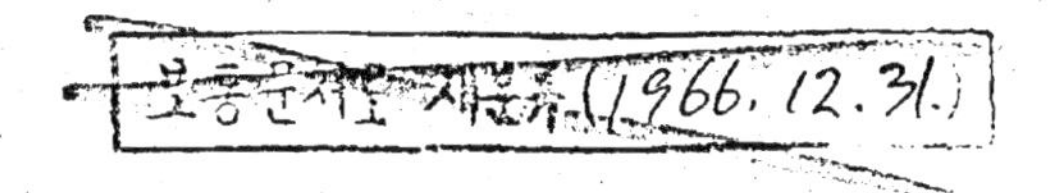

3. 제53차 회의, 5.28

0111

SOFA NEGOTIATION

Agenda for the 53rd Session

14:00 May 28,

1. Continuation of Discussions on:

   a. Local Procurement Article

   b. Foreign Exchange Controls Article

   c. Military Payment Certificates Article

   d. Customs Article

2. Other Business

3. Agenda and Date of the Next Meeting

4. Press Release

0112

기 안 지

관리 1474

기 안 자	미주과 이근팔	전화번호		공 보	필 요	불필요
	과장	국장	차관	장관		
협조자 서 명					보존 년한	
기 안 년월일	1964. 6. 22	시 행 년월일		통 제 관	정 서	기 장
분류기호 문서번호	외구미 722.2 —					
경 유 수 신 참 조	대 통 령: 참조 비서실장 국 무 총 리: 참조 비서실장	발 신	장 관			
제 목	제 53 차 주둔군지위협정 체결 교섭 실무자회의 보고					

1964. 5. 28. 하오 2 시 부터 동 4 시 15 분 까지 외무부 제 1 회의실에서 개최된 제 53 차 주둔군지위협정 체결 교섭 실무자회의에서 토의된 내용을 별첨과 같이 보고합니다.

유 첨: 제 53 차 주둔군지위협정 체결 교섭실무자회의 보고서.

끝.

1966. 12. 31. 에 예고문에 의거 일반문서로 재분류됨

첨부물에서 분리되면 보통문서로 재분류

공통서식 1—1 (갑) (16절지)

0113

제 53 차

한·미간 주둔군지위협정 체결 교섭 실무자회의

보 고 서

1. 일 시: 1964 년 5 월 28 일 하오 2 시 부터 4 시 15 분 까지.

2. 장 소: 외무부 제 1 회의실

3. 토의사항:

가: 현지조달

양측은 주한미군이 한국내에서 필요로 하는 자재 공급품 장비 건축 사업을 포함한 용역 조달을 위하여 [illegible] 용역 공급자 또는 제공자의 선택상 제약을 받음이 없이 계약을 체결할 수 있으며 필요한 경우에는 한국정부를 통하여서도 조달할 수 있다는 원칙에 합의하였으며 (미측이) 제시한 두개의 양해사항 즉

(1) 미군이 조달하는 물자 용역등에 대한 면세조치가 합동위원회에서 논의되고 있는 기간은 한국당국은 과세조치를 보류할 것과

(2) 미군인이 공무여행차 우리 나라의 철도 또는 항공기등 교통 시설을 이용하는 경우에 교통세를 현행제도에 따라 면제 하는데

우리측이 합의함으로서 양측은 현지조달조항에 관하여 완전합의를 보았다.

나. 외환통제

(1) 미측은 미군에 적용될 환율을" 불법적이 않인 최고환율" 로 할 것을 주장하고 있는데 대하여 우리측은 동 주장이 우리 나라의 2중 환율을 전제로 하고 있으며 우리 나라 현제도는 "외환은행에서 적용되는 매입률"로 하면 미측의 요구를 ~~충족히~~ 충족시킬 수 있음을 지적하였음.

(2) 미측은 우리측 제안에 대하여 현제도 하에서는 타당하나 장구한 기간 존속할 지위협정을 위하여서 예상할 수 있는 제도상의 변경에 대비하여 "최고율"을 주장하는 것이라고 설명하고 우리 제안을 수락 할 수 없다고 하였음.

다. 군표

(1) 미측은 군표의 불법거래자를 "미국법이 허용하는 범위내"에서만 처벌하려는데 대하여 우리측은 미군법의 적용을 받지 않는 가족 기타 민간인은 한국법에 의하여 처벌되어야 한다고 주장하~~고 미측도 이를 시인하였다.~~였는

(

0114

64-(3)-(2)

0115

(2) 양측은 한국정부나 또는 기타 법이 허용하지 않는 자가 소유하게될 군표에 대하여 미측이 하등의 의무를 부담하는 것이 아니라는데 합의를 보았다.

(3) 우리측은 협정 발효 전에 한국정부가 소유하고 있는 군표의 처리에 관하여 미측과 상호 합의 하에 행할 것을 양해 사항으로 남길 것을 주장하였는바 미측은 어떠한 형태의 의무라도 부담하게 될 양해사항의 삽입에 동의할 수 없다는 입장을 계속 취하였다.

바. 관세업무

(1) 양측은 미측이 군사화물의 정의에 포함할 것을 주장하는 비세출자금기관 앞으로 탁송되는 화물이 포장 또는 표식등에 의하여 식별할 수 있음을 확인하였으며

(2) 우리측은 비세출자금기관 앞으로 탁송되는 화물에 대하여서는 미군이 한국세관에 반듯이 신고를 해야하며 또한 세관당국이 필요로 하는 정보를 자동적으로 미군으로 하여금 제출케 하는 제도를 확립하는 것이 미측 주장을 검토할 수 있는 전제가 ~~되어야~~ 된다고 주장하였다.

4. 기타 사항: 차기 회의일자: 1964 년 6 월 5 일(금요일) 하오 3 시. 끝

~~보통문서로 재분류(1966.12.31.)~~

1966.12.31에 예고문에 의거 일반문서로 재분류됨

0116

0117

STATUS OF FORCES NEGOTIATIONS: 53rd Meeting

SUBJECTS:
1. Local Procurement
2. Foreign Exchange Controls
3. Military Payment Certificates
4. Customs

PLACE: Ministry of Foreign Affairs

DATE: May 28, 1964

PARTICIPANTS:

Republic of Korea

CHANG Sang-mun
KU Chung-hoe
Major YI Kae-hun, ROKA
O Chae-hi
YI Kae-chol
YI Kun-pal (Interpreter)
CHO Chung-hyun
HWANG Yong-chae

United States

Philip C. Habib
Brig. General G.G. O'Connor, USA
Colonel Howard Smigelow, USA
Captain John Wayne, USN
Colonel Kenneth C. Crawford, USA
Benjamin A. Fleck
Robert A. Kinney
Lt. Colonel Charles Wright, USA
Robert A. Lewis

0118

Local Procurement

1. Mr. Chang opened the meeting by stating that the revision of Paragraph 1 of the Local Procurement Article and the two understandings proposed by the U.S. negotiators at the 51st meeting were acceptable to the Korean negotiators, provided the U.S. negotiators would agree to include in the Agreed Joint Summary a statement to the effect that the inclusion of the word "services" in Paragraph 1 would not in any way affect the provisions of the Labor Procurement Article. Mr. Habib replied that this understanding was acceptable to the U.S. negotiators. Full agreement was thereupon reached on the Local Procurement Article.

Foreign Exchange Controls

2. Turning to the Foreign Exchange Controls Article, Mr. Chang said that the only remaining point of difference was to be found in the Agreed Minute. The U.S. draft used the term "highest rate" while the Korean draft used the term "basic rate". In order to resolve this difference, the Korean negotiators proposed that instead of either of the foregoing terms, the phraseology "buying rate of the foreign exchange bank" be used. He pointed out that since the adoption of the new conversion system, there is only one buying rate now applicable.

3. Mr. Habib said that the U.S. negotiators would study the Korean proposal. However, their initial reaction was that the proposal did not meet their requirement. The proposition set forth in the U.S. draft of the Agreed Minute was very simple. It would provide that funds would be converted by the U.S. armed forces "in accordance with the Korean Foreign Exchange Control Law and regulations" and at the highest rate which is not unlawful. The Korean negotiators were suggesting that the present buying rate at the Bank of Korea is the highest buying rate which is not unlawful. The U.S. negotiators agreed that this was a fact at that moment. However, laws can be changed and adjustments in rates can be made unilaterally. The purpose of the U.S. draft was to provide in advance for any such change in the future, in order to avoid

0119

discriminatory rates. The Korean proposal does not take into account the long-term nature of the Status of Forces Agreement or the necessity to provide for changes in the law without changing the purpose of the Agreement. The reluctance of the Korean negotiators to agree to the establishment of this principle led the U.S. negotiators to suspect that there may be some intention on the part of the Korean authorities to alter the exchange rate in the future, to the detriment of the U.S. armed forces. Naturally, the U.S. negotiators wished to preclude such alteration. If necessary, the U.S. negotiators would submit the Korean proposal to Washington, but the reply from Washington would certainly be identical with the position just expressed.

4. Mr. Chang replied that the language proposed by the Korean negotiators would meet the requirements of the U.S. authorities under the present exchange system and would guarantee that there would be no discriminatory treatment of the U.S. armed forces. If any changes in the exchange rate should occur in the future, the Korean negotiators hoped that both sides would negotiate a mutually acceptable solution. If the U.S. negotiators insisted that the language of this Agreed Minute should meet all foreseeable contingencies, then the phrase "equitable rate" should suffice. The language of the U.S. draft bore the connotation that the official exchange rate is not a unitary rate. The language was therefore unacceptable to the Korean negotiators. Mr. Chang said they would consider this question further and comment at the next meeting.

5. Mr. Habib replied that the U.S. negotiators fully understood the present system. He pointed out that it is not unusual in many countries for various exchange rates to exist simultaneously. The U.S. negotiators were not prepared to agree that if the rate is changed, the rate charged to the U.S. armed forces would be subject to negotiation. He pointed out that there is no Status of Forces Agreement under the provisions of which the system proposed by the U.S. negotiators is not the practice. The Korean negotiators could not expect the U.S. negotiators to agree to a loophole which might require the U.S. armed forces to convert at an unfavorable rate. The unwillingness

0120

8.

Accordingly, the Korean negotiators proposed the insertion of the phrase "subject to the Military Law of the United States" after the word "dependents" in Para. 1(d) of the Korean draft.

The Korean negotiators believed that the U.S. authorities could punish the member of the U.S. armed forces and civilian component without the phrase "to the extent authorized by the U.S. Law". Therefore, the Korean negotiators have reached the conclusion that the phrase " to the extent authorized by the U.S. Law" should be deleted from Para. 1(b) of the U.S. draft.

0121

of the Korean negotiators to agree to this principle made the U.S. negotiators all the more certain that it was a required principle.

6. Mr. Chang stated that the Korean negotiators did not intend that the U.S. armed forces should be subject to unfavorable treatment. They believed that the principles expressed in both drafts are identical. The difficulty was a purely technical one of finding suitable language. To use the term "highest rate" implied that there was more than one official rate.

7. Mr. Habib pointed out that it was not a question of official or unofficial rates. There could be a legal rate which was higher than the "official" rate. In any case, the U.S. negotiators agreed to study this matter for further discussion at a later meeting.

Military Payment Certificates

8. Turning to the Military Payment Certificates Article, Mr. Chang stated that there were three points at issue. The first was the phrase in Paragraph 1(b) of the U.S. draft: "to the extent authorized by United States law". This language did not clarify how those persons not subject to U.S. military law would ~~be arrested and punished~~ if they abuse privileges relating to MPC. The Korean negotiators recalled that Colonel Solf had sought to clarify this point by stating that the U.S. armed forces could take administrative measures against such persons. The Korean negotiators were of the opinion that such administrative actions should not preclude the ROK authorities from punishing such offenders. In short, persons not subject to U.S. military law should be subject to trial and punishment in accordance with ROK law.

9. Secondly, Mr. Chang continued, there was disagreement over the phrase in Paragraph 1(d) of the Korean draft "after the date of coming into force of this agreement". The Korean negotiators now agreed to the deletion of this phrase.

10. Thirdly, there was disagreement over the Agreed Minutes tabled by each side. The Korean negotiators requested that ~~the~~ U.S. negotiators withdraw the U.S. Agreed

0122

Minute and agree to insertion of the Korean Agreed Minute in the Agreed Joint Summary.

11. With regard to the first point made by Mr. Chang, Mr. Habib replied that the recollection of the Korean negotiators was quite correct and that the U.S. negotiators had explained why the inclusion of the phrase "to the extent authorized by United States law" was necessary. The Korean negotiators were seeking to be reassured that inclusion of this phrase would in no way derogate from the jurisdictional authority of the ROK Government over persons not subject to U.S. law. He pointed out that jurisdictional authority is determined by the provisions of the Criminal Jurisdiction Article. There is nothing in either the U.S. draft or the Korean draft of the MPC Article which would affect that authority.

12. Mr. Habib welcomed the agreement of the Korean negotiators to delete the phrase "after the date of coming into force of this agreement".

13. With regard to the third point raised by Mr. Chang, Mr. Habib replied that the U.S. negotiators were willing to delete the U.S. Agreed Minute if the Korean negotiators would agree to delete the Korean Agreed Minute. The U.S. negotiators wished to remove from the SOFA the whole question of compensation for MPC's held by unauthorized persons. Furthermore, they could not agree to the inclusion of any language which might be construed as indicating an obligation on the part of the U.S. authorities to compensate illegal holders of MPC's.

14. Mr. Chang replied that the U.S. negotiators appeared to have misunderstood the proposal made by the Korean negotiators. The Korean negotiators had proposed deletion of the U.S. Agreed Minute and inclusion of the Korean Agreed Minute in the Agreed Joint Summary.

15. Mr. Habib stated that the U.S. negotiators had understood very well the Korean proposal. He said the U.S. negotiators could not object if the Korean negotiators proposed to include in the Agreed Joint Summary language indicating that the Korean authorities had no intention of abandoning their intention to raise the

0123

question of compensation for discussion at some future date. However, the U.S. negotiators could not agree to the inclusion of any language which would imply an obligation on the U.S. authorities to pay compensation. With that understanding, the U.S. negotiators were prepared to delete both Agreed Minutes. The U.S. negotiators would study the matter further to see whether some alternative wording might not be drafted for inclusion in the Agreed Joint Summary instead of the Korean Agreed Minute. Mr. Chang expressed the desire of the Korean negotiators that whatever alternative wording was developed would incorporate the spirit of the Korean Agreed Minute.

Customs

16. Turning to the Customs Article, Mr. Habib recalled that full agreement had been reached on this article, except for Paragraph 5(a) and Agreed Minutes 2, 3, and 7. He inquired whether the Korean negotiators were prepared to accept Agreed Minute 3 of the U.S. draft, including the proposed additional sentence.

17. Mr. Chang said the Korean negotiators wished to ask a few questions concerning the proposed additional sentence. First, was cargo consigned to the non-appropriated fund organizations clearly distinguishable from other cargo in terms of packing or markings on them? Secondly, were the U.S. authorities prepared to provide for NAFO cargo packing lists as well as invoices and other documents which the Korean customs authorities might deem necessary?

18. Mr. Habib replied that cargo consigned to non-appropriated fund organizations is clearly distinguishable from other cargo in terms of markings and documentation. According to the terms of the U.S. draft, the Joint Committee will provide information pertinent to such cargo on request. He said the U.S. authorities fully intend to live up to the obligations placed upon them by the provisions of this article. There was no intent to conceal what is normally considered to be pertinent information.

19. Mr. Chang then indicated that the Korean negotiators desired that all pertinent information regarding NAFO cargo should be provided auto-

0124

21. Mr. Chang said it was the responsibility of the negotiators to decide on the principle whether the pertinent information be provided to the Korean side on an automatic basis or not. If the U.S. negotiators would agree to the principle, the Korean negotiators were prepared to consider the U.S. additional sentence in order to settle the argument on Agreed Minute 3 of the U.S. draft.

22. Mr. Habib asked if the Korean negotiators would be satisfied in case the U.S. negotiators assured the Korean side that pertinent information will be furnished to the Korean Authorities on an automatic basis upon request through the Joint Committee. Mr. Chang indicated the possibility of acceptance by the Korean negotiators of the assurance made by Mr. Habib provided that the U.S. side would eliminate the procedure of going through the Joint Committee.

0125

matically to the Korean customs officials, without going through the Joint Committee. If the Korean customs authorities detected something amiss, then they would take the matter to the Joint Committee but they did not want to have to request the Joint Committee for information every time a ship came into port. Therefore, they wished to establish the principle in the SOFA that the pertinent information, including invoices, packing lists, and customs declarations would be provided routinely to the Korean customs officials on an automatic basis by the U.S. armed forces.

20. In reply to these arguments, Mr. Habib stated that the U.S. negotiators were negotiating on the principle that the Joint Committee would be responsible for administering the Status of Forces Agreement. They were unwilling, therefore, to include administrative details of the type desired by the Korean negotiators in the Agreement itself. What the Korean negotiators were proposing would prove to be an administrative nightmare. There was nothing in the U.S. draft which would prevent the establishment of a system such as that proposed by the Korean negotiators. However, it was the responsibility of the Joint Committee, not the negotiators, to decide how the SOFA was to be administered. Therefore, the Joint Committee should decide what constituted "pertinent" information and by what means that information would be provided to the Korean authorities.

23. At this point, it was agreed to adjourn the meeting. The next meeting was scheduled for June 4 at 2:00 p.m.

21.
22.

0126

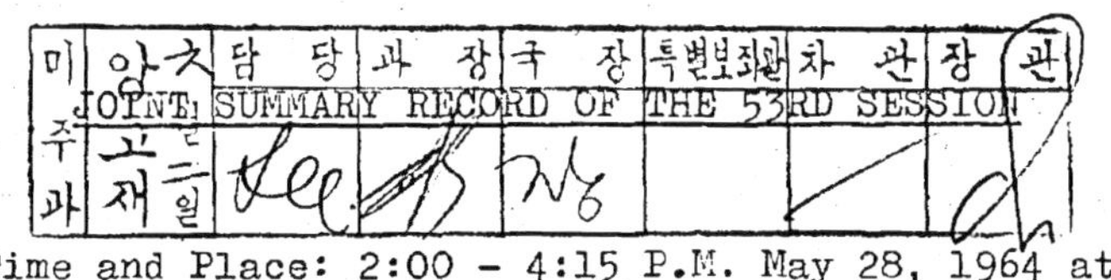

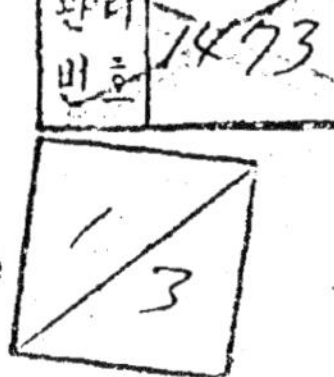

1. Time and Place: 2:00 - 4:15 P.M. May 28, 1964 at the Foreign Ministry's Conference Room (No.1)

2. Attendants:

ROK Side:

Mr. Chang, Sang Moon	Director European and American Affairs Bureau
Mr. Koo, Choong Whay	Chief, American Section Ministry of Foreign Affairs
Mr. Oh, Jae Hee	Chief, Treaty Section Ministry of Foreign Affairs
Mr. Cho, Choong Hoon	Chief Customs Section Ministry of Finance
Maj. Lee, Kye Hoon	Military Affairs Section Ministry of National Defense
Mr. Ahn, Yun Gi	3rd Secretary Ministry of Foreign Affairs
Mr. Lee, Kae Chul	3rd Secretary Ministry of Foreign Affairs
Mr. Lee, Keun Pal (Rapporteur and Interpreter)	3rd Secretary Ministry of Foreign Affairs
Mr. Park, Won Chul	3rd Secretary Ministry of Foreign Affairs
Mr. Hwang, Young Jae	3rd Secretary Ministry of Foreign Affairs

U.S. Side:

Mr. Philip C. Habib	Counselor American Embassy
Brig. Gen. G.G. O'Connor	Deputy Chief of Staff 8th U.S. Army
Col. Howard Smigelow	Deputy Chief of Staff 8th U.S. Army
Capt. John Wayne	Assistant Chief of Staff USN/K
Col. Kenneth C. Crawford	Staff Judge Advocates Office 8th U.S. Army

0127

Mr. Benjamin A. Fleck (Rapporteur and Press Officer)	First Secretary American Embassy
Mr. Robert A. Kinney	J-5 8th U.S. Army
Lt. Col. Charles Wright	Staff Judge Advocate's Office 8th U.S. Army
Mr. Robert A. Lewis	2nd Secretary American Embassy
Mr. Edward Hurwitz	2nd Secretary American Embassy

Local Procurement

1. Mr. Chang opened the meeting by stating that the revision of Paragraph 1 of the Local Procurement Article and the two understandings proposed by the U.S. negotiators at the 51st meeting were acceptable to the Korean negotiators, provided the U.S. negotiators would agree to include in the Agreed Joint Summary a statement to the effect that the inclusion of the word "services" in Paragraph 1 would not in any way affect the provisions of the Labor Procurement Article. Mr. Habib replied that this understanding was acceptable to the U.S. negotiators. Full agreement was thereupon reached on the Local Procurement Article.

Foreign Exchange Controls

2. Turning to the Foreign Exchange Controls Article, Mr. Chang said that the only remaining point of difference was to be found in the Agreed Minute. The U.S. draft used the term "highest rate" while the Korean draft used the term "basic rate." In order to resolve this difference, the Korean negotiators proposed that instead of either of the foregoing terms, the phraseology "buying rate of the foreign exchange bank" be used. He pointed out that since the adoption of the new conversion system, there is only one buying rate now applicable.

0128

3. Mr. Habib said that the U.S. negotiators would study the Korean proposal. However, their initial reaction was that the proposal did not meet their requirement. The proposition set forth in the U.S. draft of the Agreed Minute was very simple. It would provide that funds would be converted by the U.S. armed forces "in accordance with the Korean Foreign Exchange Control Law and regulations" and at the highest rate which is not unlawful. The Korean negotiators were suggesting that the present buying rate at the Bank of Korea is the highest buying rate which is not unlawful. The U.S. negotiators agreed that this was a fact at that moment. However, laws can be changed and adjustments in rates can be made unilaterally. The purpose of the U.S. draft was to provide in advance for any such changes or adjustments in the future, in order to avoid discriminatory rates. The Korean proposal does not take into account the long-term nature of the Status of Forces Agreement or the necessity to provide for changes in the law without changing the purpose of the Agreement. The reluctance of the Korean negotiators to agree to the establishment of this principle led the U.S. negotiators to suspect that there may be some intention on the part of the Korean authorities to alter the exchange rate in the future to the detriment of the U.S. armed forces. Naturally, the U.S. negotiators wished to preclude such alteration. If necessary, the U.S. negotiators would submit the Korean proposal to Washington, but the reply from Washington would certainly be identical with the position just expressed.

4. Mr. Chang replied that the language proposed by the Korean negotiators would meet the requirements of the U.S.

authorities under the present exchange system and would guarantee that there would be no discriminatory treatment of the U.S. armed forces. If any changes in the exchange rate should occur in the future, the Korean negotiators hoped that both sides would negotiate a mutually acceptable solution. If the U.S. negotiators insisted that the language of this Agreed Minute should meet all foreseeable contingencies, then the phrase "equitable rate" should suffice. The language of the U.S. draft bore the connotation that the official exchange rate is not a unitary rate. The language was therefore unacceptable to the Korean negotiators. Mr. Chang said they would consider this question further and comment at the next meeting.

5. Mr. Habib replied that the U.S. negotiators fully understood the present system. He pointed out that it is not unusual in many countries for various exchange rates to exist simultaneously. The U.S. negotiators were not prepared to agree that if the rate is changed, the rate charged to the U.S. armed forces would be subject to negotiation. He pointed out that there is no Status of Forces Agreement under the provisions of which the system proposed by the U.S. negotiators is not the practice. The Korean negotiators could not expect the U.S. negotiators to agree to a loophole which might require the U.S. armed forces to convert at an unfavorable rate. The unwillingness of the Korean negotiators to agree to this principle made the U.S. negotiators all the more certain that it was a required principle.

6. Mr. Chang stated that the Korean negotiators did not intend that the U.S. armed forces should be subject to unfavorable treatment. They believed that the principles expressed in both drafts are identical. The difficulty was a purely technical one of finding suitable language. To

0130

use the term "highest rate" implied that there was more than one official rate.

7. Mr. Habib pointed out that it was not a question of official or unofficial rates. There could be a legal rate which was higher than the "official" rate. In any case, the U.S. negotiators agreed to study this matter for further discussion at a later meeting.

Military Payment Certificates

8. Turning to the Military Payment Certificates Article, Mr. Chang stated that there were three points at issue. The first was the phrase in Paragraph 1(b) of the U.S. draft: "to the extent authorized by United States law". This language did not clarify how those persons not subject to U.S. military law would be arrested and punished if they abuse privileges relating to MPC. The Korean negotiators recalled that Colonel Solf had sought to clarify this point by stating that the U.S. armed forces could take administrative measures against such persons. The Korean negotiators were of the opinion that such administrative actions should not preclude the ROK authorities from punishing such offenders. In short, persons not subject to U.S. military law should be subject to trial and punishment in accordance with ROK law. Accordingly, the Korean negotiators proposed the insertion of the phrase "subject to the Military Law of the United States" after the word "dependents" in Para. 1(d) of the Korean draft. The Korean negotiators believed that the U.S. authorities could punish the members of the U.S. armed forces and civilian component without the phrase "to the extent authorized by the U.S. Law".

Therefore, the Korean negotiators have reached the conclusion that the phrase "to the extent authorized by the U.S. Law" should be deleted from Para. 1(b) of the U.S. draft.

9. Secondly, Mr. Chang continued, there was disagreement over the phrase in Paragraph 1(d) of the Korean draft "after the date of coming into force of this agreement". The Korean negotiators now agreed to the deletion of this phrase.

10. Thirdly, there was disagreement over the Agreed Minutes tabled by each side. The Korean negotiators requested that the U.S. negotiators withdraw the U.S. Agreed Minute and agree to insertion of the Korean Agreed Minute in the Agreed Joint Summary.

11. With regard to the first point made by Mr. Chang, Mr. Habib replied that the recollection of the Korean negotiators was quite correct and that the U.S. negotiators had explained why the inclusion of the phrase "to the extent authorized by United States law" was necessary. The Korean negotiators were seeking to be reassured that inclusion of this phrase would in no way derogate from the jurisdictional authority of the ROK Government over persons not subject to U.S. law. He pointed out that jurisdictional authority is determined by the provisions of the Criminal Jurisdiction Article. There is nothing in either the U.S. draft or the Korean draft of the MPC article which would affect that authority.

12. Mr. Habib welcomed the agreement of the Korean negotiators to delete the phrase "after the date of coming into force of this agreement".

0132

13. With regard to the third point raised by Mr. Chang, Mr. Habib replied that the U.S. negotiators were willing to delete the U.S. Agreed Minute if the Korean negotiators would agree to delete the Korean Agreed Minute. The U.S. negotiators wished to remove from the SOFA the whole question of compensation for MPC's held by unauthorized persons. Furthermore, they could not agree to the inclusion of any language which might be construed as indicating an obligation on the part of the U.S. authorities to compensate illegal holders of MPC's.

14. Mr. Chang replied that the U.S. negotiators appeared to have misunderstood the proposal made by the Korean negotiators. The Korean negotiators had proposed deletion of the U.S. Agreed Minute and inclusion of the Korean Agreed Minute in the Agreed Joint Summary.

15. Mr. Habib stated that the U.S. negotiators had understood very well the Korean proposal. He said the U.S. negotiators could not object if the Korean negotiators proposed to include in the Agreed Joint Summary language indicating that the Korean authorities had no intention of abandoning their intention to raise the question of compensation for discussion at some future date. However, the U.S. negotiators could not agree to the inclusion of any language which would imply an obligation on the U.S. authorities to pay compensation. With that understanding, the U.S. negotiators were prepared to delete both Agreed Minutes. The U.S. negotiators would study the matter further to see whether some alternative wording might not be drafted for inclusion in the Agreed Joint Summary instead of the Korean Agreed Minute. Mr. Chang expressed the desire of the Korean negotiators that whatever alternative wording was developed would incorporate the spirit of the Korean

Agreed Minute.

Customs

16. Turning to the Customs Article, Mr. Habib recalled that full agreement had been reached on this article, except for Paragraph 5(a) and Agreed Minutes 2,3 and 7. He inquired whether the Korean negotiators were prepared to accept Agreed Minute 3 of the U.S. draft, including the proposed additional sentence.

17. Mr. Chang said the Korean negotiators wished to ask a few questions concerning the proposed additional sentence. First, was cargo consigned to the non-appropriated fund organizations clearly distinguishable from other cargo in terms of packing or markings on them? Secondly, were the U.S. authorities prepared to provide for NAFO cargo packing lists as well as invoices and other documents which the Korean customs authorities might deem necessary?

18. Mr. Habib replied that cargo consigned to non-appropriated fund organizations is clearly distinguishable from other cargo in terms of markings and documentation. According to the terms of the U.S. draft, the Joint Committee will provide information pertinent to such cargo on request. He said the U.S. authorities fully intend to live up to the obligations placed upon them by the provisions of this article. There was no intent to conceal what is normally considered to be pertinent information.

19. Mr. Chang then indicated that the Korean negotiators desired that all pertinent information regarding NAFO cargo should be provided automatically to the Korean customs officials, without going through the Joint Committee. If the Korean customs authorities detected something amiss, then they would take the matter to the Joint Committee but they

0134

did not want to have to request the Joint Committee for information every time a ship came into port. Therefore, they wished to establish the principle in the SOFA that the pertinent information, inclduding invoices, packing lists, and customs declarations would be provided routinely to the Korean customs officials on an automatic basis by the U.S. armed forces.

20. In reply to these arguments, Mr. Habib stated that the U.S. negotiators were negotiating on the principle that the Joint Committee would be responsible for administering the Status of Forces Agreement. They were unwilling, therefore, to include administrative details of the type desired by the Korean negotiators in the Agreement itself. What the Korean negotiators were proposing would prove to be an administrative nightmare. There was nothing in the U.S. draft which would prevent the establishment of a system such as that proposed by the Korean negotiators. However, it was the responsibility of the Joint Committee, not the negotiators, to decide how the SOFA was to be administered. Therefore, the Joint Committee should decide what constituted "pertinent" information and by what means that information would be provided to the Korean authorities.

21. Mr. Chang said it was the responsibility of the negotiators to decide on the principle whether the pertinent information be provided to the Korean side on an automatic basis or not. If the U.S. negotiators would agree to the principle, the Korean negotiators were prepared to consider the U.S. additional sentence in order to settle the argument on Agreed Minute 3 of the U.S. draft.

0135

22. Mr. Habib asked if the Korean negotiators would be satisfied in case the U.S. negotiators assured the Korean side that pertinent information will be furnished to the Korean Authorities on an automatic basis upon request through the Joint Committee. Mr. Chang indicated the possibility of acceptance by the Korean negotiators of the assurance made by Mr. Habib provided that the U.S. side would eliminate the procedure of going through the Joint Committee.

23. At this point, it was agreed to adjourn the meeting. The next meeting was scheduled for June 5 at 3:00 p.m.

4. 제54차 회의, 6.9

0137

ARTICLE ____

TAXATION

1. The United States armed forces shall not be subject to taxes or similar charges on property held, used or transferred by such forces in Korea.

2. Members of the United States armed forces, the civilian component, and their dependents shall not be liable to pay any Korean taxes to the Government of Korea or to any other taxing agency in Korea on income received as a result of their service with or employment by the United States armed forces, including the activities provided for in Article ____. Persons in Korea solely by reason of being members of the United States armed forces, the civilian component, or their dependents shall not be liable to pay any Korean taxes to the Government of Korea or to any taxing agency in Korea on income derived from sources outside of Korea, nor shall periods during which such persons are in Korea be considered as periods of residence or domicile in Korea for the purpose of Korean taxation. The provisions of this Article do not exempt such persons from payment of Korean taxes on income derived from Korean sources, other than those sources referred to in the first sentence of this paragraph, nor do they exempt United States citizens who claim Korean residence for United States income tax purposes from

0138

payment of Korean taxes on income.

3. Members of the United States armed forces, the civilian component, and their dependents shall be exempt from taxation in Korea on the holding, use, transfer inter se, or transfer by death of movable property, tangible or intangible, the presence of which in Korea is due solely to the temporary presence of these persons in Korea, provided that such exemption shall not apply to property held for the purpose of investment or the conduct of business in Korea or to any intangible property registered in Korea.

ARTICLE

LICENSING OF MOTOR VEHICLES

1. Korea shall accept as valid, without a driving test or fee, the driving permit or license or military driving permit issued by the United States, or political subdivision thereof, to a member of the United States armed forces, the civilian component, and their dependents.

2. Official vehicles of the United States armed forces and the civilian component shall carry distinctive numbered plates or individual markings which will readily identify them.

3. Privately owned vehicles of members of the United States armed forces, the civilian component and their dependents may be licensed or registered, and shall be provided with license plate or other identification as appropriate, by the United States. The authorities of the United States shall take adequate safety measures for, and shall assure the technical supervision of, the vehicles licensed by them and shall, where necessary, and at the request of the Government of the Republic of Korea, furnish the name and address of the owner of a vehicle licensed by them.

0140

ARTICLE

3. The Government of the Republic of Korea will license and register those vehicles privately owned by members of the United States armed forces, the civilian component, or dependents. The names of the owners of such vehicles and such other pertinent information as is required by Korean law to effect the licensing and registration of such vehicles, shall be furnished to the Government of the Republic of Korea by officials of the United States Government through the Joint Committee. Except for the actual cost of the issuance of license plates, members of the United States armed forces, the civilian component, and their dependents shall be exempt from the payment of all fees and charges relating to the licensing, registration, or operation of vehicles in the Republic of Korea and, in accordance with the provisions of Article ____, from the payment of all taxes relating thereto.

0141

Jan 9, 64

2. No Korean tax shall be imposed on sales of merchandise or services by such organizations, except as provided in paragraph 1 (b) of this article. Purchases within the Republic of Korea of merchandise and supplies by such organizations shall be subject to the Korean taxes to which other purchasers of such merchandise and supplies are subject unless otherwise agreed between the two Governments.

0142

ARTICLE

Non-Appropriated Fund Activities

1. Military exchanges, messes, social clubs, theaters, newspapers and other non-appropriated fund activities authorized and regulated by the United States military authorities may be established by the United States armed forces for the use of members of such forces, the civilian component, and their dependents. Except as otherwise provided in this Agreement, such activities shall not be subject to Korean regulations, licenses, fees, taxes, or similar controls.

2. No Korean tax shall be imposed on sales of merchandise or services by such activities. Purchases within Korea of merchandise and supplies by such activities shall be subject to the Korean taxes to which other purchasers of such merchandise and supplies are subject and at rates no less favorable than those imposed on other purchasers.

3. Except as such disposal may be permitted by the United States and Korean authorities in accordance with mutually agreed conditions, goods which are sold by such activities shall not be disposed of in Korea to persons not authorized to make purchases from such activities.

4. The activities referred to in this Article shall, after consultation between the representatives of the two Governments in the Joint Committee, provide such information to the Republic of Korea tax authorities as is required by Korean tax legislation.

0143

June 9, '64

PROPOSED STATEMENT FOR JOINT AGREED SUMMARY

The ROK and U.S. negotiators agree that nothing in the Status of Forces Agreement in any way prevents the appropriate authorities of either the Republic of Korea or the U.S. from raising any appropriate matter at any time with each other. The U.S. negotiators recognize the desire of the ROK authorities to discuss the disposal of MPC's under custody of the ROK Government. However, both the ROK and U.S. negotiators have agreed to remove from the SOFA text any reference to the question of compensation for MPC's held by unauthorized persons. This agreement does not prejudice the position of either party in connection with discussion of this question through other channels.

0144

ARTICLE

MILITARY PAYMENT CERTIFICATES

1. (a) United States military payment certificates denominated in dollars may be used by persons authorized by the United States for internal transactions. The Government of the United States will take appropriate action to insure that authorized personnel are prohibited from engaging in transactions involving military payment certificates except as authorized by United States regulations. The Government of Korea will take necessary action to prohibit unauthorized persons from engaging in transactions involving military payment certificates and with the aid of United States authorities will undertake to apprehend and punish any person or persons under its jurisdiction involved in the counterfeiting or uttering of counterfeit military payment certificates.

(b) It is agreed that the United States authorities will to the extent authorized by United States law, apprehend and punish members of the United States armed forces, the civilian component, or their dependents, who tender military payment certificates to unauthorized persons and that no obligation will be due to such unauthorized persons or to the Government of Korea or its agencies from the United States or any of its agencies as a result of any unauthorized use of military payment certificates within Korea.

0145

2. In order to exercise control of military payment certificates the United States may designate certain American financial institutions to maintain and operate, under United States supervision, facilities for the use of persons authorized by the United States to use military payments certificates. Institutions authorized to maintain military banking facilities will establish and maintain such facilities physically separated from their Korean commercial banking business, with personnel whose sole duty is to maintain and operate such facilities. Such facilities shall be permitted to maintain United States currency bank accounts and to perform all financial transactions in connection therewith including receipt and remission of funds to the extent provided by Article .... paragraph 2, of this Agreement.

0146

FOREIGN EXCHANGE CONTROLS

AGREED MINUTE

Payment in Korea by the United States armed forces including those activities provided in Article ______, to persons other than members of the United States armed forces, civilian component, their dependents and those persons referred to in Article ______ shall be effected in accordance with the Korean Foreign Exchange Control Law and regulations. The funds to be used for these transactions shall be convertible into currency of the Republic of Korea at the highest rate in terms of the number of Korean Won per United States dollar which, at the time the conversion is made, is not unlawful in the Republic of Korea.

0147

ARTICLE XIX - Military Payment Certificates

AGREED MINUTE

Inasmuch as United States Military Payment Certificates are property of the United States Government, any Military Payment Certificates which are in, or come into, the possession of the Government of the Republic of Korea shall be returned without compensation to the authorities of the United States armed forces as expeditiously as practicable.

0148

ARTICLE

1. Members of the United States armed forces, the civilian component and their dependents, shall be subject to the foreign exchange controls of the Government of the Republic of Korea.

2. The preceding paragraph shall not be construed to preclude the transmission into or out of Korea of United States dollars or dollar instruments representing the official funds of the United States or realized as a result of service or employment in connection with this Agreement by members of the United States armed forces and the civilian component, or realized by such persons and their dependents from sources outside Korea.

3. The United States authorities shall take suitable measures to preclude the abuse of the privileges stipulated in the preceding paragraphs or circumvention of the Korean foreign exchange controls.

0149

관리번호 1476

기 안 지

기 안 자	미주과 이근팔	전화번호		공 보	필요 불필요
	과장	국장	차관	장관	
협조자 서명				보존년한	
기안 년월일	1964. 6. 10.	시행 년월일	통제관 검열	정서기장	
분류기호 문서번호	외구미 722.2 —				
경유 수신 참조	대통령: 참조: 비서실장 국무총리: 참조: 비서실장	발신	장관		
제 목	제 54 차 주둔군지위협정 체결 교섭 실무자회의 보고				

1964. 6. 9. 하오 3 시부터 동 4 시 15 분까지 외무부 제 1 회의실에서 개최된 제 54 차 주둔군지위협정 체결 교섭 실무자회의에서 토의된 내용을 별첨과 같이 보고합니다.

유 첨: 제 54 차 주둔군지위협정 체결 교섭실무자회의 보고서.

끝.

첨부물에서 분리되면 보통문서로 재분류

1964. 6. 1. 예고문에 의거 일반문서로 재분류됨

발송 No. 263 1964. 6. 12. 외무부

공통서식 1—1 (갑) (16절지)

0150

제 54 차

한• 미간 주둔군지위협정 체결 교섭실무자회의

보 고 서

1. 일 시: 1964 년 6 월 9 일 하오 3 시 부터 동 4 시 15 분 까지.

2. 장 소: 외무부 제1 회의실

3. 토의사항:

가. 군표

(1) 미측은 본 협정 발효 이전에 한국정부가 보유하고 있는 미군표의 처리에 관하여 양측이 동 문제를 본 협정의 대상으로 부터 제외하되 별도 경로를 통하여 동 문제를 토의하는 것을 저해하지는 않을 것이라는 양해 하에 군표의 처리방안에 관한 쌍방 주장을 다 같이 철회할 것을 제안하였다.

(2) 우리측은 미측의 제안이 건설적이라고 지적하고 양측의 입장이 원칙적으로 접근하였음을 시인하면서 미측 제안을 검토하여 다음 회의에서 태도를 밝힐 것이라고 답변하였다.

나. 외환통제

(1) 우리측은 미측이 외환율을 불법적이 않인 최고환율로 할 것을 주장하고 있는데 대하여 동안이 우리 나라 현실환율제도 하에서는 타당하지 못하며 따라서 "외환은행에서 적용되는 매입율"로 할 것을 계속 주장하였으나 미측은 예상할 수 있는 외환제도 상의 변경에 대비하여 미측 요망을 충족시킬 수 없을 것이라는 이유로 우리 제안을 수락할 수 없다고 고집하였다.

(2) 우리측은 미측의 이와 같은 태도에 감하여 미측이 주장하는 바와 같이 "불법적이 않인 최고환율"로 하되 "외환은행에서 적용되는 환율"일 것을 주장하고 현제도 하에서는 외환매입율 이외에 외환증서의 자유매매율이 있는 고로 "불법적이 않인 최고율"이라고 만 한다면 외환증서의 자유매매율을 포함할 가능성이 있어 수락할 수 없음을 명백히 하였다.

(3) 우리측은 또한 질문을 통하여 미측이 외환은행의 매입율 보다 높은 외환증서의 자유매매율의 적용을 원하고 있음을 확인하였다.

0151

64. 3-11

14-3-20 (2)　　미국·은 110-7(2)

0152

다. 관세업무

(1) 우리측은 미군당국이 비세출자금기관 앞으로 탁송되는 화물에 관한 필요한 정보를 한국관세당국에 자동적으로 제공할 것을 제안하고 미측이 우리 제안을 수락한다면 우리측도 군사화물의 정의에 관한 미측의 주장을 고려할 것을 시사하였다.

4. 기타 사항:

가. 차기 회의 일자: 1964. 6. 19. 하오 2 시 부터. 끝.

64-3-20 (2)

마이크로 110-7 (2)

0154

STATUS OF FORCES NEGOTIATIONS: 54th Meeting

Subjects: 1. Military Payment Certificates
2. Foreign Exchange Controls
3. Customs

Place: Ministry of Foreign Affairs

Date: June 9, 1964

Participants:

Republic of Korea	United States
CHANG Sang-mun	Philip C. Habib
Chung-hoe	Brig. General G.G. O'Connor, USA
Colonel KIM Won-kil, ROKA	Colonel Howard Smigelow, USA
O Chae-hi	Colonel Kenneth C. Crawford, USA
CHO Chung-hyun	Frank R. La Macchia
YI Kun-pal (Interpreter)	Benjamin A. Fleck
YI Kae-chol	Robert A. Kinney
CHUNG U-yong	Lt. Colonel Charles Wright, USA
HWANG Yong-chae	Robert A. Lewis

0155

1. Mr. Habib opened the meeting by introducing Mr. La Macchia, who was joining the U.S. negotiating team in place of Mr. Sartorius. Mr. Chang welcomed Mr. La Macchia on behalf of the Korean negotiators.

Military Payment Certificates Article

2. Taking up the first item on the agenda, the MPC Article, Mr. Chang asked if the U.S. negotiators had any comments to make. Mr. Habib replied that at the 53rd meeting, the Korean negotiators had suggested the inclusion in the Agreed Joint Summary of a statement referring to the desire of the ROK Government to obtain compensation for Military Payment Certificates in its possession. The U.S. negotiators understood that the Korean negotiators, in making that suggestion, were indicating their willingness to set aside the question of compensation from the Status of Forces Agreement by removing from the text of the Agreement any reference to the question. At the same time, the U.S. negotiators were compelled to make clear the position of the U.S. Government that it was under no obligation to pay such compensation. Each ide, therefore, was trying not to prejudice its position while recognizing that the SOFA was not the instrument by which a solution to this problem would ultimately be found.

3. In an attempt to meet the needs of both sides, Mr. Habib continued, the S. negotiators had formulated language which they proposed as an understanding to be placed in the Agreed Joint Summary. He thereupon tabled the following language:

> "The ROK and U.S. negotiators agree that nothing in the Status of Forces Agreement in any way prevents the appropriate authorities of either the Republic of Korea or the United States from raising any appropriate matter at any time with each other. The U.S. negotiators recognize the desire of the ROK authorities to discuss the disposal of Military Payment Certificates under custody of the ROK Government. However, both the ROK and U.S. negotiators have agreed to remove from the SOFA text any reference to the question of compensation for Military Payment Certificates held by unauthorized persons. This agreement does not prejudice the position of either party in connection with discussion of this question through other channels."

0156

4. Mr. Chang commented that the ROK negotiators believed this proposal to be

He explained that under the present system there is a market rate which is neither unlawful nor identical with the bank rate and upon which the bank rate is based. It should be noted that if the market rate should be higher than the bank rate, then a literal interpretation of the U.S. language would naturally lead to application of the market rate rather than the bank rate, even though the Korean negotiators believe the intention of the U.S. side is otherwise.

0157

a very constructive suggestion. They wished to know whether the term "any appropriate matter" was intended to include "the question of compensation for Military Payment Certificates held by unauthorized persons". Upon being assured by Mr. Habib that the former term was intended to include the latter, Mr. Chang stated that the Korean negotiators would consider this proposal and comment upon it at a later meeting.

5. Mr. Habib then referred to the proposal of the Korean negotiators to delete from Paragraph 1(b) of the U.S.draft the phrase "to the extent authorized by U.S. law" and to insert after the word "dependents" the phrase "subject to the Military Law of the United States". He commented that resolution of this point would have to await agreement on the equivalent point in the Criminal Jurisdiction Article. The U.S. negotiators, therefore, would reserve comment on the Korean proposals until agreement had been reached on the relevant provisions of the Criminal Jurisdiction Article.

Foreign Exchange Controls

6. Turning to the Foreign Exchange Controls Article, Mr. Chang restated the position of the Korean negotiators that the ROK Government had no intention whatsoever of imposing discriminatory rates on the U.S. armed forces. In an attempt to satisfy the needs of the U.S. negotiators, the ROK negotiators had tabled at the last meeting a suggested revision of the Agreed Minute which would provide that funds would be convertible "at the buying rate of the Foreign Exchange bank". This proposal had not been agreed to by the U.S. negotiators. The Korean negotiators wished to make clear the reasons for their inability to accept the language proposed by the U.S. negotiators: "at the highest rate .... which, at the time the conversion is made, is not unlawful in the Republic of Korea." He explained that under the present system there is a market rate ~~as well as the bank rate.~~ A literal interpretation of the U.S. language would ~~mean~~ that if the market rate should be higher than the bank rate, then ~~the U.S. forces would convert at the market rate.~~ This was why the U.S. language is unacceptable to the Korean negotiators.

7. Mr. Habib replied that at the present time the bank rate may be the highest rate. However, it will not necessarily remain so indefinitely. Therefore, there is a possibility of discriminatory rates being charged at some future time. The Korean negotiators were trying to make the current system fit the problem, while the U.S. negotiators were trying to devise language to meet possible future problems. If a rate were "lawful", it must have been provided for in ROK laws and regulations. If it has been so provided for, the U.S. armed forces should be able to take advantage of it. So far, the Korean negotiators had not proposed language which would ensure that discrimination ould not take place, ~~but the language which they had suggested would provide~~ only ~~that discrimination would not take place under the present exchange system.~~ If the Korean negotiators accepted the premise that no discriminatory rates would be imposed upon the U.S. armed forces, the U.S. negotiators knew of no simpler way of stating this premise than in the language which they had proposed..

8. Mr. Chang reiterated the assurances previously given by the ROK negotiators that the U.S. armed forces will not be discriminated against. He asked whether the armed forces would demand conversion at the market rate if the market rate became higher than the bank rate.

9. Mr. Habib replied that the U.S. negotiators would study this question. however, Their preliminary answer was in the affirmative, since the whole purpose of the present certificate system of exchange was to provide a floating and realistic exchange rate, based on market demand. After consultation and thorough study of this question, the U.S. negotiators would give their considered views at a later meeting.

10. Mr. Chang thanked Mr. Habib for his reply and stated that the point raised by Mr. Habib was exactly the reason why the U.S. language was unacceptable. The ROK negotiators were not prepared to agree to conversion by the U.S. armed forces outside of the foreign exchange banks. In a further effort to resolve the differences over this question, the Korean negotiators wished to propose another formulation. They were prepared to accept the U.S. draft of ~~the Agreed Minute~~, with the addition after the word

0159

since the Korean negotiators were making a great concession from their original position and the additional sentence proposed by the U.S. negotiators was the counter-proposal to the Korean agreed minute regarding the information on NAFO goods. In this connection, Mr. Chang stated that the agreed minute should cover the following three points:

a. Certain information on all cargo consigned to non-appropriated fund organizations shall be furnished automatically to the Korean authorities.

b. In specific cases, additional information which the Korean authorities may deem necessary shall be furnished to the Korean authorities upon request through the Joint Committee.

c. The extent of the information to be furnished automatically to the Korean authorities shall be determined by the Joint Committee.

Therefore, the Korean negotiators would appreciate it if the U.S. negotiators would take into consideration the three points proposed by the Korean side. The Korean negotiators believe that the both sides would be able to work out mutually acceptable language on the basis of the three points for the proposed additional sentence of U.S. agreed minute #3.

0160

"unlawful" of the phrase "and is applicable in transactions at foreign exchange banks", and also with the understanding that the phrase "highest rate" refers to the buying rate of the banks and not to the selling rate. This addition was made with a view to avoid any possible misunderstanding that "the highest rate" may refer to the market rate, which is also not unlawful.

11. Mr. Habib stated that the U.S. negotiators would study this proposal and reply at a later meeting.

Customs

12. Turning to the Customs Article, Mr. Habib reviewed the discussion at the previous meeting of Agreed Minute #3. The Korean negotiators had proposed that ~~a statement be included in the Agreed Joint Summary to the effect that~~ the U.S. armed forces ~~would~~ provide information regarding cargo consigned to non-appropriated fund organizations on an automatic basis. The U.S. negotiators were prepared to agree to this proposal, provided that it was made clear that the process of providing such information would be regulated and controlled through requests made to the Joint Committee. The Agreed Joint Summary could show that the negotiators agreed to the principle of automaticity and to the automatic provision of pertinent information through the Joint Committee. This would then mean complete agreement on Agreed Minute #3.

13. Mr. Chang replied that the ROK negotiators understood the U.S. position. The ROK negotiators also agreed to the principle of automaticity but believed that it was necessary to have such agreement recorded in the Agreed Minute itself, rather than in the Agreed Joint Summary, since the Korean neg... To that end, they proposed the following language as a substitution for the additional sentence previously proposed for Agreed Minute #3 by the U.S. negotiators:

> "Pertinent information on all cargo consigned to non-appropriated fund organizations shall routinely be furnished to the Korean authorities and on specific cases, additional information shall be provided to the Korean authorities upon request through the Joint Committee. The extent of pertinent information shall be determined by the Joint Committee."

14. Mr. Habib pointed ~~out~~ that this proposal was considerably different from

0161

the proposal made by the Korean negotiators at the previous meeting. The U.S. negotiators had replied to the previous proposal. With regard to this latest proposed language, the U.S. negotiators wondered what was meant by the phrase "additional information"?

15. Mr. Chang replied that "pertinent information" referred to that information which would be supplied on a routine basis, while "additional information" referred to that information which would not be supplied on a routine basis.

16. Mr. Habib stated that the English translation of the Korean proposal was defective. Perhaps more suitable wording could be worked out. The U.S. negotiators would study the proposal and reply at a later meeting.

17. At this point the meeting was adjourned. The next meeting was scheduled for June 19 at 3:00 p.m.

0162

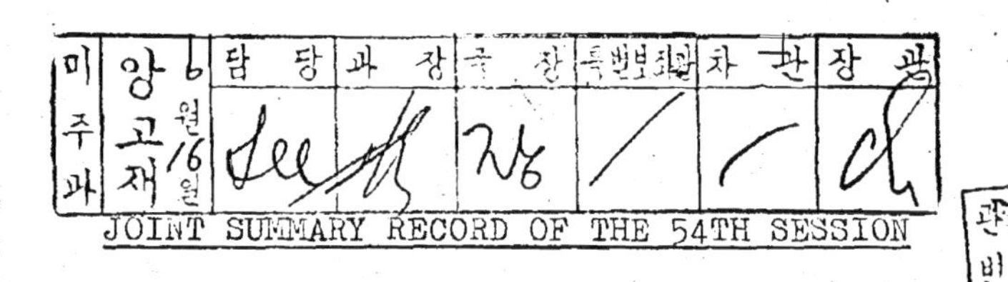

JOINT SUMMARY RECORD OF THE 54TH SESSION

1. Time and Place: 3:00 - 4:15 P.M. June 9, 1964 at the Foreign Ministry's Conference Room (No.1)

2. Attendants:

ROK Side:

Mr. Chang, Sang Moon	Director European and American Affairs Bureau
Mr. Koo, Choong Whay	Chief, American Section Ministry of Foreign Affairs
Mr. Oh, Jae Hee	Chief, Treaty Section Ministry of Foreign Affairs
Mr. Cho, Choong Hoon	Chief Customs Section Ministry of Finance
Col. Kim, Won Kil	Chief Military Affairs Section Ministry of National Defense
Mr. Chung, Woo Young	3rd Secretary Ministry of Foreign Affairs
Mr. Ahn, Yun Gi	3rd Secretary Ministry of Foreign Affairs
Mr. Lee, Kae Chul	3rd Secretary Ministry of Foreign Affairs
Mr. Lee, Keun Pal (Rapporteur and Interpreter)	3rd Secretary Ministry of Foreign Affairs
Mr. Park, Won Chul	3rd Secretary Ministry of Foreign Affairs
Mr. Hwang, Young Jae	3rd Secretary Ministry of Foreign Affairs

U.S. Side:

Mr. Philip C. Habib	Counselor American Embassy
Brig. Gen. G.G. O'Connor	Deputy Chief of Staff 8th U.S. Army
Col. Howard Smigelow	Deputy Chief of Staff 8th U.S. Army
Col. Kenneth C. Crawford	Staff Judge Advocates Office 8th U.S. Army

0163

Mr. Frank R. La Macchia	First Secretary American Embassy
Mr. Benjamin A. Fleck (Rapporteur and Press Officer)	First Secretary American Embassy
Mr. Robert A. Kinney	J-5 8th U.S. Army
Lt. Col. Charles Wright	Staff Judge Advocate's Office 8th U.S. Army
Mr. Robert A. Lewis	2nd Secretary American Embassy
Mr. Edward Hurwitz	2nd Secretary American Embassy

1. Mr. Habib opened the meeting by introducing Mr. La Macchia, who was joining the U.S. negotiating team in place of Mr. Sartorius. Mr. Chang welcomed Mr. La Macchia on behalf of the Korean negotiators.

Military Payment Certificates Article

2. Taking up the first item on the agenda, the MPC Article, Mr. Chang asked if the U.S. negotiators had any comments to make. Mr. Habib replied that at the 53rd meeting, the Korean negotiators had suggested the inclusion in the Agreed Joint Summary of a statement referring to the desire of the ROK Government to obtain compensation for Military Payment Certificates in its possession. The U.S. negotiators understood that the Korean negotiators, in making that suggestion, were indicating their willingness to set aside the question of compensation from the Status of Forces Agreement by removing from the text of the Agreement any reference to the question. At the same time, the U.S. negotiators were compelled to make clear the position of the U.S. Government that it was under no obligation to pay

0164

such compensation. Each side, therefore, was trying not to prejudice its position while recognizing that the SOFA was not the instrument by which a solution to this problem would ultimately be found.

3. In an attempt to meet the needs of both sides, Mr. Habib continued, the U.S. negotiators had formulated language which they proposed as an understanding to be placed in the Agreed Joint Summary. He thereupon tabled the following language:

> "The ROK and U.S. negotiators agree that nothing in the Status of Forces Agreement in any way prevents the appropriate authorities of either the Republic of Korea or the United States from raising any appropriate matter at any time with each other. The U.S. negotiators recognize the desire of the ROK authorities to discuss the disposal of Military Payment Certificates under custody of the ROK Government. However, both the ROK and U.S. negotiators have agreed to remove from the SOFA text any reference to the question of compensation for Military Payment Certificates held by unauthorized persons. This agreement does not prejudice the position of either party in connection with discussion of this question through other channels."

4. Mr. Chang commented that the ROK negotiators believed this proposal to be a very constructive suggestion. They wished to know whether the term "any appropriate matter" was intended to include "the question of compensation for Military Payment Certificates held by unauthorized persons". Upon being assured by Mr. Habib that the former term was intended to include the latter, Mr. Chang stated that the Korean negotiators would consider this proposal and comment upon it at a later meeting.

5. Mr. Habib then referred to the proposal of the Korean negotiators to delete from Paragraph 1(b) of the U.S. draft the phrase "to the extent authorized by U.S. law" and to insert after the word "dependents" the phrase "subject to the Military Law of the United States." He

commented that resolution of this point would have to await agreement on the equivalent point in the Criminal Jurisdiction Article. The U.S. negotiators, therefore, would reserve comment on the Korean proposals until agreement had been reached on the relevant provisions of the Criminal Jurisdiction Article.

Foreign Exchange Controls

6. Turning to the Foreign Exchange Controls Article, Mr. Chang restated the position of the Korean negotiators that the ROK Government had no intention whatsoever of imposing discriminatory rates on the U.S. armed forces. In an attempt to satisfy the needs of the U.S. negotiators, the ROK negotiators had tabled at the last meeting a suggested revision of the Agreed Minute which would provide that funds would be convertible "at the buying rate of the foreign exchange bank". This proposal had not been agreed to by the U.S. negotiators. The Korean negotiators wished to make clear the reasons for their inability to accept the language proposed by the U.S. negotiators: "at the highest rate ... which, at the time the conversion is made, is not unlawful in the Republic of Korea." He explained that under the present system there is a market rate which is neither unlawful nor identical with the bank rate and upon which the bank rate is based. It should be noted that if the market rate should be higher than the bank rate, then a literal interpretation of the U.S. language would naturally lead to application of the market rate rather than the bank rate, even though the Korean negotiators believe the intention of the U.S. side is otherwise. This was why the U.S. language is unacceptable to the Korean negotiators.

0166

7. Mr. Habib replied that at the present time the bank rate may be the highest rate. However, it will not necessarily remain so indefinitely. Therefore, there is a possibility of discriminatory rates being charged at some future time. The Korean negotiators were trying to make the current system fit the problem, while the U.S. negotiators were trying to devise language to meet possible future problems. If a rate were "lawful", it must have been provided for in ROK laws and regulations. If it has been so provided for, the U.S. armed forces should be able to take advantage of it. So far, the Korean negotiators had not proposed language which would ensure that discrimination would not take place. If the Korean negotiators accepted the premise that no discriminatory rates would be imposed upon the U.S. armed forces, the U.S. negotiators knew of no simpler way of stating this premise than in the language which they had proposed.

8. Mr. Chang reiterated the assurances previously given by the ROK negotiators that the U.S. armed forces will not be discriminated against. He asked whether the armed forces would demand conversion at the market rate if the market rate became higher than the bank rate.

9. Mr. Habib replied that the U.S. negotiators would study this question. However, their preliminary answer was in the affirmative since the whole purpose of the present certificate system of exchange was to provide a floating and realistic exchange rate, based on market demand. After consultation and thorough study of this question, the U.S. negotiators would give their considered views at a later meeting.

0167

10. Mr. Chang thanked Mr. Habib for his reply and stated that the point raised by Mr. Habib was exactly the reason why the U.S. language was unacceptable. The ROK negotiators were not prepared to agree to conversion by the U.S. armed forces outside of the foreign exchange banks. In a further effort to resolve the differences over this question, the Korean negotiators wished to propose another formulation. They were prepared to accept the U.S. draft of the Agreed Minute, with the addition after the word "unlawful" of the phrase "and is applicable in transactions at foreign exchange banks", and also with the understanding that the phrase "highest rate" refers to the buying rate of the banks and not to the selling rate. This addition was made with a view to avoid any possible misunderstanding that "the highest rate" may refer to the market rate which is also not unlawful.

11. Mr. Habib stated that the U.S. negotiators would study this proposal and reply at a later meeting.

Customs

12. Turning to the Customs Article, Mr. Habib reviewed the discussion at the previous meeting of Agreed Minute #3. The Korean negotiators had proposed that the U.S. armed forces provide information regarding cargo consigned to non-appropriated fund organizations on an automatic basis. The U.S. negotiators were prepared to agree to this proposal, provided that it was made clear that the process of providing such information would be regulated and controlled through requests made to the Joint Committee. The Agreed Joint Summary could show that the negotiators agreed to the principle of automaticity and to the automatic provision

0168

of pertinent information through the Joint Committee. This would then mean complete agreement on Agreed Minute #3.

13. Mr. Chang replied that the ROK negotiators understood the U.S. position. The ROK negotiators also agreed to the principle of automaticity but believed that it was necessary to have such agreement recorded in the Agreed Minute itself, rather than in the Agreed Joint Summary since the Korean negotiators were making a great concession from their original position and the additional sentence proposed by the U.S. negotiators was the counter-proposal to the Korean agreed minute regarding the information on NAFO goods. To that end, they proposed the following language as a substitution for the additional sentence previously proposed for Agreed Minute #3 by the U.S. negotiators:

> "Pertinent information on all cargo consigned to non-appropriated fund organizations shall routinely be furnished to the Korean authorities and on specific cases, additional information shall be provided to the Korean authorities upon request through the Joint Committee. The extent of pertinent information shall be determined by the Joint Committee."

14. Mr. Habib pointed out that this proposal was considerably different from the proposal made by the Korean negotiators at the previous meeting. The U.S. negotiators had replied to the previous proposal. With regard to this latest proposed language, the U.S. negotiators wondered what was meant by the phrase "additional information"?

15. Mr. Chang replied that "pertinent information" referred to that information which would be supplied on a routine basis, while "additional information" referred to that information which would not be supplied on a routine basis.

0169

16. Mr. Habib stated that the English translation of the Korean proposal was defective. Perhaps more suitable wording could be worked out. The U.S. negotiators would study the proposal and reply at a later meeting.

17. At this point the meeting was adjourned. The next meeting was scheduled for June 19 at 3:00 p.m.

5. 제55차 회의, 6. 19

0171

SOFA NEGOTIATION

Agenda for the 54th Session

15:00 June 9, 1964

1. Continuation of Discussions on:
   a. Military Payment Certificates Article
   b. Foreign Exchange Controls Article
   c. Customs Article
2. Other Business
3. Agenda and Date of the Next Meeting
4. Press Release

0172

기 안 용 지

관리번호 1478

자체통제		기안처	미주과 이근팔	전화번호	근거서류접수일자

과장	국장	차관	장관		
(서명)	(서명)	(서명)	(서명)		

관계관 서명						
기안년월일	1964. 6. 22.	시행년월일	검열 1964. 6. 토제관 종결	보존년한		정서기장
분류기호	외구미 722.2—	전체통제				
경유 수신 참조	대통령 참조: 비서실장 국무총리 참조: 비서실장		발신	장관		
제목	제 55 차 주둔군지위협정 체결 교섭실무자회의 보고					

1964. 6. 19. 하오 3시부터 동 5시 까지 외무부 제 1 회의실에서 개최된 제 55 차 주둔군지위협정 체결 교섭 실무자회의에서 토의된 내용을 별첨과 같이 보고합니다.

유 첨: 제 55 차 주둔군지위협정 체결 교섭실무자회의 보고서 1부. 끝.

보통문서로 재분류(1966. 12. 31.)

1966, 12. 31 예고문에 의거 일반문서로 재분류됨

승인서식 1-1-3 (11-00900-03) (195mm×265mm16절지)

0173

제 55 차

한.미 간 주둔군지위협정 체결 교섭실무자회의

보 고 서

1. 일 시: 1964 년 6 월 19 일 하오 3 시 부터 동 5 시 까지.

2. 장 소: 외무부 제 1 회의실

3. 토의사항:

가. 보호조치

(1) 미국측은 미군대 군대구성원 군속 군계약자 및 그들의 가족과 재산의 안전과 보호를 위하여 한국당국이 입법조치를 포함한 필요한 조치를 취할 것을 요구하고 있다.

(2) 우리측은 그들의 안전과 보호를 위하여 한국정부가 필요하다고 인정하는 조치를 취하는데 협조할 것이며 미국정부 재산 및 공문서의 안전 및 보호와 범법자의 처벌을 위하여 입법조치 기타 필요한 조치를 취할 용의가 있으나 개인의 재산 및 신체의 보호를 위하여 입법조치 까지 취할 수는 없다고 주장 하였다.

나. 군표

(1) 양측은 협정 발효 이전에 한국정부가 보유하고 있는 미군표의 처리문제를 본 협정의 대상으로 부터 제외하되 당사국의 일방이 별도로 논의할 것을 제의하는 것은 무방하다는 것을 양해사항 으로 채택하는데 합의를 보았다.

(2) 양측은 기타 한국측이 제 54 차 회의에서 제안한 다음과 같은 문제는 형사재판관할권규정과 관련이 있음으로 동 관계규정에서 합의를 볼 때 까지 논의를 보류하기로 하였다.

(ㄱ) 미군당국이 군표관계 범법자를 처벌함에 있어서 "미국법의 허용하는 범위 내에서" 만 처벌하려는 것은 부당함으로 제한적 용어를 삭제할 것 및

(ㄴ) 미군이 처벌할 수 있는 대상자 중 군인 및 군속의 가족에 대하여서는 "미군법에 복하는 가족" 이라고 규정할 것.

0174

64-3-1(1)

64-3-21(2) 미국문 110-6(2)

0175

다. 관세

(1) 미측은 비세출자금기관 앞으로 탁송되는 화물에 관한 필요한 정보를 한국당국에 정기적으로 제공할 것과 그 정보의 범위는 합동위원회에서 결정할 것을 제의함으로서 우리측 주장에 상당히 접근하였다.

(2) 그러나 우리측은 자동적으로 제공되는 정보 이외에 수시 한국당국이 필요하다고 인정하는 추가적 정보를 합동위원회를 통하여 요청하면 미군당국은 제공하여야 한다는 원칙을 미측 제안에 반영시킬 것을 주장하였으며 미측은 이를 고려할것 이라고 대답하였다.

라. 외환관리

(1) ~~한국측의~~ 우리측은 제 54 차 회의에서 미측이 주장하여 온바와 같이 미측의 외환 매매에 적용될 환율을 "불법적이 않인 최고환율"로 하되 "외환은행에서 적용되는 환율"일 것을 제안한데 대하여 미측은 다음과 같은 이유를 들어 우리 제안을 수락할 수 없다고 말하고 계속 "불법적이 않인 최고환율"로 할 것을 고집하였다.

(ㄱ) 외환증서의 자유시장율이 외환은행에서 적용되는 환율 보다 현저하게 높아 질 경우에 외환은행에서 적용되는 환율을 미군에게 적용하는 것은 차별적 대우가 되며

(ㄴ) 현 환율제도는 한국정부에서 조절할 수 있기 때문에 미측에 불리한 환율이 적용될 염려가 있다.

(2) 우리측은 미국측에 차별대우를 할 의도는 없으며 미군이 외환를 매매하는데 있어서 외환은행에서 적용되는 환율 이외에 또 별개의 환율의 적용이 있을 수 없음을 주장하였다.

4. 기타 사항: 차기회의 일자: 1964 년 6 월 26 일 하오 3 시 부터. 끝.

0176

66-3-14

14-3-21(2)　미주, 1문 110-6(2)

0177

STATUS OF FORCES NEGOTIATIONS: 55th Meeting

SUBJECTS:
1. Security Measures
2. Military Payment Certificates
3. Customs
4. Foreign Exchange Controls

PLACE: Ministry of Foreign Affairs

DATE: June 9, 1964

PARTICIPANTS:

Republic of Korea	United States
CHANG Sang-mun	Philip C. Habib
KU Chung-hoe	Brig. General G.G. O'Connor, USA
CHO Chung-hun	Colonel Howard Smigelow, USA
Major YI Kae-hun, ROKA	~~Colonel Kenneth C.~~
YI Kae-chol	Captain John Wayne, USN
YI Kun-pal (Interpreter)	Colonel Kenneth C. Crawford, USA
HWANG Yong-chae	Frank R. La Macchia
	Benjamin A. Fleck
	Robert A. Kinney
	Lt. Colonel Charles Wright, USA
	Robert A. Lewis
	Kenneth Campen, (Interpreter)

0178

Security Measures

1. The meeting was begun with a discussion of the Security Measures Article. Mr. Habib recalled that the article was last discussed at the 48th negotiating meeting, at which time the Korean negotiators had counter-proposed certain language in response to a U.S. revision of the article which had previously been discussed informally. The Korean counter-proposal differed from the U.S. revision in that the former would provide that "the Republic of Korea will take such actions as it deems necessary" whereas the latter would provide that "the Republic of Korea will take such actions as may be necessary". The Korean negotiators had indicated that their proposed language had a precedent in the SOFA with the Federal Republic of Germany. The U.S. negotiators wished to point out that while Article 29 of the German SOFA uses the words "it deems", that article deals with legislative measures only and does not include the basic commitment to cooperate with the U.S. armed forces in ensuring the security and protection of persons and property. That broader commitment is contained in Paragraph 2(b) of Article 3 of the German SOFA. The language of the latter article is analogous to that of the revision proposed by the U.S. negotiators. In some ways, Mr. Habib continued, the language of the German SOFA is more restrictive than that being proposed by the U.S. negotiators. For example, Paragraph 2 of Article 3 of the German SOFA uses the words "the cooperation provided for in paragraph 1 of this article shall xtend..."

2. Mr. Habib stated that the problem in connection with this article was one of principle. The Korean negotiators wanted to give the ROK Government unilateral responsibility for security measures rather than providing for a cooperative effort by both sides. The purpose of this article is to provide an explicit understanding that certain security measures will be taken for the protection of the American elements involved. Inasmuch as the ROK Government was already taking such measures and was likely to continue to do so, the Korean negotiators appeared to be creating a problem where none existed. The U.S. negotiators suggested that the Korean negotiators examine

carefully Article 3 of the German SOFA as well as Article 29. These two articles together set a clear precedent.

3. Mr. Chang replied that the wording of the German SOFA appeared to be stricter than that proposed by the Korean negotiators. The Korean negotiators did not think it appropriate to adopt language which would provide for the passage of legislation "to ensure the punishment of offenders".

4. Mr. Habib replied that there was no mention of legislation in the revision proposed by the U.S. negotiators. He also pointed out again that Article 29 of the German SOFA, on which the Korean negotiators were apparently basing their counter-proposal, was restricted specifically to legislation. He recalled that the U.S. negotiators had formulated their proposed revision in response to earlier objections by the Korean negotiators to the inclusion in the article of any reference to legislation regarding the protection of persons, dependents, and their property.

5. Mr. Chang asked if the phrase "such actions as may be necessary" could be construed to include legislation.

6. In reply, Mr. Habib referred to the Agreed Joint Summary of the 48th negotiating session, which revealed that the U.S. negotiators had already answered this question as follows: "The U.S. negotiators did not believe that a commitment to legislation was necessary in the article but they did want the negotiating record to show that 'such actions' would include legislation, when appropriate; for example, to ensure the security of U.S. Government property".

7. Mr. Chang stated that the revision proposed by the U.S. negotiators included provision for legislation covering persons and their property. This would place a great obligation on the ROK Government. The Korean negotiators believed the original draft was clearer because it divided the actions to be taken by the ROK Government into two distinguishable categories. The Korean negotiators, therefore, proposed that the original drafts of this article be used as the bases for further negotiation.

8. Mr. Habib asked whether the Korean negotiators were proposing to return

0180

to the position which they had adopted at the 46th negotiating meeting, at which they had made certain proposals with regard to the original drafts. Mr. Chang replied affirmatively. Mr. Habib then stated that the U.S. negotiators were willing to return to the original drafts for further negotiation. However, this brought the negotiators back to the same old problem - the Korean negotiators were unwilling to agree to an assurance of cooperative effort to ensure the protection of U.S. persons and their property. Instead of a provision calling for cooperation, the Korean negotiators were insisting on provision for unilateral determination by the ROK Government of what steps would be necessary.

9. Mr. Habib stated the U.S. negotiators were prepared to agree to adoption of the original U.S. draft of the article, with the deletion of the phrase "of the persons referred to in this paragraph, and their property", as proposed by the Korean negotiators, provided the Korean negotiators would agree to the inclusion in the negotiating record of the following understanding:

> "In cooperating with each other under this Article the two governments agree that each will take such measures as may be necessary to ensure the security and protection of the U.S. Armed Forces, the members thereof, the civilian component, the persons who are present in the Republic of Korea pursuant to the article dealing with Invited Contractors, their dependents and their property."

10. Mr. Chang asked if the phrase "such measures" in the proposed understanding could be construed to include legislation. Mr. Habib said that the phrase could include legislation, if and when legislation was appropriate. Mr. Chang stated that if that were the case, the language was unacceptable to the Korean negotiators.

11. Mr. Habib stated that the U.S. negotiators had come a long way toward meeting the position of the Korean negotiators. However, the armed forces needed to have some sense of security and also needed language in this article which would give them recourse to the ROK Government.

12. Mr. Chang replied that existing ROK laws fully protect the persons, dependents and their property.

0181

Therefore, the Korean negotiators thought it was not necessary to bind the ROK Government to seek legislation regarding the protection of invited contractors, dependents, and their property.

13. Mr. Habib commented that no other government with which a SOFA has been negotiated has balked at seeking legislation, if such legislation was necessary or appropriate. He urged the Korean negotiators to study the precedents.

14. Mr. Chang stated that the discussion had clarified the points of difference with regard to this article. The Korean negotiators could not accept the proposal made by the U.S. negotiators if that proposal included provision for legislation to ensure the protection of persons, dependents, and their property.

Military Payment Certificates

15. Turning to the article dealing with Military Payment Certificates, Mr. Chang stated that the Korean negotiators accepted the understanding proposed by the U.S. negotiators at the 54th meeting for inclusion in the Agreed Joint Summary (see Paragraph 3, Agreed Joint Summary, 54th Negotiating Meeting). He noted that there still remained an unresolved question of language in Paragraph 1(b) of the article.

16. Mr. Habib recalled that at the 54th meeting the U.S. negotiators had indicated resolution of this question would depend upon agreement on the equivalent point in the Criminal Jurisdiction Article. When agreement was reached on the latter article, this point would be resolved. Therefore, the U.S. negotiators suggested that the Military Payment Certificates Article be set aside until agreement had been reached on the Criminal Jurisdiction Article. Mr. Chang agreed.

Customs

17. Turning to the Customs Article, Mr. Habib recalled that at the 54th meeting, the Korean negotiators had proposed alternative language for Agreed Minute #3. The U.S. negotiators had formulated alternative language which was more precise but which included the provisions desired by the Korean negotiators. He then tabled the

0182

following revision of Agreed Minute #3:

> "The term 'military cargo' as used in paragraph 5(c) is not confined to arms and equipment but refers to all cargo consigned to the United States armed forces (including their authorized procurement agencies and their non-appropriated fund organizations provided for in Article ____). Pertinent information on cargo consigned to non-appropriated fund organizations will be furnished on a routine basis to authorities of the Republic of Korea. The extent of the pertinent information will be determined by the Joint Committee."

18. Mr. Chang stated that the Korean negotiators would consider this proposal and comment on it at a later meeting. Mr. Habib expressed the hope that the Korean negotiators could at least agree in principle to this proposal, so that negotiations could proceed with regard to other portions of this article.

19. Mr. Chang replied that the proposal just tabled by the U.S. negotiators did not include any reference to the provision of additional information. He said the Korean negotiators sought a system whereby certain information would be provided on a routine basis and in specific cases, in addition to the routine information, other ~~additional~~ information which the Korean authorities may deem necessary should be provided on request to the Joint Committee. The Joint Committee, of course, would determine the extent of the pertinent information to be provided.

20. In reply, Mr. Habib referred to the Joint Committee Article, pointing out that under its provisions, the Korean authorities could apply to the Joint Committee at any time for whatever information they desired. There was no need, therefore, to include a redundant provision to this effect in the Agreed Minutes to the Customs Article. The Korean negotiators had asked for a provision for the delivery of information on an automatic basis to Korean authorities. The language proposed by the U.S. negotiators gave them such a provision.

Foreign Exchange Controls

21. Turning to the Article dealing with Foreign Exchange Controls, Mr. Habib recalled that at the 54th meeting, the Korean negotiators had tabled proposed additional language to be included in the Agreed Minute. The U.S. negotiators could not

agree to the Korean proposal, which did not meet the problem. Mr. Habib recalled that the Korean negotiators had suggested the possibility of the existence of a lawful exchange rate outside of the foreign exchange banks. He pointed out that the current ROK foreign exchange system provides for a floating exchange rate coupled with a market mechanism consisting of the exchange certificate system. The Korean negotiators seemed to assume that the U.S. armed forces would continue to purchase won only at the bank rate. If the bank rate were pegged at 255 won to the dollar and not permitted to float, the U.S. armed forces might be the victims of discrimination if they continued to buy at the bank rate. Traditionally, the ROK Government has operated on the basis of pegged rates. However, the new system provides the possibility of flexibility. If it operates as intended, the bank rate will be adjusted automatically to keep pace with the market rate. The foreign exchange banks, however, have the capability of adjusting the system. If the operation of the system is adjusted for other purposes, the U.S. armed forces are unwilling to pay the cost of such adjustment through the payment of discriminatory rates.

22. The language of the U.S. draft, Mr. Habib continued, requires no legislative changes by the ROK Government, nor does it impinge on the sovereign right of that government to change the operation of the foreign exchange system as it sees fit. The question of the operation of the present system will be discussed, of course, through channels other than those of the SOFA negotiations, since it is of great importance to other U.S. interests in Korea. The principle remains the same, however, insofar as the SOFA negotiations are concerned. That principle is that the U.S. armed forces intend to abide by Korean law 100% but do not intend to permit themselves to be subjected to discriminatory exchange rates.

23. Mr. Habib added that the U.S. armed forces did not wish, furthermore, to make it attractive to the ROK Government to establish discriminatory rates. He pointed out that discrimination against the U.S. armed forces would not be in the best interests

0184

of the ROK Government. Such action would force the U.S. armed forces to reconsider their policy of purchasing on the local market, would inhibit foreign exchange earnings from U.S. sources, and would foster the growth of black market activities, which both the U.S. authorities and the ROK authorities sought to avoid.

24. Mr. Chang asked if he interpreted Mr. Habib's remarks correctly to the effect that if the market rate increased in value over the bank rate, the U.S. armed forces intended to purchase at the market rate.

25. Mr. Habib, in turn, asked Mr. Chang if it were not a fact that under the present system, if the difference between the market rate and the bank rate became more than 2%, the bank rate would be adjusted automatically? Mr. Chang replied in the affirmative.

26. Mr. Habib then stated that this 2% was in fact administrative leeway which permitted the banks to avoid a situation in which the bank rate would have to be adjusted each time the market rate rose or fell by a fraction of a point. To all intents and purposes, so long as the 2% provision was operative, there was little difference between the market rate and the bank rate. However, if the market rate were permitted to rise to 15% or 20% higher than the bank rate without any adjustment in the bank rate, why should the U.S. armed forces not be able to buy at the higher rate? Why would the ROK Government want to discriminate against them?

27. Mr. Chang stated that the reluctance of the U.S. negotiators to agree to the additional language proposed by the Korean negotiators implied that the U.S. armed forces were thinking of purchasing foreign exchange outside the foreign exchange banks. Mr. Habib replied that the U.S. armed forces would prefer not to purchase outside the foreign exchange banks. However, trading in foreign exchange certificates is legal under the present system. The language proposed by the Korean negotiators would open up the possibility of discriminatory rates. All the U.S. armed forces wanted was to be able to purchase at the highest rate which is not unlawful.

0185

They had no intention or desire to do anything other than abide by ROK laws.

28. It was agreed to hold the next meeting on June 26 at 3:00 p.m.

JOINT SUMMARY RECORD OF THE 55TH SESSION

1. Time and Place: 3:00 - 5:00 P.M. June 19, 1964 at the Foreign Ministry's Conference Room (No.1)

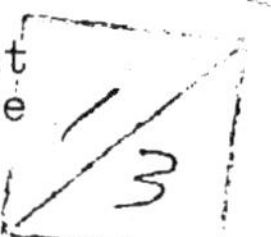

2. Attendants:

ROK Side:

Mr. Chang, Sang Moon	Director European and American Affairs Bureau
Mr. Koo, Choong Whay	Chief, American Section Ministry of Foreign Affairs
Mr. Cho, Choong Hoon	Chief Customs Section Ministry of Finance
Maj. Lee, Kye Hoon	Chief Military Affairs Section Ministry of National Defense
Mr. Ahn, Yun Gi	3rd Secretary Ministry of Foreign Affairs
Mr. Lee, Kae Chul	3rd Secretary Ministry of Foreign Affairs
Mr. Lee, Keun Pal (Rapporteur and Interpreter)	3rd Secretary Ministry of Foreign Affairs
Mr. Park, Won Chul	3rd Secretary Ministry of Foreign Affairs

U.S. Side:

Mr. Philip C. Habib	Counselor American Embassy
Brig. Gen. G.G. O'Connor	Deputy Chief of Staff 8th U.S. Army
Col. Howard Smigelow	Deputy Chief of Staff 8th U.S. Army
Capt. John Wayne	Assistant Chief of Staff USN/K.S. Army
Col. Kenneth C. Crawford	Staff Judge Advocates Office 8th U.S. Army

미주과	양 고 재 6월 19일	담 당	과 장	국 장	특별보좌관	차 관	장 관
		Lee					

0187

Mr. Frank R. La Macchia	First Secretary American Embassy
Mr. Benjamin A. Fleck (Rapporteur and Press Officer)	First Secretary American Embassy
Mr. Robert A. Kinney	J-5 8th U.S. Army
Lt. Col. Charles Wright	Staff Judge Advocate's Office 8th U.S. Army
Mr. Robert A. Lewis	2nd Secretary American Embassy
Mr. Kenneth Campen	Interpreter American Embassy

Security Measures

1. The meeting was begun with a discussion of the Security Measures Article. Mr. Habib recalled that the article was last discussed at the 48th negotiating meeting, at which time the Korean negotiators had counter-proposed certain language in response to a U.S. revision of the article which had previously been discussed informally. The Korean counter-proposal differed from the U.S. revision in that the former would provide that "the Republic of Korea will take such actions as it deems necessary" whereas the latter would provide that "the Republic of Korea will take such actions as may be necessary". The Korean negotiators had indicated that their proposed language had a precedent in the SOFA with the Federal Republic of Germany. The U.S. negotiators wished to point out that while Article 29 of the German SOFA uses the words "it deems", that article deals with legislative measures only and does not include the basic commitment to cooperate with the U.S. armed forces in ensuring the security and protection of persons and property. The broader commitment is contained in Paragraph 2(b) of Article 3 of the German SOFA. The language of the latter

0188

article is analogous to that of the revision proposed by the U.S. negotiators. In some ways, Mr. Habib continued, the language of the German SOFA is more restrictive than that being proposed by the U.S. negotiators. For example, Paragraph 2 of Article 3 of the German SOFA uses the words "the cooperation provided for in paragraph 1 of this article shall extend ..."

2. Mr. Habib stated that the problem in connection with this article was one of principle. The Korean negotiators wanted to give the ROK Government unilateral responsibility for security measures rather than providing for a cooperative effort by both sides. The purpose of this article is to provide an explicit understanding that certain security measures will be taken for the protection of the American elements involved. Inasmuch as the ROK Government was already taking such measures and was likely to continue to do so, the Korean negotiators appeared to be creating a problem where none existed. The U.S. negotiators suggested that the Korean negotiators examine carefully Article 3 of the German SOFA as well as Article 29. These two articles together set a clear precedent.

3. Mr. Chang replied that the wording of the German SOFA appeared to be stricter than that proposed by the Korean negotiators. The Korean negotiators did not think it appropriate to adopt language which would provide for the passage of legislation "to ensure the punishment of offenders".

4. Mr. Habib replied that there was no mention of legislation in the revision proposed by the U.S. negotiators. He also pointed out again that Article 29 of the German SOFA, on which the Korean negotiators were apparently basing their counter-proposal, was restricted specifically to legislation.

He recalled that the U.S. negotiators had formulated their proposed revision in response to earlier objections by the Korean negotiators to the inclusion in the article of any reference to legislation regarding the protection of persons, dependents, and their property.

5. Mr. Chang asked if the phrase "such actions as may be necessary" could be construed to include legislation.

6. In reply, Mr. Habib referred to the Agreed Joint Summary of the 48th negotiating session, which revealed that the U.S. negotiators had already answered this question as follows: "The U.S. negotiators did not believe that a commitment to legislation was necessary in the article but they did want the negotiating record to show that 'such actions' would include legislation, when appropriate; for example, to ensure the security of U.S. Government property".

7. Mr. Chang stated that the revision proposed by the U.S. negotiators included provision for legislation covering persons and their property. This would place a great obligation on the ROK Government. The Korean negotiators believed the original draft was clearer because it divided the actions to be taken by the ROK Government into two distinguishable categories. The Korean negotiators, therefore, proposed that the original drafts of this article be used as the bases for further negotiation.

8. Mr. Habib asked whether the Korean negotiators were proposing to return to the position which they had adopted at the 46th negotiating meeting, at which they had made certain proposals with regard to the original drafts. Mr. Chang replied affirmatively. Mr. Habib then stated that the U.S. negotiators were willing to return to the original drafts for further negotiation. However, this brought the negotiators back to the same old problem - the Korean

0190

negotiators were unwilling to agree to an assurance of cooperative effort to ensure the protection of U.S. persons and their property. Instead of a provision calling for cooperation, the Korean negotiators were insisting on provision for unilateral determination by the ROK Government of what steps would be necessary.

9. Mr. Habib stated the U.S. negotiators were prepared to agree to adoption of the original U.S. draft of the article, with the deletion of the phrase "of the persons referred to in this paragraph, and their property", as proposed by the Korean negotiators, provided the Korean negotiators would agree to the inclusion in the negotiating record of the following understanding:

> "In cooperating with each other under this Article the two governments agree that each will take such measures as may be necessary to ensure the security and protection of the U.S. Armed Forces, the members thereof, the civilian component, the persons who are present in the Republic of Korea pursuant to the article dealing with Invited Contractors, their dependents and their property."

10. Mr. Chang asked if the phrase "such measures" in the proposed understanding could be construed to include legislation. Mr. Habib said that the phrase could include legislation, if and when legislation was appropriate. Mr. Chang stated that if that were the case, the language was unacceptable to the Korean negotiators.

11. Mr. Habib stated that the U.S. negotiators had come a long way toward meeting the position of the Korean negotiators. However, the armed forces needed to have some sense of security and also needed language in this article which would give them recourse to the ROK Government.

12. Mr. Chang replied that existing ROK laws fully protect the persons, dependents and their property.

0191

Therefore, the Korean negotiators thought it was not necessary to bind the ROK Government to seek legislation regarding the protection of invited contractors, dependents, and their property.

13. Mr. Habib commented that no other government with which a SOFA has been negotiated has balked at seeking legislation, if such legislation was necessary or appropriate. He urged the Korean negotiators to study the precedents.

14. Mr. Chang stated that the discussion had clarified the points of difference with regard to this article. The Korean negotiators could not accept the proposal made by the U.S. negotiators if that proposal included provision for legislation to ensure the protection of persons, dependents, and their property.

Military Payment Certificates

15. Turning to the article dealing with Military Payment Certificates, Mr. Chang stated that the Korean negotiators accepted the understanding proposed by the U.S. negotiators at the 54th meeting for inclusion in the Agreed Joint Summary (see paragraph 3, Agreed Joint Summary, 54th Negotiating Meeting). He noted that there still remained an unresolved question of language in Paragraph 1(b) of the article.

16. Mr. Habib recalled that at the 54th meeting the U.S. negotiators had indicated resolution of this question would depend upon agreement on the equivalent point in the Criminal Jurisdiction Article. When agreement was reached on the latter article, this point would be resolved. Therefore, the U.S. negotiators suggested that the Military Payment Certificates Article be set aside until agreement had been reached on the Criminal Jurisdiction Article. Mr. Chang agreed.

0192

Customs

17. Turning to the Customs Article, Mr. Habib recalled that at the 54th meeting, the Korean negotiators had proposed alternative language for Agreed Minute #3. The U.S. negotiators had formulated alternative language which was more precise but which included the provisions desired by the Korean negotiators. He then tabled the following revision of Agreed Minute #3:

> "The term 'military cargo' as used in paragraph 5(c) is not confined to arms and equipment but refers to all cargo consigned to the United States armed forces (including their authorized procurement agencies and their non-appropriated fund organizations provided for in Article ____). Pertinent information on cargo consigned to non-appropriated fund organizations will be furnished on a routine basis to authorities of the Republic of Korea. The extent of the pertinent information will be determined by the Joint Committee."

18. Mr. Chang stated that the Korean negotiators would consider this proposal and comment on it at a later meeting. Mr. Habib expressed the hope that the Korean negotiators could at least agree in principle to this proposal, so that negotiations could proceed with regard to other portions of this article.

19. Mr. Chang replied that the proposal just tabled by the U.S. negotiators did not include any reference to the provision of additional information. He said the Korean negotiators sought a system whereby certain information would be provided on a routine basis and in specific cases, in addition to the routine information, other information which the Korean authorities may deem necessary should be provided on request to the Joint Committee. The Joint Committee, of course, would determine the extent of the pertinent information to be provided.

0193

20. In reply, Mr. Habib referred to the Joint Committee Article, pointing out that under its provisions, the Korean authorities could apply to the Joint Committee at any time for whatever information they desired. There waw no need, therefore, to include a redundant provision to this effect in the Agreed Minutes to the Customs Article. The Korean negotiators had asked for a provision for the delivery of information on an automatic basis to Korean authorities. The language proposed by the U.S. negotiators gave them such a provisions.

Foreign Exchange Controls

21. Turning to the Article dealing with Foreign Exchange Controls, Mr. Habib recalled that at the 54th meeting, the Korean negotiators had tabled proposed additional language to be included in the Agreed Minute. The U.S. negotiators could not agree to the Korean proposal, which did not meet the problem. Mr. Habib recalled that the Korean negotiators had suggested the possibility of the existence of a lawful exchange rate outside of the foreign exchange banks. He pointed out that the current ROK foreign exchange system provides for a floating exchange rate coupled with a market mechanism consisting of the exchange certificate system. The Korean negotiators seemed to assume that the U.S. armed forces would continue to purchase won only at the bank rate. If the bank rate were pegged at 255 won to the dollar and not permitted to float, the U.S. armed forces might be the victims of discrimination if they continued to buy at the bank rate. Traditionally, the ROK Government has operated on the basis of pegged rates. However, the new system provides the possibility of flexibility. If it operates as intended, the bank rate will be adjusted automatically

0194

to keep pace with the market rate. The foreign exchange banks, however, have the capability of adjusting the system. If the operation of the system is adjusted for other purposes, the U.S. armed forces are unwilling to pay the cost of such adjustment through the payment of discriminatory rates.

22. The language of the U.S. draft, Mr. Habib continued, requires no legislative changes by the ROK Government, nor does it impinge on the sovereign right of that government to change the operation of the foreign exchange system as it sees fit. The question of the operation of the present system will be discussed, of course, through channels other than those of the SOFA negotiations, since it is of great importance to other U.S. interests in Korea. The principle remains the same, however, insofar as the SOFA negotiations are concerned. That principle is that the U.S. armed forces intend to abide by Korean law 100% but do not intend to permit themselves to be subjected to discriminatory exchange rates.

23. Mr. Habib added that the U.S. armed forces did not wish, furthermore, to make it attractive to the ROK Government to establish discriminatory rates. He pointed out that discrimination against the U.S. armed forces would not be in the best interests of the ROK Government. Such action would force the U.S. armed forces to reconsider their policy of purchasing on the local market, would inhibit foreign exchange earnings from U.S. sources, and would foster the growth of black market activities, which both the U.S. authorities and the ROK authorities sought to avoid.

0195

24. Mr. Chang asked if he interpreted Mr. Habib's remarks correctly to the effect that if the market rate increased in value over the bank rate, the U.S. armed forces intended to purchase at the market rate.

25. Mr. Habib, in turn, asked Mr. Chang if it were not a fact that under the present system, if the difference between the market rate and the bank rate became more than 2%, the bank rate would be adjusted automatically? Mr. Chang replied in the affirmative.

26. Mr. Habib then stated that this 2% was in fact administrative leeway which permitted the banks to avoid a situation in which the bank rate would have to be adjusted each time the market rate rose or fell by a fraction of a point. To all intents and purposes, so long as the 2% provision was operative, there was little difference between the market rate and the bank rate. However, if the market rate were permitted to rise to 15% or 20% higher than the bank rate without any adjustment in the bank rate, why should the U.S. armed forces not be able to buy at the higher rate? Why would the ROK Government want to discriminate against them?

27. Mr. Chang stated that the reluctance of the U.S. negotiators to agree to the additional language proposed by the Korean negotiators implied that the U.S. armed forces were thinking of purchasing foreign exchange outside the foreign exchange banks. Mr. Habib replied that the U.S. armed forces would prefer not to purchase outside the foreign exchange banks. However, trading in foreign exchange certificates is legal under the present system. The language proposed by the Korean negotiators would open up the possibility of discriminatory rates. All the U.S. armed forces wanted

0196

was to be able to purchase at the highest rate which is not unlawful. They had no intention or desire to do anything other than abide by ROK laws.

28. It was agreed to hold the next meeting on June 26 at 3:00 p.m.

6. 제56차 회의, 6.26

0198

SOFA NEGOTIATION

Agenda for the 56th Session

15:00 June 26, 1964

1. Continuation of Discussions on:

   a. Customs Article

   b. Invited Contractors Article

   c. Security Measures Article

2. Other Business

3. Agenda and Date of the Next Meeting

4. Press Release

0199

June 26, '64 - ?th meeting

Agreed Summary

"If the US authorities determine that there would be significant advantage for US-ROK mutual defense to utilize one or more third-country corporations as USFK-invited contractor, the authorities of the Government of the Republic of Korea shall give sympathetic consideration to a US request to extend the benefits of this agreement to such non-US corporations."

0200

관리번호 1480

기 안 용 지

자체통제		기안처	미주과 이근팔	전화번호	근거서류접수일자

	과장	국장	차관	장관		
	(서명)	(서명)	(서명)	(서명)		

관계관 서명	

기안년월일	1964. 6. 30.	시행년월일		보존년한		정서기장
분류기호	외구미 722.2—	전체통제		종결		
경유 수신 참조	대통령 참조: 비서실장 국무총리 참조: 비서실장			발신	장관	
제목	제 56 차 주둔군지위협정 체결 교섭 실무자회의 보고					

검열 1964. 7. 3. 통제관

1964. 6. 26. 하오 3 시부터 동 4 시 45 분 까지 외무부 제 1 회의실에서 개최된 제 56 차 주둔군지위협정 체결 교섭 실무자회의에서 토의된 내용을 별첨과 같이 보고합니다.

유 첨: 제 56 차 주둔군지위협정 체결 교섭 실무자회의 보고

No.302 호 1964. 7. 3.

첨부문에서 분리되면 보통문서로 재분류 외무부

1964. 6.30에 예고문에 의거 일반문서로 재분류됨

승인서식 1—1—3 (11—00900—03) (195mm×265mm16절지)

0201

제 56 차

한·미 간 주둔군지위협정 체결 교섭실무자회의

보 고 서

1. 일 시: 1964 년 6 월 26 일 하오 3 시 부터 동 4 시 45 분 까지.

2. 장 소: 외무부 제 1 회의실

3. 토의사항

가. 군계약자

(1) 양측은 군계약자의 정의를 "미국법에 의하여 조직된 법인체를 포함한 사람과 고용자로서 통상 미국내에서 거주하는 자와 그들의 가족으로 규정할 것에 합의를 보고 다음과 같은 양해사항을 유보하기로 하였다.

(가) 미당국이 제 3 국의 법인체인 군계약자를 이용하는 것이 한·미 양국의 상호 방위를 위하여 현저한 이익이 된다고 판단하는 경우 한국당국은 본협정의 특권을 그들에게 인정하기 위한 미측 요청에 대하여 호의적인 고려를 한다."

(2) 양측은 군계약자가 군계약에 참가하여 기타 미국기관과의 계약을 수행할 때에도 군계약자 규정의 적용을 받을 수 있다는 것과

(3) 미측이 협정 체결 후에는 제 3 국인인 고용인을 채용하지 않을 것이라는 양해 하에 이미 고용된 제 3 국인에 대하여서는 계약 수행을 조건으로 본 조항에 규정된 특권을 향유할 수 있다는 점에 합의를 보았다.

(4) 기타 우리측은 개인용 차량에 대하여서는 등록과 소유에 따른 각종 세금 및 수수료를 납부해야 한다는 입장인데 대하여 미측은 수수료는 납부할 용의가 있으나 세금은 그 액수가 과국의 예와 판이하게 고액임으로 납부할 수 없다고 주장하였다.

나. 보호조치

(1) 양측은 각기 종전 주장하여 온 입장에 변경이 없음을 확인하고 쌍방의 입장을 재검토하여 다음 기회에 논의하기로 하였다.

0202

64-3-14

64-3-27 (2)

0203

다. 관세업무

(1) 우리측은 군사화물이라 함은 미군대에 탁송되는 무기 및 장비 뿐만 아니라 비세출자금기관 앞으로 송부되는 화물까지 포함하며 비세출자금기관 앞으로 탁송되는 모든 화물에 관한 정보는 정기적으로 한국당국에 제공될 것이라는 미측 제안을 수락함에 있어 미측이 다음과 같은 양해사항을 수락할 것을 제안하였다.

(ㄱ) 정규적으로 제공되는 정보에는 최소한 packing lists 및 invoices 가 포함되어야 한다.

(ㄴ) 정규적으로 제공되는 정보 이외에 특별한 경우 한국당국이 필요하다고 인정하는 기타 정보를 합동위원회를 통하여 요청하면 곧 제공하여야 한다.

(2) 미측은 우리의 상기 제안 중 정규적 정보에 추가하여 기타 필요한 정보를 제공하는데에는 원칙적으로 찬의를 표명하였으나 정규적 정보의 종류까지 결정하는 것은 합동위원회에서 결정할 성질의 것이라고 상반된 입장을 취하였음으로 양측은 쌍방의 입장을 조정하기 위하여 실무자급의 비공식회의를 개최하는데 합의하였다.

4. 기타 사항: 차기 회의 일자: 1964년 7월 8일 하오 3시부터. 끝.

0204

64-3-60

64-3-23 (2)　　미국문 1105(2)

0205

STATUS OF FORCES NEGOTIATIONS: 56th Meeting

SUBJECTS:
1. Invited Contractors
2. Security Measures
3. Customs

PLACE: Ministry of Foreign Affairs

DATE: June 26, 1964

PARTICIPANTS:

Republic of Korea

CHANG Sang-mun
KU Chung-hoe
Colonel KIM Won-kil, ROKA
CHO Chung-hun
O Chae-hi
YI Kun-pal (Interpreter)
HWANG Yong-chae
PAK Won Chul
AHN Yun Gi

United States

Philip C. Habib
Brig. General G.G. O'Connor, USA
Colonel Howard Smigelow, USA
Captain John Wayne, USN
Colonel Kenneth C. Crawford, USA
Frank La Macchia
Benjamin A. Fleck
Robert A. Kinney
Lt. Colonel Charles Wright, USA
Robert A. Lewis
Kenneth Campen (Interpreter)

0206

Invited Contractors

1. Opening the meeting with the Invited Contractors Article, Mr. Habib recalled that at the 48th meeting, the Korean negotiators had indicated that if the U.S. negotia-ors would agree to the inclusion of the phrase "organized under the laws of the United States" after the word "corporations" in Paragraph 1 of the U.S. draft, the Korean negotiators would agree to the following:

a. In Paragraph 1, insertion of the words "and the dependents of such persons" following the words "United States";

b. Acceptance of Agreed Minute #2 of the U.S. draft and withdrawal of Agreed Minutes #1 and #2 of the Korean draft;

c. Acceptance of Agreed Minute #1 of the U.S. draft.

2. Mr. Habib stated that the U.S. negotiators were now prepared to accept the

Korean proposal. As a result, full agreement was now reached on Paragraph 1, which, as revised, reads as follows:

"1. Persons, including corporations organized under the laws of the United States, their employees who are ordinarily resident in the United States, and the dependents of such persons, present in Korea solely for the purpose of executing contracts with the United States for the benefit of the United States armed forces or other armed forces in Korea under the Unified Command receiving logistical support from the United States armed forces, who are designated by the Government of the United States in accordance with the provisions of paragraph 2 below, shall, except as provided in this Article, be subject to the laws and regulations of Korea."

3. Mr. Habib stated that the U.S. negotiators, in order to retain a degree of flexibility regarding third-country corporations, would like to obtain the agreement of the Korean negotiators to the inclusion in the negotiating record of the following understanding:

"If the U.S. authorities determine that there would be significant advantage for U.S. ROK mutual defense to utilize one or more third-country corporations as USFK-invited contractors, the authorities of the Government of the Repub-

0207

lic of Korea shall give sympathetic consideration to a U.S. request to extend the benefits of this agreement to such non-U.S. corporations."

Mr. Habib pointed out that a case might arise in which the use of a third-country corporation would be to the mutual advantage of the ROK and U.S. forces in carrying out their mission of defending the Republic. Stating that the U.S. negotiators had already waived any right to include third-country corporations within the provisions of this article, Mr. Habib said the proposed understanding would serve only as guidance to the Joint Committee. He pointed out that it would refer only to corporations and not to third-country nationals.

4. Mr. Habib said the U.S. negotiators also wished to confirm that references throughout the article (in paragraphs 2, 3, 4, 5, and 6) to "such persons" were references to contractors, their employees, and their dependents, as identified in paragraph 1.

5. Mr. Chang stated that the Korean negotiators appreciated the acceptance by the U.S. negotiators of the proposal made by the Korean negotiators at the 48th meeting. However, they understood that this acceptance was conditioned upon acceptance by the Korean negotiators of the understanding just proposed by the U.S. negotiators. They did not believe that the understanding would carry much weight if it were placed in the negotiating record. However, if there were indications that it would be to the mutual advantage of the two governments for defense of the Republic of Korea to engage a third-country corporation, the Korean authorities were prepared to give sympathetic consideration to such a request by the U.S. armed forces. Therefore, the Korean negotiators agreed to the understanding.

6. Mr. Habib stated that the understanding had not been proposed as a condition for acceptance of the previous Korean proposal. It was intended to serve as a guide to the Joint Committee and would show that the negotiators had considered this particular possibility.

7. Mr. Habib noted that the revised draft of the article tabled by the Korean negotiators on February 14, 1964 contained in Paragraph 2(a) the apparently inadvertent

0208

omission of the phrase "the United States for". He added that paragraph 6 of the Korean revised draft should be slightly revised to improve the style. The Korean negotiators stated, however, that inasmuch as they had already agreed to Paragraph 6 of the U.S. draft at the 32nd meeting, the text of that version of the paragraph should be considered to be the agreed text.

8. Mr. Chang asked for the U.S. position with regard to Agreed Minute #3 proposed by the Korean negotiators. Mr. Habib replied that the negotiators had already reached agreement in Paragraph 6 on the principle of exemption from taxation. This is a principle which the U.S. negotiators believe should be applied and maintained. It was not proper to levy taxes on persons who normally would expect exemption and who, indeed, are granted exemption by the terms of Paragraph 6. Furthermore, the size of the taxes levied by the Korean authorities on privately-owned automobiles was unusually large.

9. Mr. Chang replied that Korean laws and regulations require privately-owned vehicles to be registered with the local authorities. Such registration in turn required the owners to pay the local fees and assessments. Even members of the armed forces should pay such local fees but the requirement on them to do so has been waived in view of their mission. The Korean negotiators believed that privately-owned vehicles of contractors and their employees and dependents should be required to pay these local fees and assessments. Mr. Chang stated that the local assessments are, in fact, payments for the use of roads and highways.

10. Mr. Habib pointed out that the vehicles under discussion actually remained in the country for only a relatively short period. When their owners departed, the vehicles were taken out of the country. If they were not taken out, they were sold and the relevant taxes were paid at the time of the sale. The U.S. negotiators believed that the ROK Government made a distinction between taxation and registration. The U.S. negotiators were not unprepared to consider the payment of registration fees on privately owned vehicles but they wished to maintain the principle of exemption from taxation.

0209

11. Mr. Chang said the Korean negotiators understood the U.S. position. They believed that fees and taxes were closely related to the registration of vehicles. They would study the question and comment further at a later meeting.

12. Mr. Habib remarked that the U.S. negotiators were merely attempting to arrive at a position similar to that which existed in other countries. In other countries registration fees were collected but heavy taxes such as those imposed in the Republic of Korea were non-existent.

Security Measures

13. Each side indicated that its position with regard to the Security Measures Article had not changed. Neither side had any alternative proposals to suggest and it was agreed to give further study to the matter.

Customs

14. Turning to the Customs Article, Mr. Chang recalled that at the 55th meeting agreement had been reached in principle that pertinent information with regard to cargo consigned to non-appropriated fund organizations would be furnished to the Korean authorities on a routine basis. However, the Korean negotiators still desired that other information deemed necessary by the ROK customs authorities in specific cases should be furnished on request through the Joint Committee. The Korean negotiators would accept the revised Agreed Minute #3 tabled by the U.S. negotiators at the 55th meeting if the U.S. negotiators would agree to the inclusion of the following two understandings in the negotiating record:

a. Pertinent information to be provided on a routine basis shall include at least invoices and packing lists;

b. In addition to the provisions of routine information, other information which the ROK authorities may deem necessary in specific cases shall promptly be provided on request through the Joint Committee.

0210

15. In reply, Mr. Habib stated that the original proposal regarding pertinent information had been made by the Korean negotiators, in a revised version of Agreed Minute #3 tabled by them at the 54th meeting. In that proposal, the Korean negotiators themselves had suggested that the extent of the pertinent information was to be decided by the Joint Committee. The U.S. negotiators had agreed to that suggestion. In the view of the U.S. negotiators, the provision of additional information upon request to the Joint Committee is provided for in any article, paragraph, or clause of this Agreement. Mr. Habib suggested that the Korean negotiators reexamine the Joint Committee Article and all of the other commitments to provide information being made in this and other articles. Instead of the two understandings proposed by the Korean negotiators, the U.S. negotiators wished to propose the following understanding, which was stated in the simplest possible terms:

> "With respect to Agreed Minute #3, in addition to the information provided on a routine basis, other pertinent information will be provided on request through the Joint Committee."

16. Mr. Chang stated that the Korean negotiators believed there should be a statement to the effect that the pertinent information should include at least packing lists and invoices.

17. Mr. Habib pointed out that a thorough discussion of documentation had been held prior to the submission by the Korean negotiators of their proposed revised Agreed Minute #3. During that previous discussion, the Korean negotiators had indicated that they recognized the function of the Joint Committee. The U.S. negotiators had without question accepted the principle of automaticity proposed by the Korean negotiators. The U.S. negotiators, however, were not prepared at this point to begin implementation of the Agreement. That was the job of the Joint Committee. The Korean negotiators had already agreed to let the Joint Committee decide the extent of the pertinent information to be provided. If it were spelled out in this article, it might as well be spelled out in

0211

every article. The U.S. negotiators believed that implementation of the Agreement should be left to the Joint Committee.

18. Mr. Chang stated that the Korean negotiators recognized that it was the function of the Joint Committee to determine the extent of the pertinent information to be furnished. However, packing lists and invoices are essential elements of information regarding non-appropriated fund cargo. U.S. objections to mentioning them specifically were of concern to the Korean negotiators, lest the Joint Committee might not agree to include them as components of the pertinent information.

19. Mr. Habib pointed out that he had said nothing that could be so construed. He pointed out that there might be other kinds of documentation which would be better than packing lists. Was it the intention of the Korean negotiators that every sealed container entering the Republic of Korea be opened in order to obtain the packing list? Such a procedure would be administratively unsound and extremely unwise from the point of view of security.

20. Mr. Chang stated that the Korean negotiators would study the U.S. counter-proposal and comment at a later meeting.

21. The next meeting was scheduled for July 8 at 3:00 p.m.

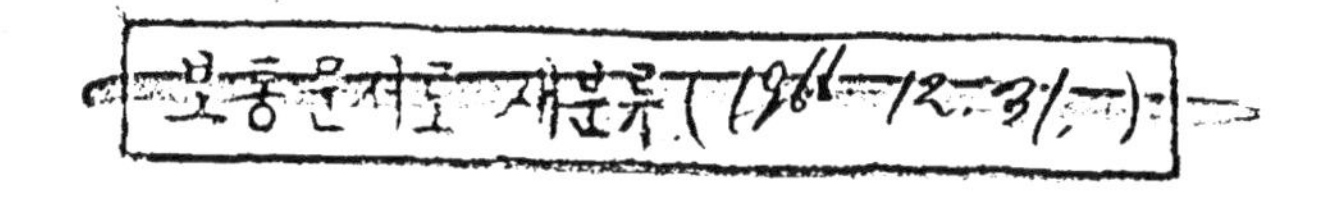

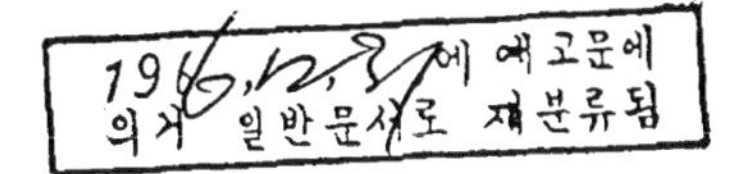

0212

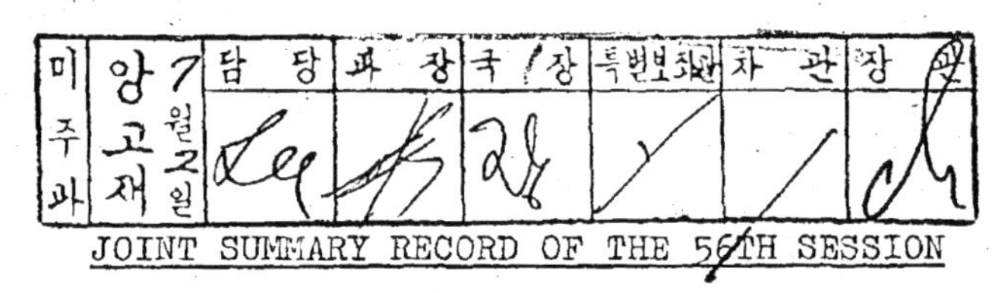

JOINT SUMMARY RECORD OF THE 56TH SESSION

1. Time and Place: 3:00 - 4:45 P.M. June 26, 1964 at the Foreign Ministry's Conference Room (No.1)

2. Attendants:

ROK Side:

Mr. Chang, Sang Moon	Director European and American Affairs Bureau
Mr. Koo, Choong Whay	Chief, America Section Ministry of Foreign Affairs
Mr. Cho, Choong Hoon	Chief Customs Section Ministry of Finance
Col. Kim, Won Kil	Chief Military Affairs Section Ministry of National Defense
Mr. Oh, Jae Hee	Chief, Treaty Section Ministry of Foreign Affairs
Mr. Ahn, Yun Gi	3rd Secretary Ministry of Foreign Affairs
Mr. Lee, Keun Pal (Rapporteur and Interpreter)	3rd Secretary Ministry of Foreign Affairs
Mr. Hwang, Young Jae	3rd Secretary Ministry of Foreign Affairs
Mr. Park, Won Chul	3rd Secretary Ministry of Foreign Affairs

U.S. Side:

Mr. Philip C. Habib	Counselor American Embassy
Brig. Gen. G.G. O'Connor	Deputy Chief of Staff 8th U.S. Army
Col. Howard Smigelow	Deputy Chief of Staff 8th U.S. Army
Capt. John Wayne	Assistant Chief of Staff USN/K
Col. Kenneth C. Crawford	Staff Judge Advocate 8th U.S. Army

0213

Mr. Frank R. La Macchia	First Secretary American Embassy
Mr. Benjamin A. Fleck (Rapporteur and Press Officer)	First Secretary American Embassy
Mr. Robert A. Kinney	J-5 8th U.S. Army
Lt. Col. Charles Wright	Staff Judge Advocate's Office 8th U.S. Army
Mr. Robert A. Lewis	2nd Secretary American Embassy
Mr. Kenneth Campen	Interpreter

Invited Contractors

1. Opening the meeting with the Invited Contractors Article, Mr. Habib recalled that at the 48th meeting, the Korean negotiators had indicated that if the U.S. negotiators would agree to the inclusion of the phrase "organized under the laws of the United States" after the word "corporations" in Paragraph 1 of the U.S. draft, the Korean negotiators would agree to the following:

a. In Paragraph 1, insertion of the words "and the dependents of such persons" following the words "United States";

b. Acceptance of Agreed Minute #2 of the U.S. draft and withdrawal of Agreed Minutes #1 and #2 of the Korean draft;

c. Acceptance of Agreed Minute #1 of the U.S. draft.

2. Mr. Habib stated that the U.S. negotiators were now prepared to accept the Korean proposal. As a result, full agreement was now reached on Paragraph 1, which, as revised, reads as follows:

"1. Persons, including corporations organized under the laws of the United States, their employees who are ordinarily resident in the United States, and the dependents of such persons, present in Korea solely for the purpose of executing contracts with the United States for the benefit of the United States armed forces or other armed forces in Korea under the Unified

0214

Command receiving logistical support from the United States armed forces, who are designated by the Government of the United States in accordance with the provisions of paragraph 2 below, shall, except as provided in this Article, be subject to the laws and regulations of Korea."

3. Mr. Habib stated that the U.S. negotiators, in order to retain a degree of flexibility regarding third-country corporations, would like to obtain the agreement of the Korean negotiators to the inclusion in the negotiating record of the following understanding:

"If the U.S. authorities determine that there would be significant advantage for U.S.-ROK mutual defense to utilize one or more third-country corporations as USFK-invited contractors, the authorities of the Government of the Republic of Korea shall give sympathetic consideration to a U.S. request to extend the benefits of this agreement to such non-U.S. corporations."

Mr. Habib pointed out that a case might arise in which the use of a third-country corporation would be to the mutual advantage of the ROK and U.S. forces in carrying out their mission of defending the Republic. Stating that the U.S. negotiators had already waived any right to include third-country corporations within the provisions of this article, Mr. Habib said the proposed understanding would serve only as guidance to the Joint Committee. He pointed out that it would refer only to corporations and not to third-country nationals.

4. Mr. Habib said the U.S. negotiators also wished to confirm that references throughout the article (in paragraphs 2, 3, 4, 5 and 6) to "such persons" were references to contractors, their employees, and their dependents, as identified in paragraph 1.

5. Mr. Chang stated that the Korean negotiators appreciated the acceptance by the U.S. negotiators of the proposal made by the Korean negotiators at the 48th meeting.

0215

However, they understood that this acceptance was conditioned upon acceptance by the Korean negotiators of the understanding just proposed by the U.S. negotiators. They did not believe that the understanding would carry much weight if it were placed in the negotiating record. However, if there were indications that it would be to the mutual advantage of the two governments for defense of the Republic of Korea to engage a third-country corporation, the Korean authorities were prepared to give sympathetic consideration to such a request by the U.S. armed forces. Therefore, the Korean negotiators agreed to the understanding.

6. Mr. Habib stated that the understanding had not been proposed as a condition for acceptance of the previous Korean proposal. It was intended to serve as a guide to the Joint Committee and would show that the negotiators had considered this particular possibility.

7. Mr. Habib noted that the revised draft of the article tabled by the Korean negotiators on February 14, 1964 contained in Paragraph 2(a) the apparently inadvertent omission of the phrase "the United States for". He added that paragraph 6 of the Korean revised draft should be slightly revised to improve the style. The Korean negotiators stated, however, that inasmuch as they had already agreed to Paragraph 6 of the U.S. draft at the 32nd meeting, the text of that version of the paragraph should be considered to be the agreed text.

8. Mr. Chang asked for the U.S. position with regard to Agreed Minute #3 proposed by the Korean negotiators. Mr. Habib replied that the negotiators had already reached agreement in Paragraph 6 on the principle of exemption from

0216

taxation. This is a principle which the U.S. negotiators believe should be applied and maintained. It was not proper to levy taxes on persons who normally would expect exemption and who, indeed, are granted exemption by the terms of Paragraph 6. Furthermore, the size of the taxes levied by the Korean authorities on privately-owned automobiles was unusually large.

9. Mr. Chang replied that Korean laws and regulations require privately-owned vehicles to be registered with the local authorities. Such registration in turn required the owners to pay the local fees and assessments. Even members of the armed forces should pay such local fees but the requirement on them to do so has been waived in view of their mission. The Korean negotiators believed that privately-owned vehicles of contractors and their employees and dependents should be required to pay these local fees and assessments. Mr. Chang stated that the local assessments are, in fact, payments for the use of roads and highways.

10. Mr. Habib pointed out that the vehicles under discussion actually remained in the country for only a relatively short period. When their owners departed, the vehicles were taken out of the country. If they were not taken out, they were sold and the relevant taxes were paid at the time of the sale. The U.S. negotiators believed that the ROK Government made a distinction between taxation and registration. The U.S. negotiators were not unprepared to consider the payment of registration fees on privately owned vehicles but they wished to maintain the principle of exemption from taxation.

11. Mr. Chang said the Korean negotiators understood the U.S. position. They believed that fees and taxes were closely

0217

related to the registration of vehicles. They would study the question and comment further at a later meeting.

12. Mr. Habib remarked that the U.S. negotiators were merely attempting to arrive at a position similar to that which existed in other countries. In other countries registration fees were collected but heavy taxes such as those imposed in the Republic of Korea were non-existent.

Security Measures

13. Each side indicated that its position with regard to the Security Measures Article had not changed. Neither side had any alternative proposals to suggest and it was agreed to give further study to the matter.

Customs

14. Turning to the Customs Article, Mr. Chang recalled that at the 55th meeting agreement had been reached in principle that pertinent information with regard to cargo consigned to non-appropriated fund organizations would be furnished to the Korean authorities on a routine basis. However, the Korean negotiators still desired that other information deemed necessary by the ROK Customs authorities in specific cases should be furnished on request through the Joint Committee. The Korean negotiators would accept the revised Agreed Minute #3 tabled by the U.S. negotiators at the 55th meeting if the U.S. negotiators would agree to the inclusion of the following two understandings in the negotiating record:

a. Pertinent information to be provided on a routine basis shall include at least invoices and packing lists;

b. In addition to the provisions of routine information, other information which the ROK authorities may

0218

deem necessary in specific cases shall promptly be provided on request through the Joint Committee.

15. In reply, Mr. Habib stated that the original proposal regarding pertinent information had been made by the Korean negotiators, in a revised version of Agreed Minute #3 tabled by them at the 54th meeting. In that proposal, the Korean negotiators themselves had suggested that the extent of the pertinent information was to be decided by the Joint Committee. The U.S. negotiators had agreed to that suggestion. In the view of the U.S. negotiators, the provision of additional information upon request to the Joint Committee is provided for in any article, paragraph, or clause of this Agreement. Mr. Habib suggested that the Korean negotiators reexamine the Joint Committee Article and all of the other commitments to provide information being made in this and other articles. Instead of the two understandings proposed by the Korean negotiators, the U.S. negotiators wished to propose the following understanding, which was stated in the simplest possible terms:

> "With respect to Agreed Minute #3, in addition to the information provided on a routine basis, other pertinent information will be provided on request through the Joint Committee."

16. Mr. Chang stated that the Korean negotiators believed there should be a statement to the effect that the pertinent information should include at least packing lists and invoices.

17. Mr. Habib pointed out that a thorough discussion of documentation had been held prior to the submission by the Korean negotiators of their proposed revised Agreed Minute #3. During that previous discussion, the Korean

0219

negotiators had indicated that they recognized the function of the Joint Committee. The U.S. negotiators had accepted without question the principle of automaticity proposed by the Korean negotiators. The U.S. negotiators, however, were not prepared at this point to begin implementation of the Agreement. That was the job of the Joint Committee. The Korean negotiators had already agreed to let the Joint Committee decide the extent of the pertinent information to be provided. If it were spelled out in this article, it might as well be spelled out in every article. The U.S. negotiators believed that implementation of the Agreement should be left to the Joint Committee.

18. Mr. Chang stated that the Korean negotiators recognized that it was the function of the Joint Committee to determine the extent of the pertinent information to be furnished. However, packing lists and invoices are essential elements of information regarding non-appropriated fund cargo. U.S. objections to mentioning them specifically were of concern to the Korean negotiators, lest the Joint Committee might not agree to include them as components of the pertinent information.

19. Mr. Habib pointed out that he had said nothing that could be so construed. He pointed out that there might be other kinds of documentation which would be better than packing lists. Was it the intention of the Korean negotiators that every sealed container entering the Republic of Korea be opened in order to obtain the packing list? Such a procedure would be administratively unsound and extremely unwise from the point of view of security.

20. Mr. Chang stated that the Korean negotiators would study the U.S. counter-proposal and comment at a later meeting.

21. The next meeting was scheduled for July 8 at 3:00 p.m.

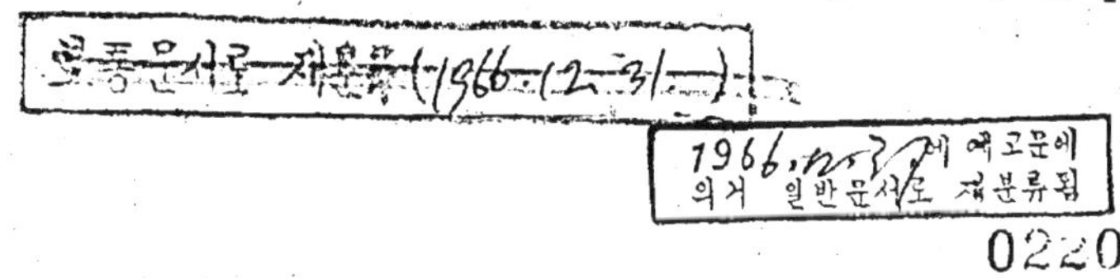

0220

외교문서 비밀해제: 주한미군지위협정(SOFA) 8
주한미군지위협정(SOFA) 서명 및 발효 8

초판인쇄 2024년 03월 15일
초판발행 2024년 03월 15일

지은이 한국학술정보(주)
펴낸이 채종준
펴낸곳 한국학술정보(주)
주 소 경기도 파주시 회동길 230(문발동)
전 화 031-908-3181(대표)
팩 스 031-908-3189
홈페이지 http://ebook.kstudy.com
E-mail 출판사업부 publish@kstudy.com
등 록 제일산-115호(2000. 6. 19)

ISBN 979-11-7217-019-6 94340
979-11-7217-011-0 94340 (set)

책에 대한 더 나은 생각, 끊임없는 고민, 독자를 생각하는 마음으로 보다 좋은 책을 만들어갑니다.